AF412007

Apocalypse

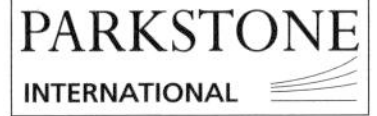

Author:
Camille Flammarion, extract from *La Fin du monde* (The End of the World)

Page 6:
Hieronymus Bosch
The Temptation of Saint Anthony (triptych, central panel)
1505-1506
Oil on panel
Museu Nacional de Arte Antiga, Lisbon

Layout:
Baseline Co. Ltd
61A-63A Vo Van Tan Street
4th Floor
District 3, Ho Chi Minh City
Vietnam

ISBN: 978-1-906981-46-4

Printed in Italy

Through me the way into the suffering city,
Through me the way to the eternal pain,
Through me the way that runs among the lost.
Justice urged on my high artificer;
My maker was divine authority,
The highest wisdom, and the primal love.
Before me nothing but eternal things were made,
And I endure eternally.
Abandon every hope, ye who enter here.

– Dante Alighieri, *Divine Comedy*
Inscription on the Gate to Hell, Canto III

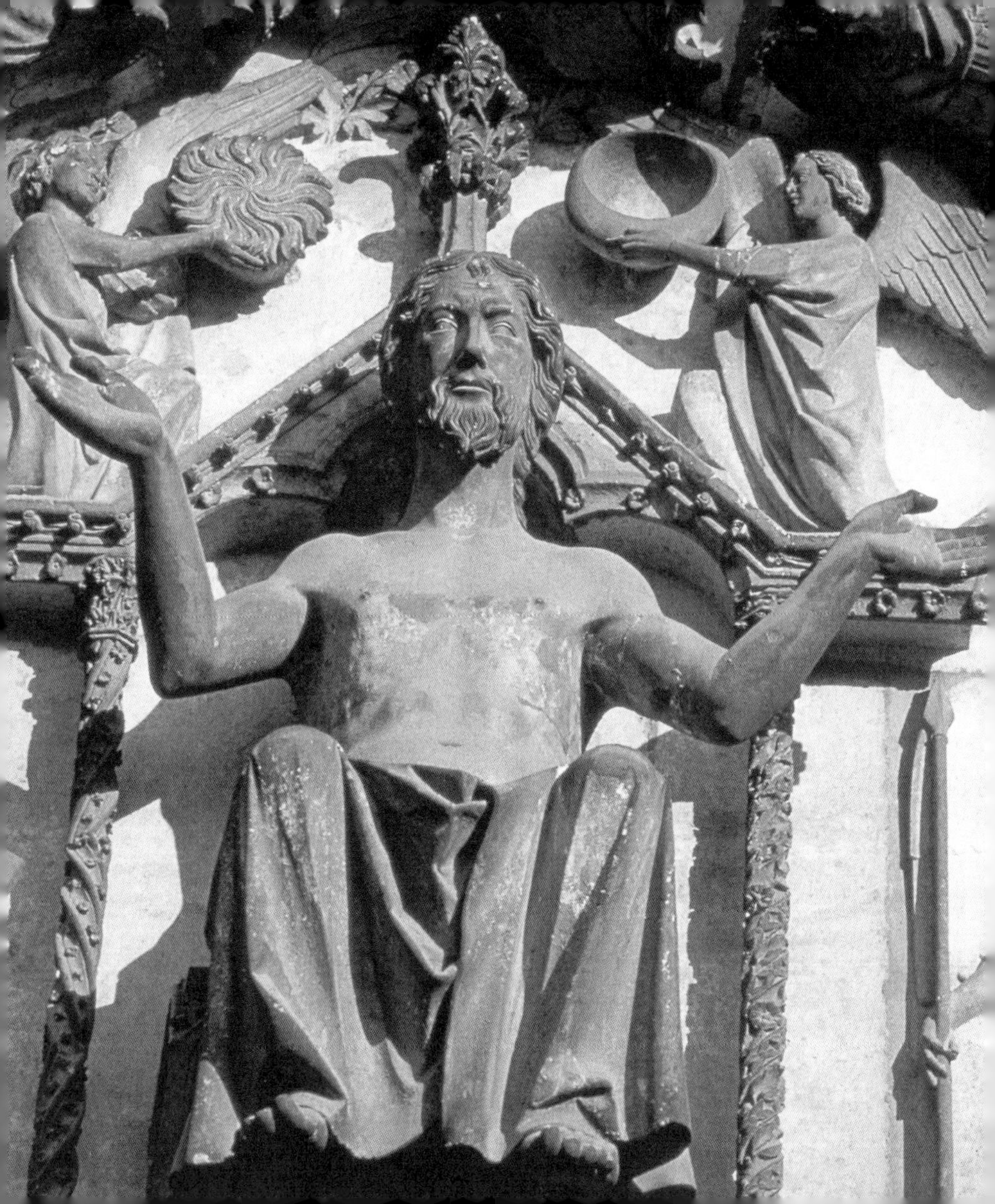

Selected Dates of Apocalyptic Predictions

c. 34 CE	The first Christian church awaits the return of Jesus Christ, basing their expectation on Jesus' own words: "Truly, I say to you, there are some standing here who will not taste death until they see the Son of Man coming in his kingdom."
31 December 999	At the end of the first millennium a wave of panic and apocalyptic gloom swept through the Christian West. Pope Sylvester II supposedly celebrated a fearful mass on the eve of the New Year, fully expecting the world to end.
1000	Taking the year 0 as the beginning of God's millennial kingdom, apocalypticists expected the year 1000 to bring the return of Satan and his last rebellion. Again, Europe was swept by mass hysteria and panic.
1033	Monk and chronicler Rodulfus Glaber of Burgundy modified the calculations of previous apocalypticists, using the year of Jesus' death as the beginning of God's kingdom on earth and wrote about the coming end-times. His expectation was strongly fuelled by his observations of society: a drought plagued Europe and the result was something that many saw as a "decline of civilisation". This era saw many reports about cannibalism, heretical activities, and satanic worship.
1186	In 1184, a strange letter made its rounds through intellectual circles, announcing that the world would be severely depopulated two years later due to natural catastrophes caused by a specific constellation of planets. Variants of the so-called "Toledo Letter" were still circulated, even centuries later.
1666	The obvious numerical connection of this date to the number of the beast leads many believers once more to assume that the apocalypse would finally begin. In the front row of these believers was Christopher Columbus, who thought that his last voyage would carry him to paradise. A severe drought in England and the Great Fire of London added to the apocalyptic mood of 1666.
1874	The Jehovah's Witnesses, who had recently emerged from the Bible Student Movement, starts a long series of apocalypse predictions with announcing the end for 1874. Before the central council distanced itself from any kind of prediction, several more years were marked for Armageddon and rapture: 1878, 1881, 1910, 1914, 1918, 1925, 1941, 1974, 1981 and 1999.

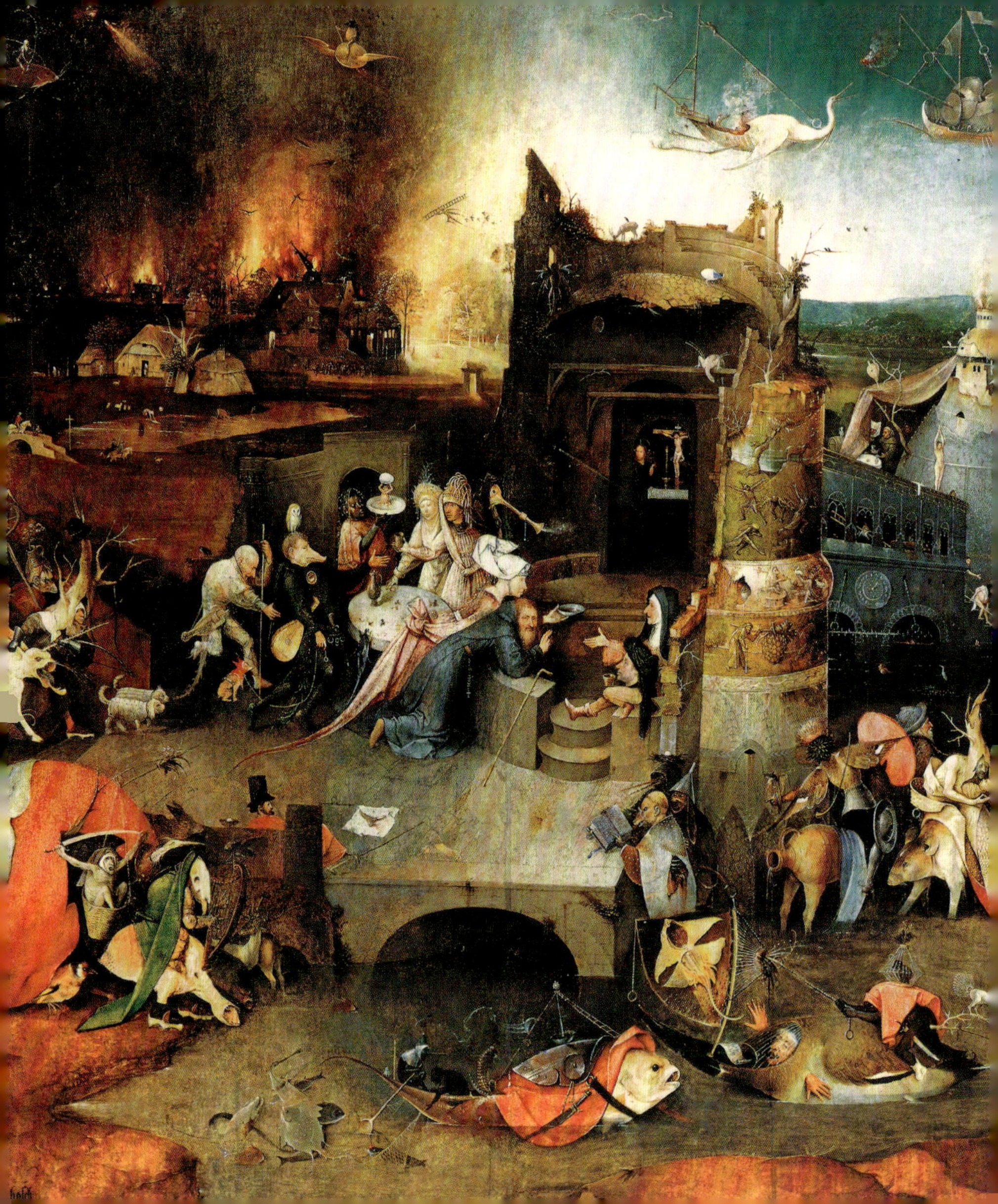

18 May 1910	The reappearance of Halley's Comet, which was rumoured to destroy humanity by releasing cyanide gas into earth's atmosphere, causes panic once more. A few con-men used this fully unfounded fear to sell "comet pills" to unassuming people with the promise that they would protect them from the poisonous gas.
1969	Infamous hippy-sectarian Charles Manson was obsessed by the idea that the world was determined to end in a full-scale race war. Not only did he prophesise these events, but he actively attempted to make them come to pass by commanding his disciples to commit high-profile murders and blame African Americans for the crimes. Manson is currently serving a life-sentence in a Californian jail.
1999-2000	Similarly to the years 999 and 1000, the years before the third millennium brought a flood of apocalyptic forecasts and revisions of old predictions. Meteors hitting earth, natural catastrophes destroying large parts of the world, the usual religiously inspired raptures or aliens visiting/invading the planet – these are just some of the possible scenarios that were named. Well-known prophets of doom were Nostradamus, Isaac Newton and fashion designer Paco Rabanne.
21 March 2011	Radio-preacher Harold Camping, after having failed with his apocalypse-prediction for 1994, announces rapture again for 21 May 2011. Although this announcement was met with general derision, his followers quit their jobs and donated large sums of money to help finance an awareness-campaign for the coming Judgement Day.
21/23 December 2012	According to the counting-system of the Mayan calendar, 21 or 23 December 2012 sees the reappearance of a specific date that also marks the first day of creation. Many esoteric and pseudo-scientific interpretations assume this to be an indicator of yet another apocalypse. These theories were made popular by the catastrophe movie *2012*.
2076	The writings of Beda Venerabilis, a Northumbrian monk, foretell that the 6000th year since the biblical creation will be the year 2076. Believing that God created the world only to last 6000 years, he assumed this to be the final year on earth. Correspondingly, 2076 also marks the year 1500 in the Islamic calendar which holds an apocalyptic relevance for some Sufi-groups.

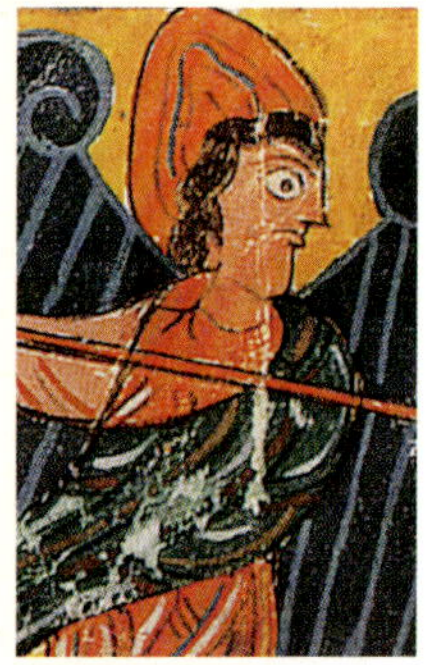

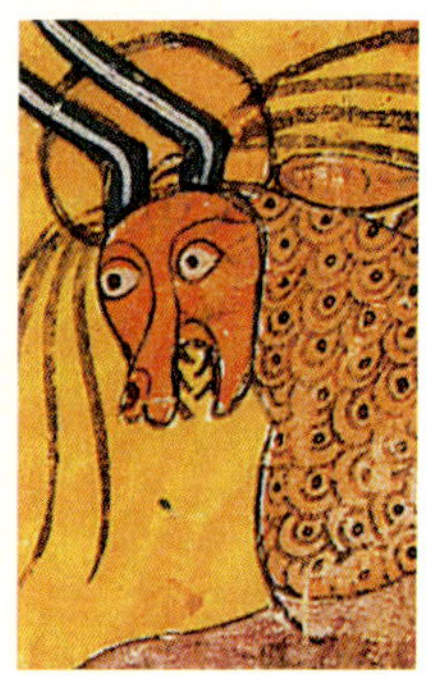

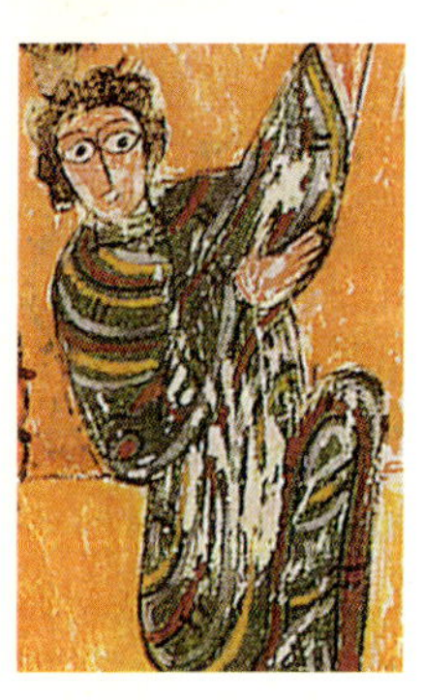

Beliefs about the end of the world through the ages

Here we will explore the curious phenomenon of the fear of the end of the world which has repeatedly appeared throughout the ages. All over the world and in every language, there has never been a more widely discussed subject.

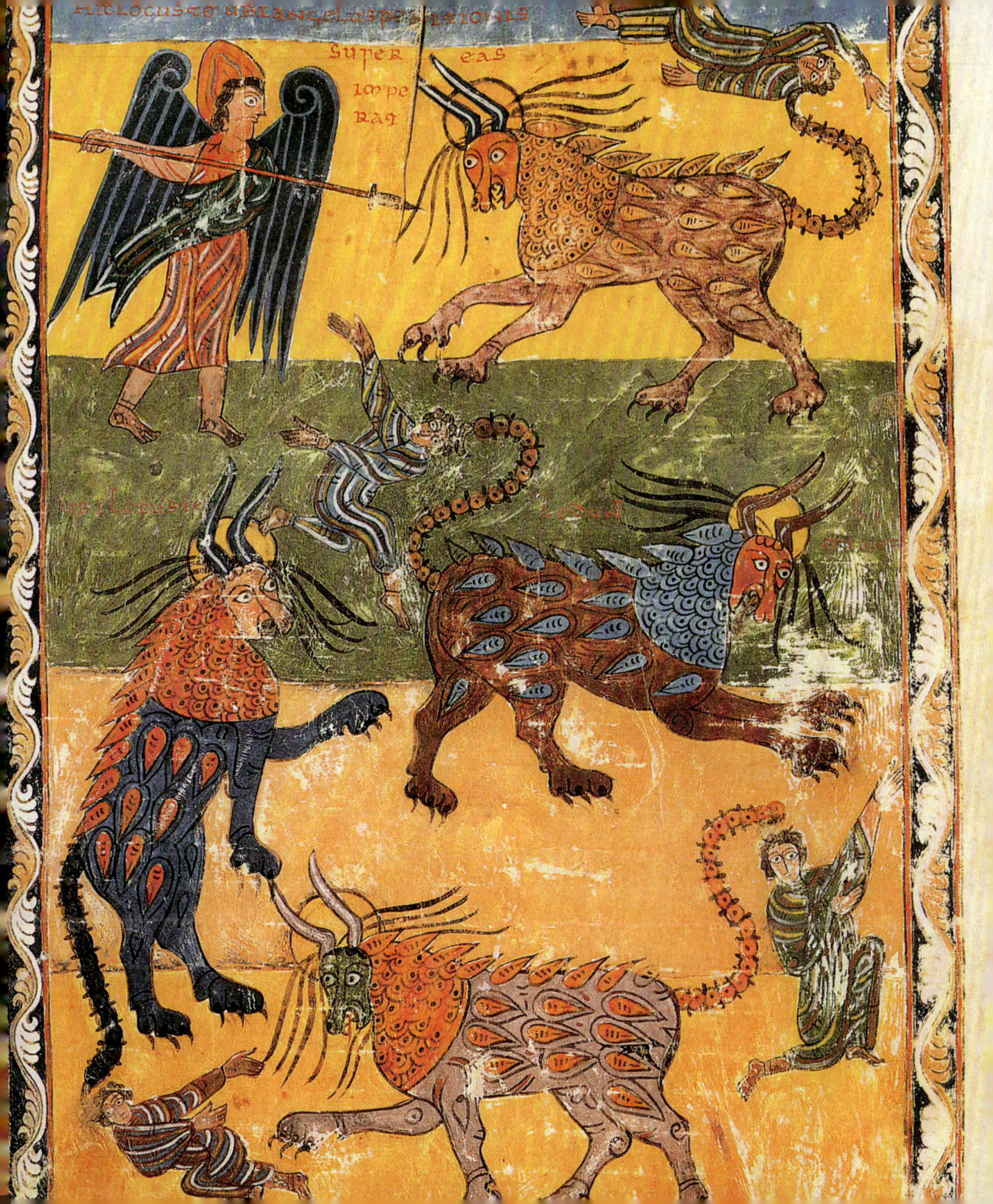

HIC LOCUSTE UBI ANGELUS PO ... ETIONIS
SUPER EAS IMPE RAT
UBI LOCUSTE
LEVUL

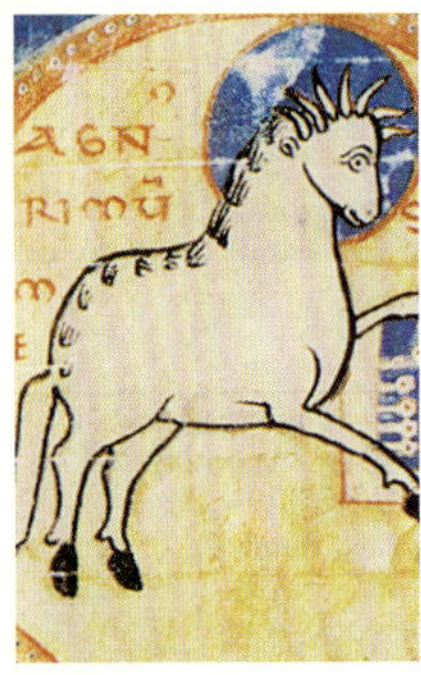

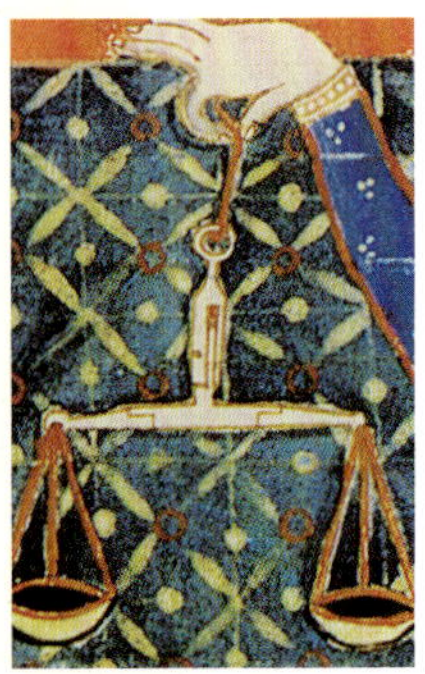

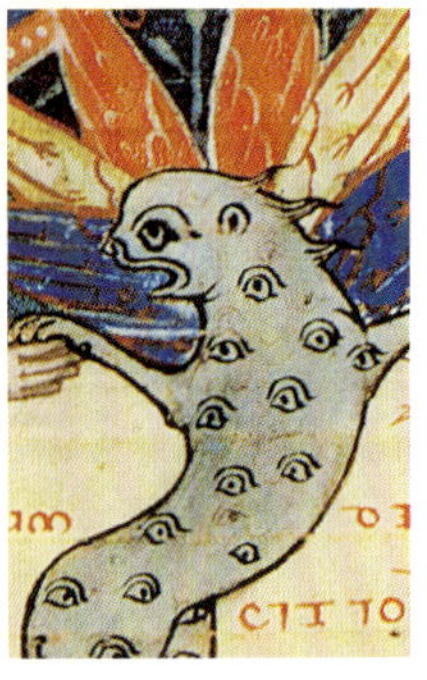

As to the dogma "Credo Resurrectionem Carnis", the addresses of the fathers of the Church before the council assembled in the Sistine Chapel in Rome, were, on the whole, in accord with the opinion expressed by the cardinal archbishop of Paris. The clause "et vitam setemam" was tacitly ignored in view of the possible discoveries in

The Four Horsemen Appear
at the Opening of the First Four Seals

Attributed to Stephanus Garsia Placidus, c. 1060
Illustration from the Beatus of Saint-Sever manuscript
Illumination on parchment
Bibliothèque Nationale de France, Paris

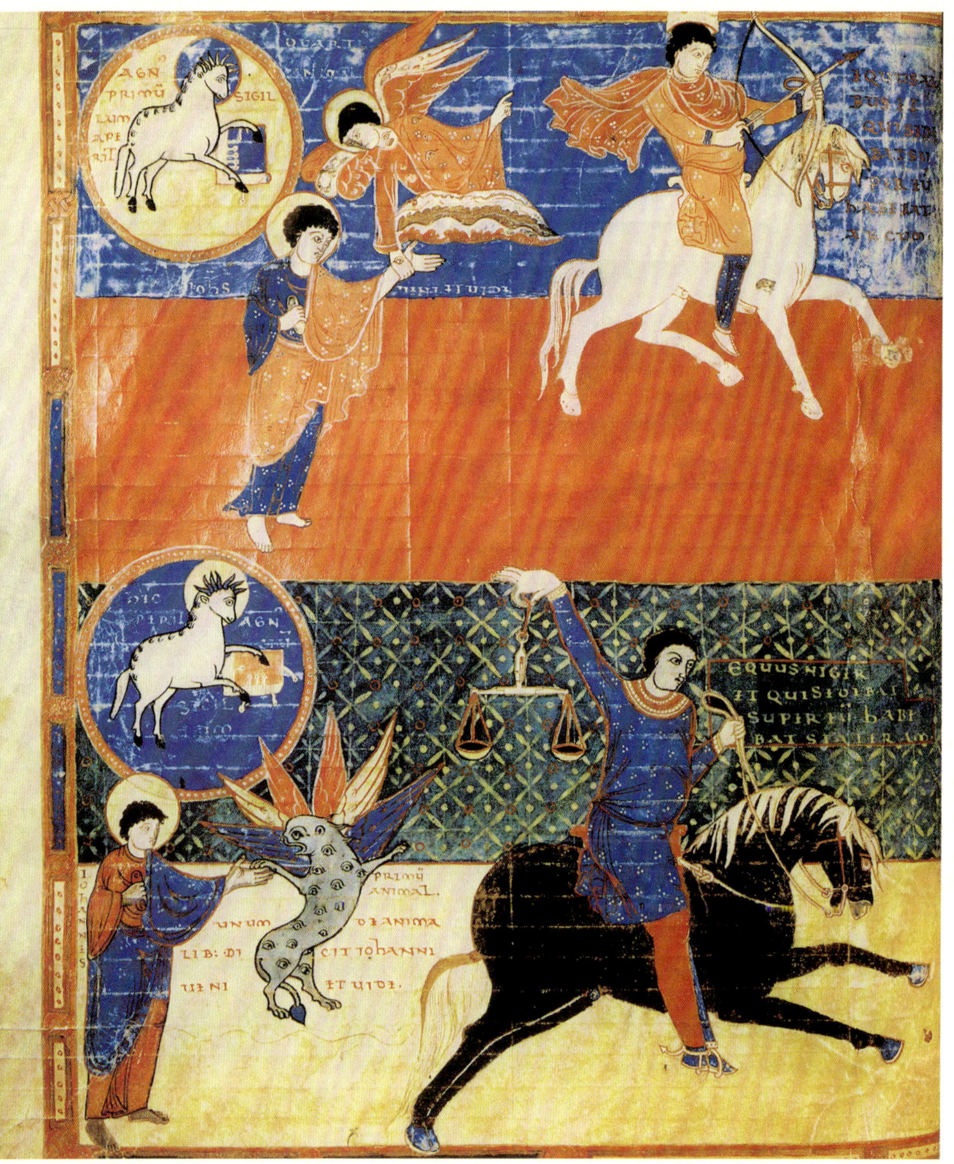

AGNUS PRIMUM SIGIL
LUM APE
RII
QUART

IOHS
IORERA
DUS
AD SIM
DISU
ET U
BAT
ARCUO
DIC
PIPLI
AGN
SOL
IOHANNES
PRIMUM
ANIMAL
DE ANIMA
LIB: DI
CIT IOHANNI
TIENI
ET UIDI.
EQUUS NIGIR
ET QUI SIDIBAT
SUPIR EU HABE
BAT STATIRAM

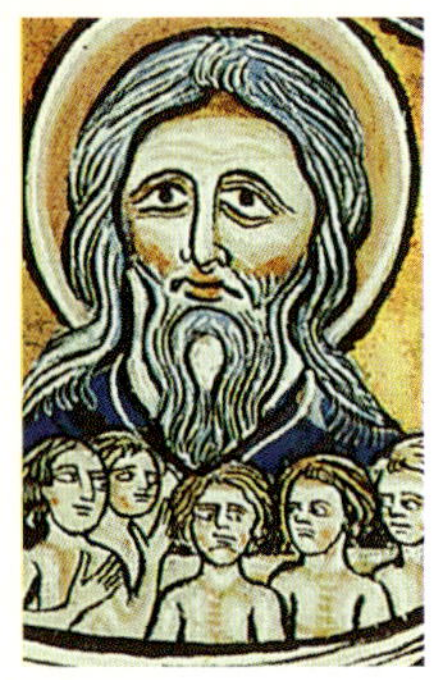

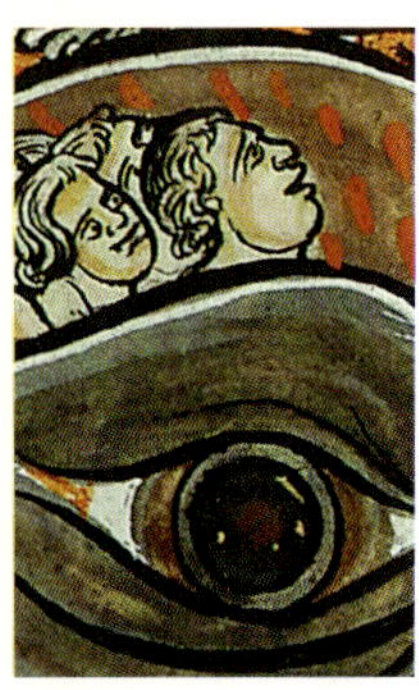

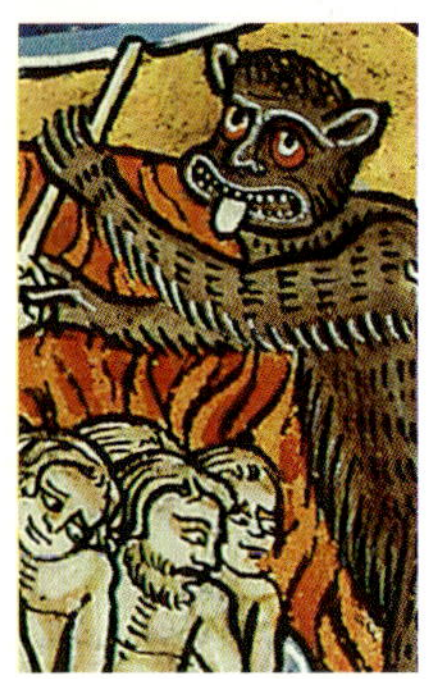

astronomy and psychology. As it were, these addresses epitomised the history of the doctrine of the end of the world as held by the Christian Church throughout the centuries.

This history is interesting, for it is also the history of the human mind face to face with its own destiny, and we believe it of sufficient importance to devote ample attention to it.

Page from the Psalter of Blanche of Castile

c. 1230
Illuminated manuscript, 28 x 22 cm
Bibliothèque de l'Arsenal, Paris

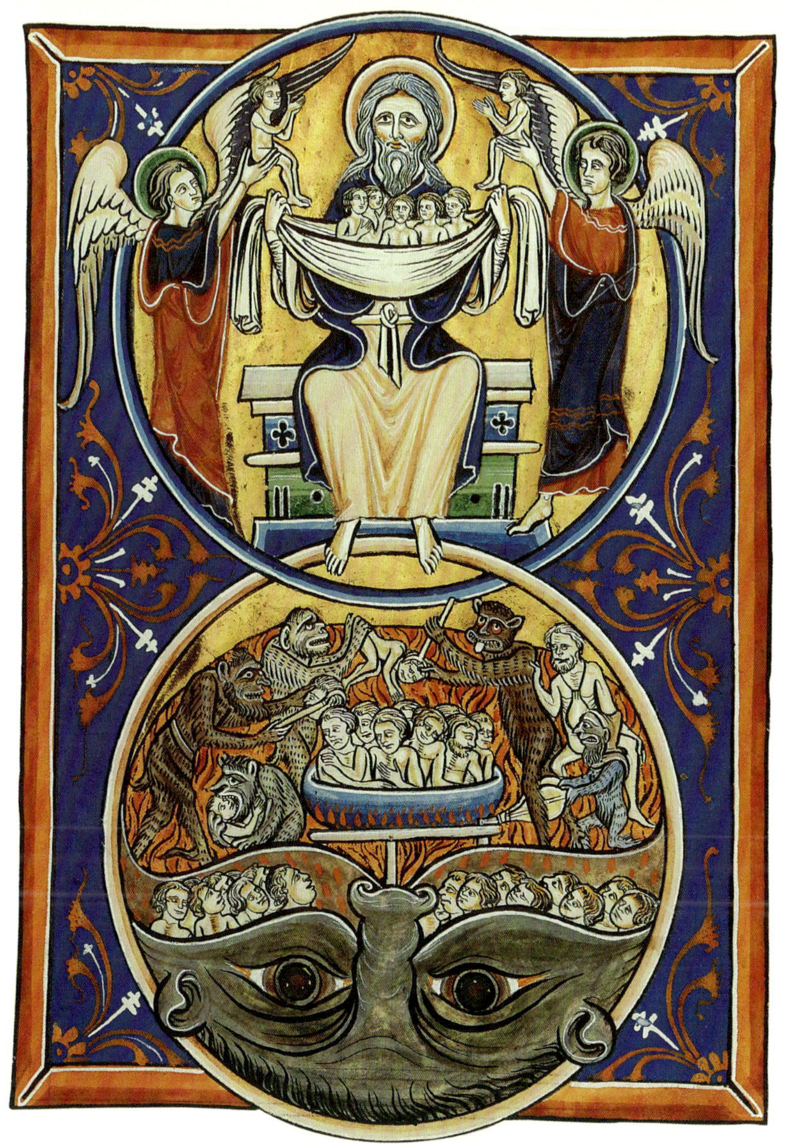

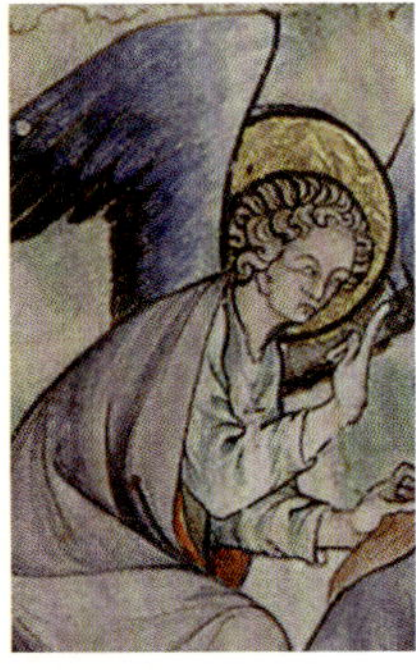

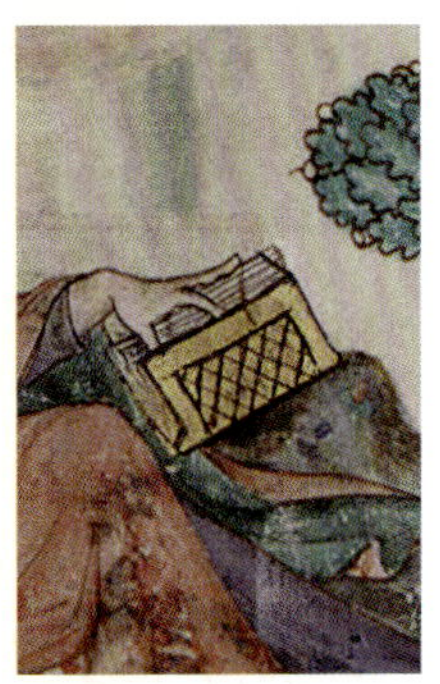

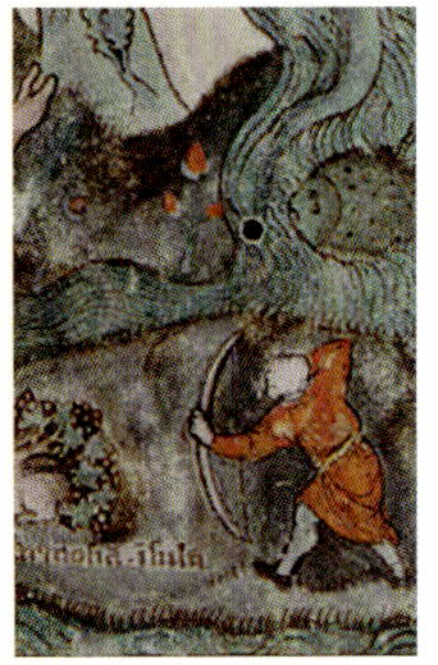

The existence of a profound and tenacious faith is as old as the centuries, and it is a notable fact that all religions, irrespective of Christian dogma, have opened the same door from this mortal life upon the unknown which lies beyond, it is the door in the *Divine Comedy* by Dante, although the conceptions of paradise,

John on Patmos Woken by the Angel

Illustration from "The Douce Apocalypse", c. 1270
Illumination
University of Oxford, Bodleian Library, Oxford

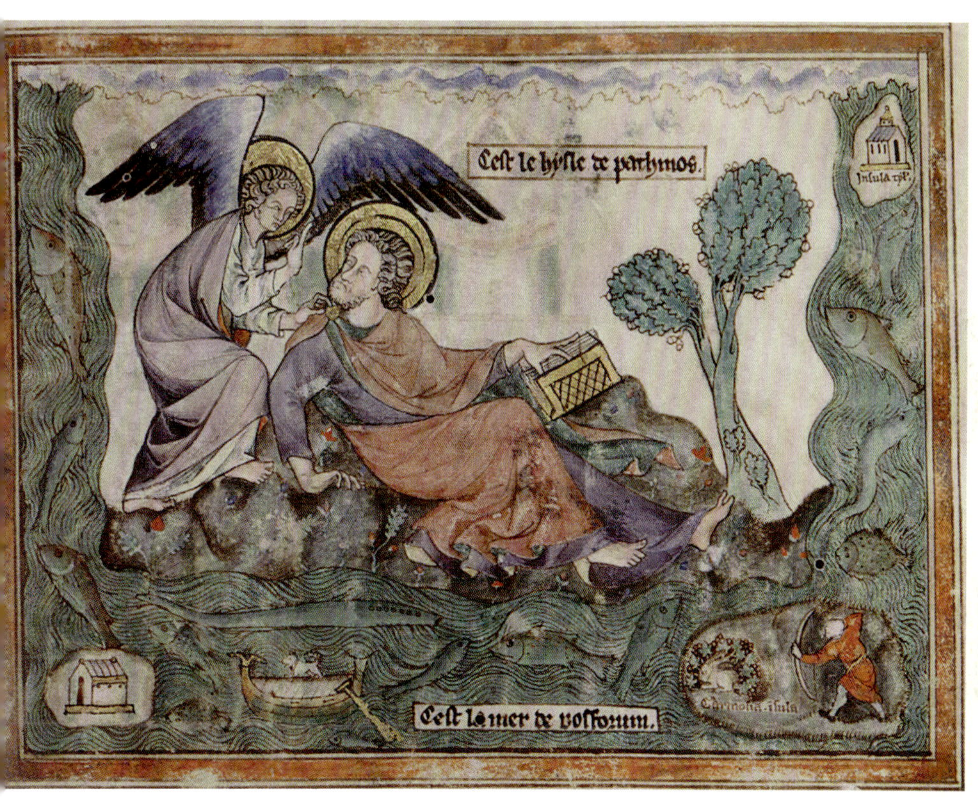

Cest le hÿsle de pathmos.
Insula tÿl.
Cest la mer de voffonum.
Chuinona insula

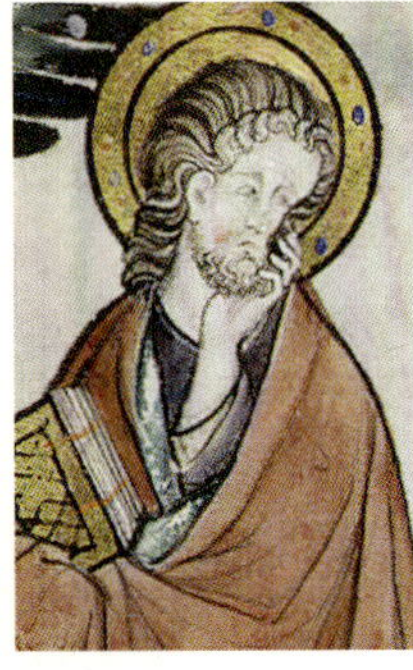

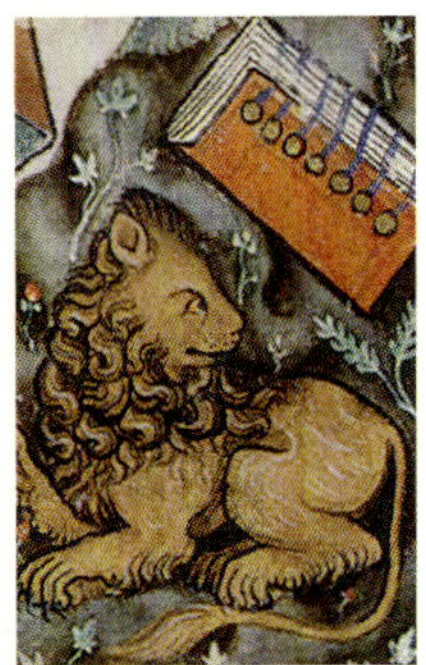

hell, and purgatory peculiar to the Christian Church, are not universal.

Zoroaster and the Zend-Avesta taught that the world would perish by fire. The same idea is found in the Epistle of St Peter. It seems that the traditions of Noah and of Deucalion, according to which the first great disaster to humanity came by flood, indicated that the second great disaster would be

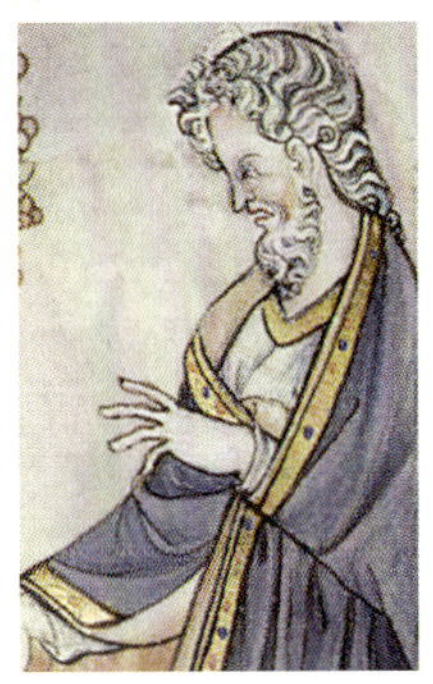

Illustration from "The Douce Apocalypse", c. 1270
Illumination
University of Oxford, Bodleian Library, Oxford

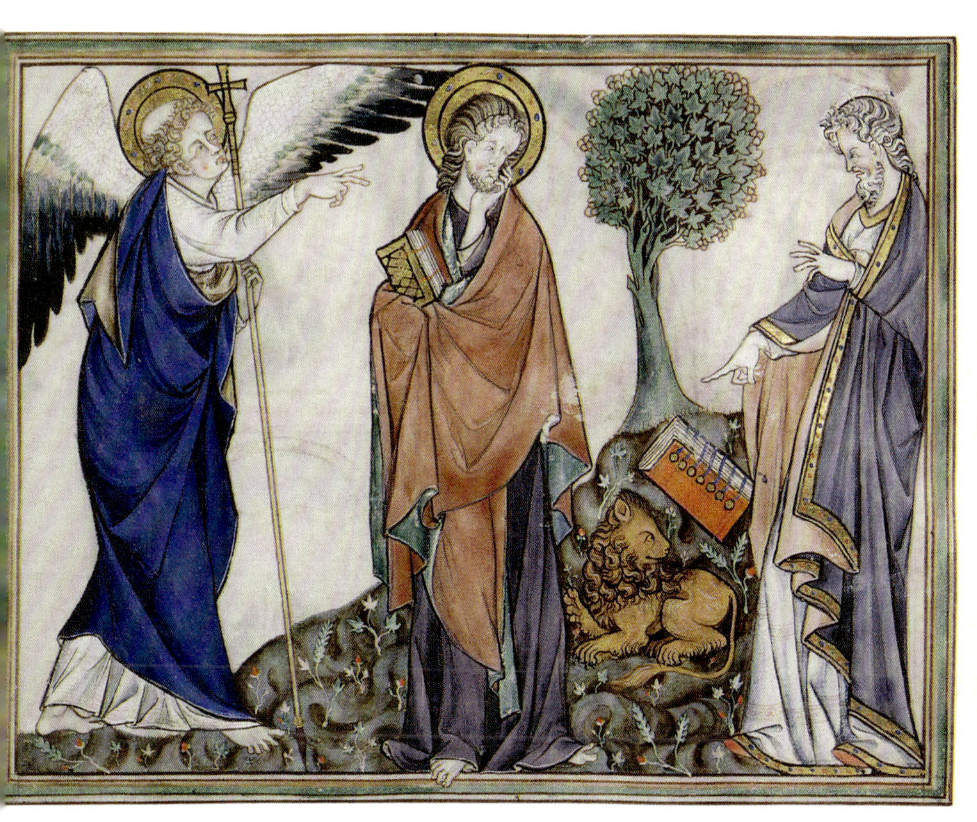

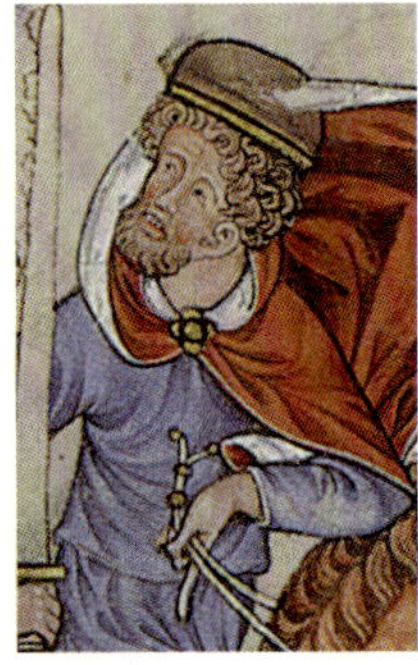

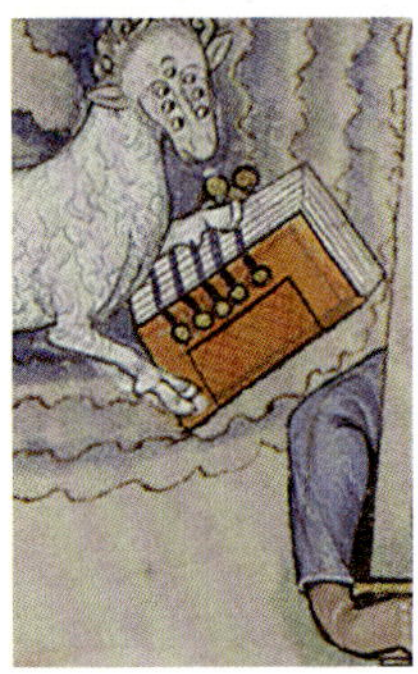

of an exactly opposite character. Among the Romans, Lucretius, Cicero, Virgil, and Ovid all also announce the future destruction of Earth by fire.

According to Jesus, the generation which he addressed would not die before the previously mentioned disaster occurred. St Paul, the real founder of Christianity, believed deeply in the

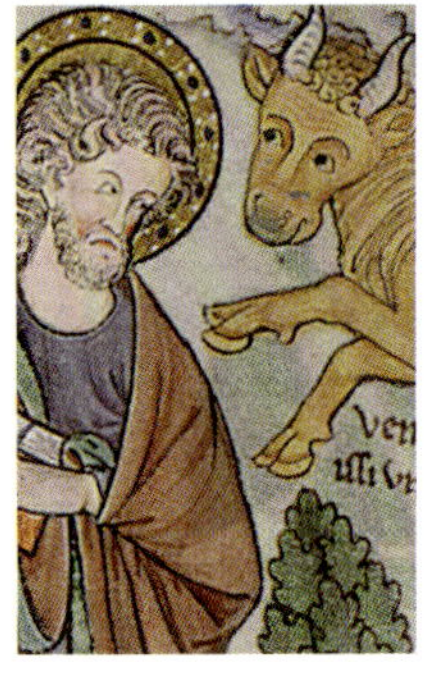

The Second Seal – The Red Horse

Illustration from "The Douce Apocalypse", c. 1270
Illumination
University of Oxford, Bodleian Library, Oxford

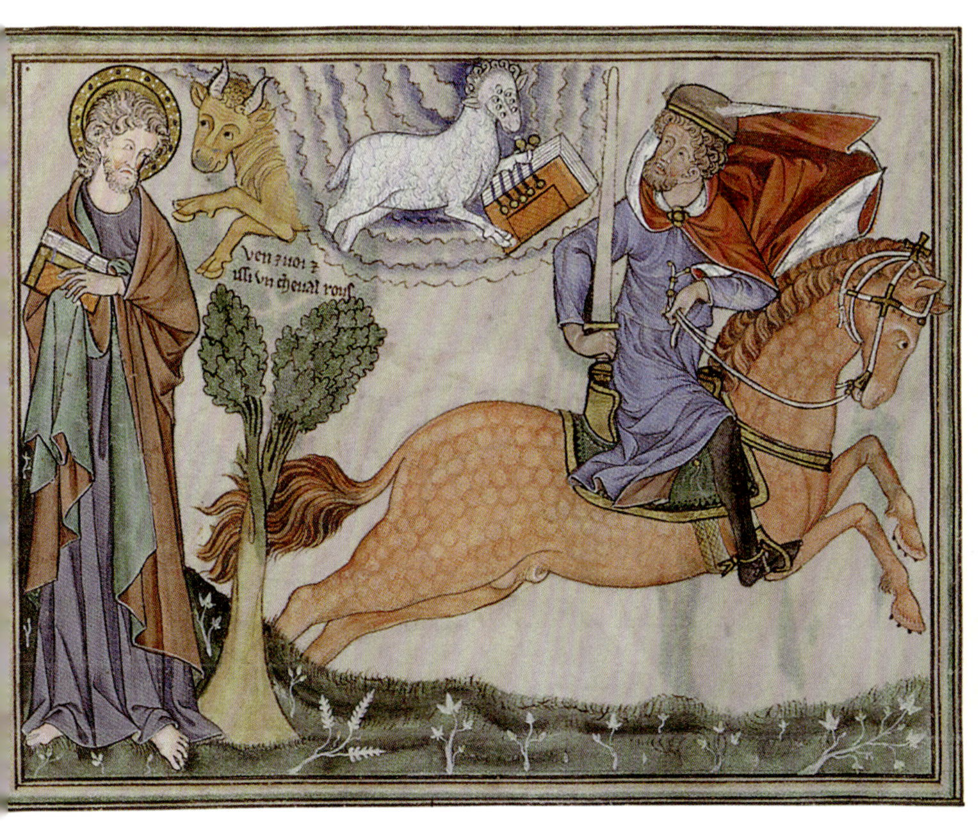

ven ʒuoit ʒ
uši un cheual rous

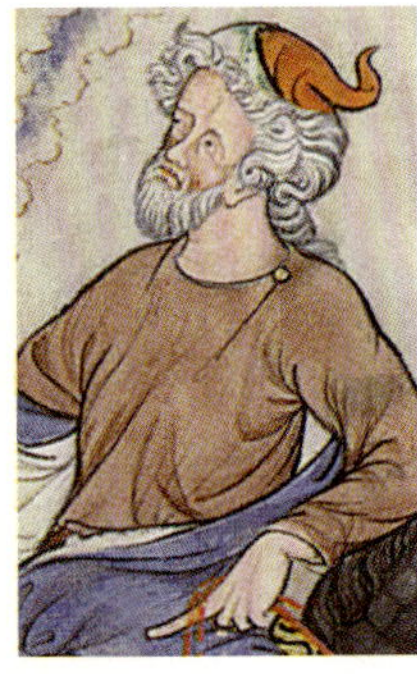

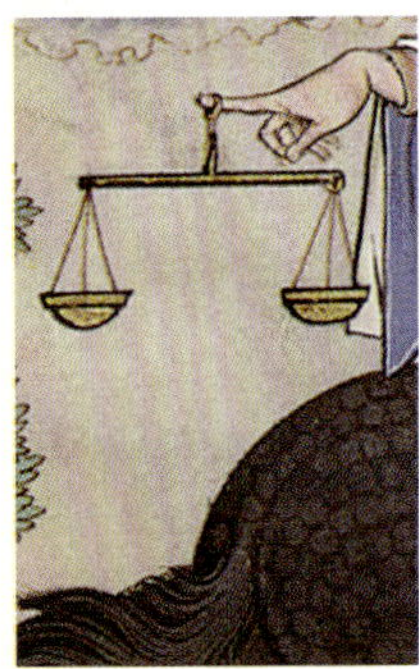

resurrection and the coming end of the world, making it a fundamental dogma of the new church. He referenced it eight or nine times in his first epistle to the Corinthians.

Unfortunately for the prophecy, Jesus' disciples, whom he had assured would not die before his accession, died one after the other under the common law. St Paul, who did not know

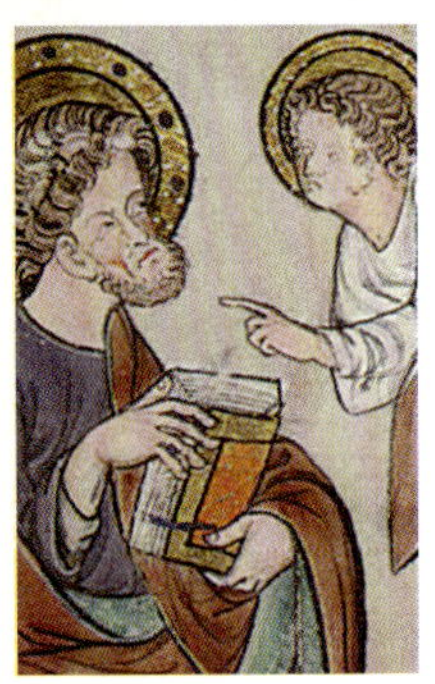

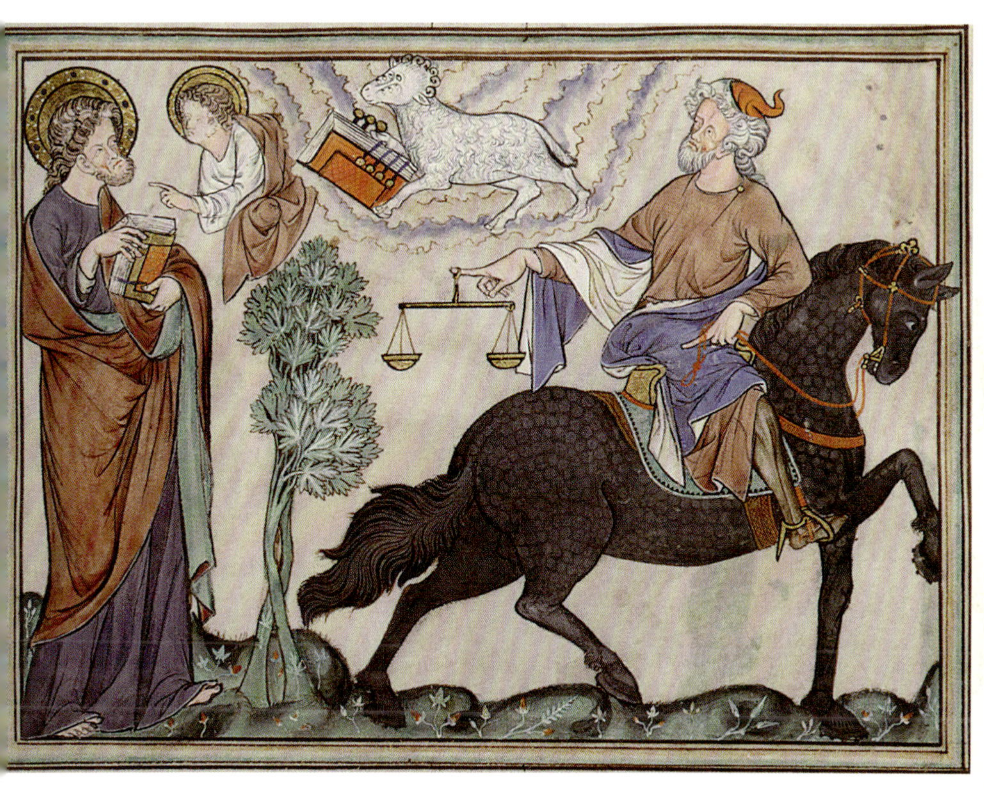

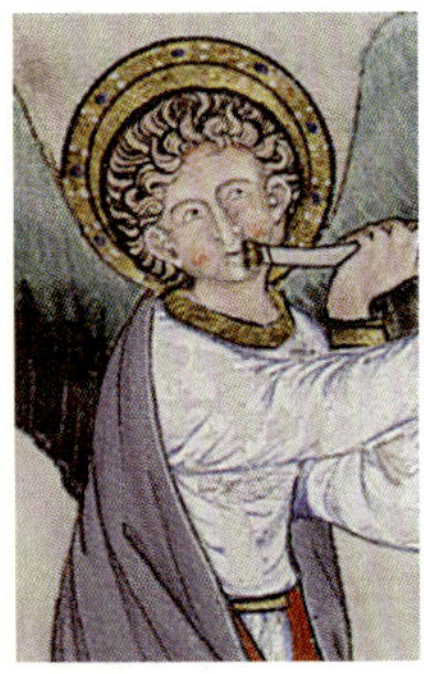

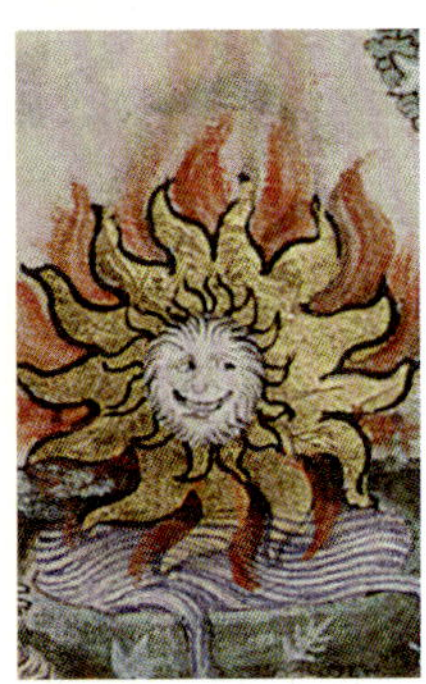

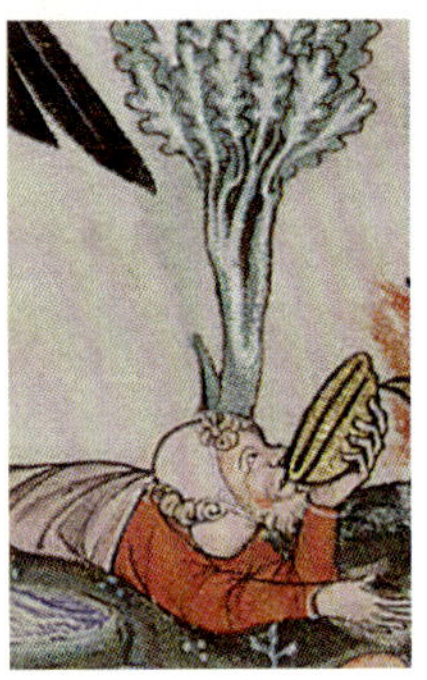

Jesus personally, but was a staunch supporter of the fledgling Christian church, was believed to have lived until the Great Commission (Jesus' appearance to his eleven disciples on Galilee). Naturally, however, they all died, and thus the end of the world, as predicted by the definitive coming of the Messiah, did not happen.

Illustration from "The Douce Apocalypse", c. 1270
Illumination
University of Oxford, Bodleian Library, Oxford

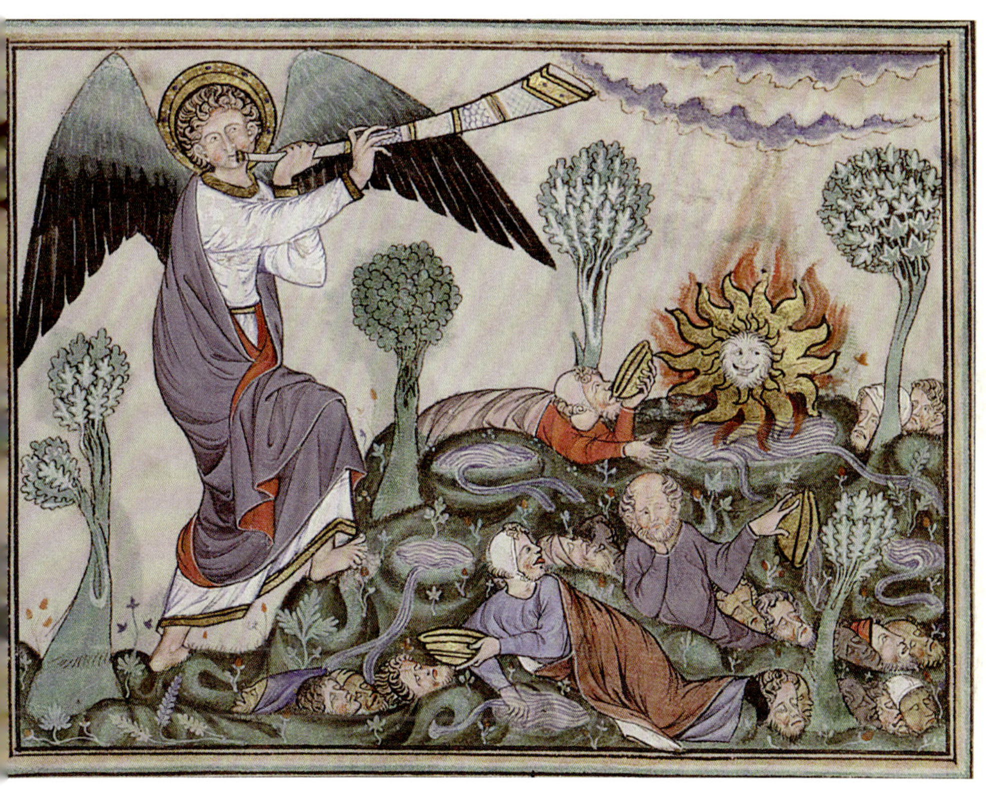

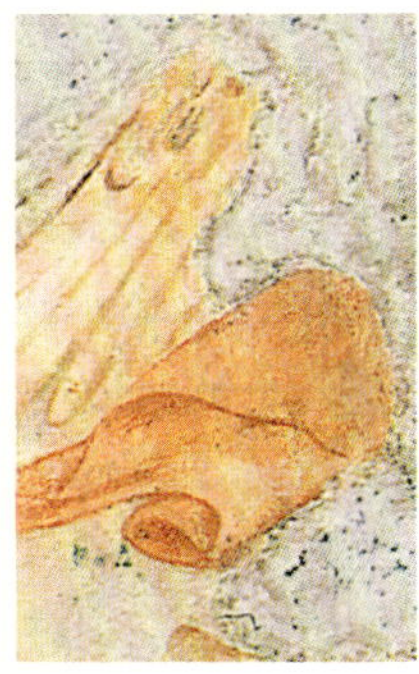

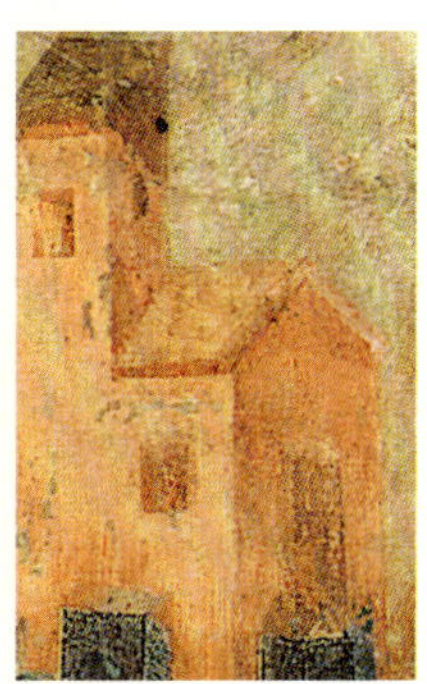

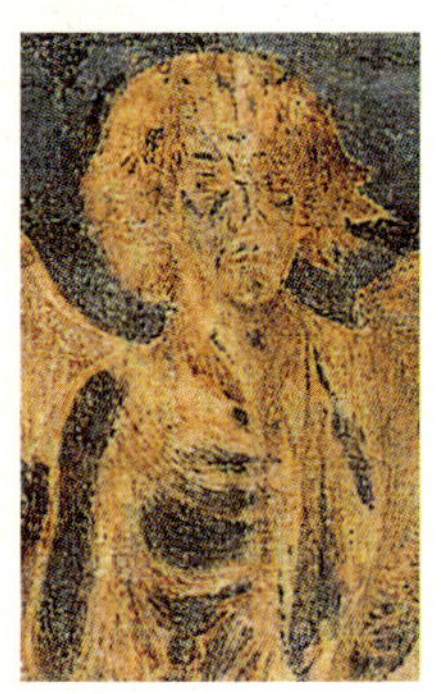

Belief in the end of the world did not simply disappear, however. Believers decided to stop taking the prediction literally, seeking instead new interpretations. However, belief in the Gospel suffered as a result. We devoutly buried the dead, laid out in coffins with reverence rather than being burned by fire, and it was written on their tombs that they would rest there until the resurrection.

The Angel of the Sixth Seal
and The Four Angels
at the Four Corners of the Earth

Cimabue
Fresco
Basilica di San Francesco d'Assisi, Assisi

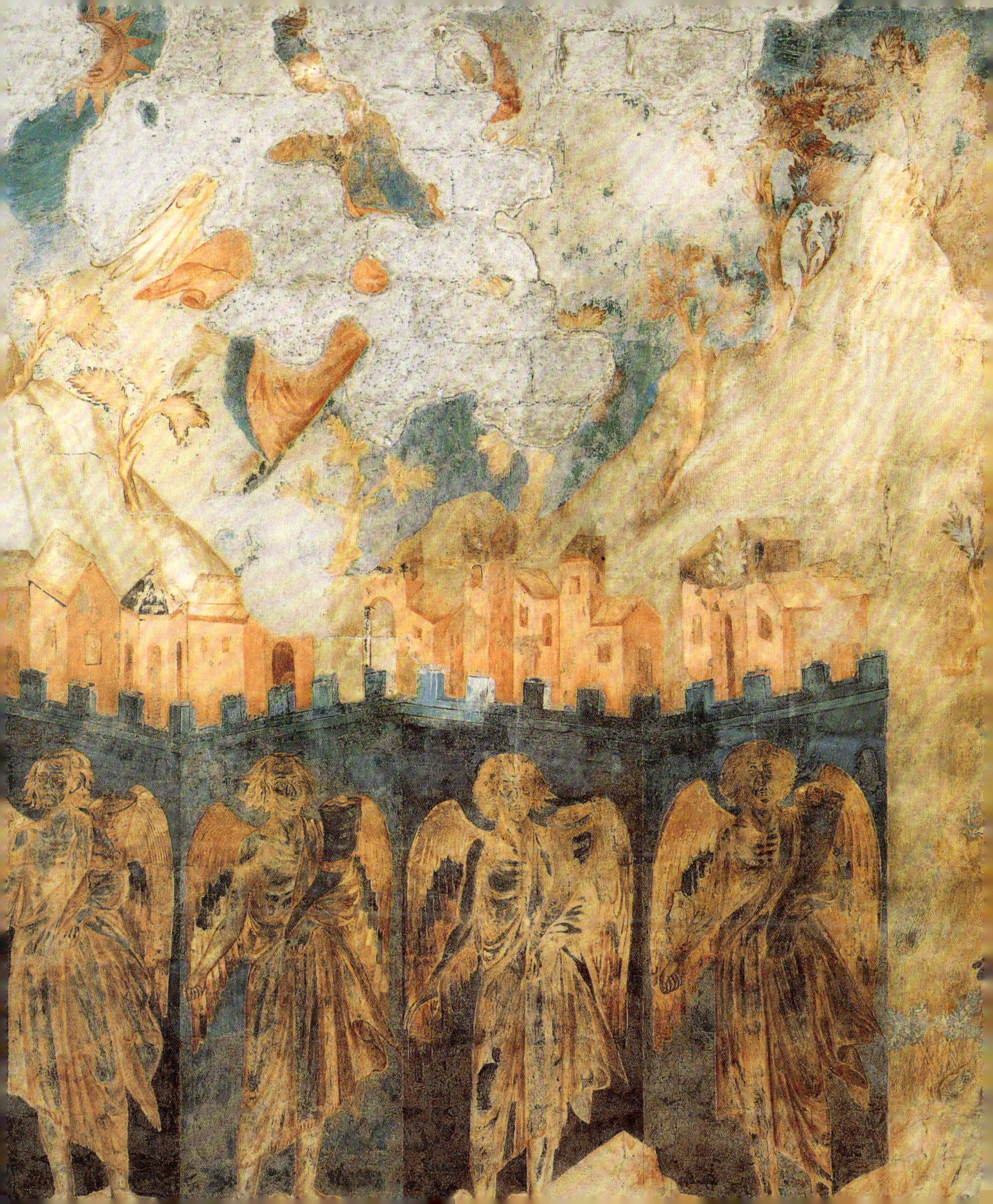

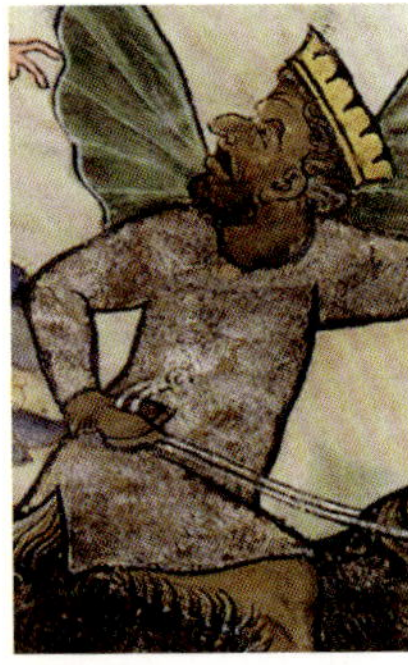

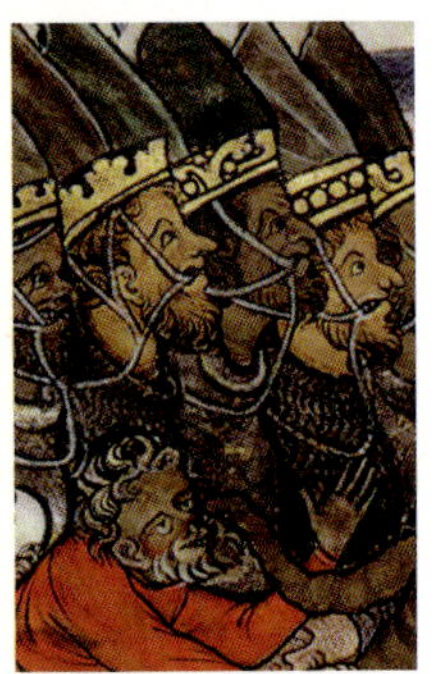

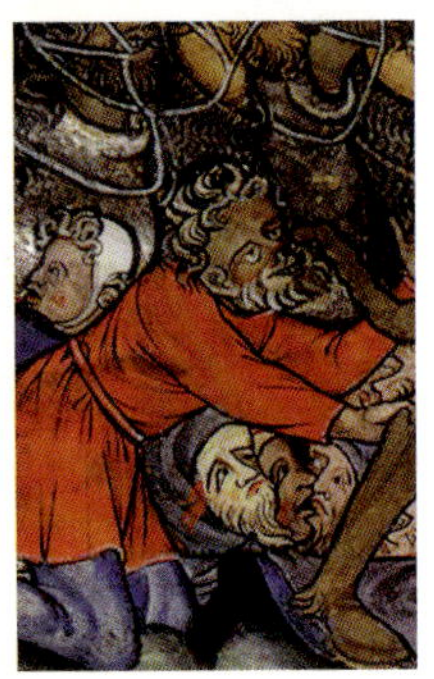

Jesus would "soon" return to judge "the living and the dead". The Christian word of recognition was *Maran atha*, "the Lord will come".

The apostles Peter and Paul most likely died in the year 64 CE, during the horrible slaughter ordered by Nero after the burning of Rome, set on fire at his command and whose destruction he attributed to the Christians so that he might have

Illustration from "The Douce Apocalypse", c. 1270
Illumination
University of Oxford, Bodleian Library, Oxford

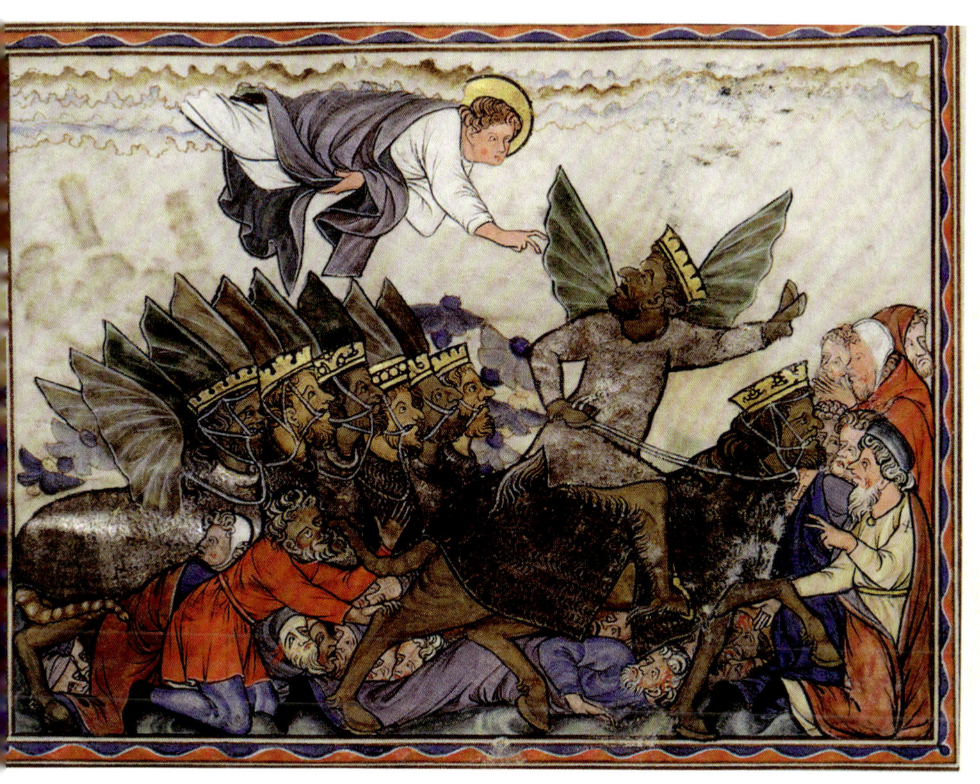

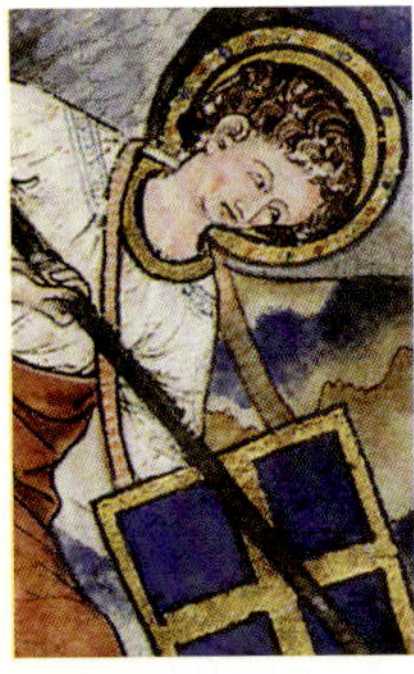

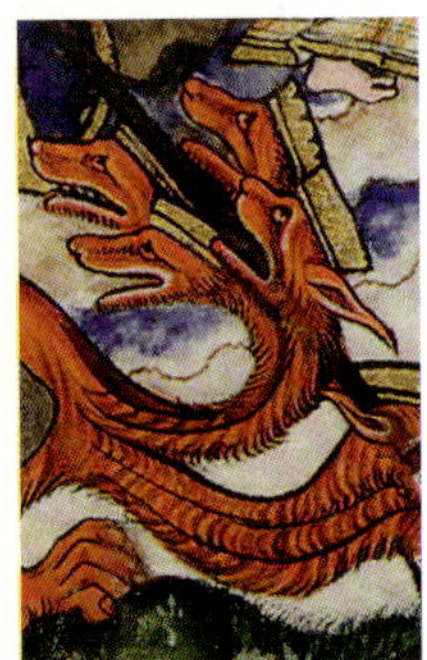

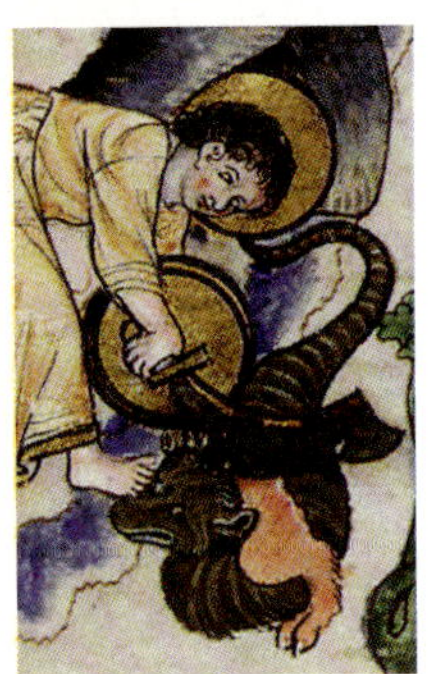

a pretext for new persecutions. St John wrote his *Apocalypse* (The Book of Revelation) in the year 69 CE. The reign of Nero was a bloody one, and martyrdom seemed to be the natural consequence of a virtuous life. Prodigies appeared on every hand; there were comets, falling stars, eclipses, showers of blood, monsters, earthquakes, famines, pestilences,

The War in Heaven

Illustration from "The Douce Apocalypse", c. 1270
Illumination
University of Oxford, Bodleian Library, Oxford

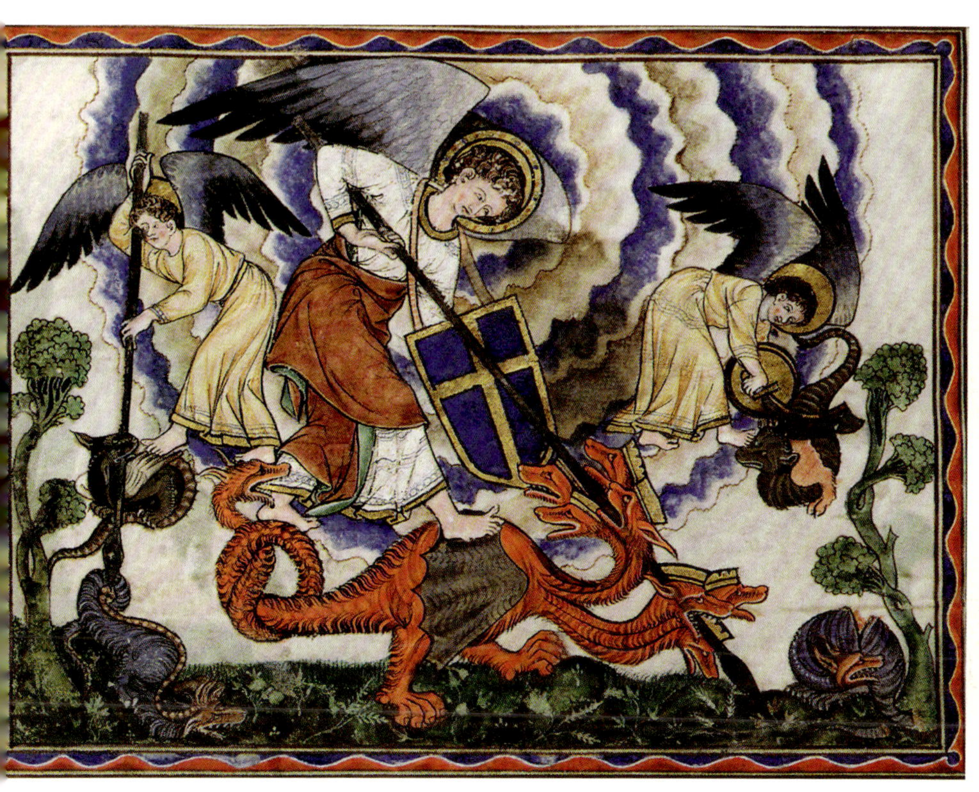

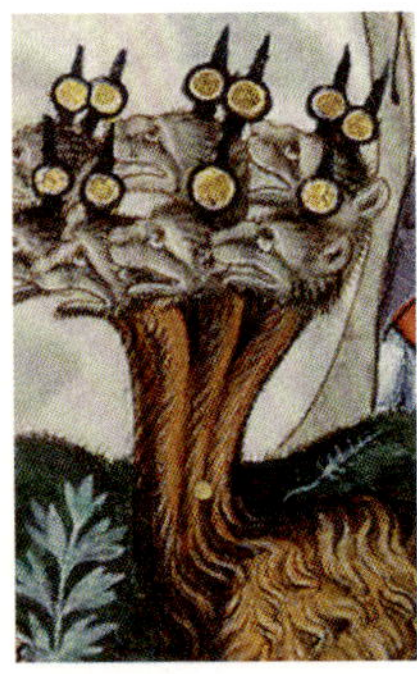

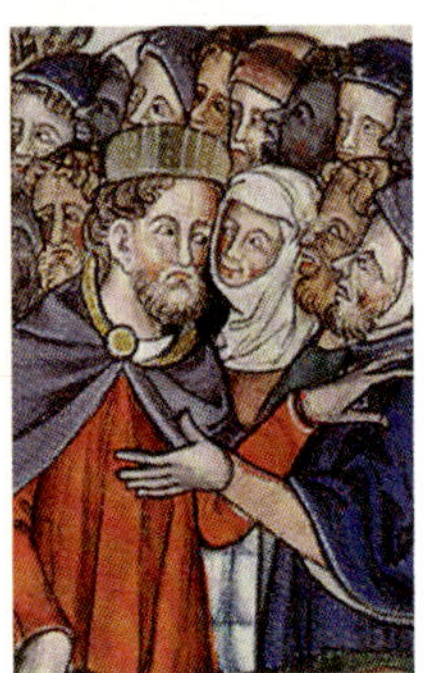

and above all, there was the Jewish war and the destruction of Jerusalem.

Never, perhaps, were so many horrors, so much cruelty and madness, so many catastrophes, crowded into so short a period as in the years 64-69 CE. The little church of Christ was apparently dispersed. It was impossible to remain in Jerusalem. The horrors of the reign of

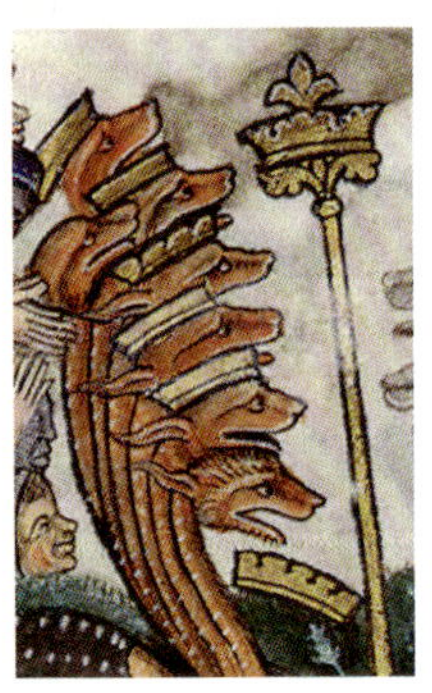

The Dragon Delegates Power
to the Beast Who Comes from the Sea

Illustration from "The Douce Apocalypse", c. 1270
Illumination
University of Oxford, Bodleian Library, Oxford

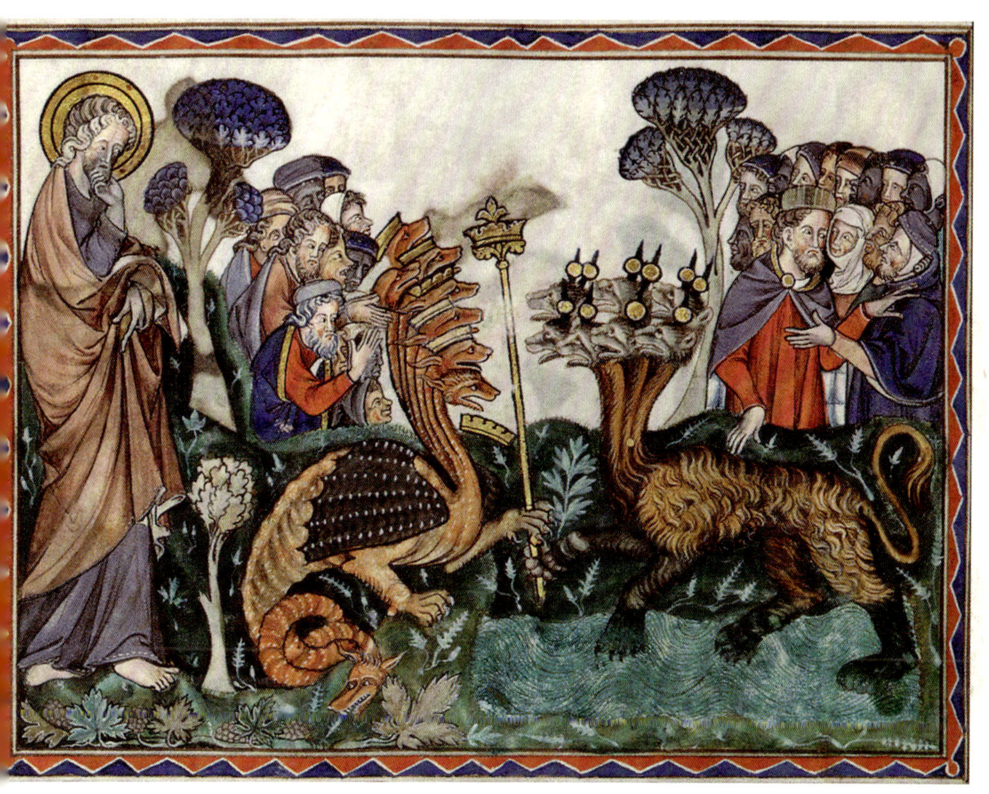

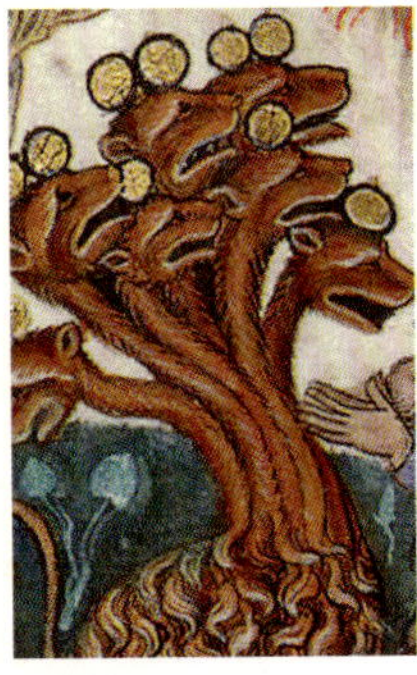

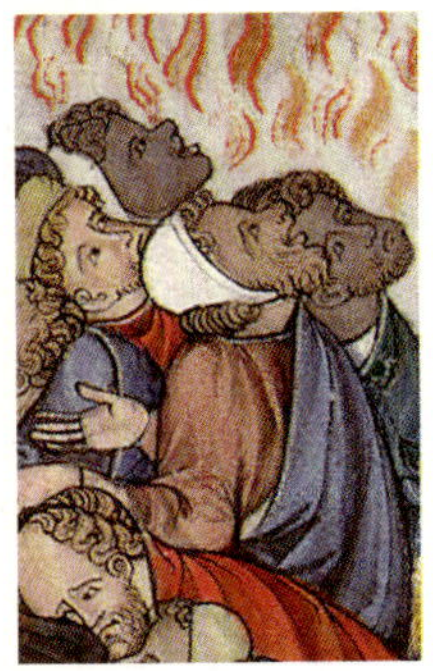

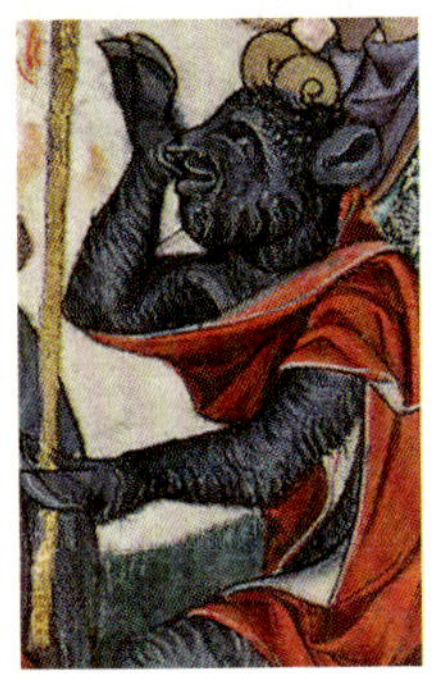

terror of 1793 and of the Commune of 1871 were nothing in comparison with those of the Jewish civil war. The Jesus' family was obliged to leave the Holy City and to seek safety in flight. False prophets appeared, thus verifying former prophecies. Vesuvius was preparing the terrible eruption of the year 79 CE, and already, in 63 CE, Pompeii had been destroyed by an earthquake.

The False Prophet Rises
from the Earth, Calls Down Fire
and Orders the Worship of the Beast

Illustration from "The Douce Apocalypse", c. 1270
Illumination
University of Oxford, Bodleian Library, Oxford

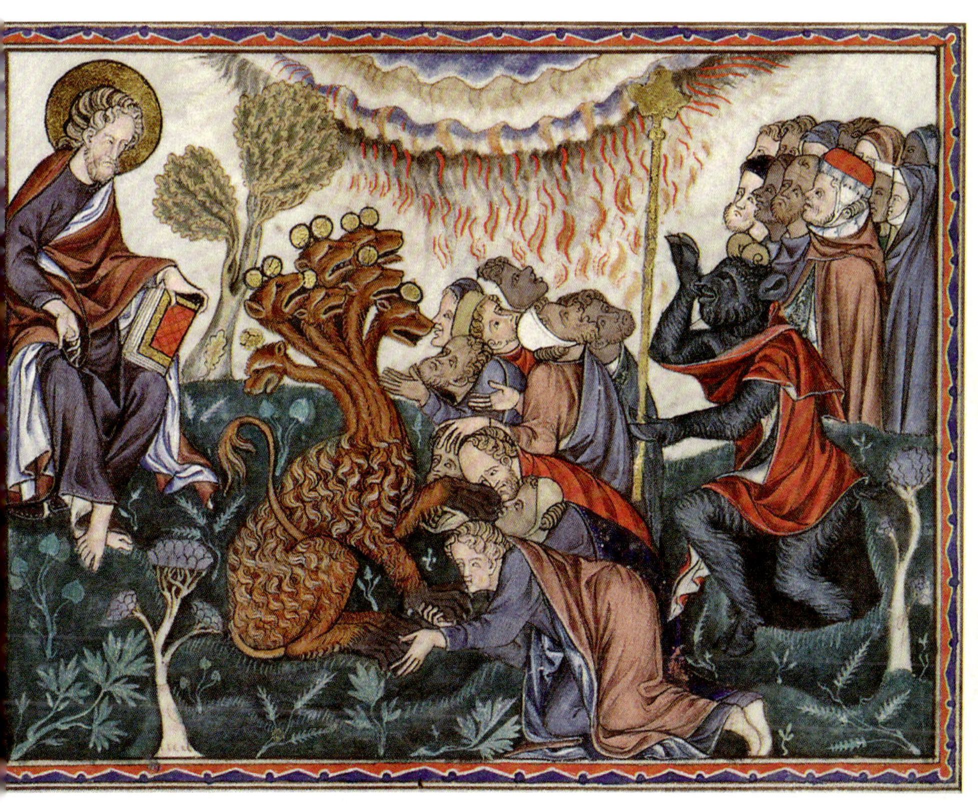

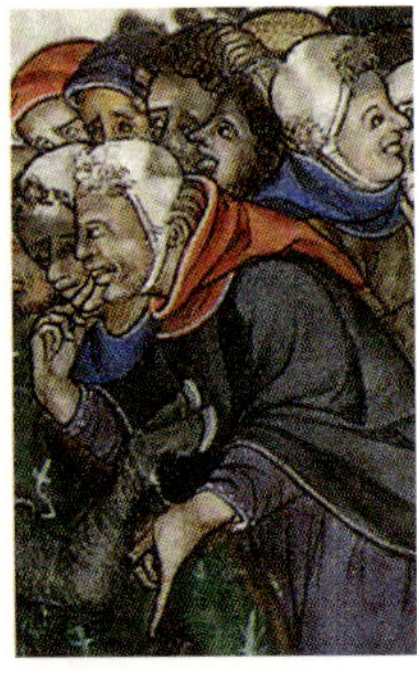

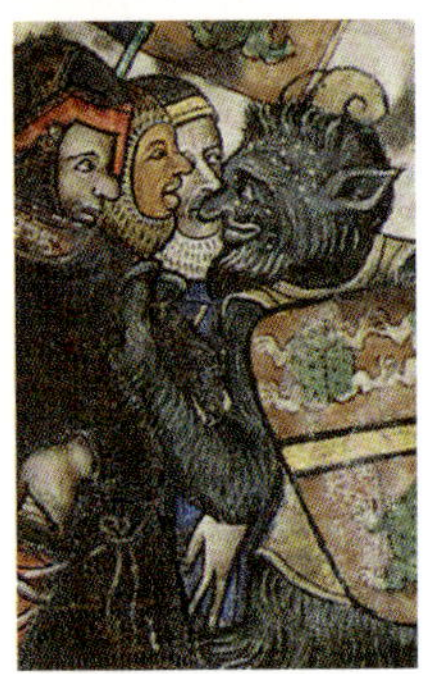

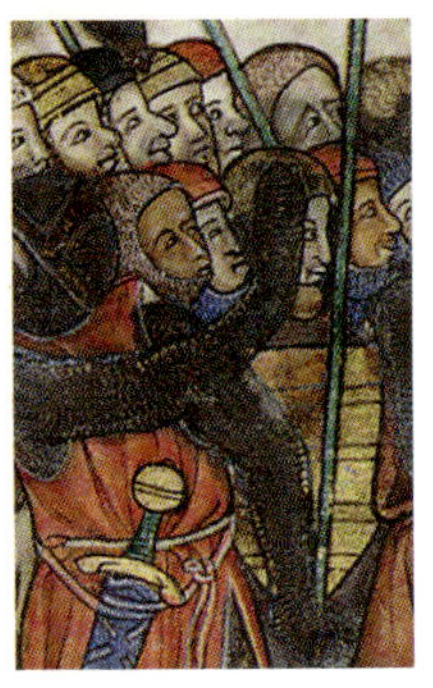

There was every indication that the end of the world was at hand. Nothing was wanting. The *Apocalypse* announced that Jesus would descend on a throne of clouds and the martyrs would rise first. The Angel of Mercy would await God's command.

But a calm followed the storm. The terrible Jewish war came to an end; Nero fell before

Illustration from "The Douce Apocalypse", c. 1270
Illumination
University of Oxford, Bodleian Library, Oxford

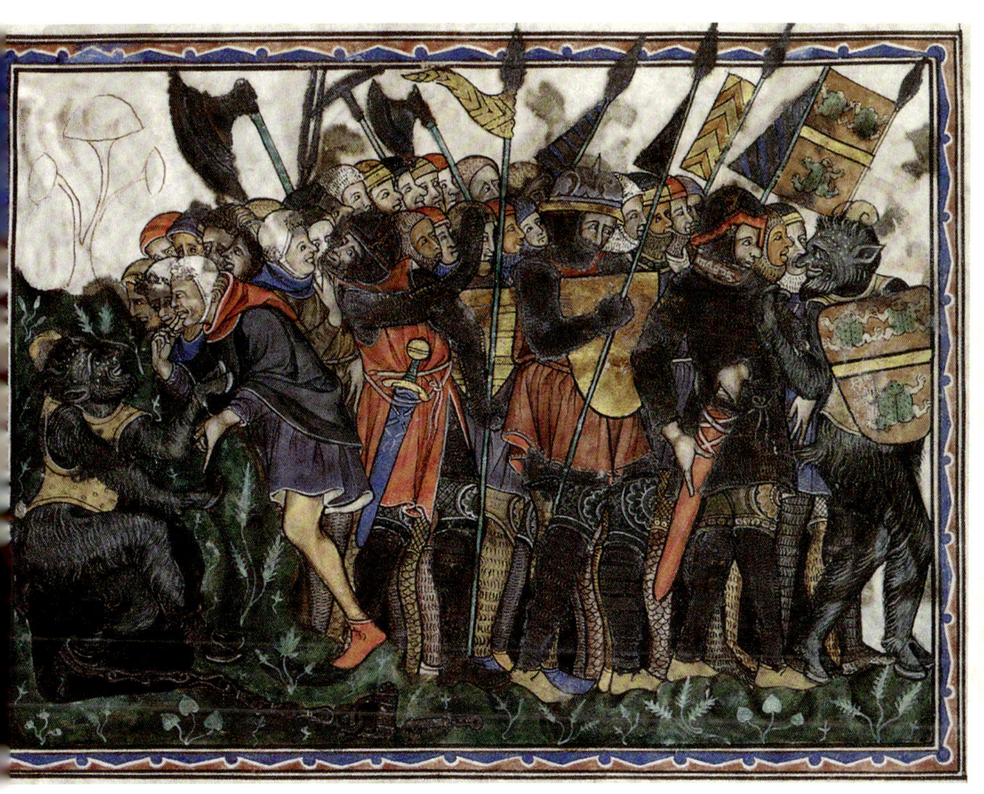

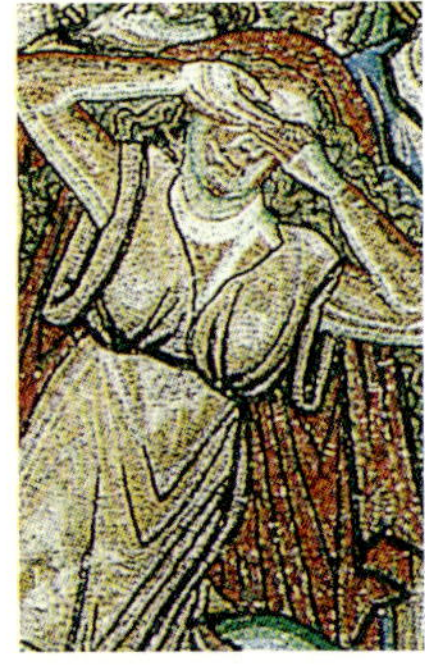

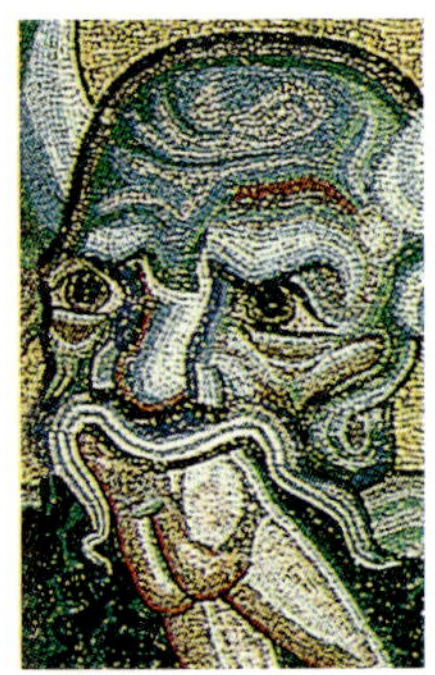

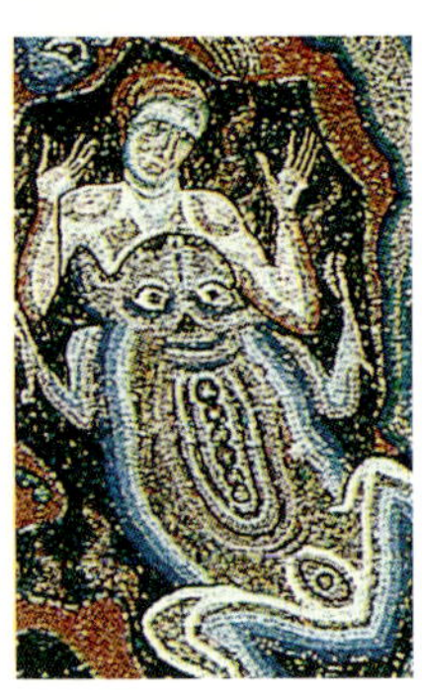

Galba; under Vespasian and Titus, peace, in the year 71 CE succeeded war, and – the end of the world still did not come to pass.

Once more, it became necessary to reinterpret the words of the evangelists. The coming of Christ was put off until after the fall of the Roman Empire, and thus considerable margin was given to the commentator. A firm belief in a final and even an

The Infernal Chaos around Satan

Atributted to Coppo di Marcovaldo, c. 1270
Mosaic
Battistero di San Giovanni, Florence

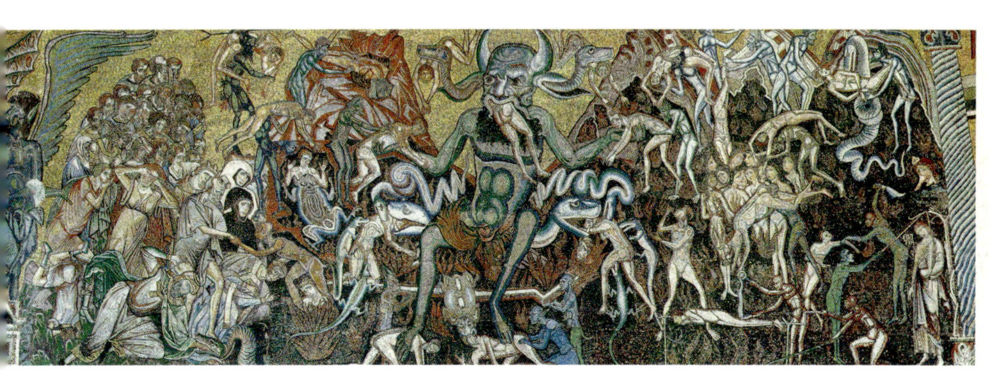

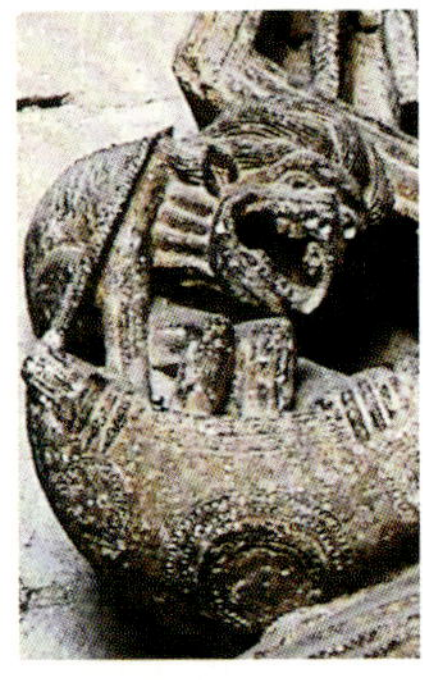

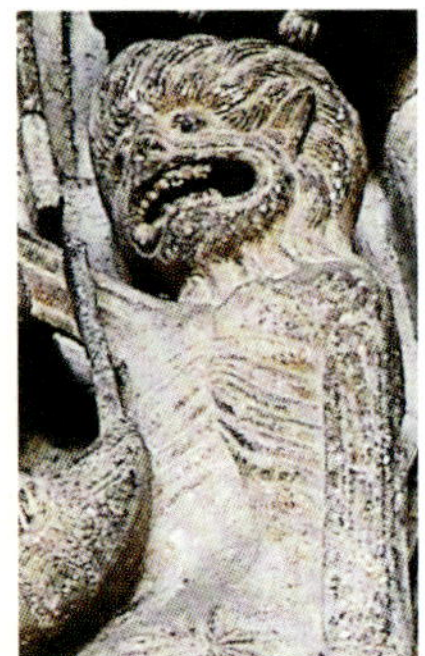

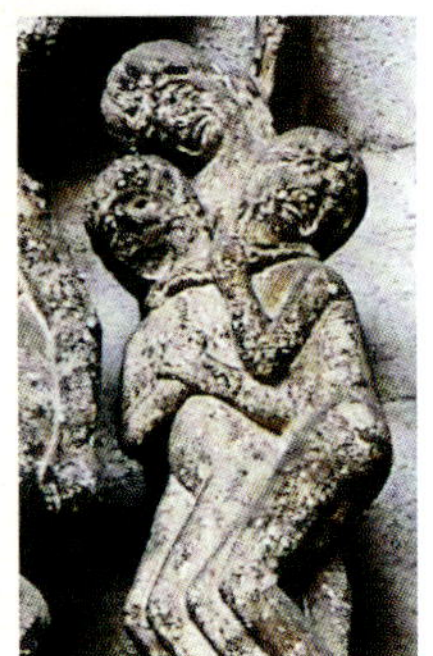

imminent catastrophe persisted, but it was embedded in vague terms, which robbed the spirit as well as the letter of the prophecy of all precision. Still, the conviction remained.

St Augustine devotes the 20th book of the *City of God* (426) to the regeneration of the world, the resurrection, the last judgement, and

Last Judgement (tympanum, west portal, detail)

Gislebertus, c. 1120-1135
Cathédrale Saint-Lazare, Autun

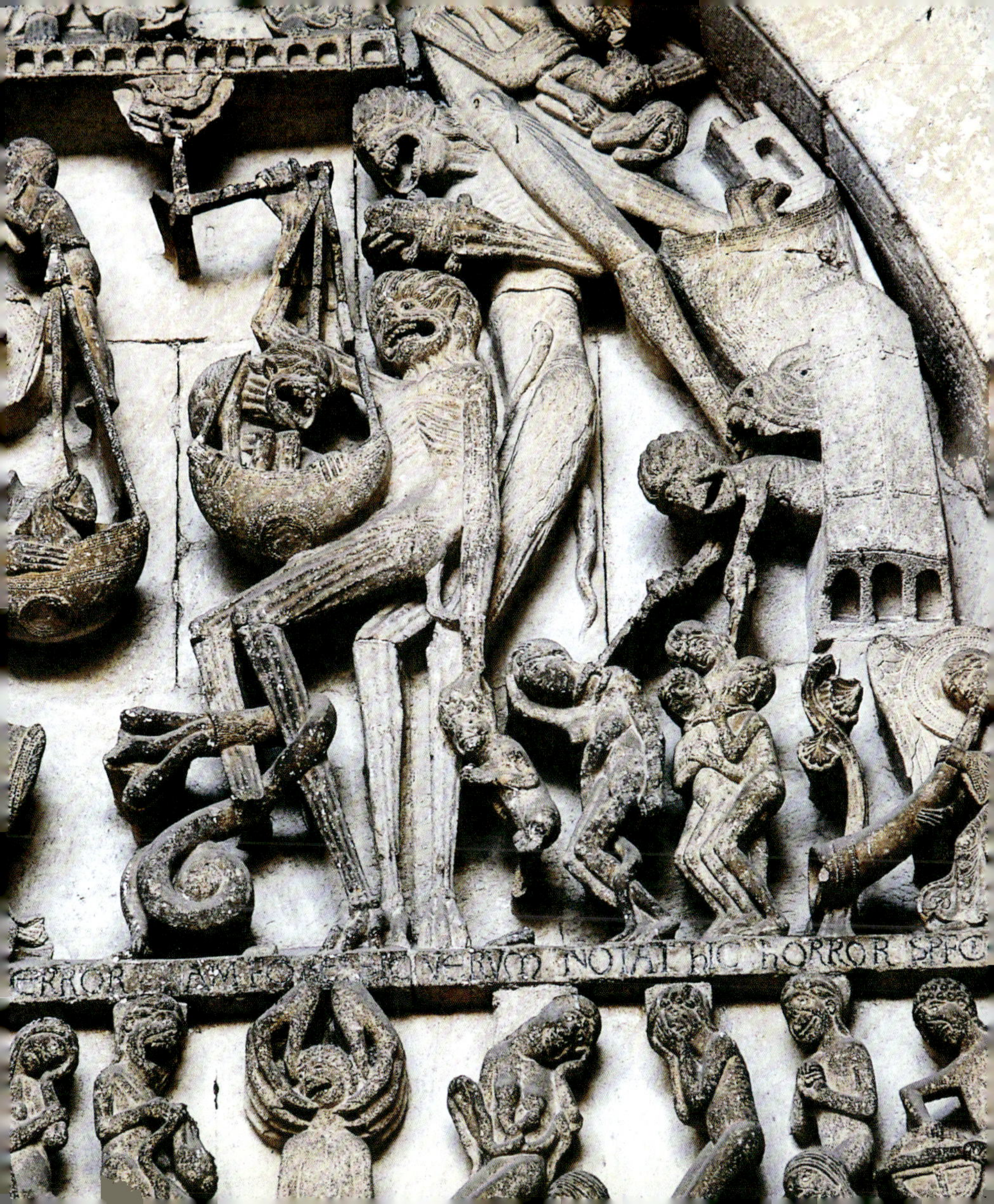

ERROR AVICO .... NERVM NOTAT HIC HORROR SPE

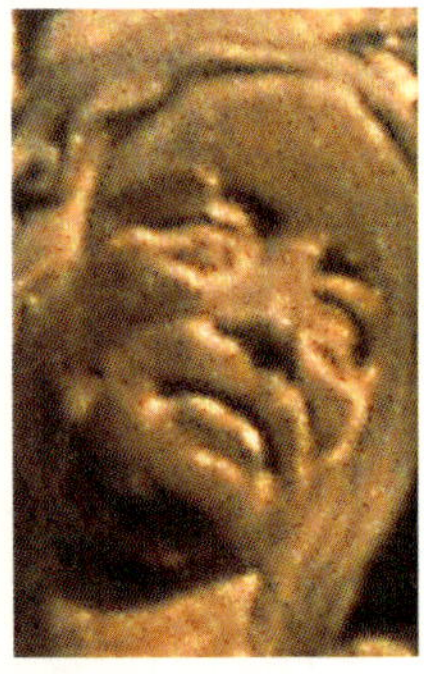

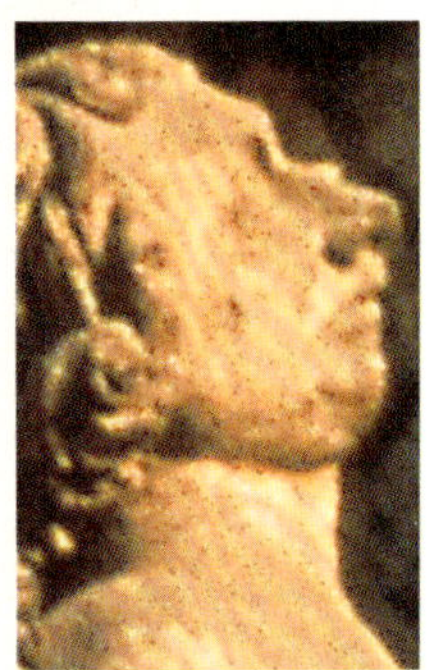

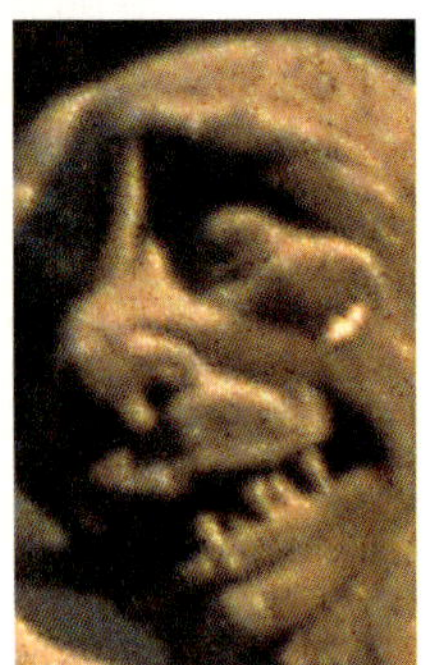

the New Jerusalem; in the 21st book he describes the everlasting torments of hell-fire. A witness to the fall of Rome and the Empire, the Bishop of Carthage believed these events to be the first act of the drama. But the Kingdom of God would continue for a thousand more years before the rise of Satan.

Last Judgement (tympanum), Bourges Cathedral

c. 1270
Sculpture
Cathédrale Saint-Étienne de Bourges, Bourges

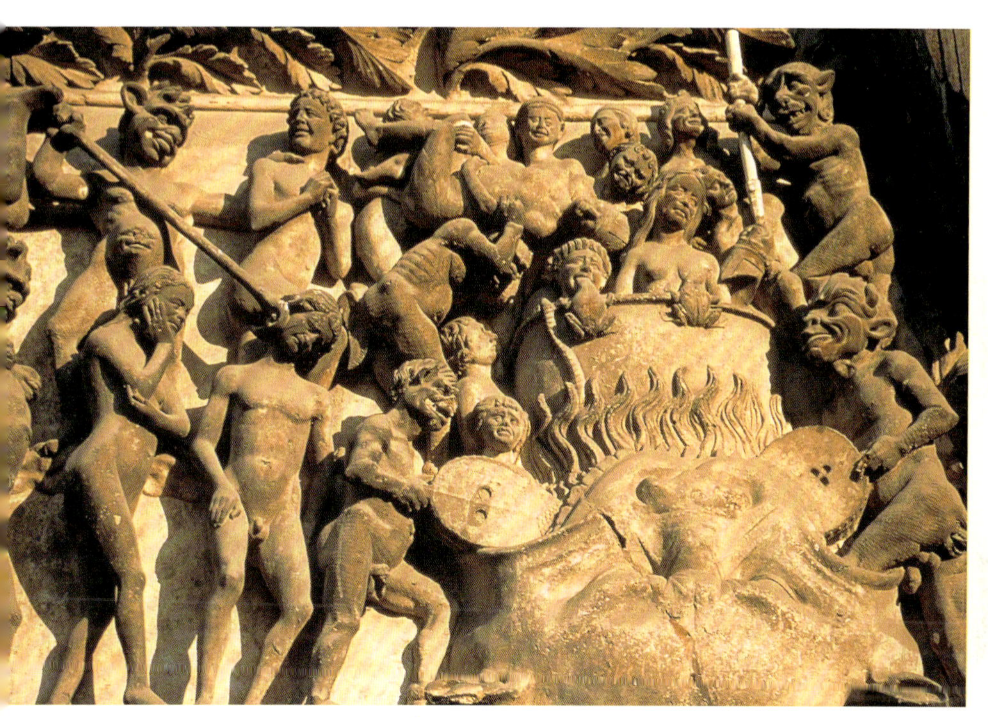

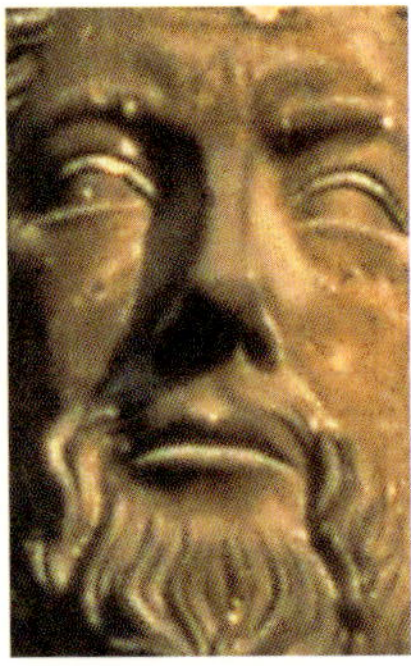

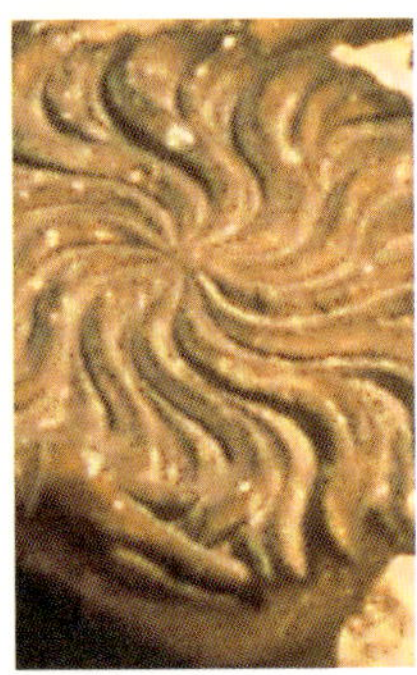

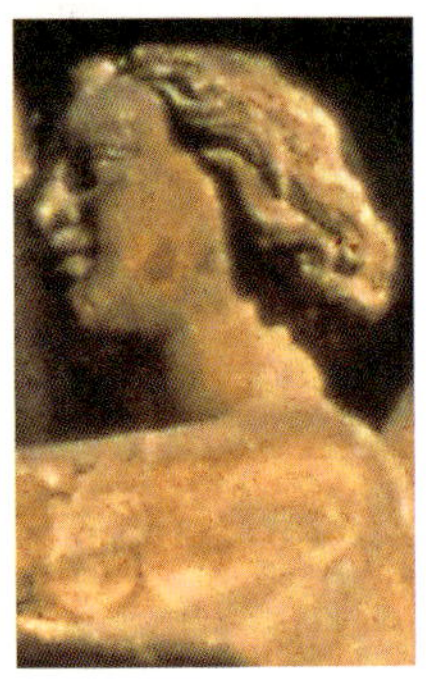

St Gregory, Bishop of Tours (573), the first historian of the Franks, began his history as follows:

As I am about to relate the wars of the kings with hostile nations, I feel impelled to declare my belief. The terror with which men await the end of the world decides me to chronicle the years already passed,

Last Judgement, Christ Enthroned

c. 1270
Sculpture
Cathédrale Saint-Étienne de Bourges, Bourges

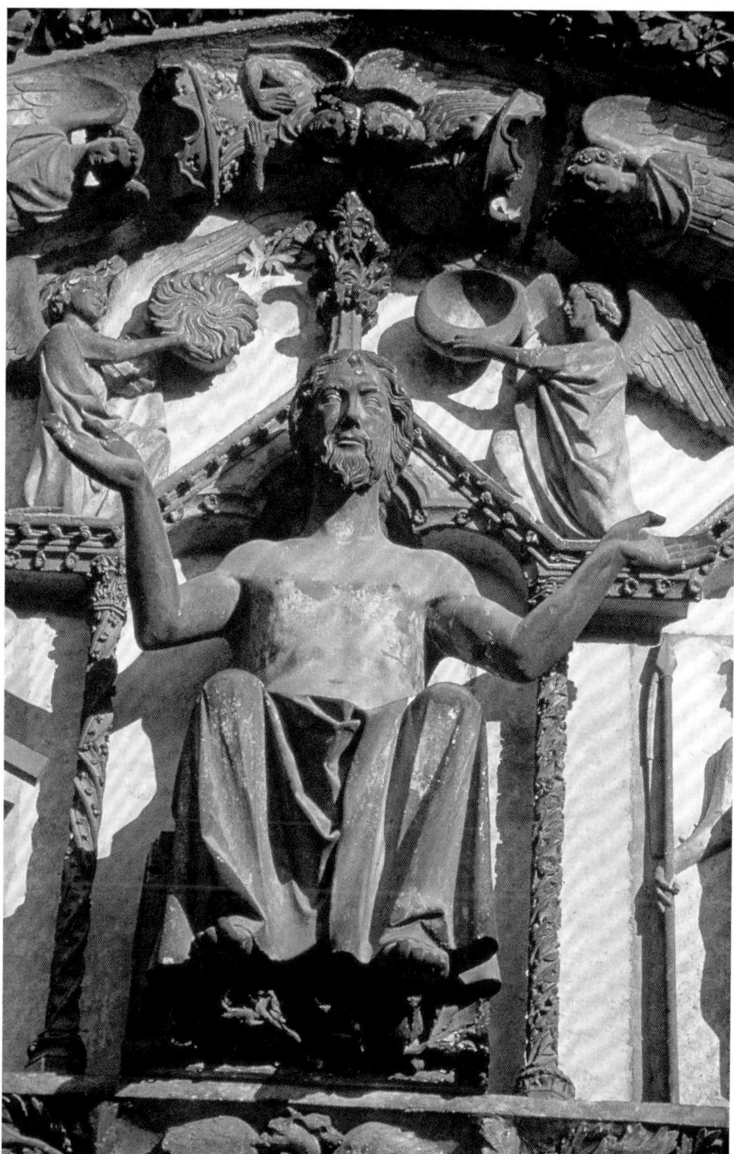

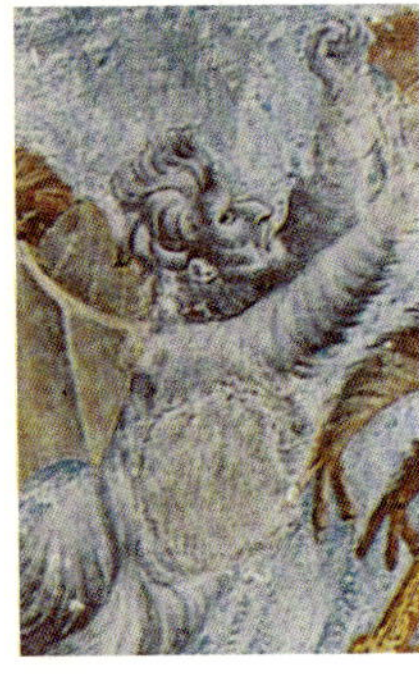

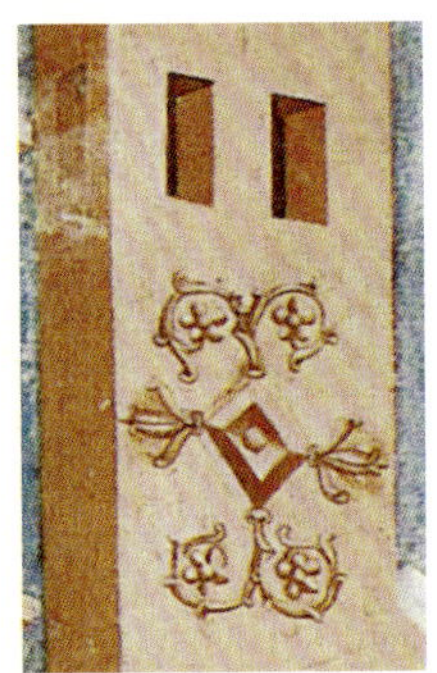

that thus one may know exactly how many have elapsed since the beginning of the world.

The saviour had come to deliver mankind. What was he waiting for, transportation to Heaven? This Christian tradition was perpetuated year on year and century on century, despite

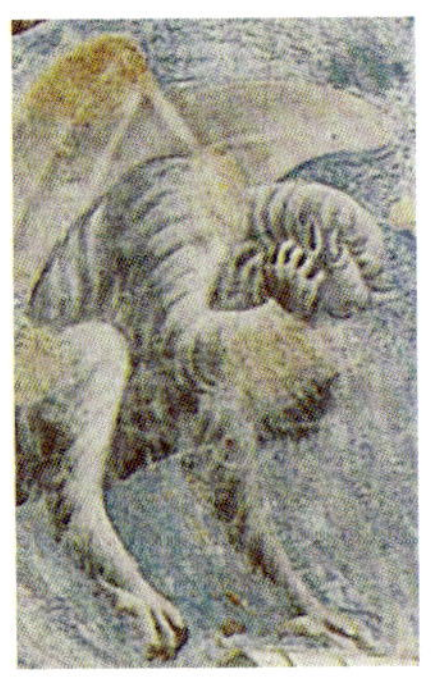

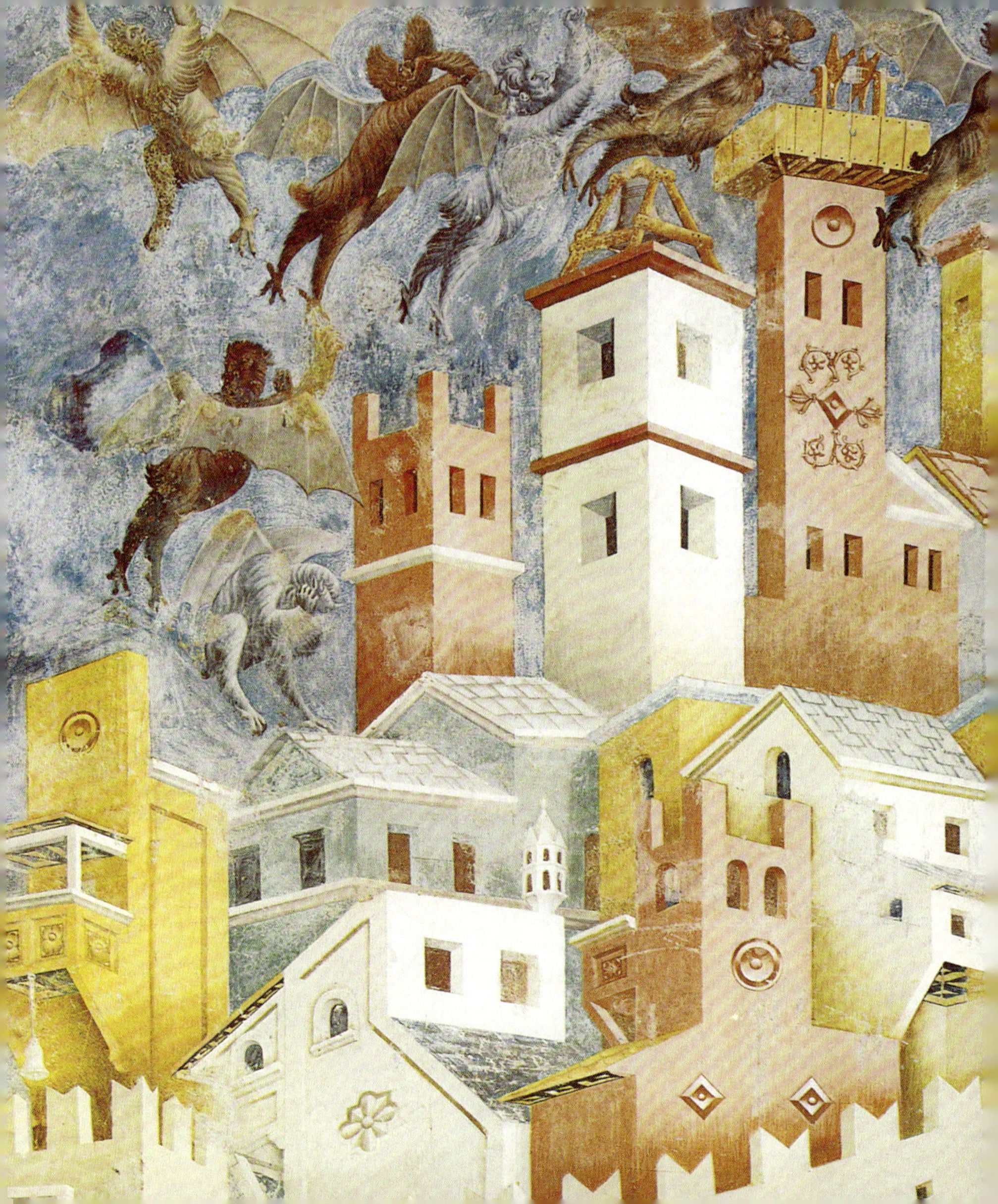

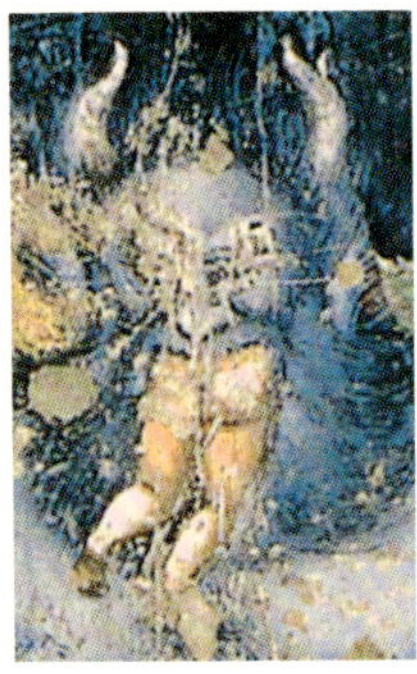

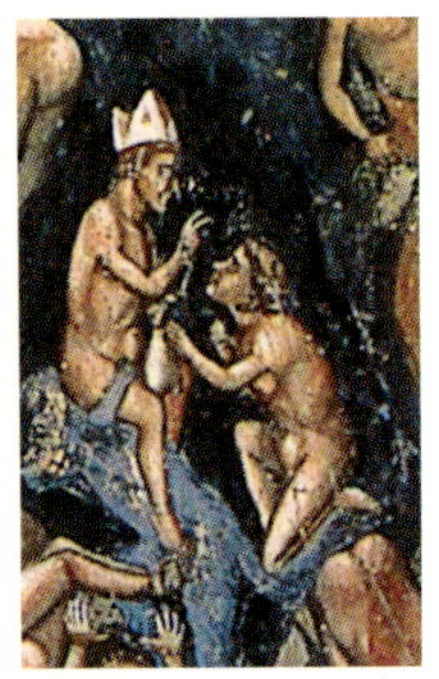

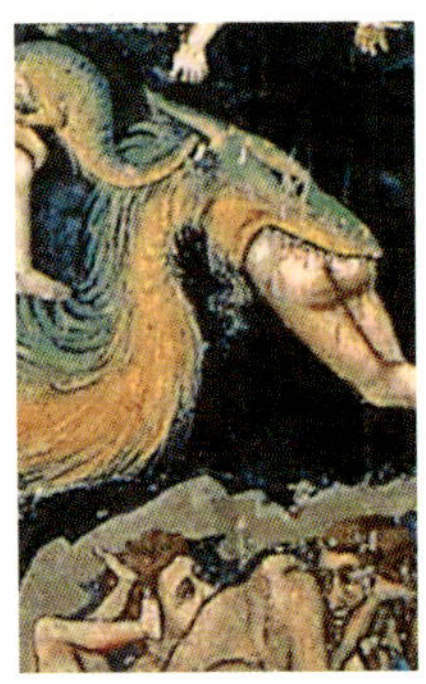

nature's evidence to the contrary. Every catastrophe, earthquake, epidemic, famine, and flood, every phenomenon, eclipse, comet, storm, sudden darkness, and tempest, was regarded as the forerunner and herald of the final cataclysm. Trembling like leaves agitated by the wind, the faithful awaited the coming

The Last Judgement (detail)

Giotto di Bondone, 1302-1305
Fresco
Capella degli Scrovegni (Arena Chapel), Padua

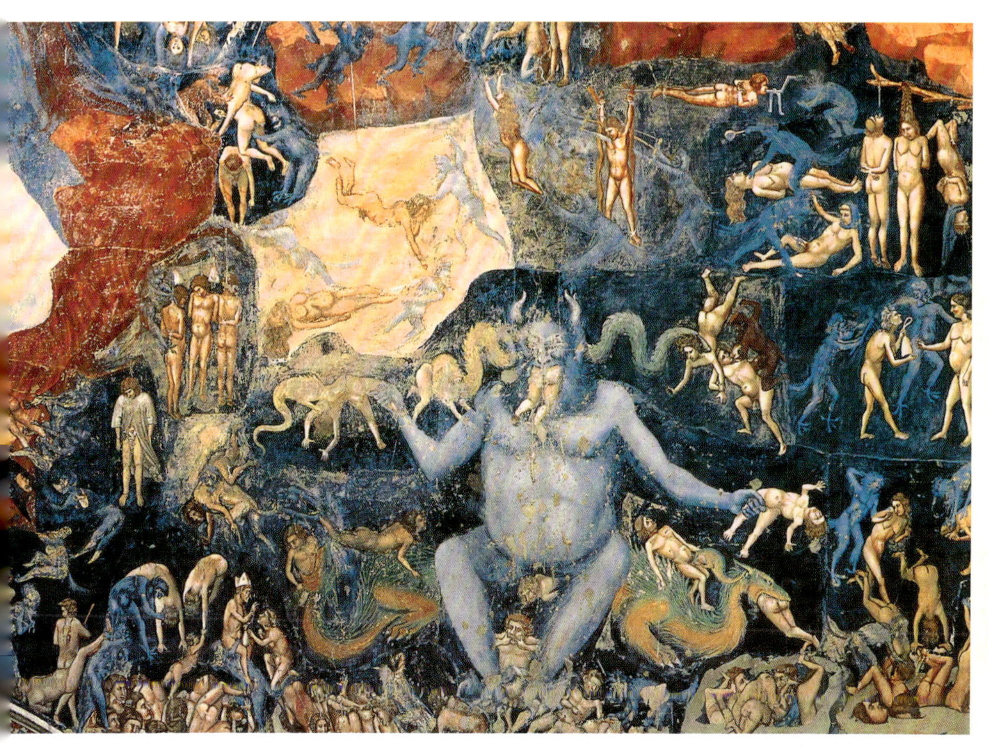

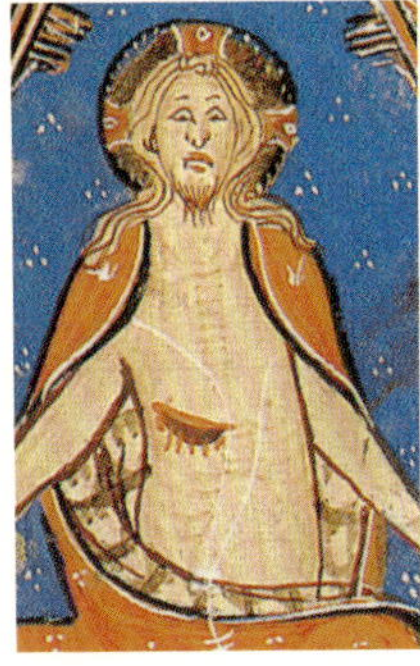

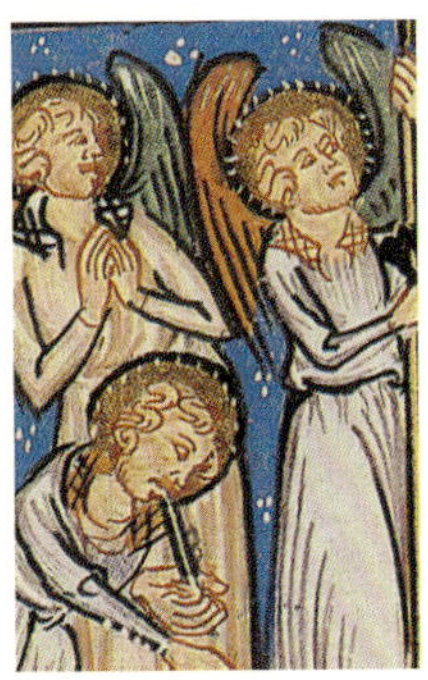

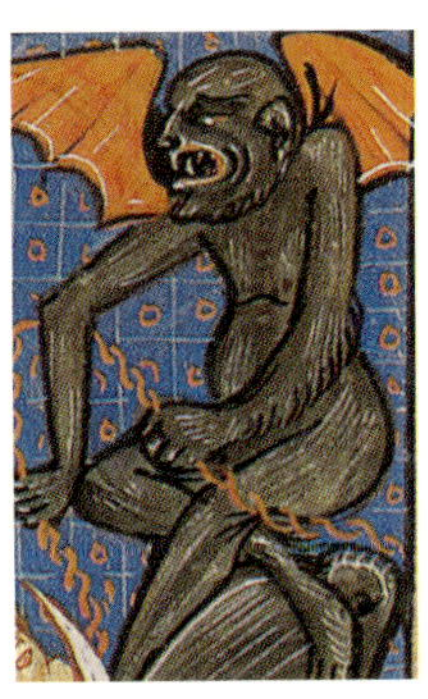

judgement while preachers successfully maintained this dreaded fear which was so deeply rooted in every heart.

But, as generation after generation passed, it became necessary to redefine, once again, the wide-spread theory, and it was around this time that the idea of a millennium took form in the minds of commentators. There were many sects

The Last Judgement

14th century
Illuminated manuscript

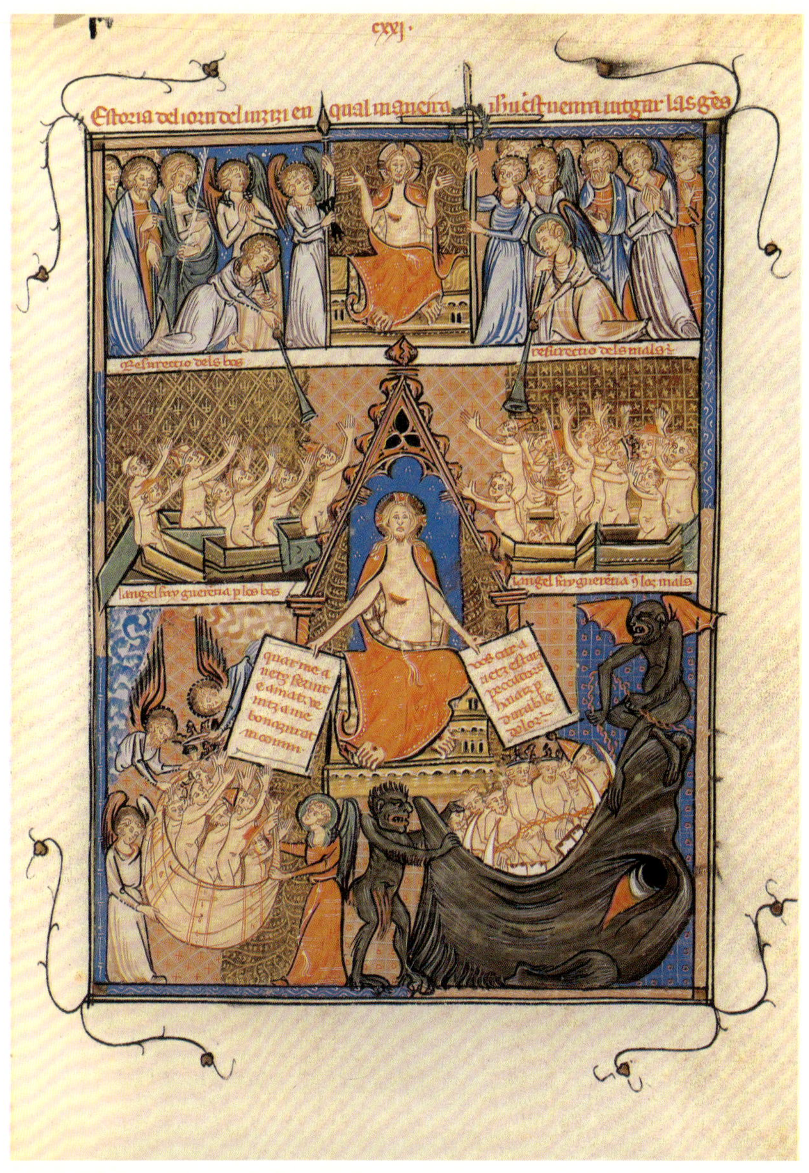
Estoria del iorn del iuzizi en qual manera ihu xrist uenra iutgar las gens
resurrectio dels bos
resurrectio dels mals
l angel fay guerentia p los bos
l angel fay guerentia y los mals
quar me a netz faim e amat e iga me bonaiurat m cō rū
uos aiaz a ter eternaumos huas p durable dolor

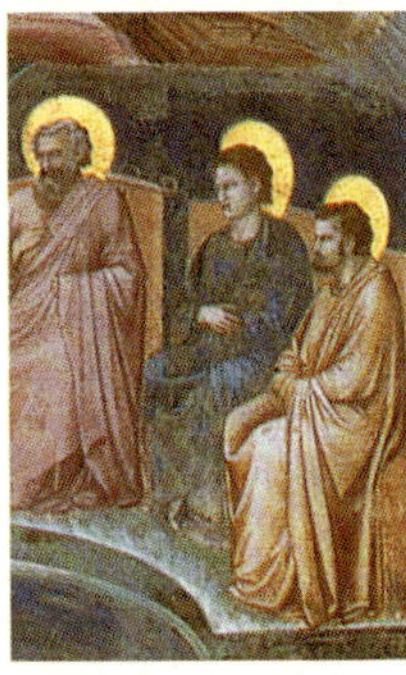

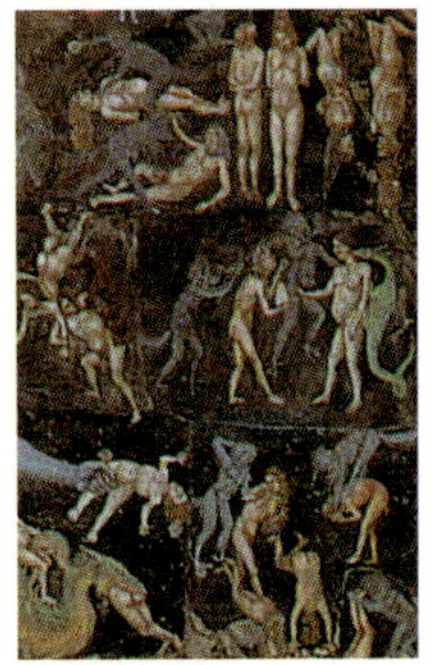

which believed that Christ would reign with the saints on Earth a thousand years before the Day of Judgement. St Irenus, St Papias, and St Sulpicius Severus shared this belief, which became exaggerated and overblown in the minds of many who looked forward to a day of general rejoicing for the elect and a reign of pleasure.

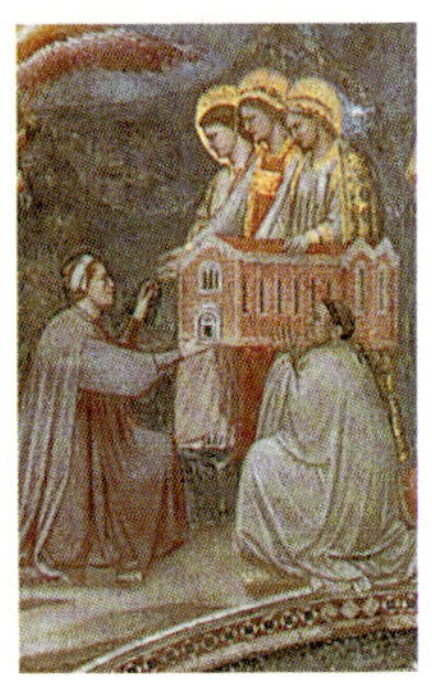

The Last Judgement

———————————————————

Giotto di Bondone, 1303-1305
Fresco
Capella degli Scrovegni (Arena Chapel), Padua

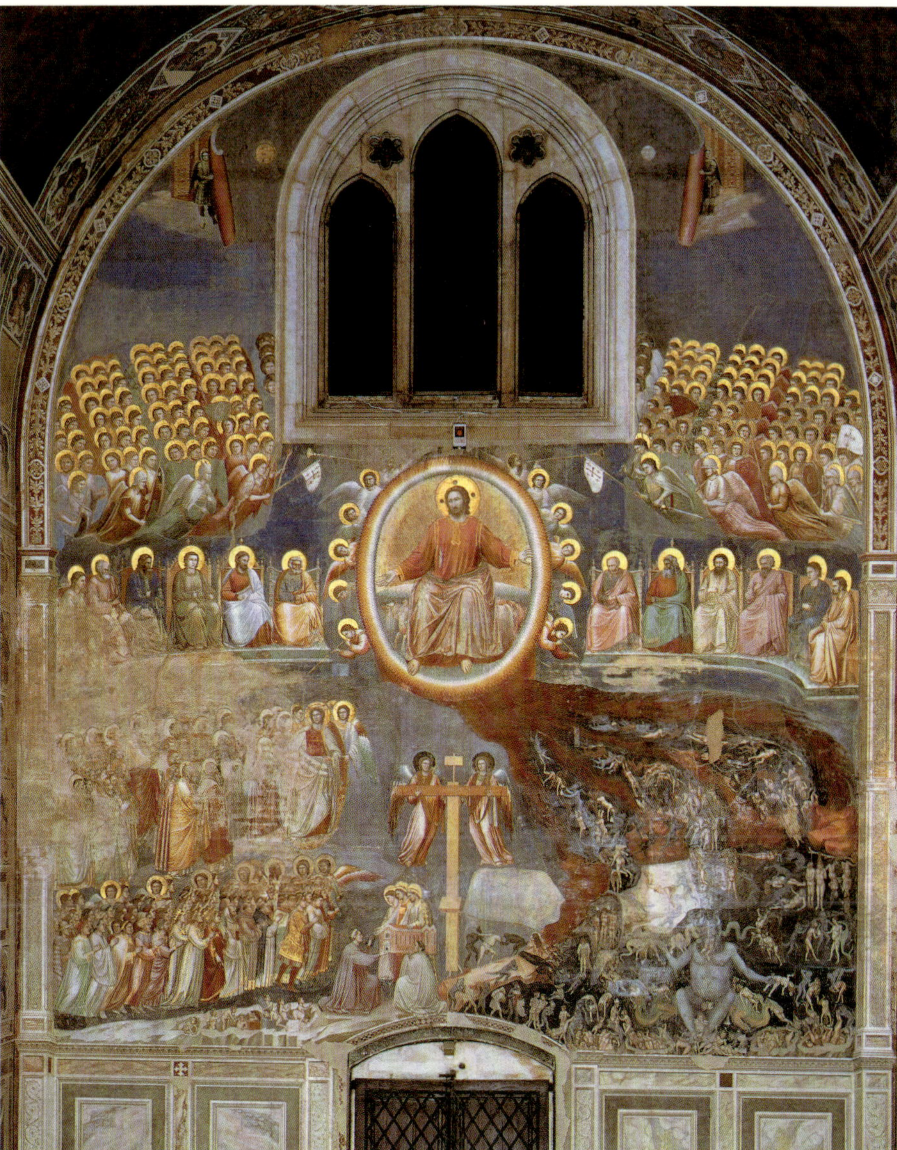

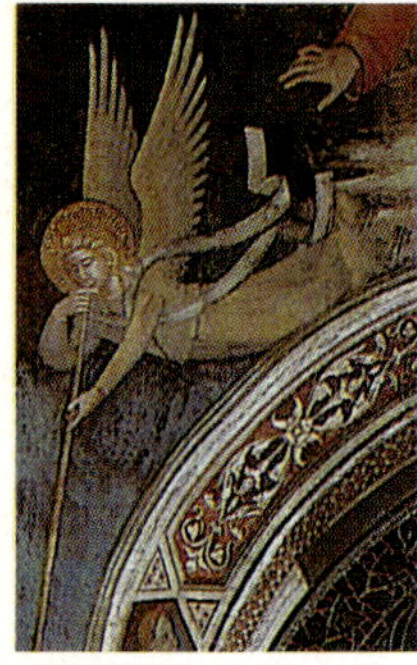

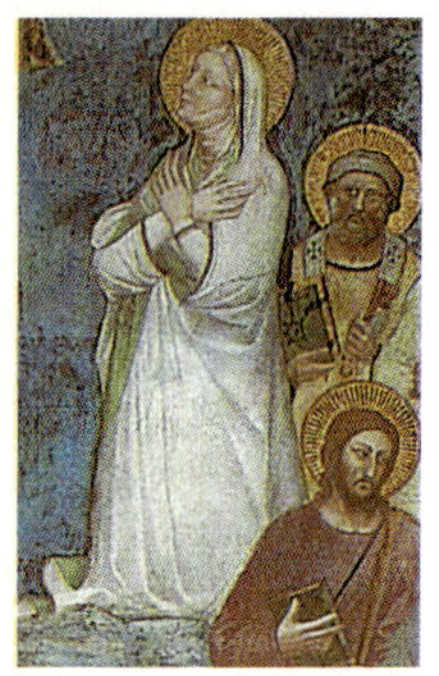

St Jerome and St Augustine did much to discredit these views, but did not attack the central doctrine of a resurrection. Comments about the apocalypse continued to flourish through the sombre darkness of the Middle Ages, and in the 10th century the belief gained ground that the year 1000 was to usher in the great change.

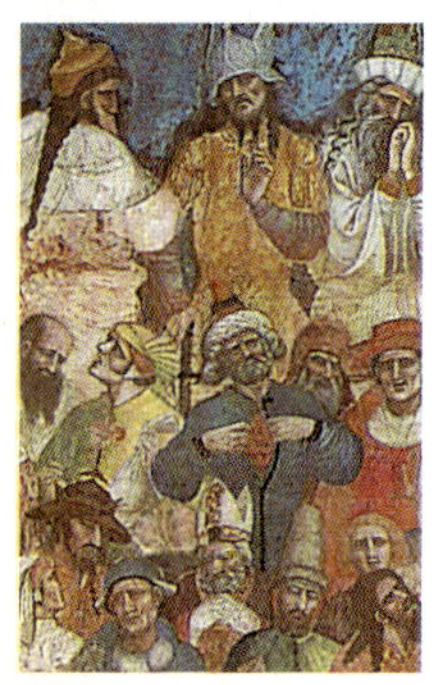

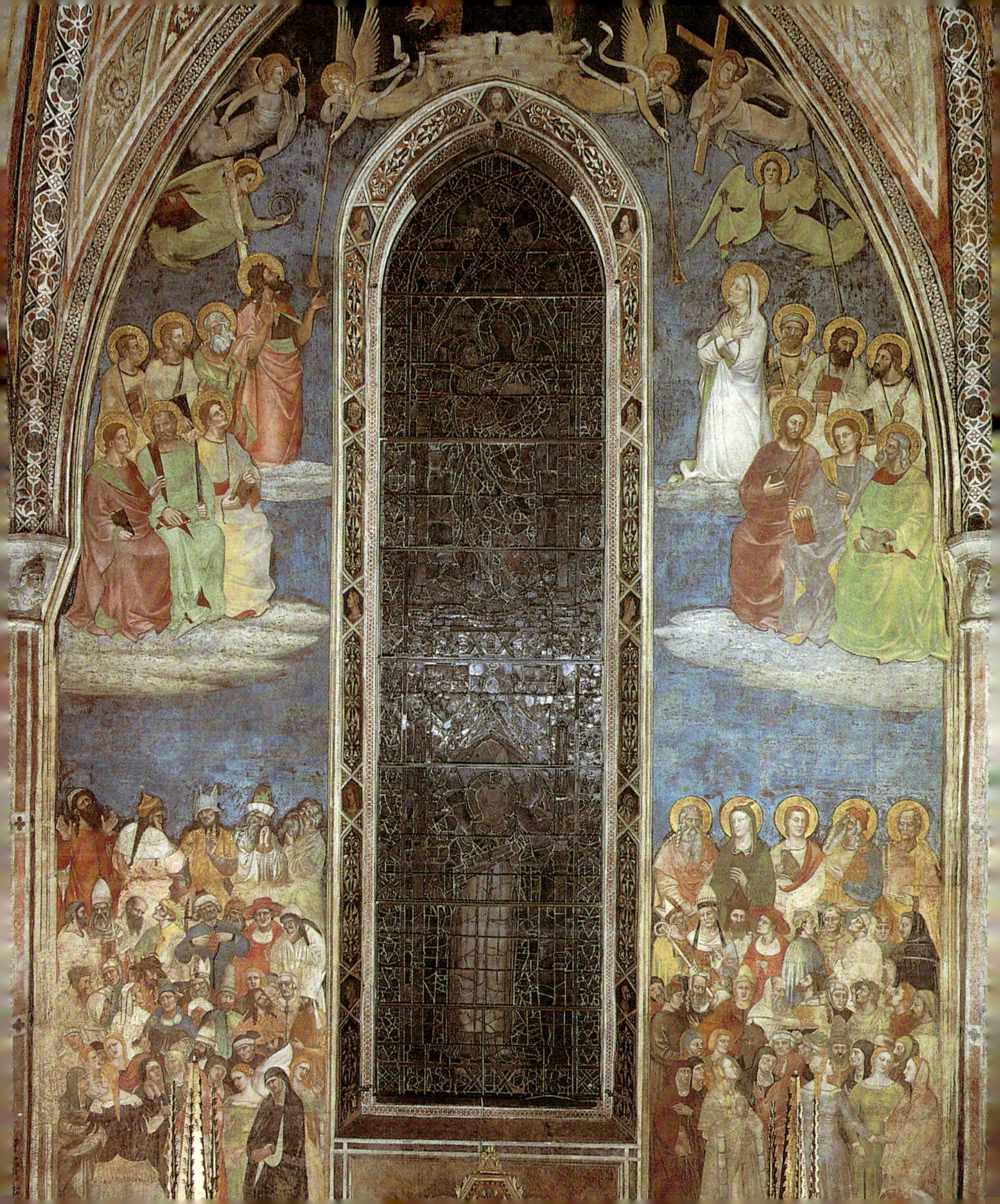

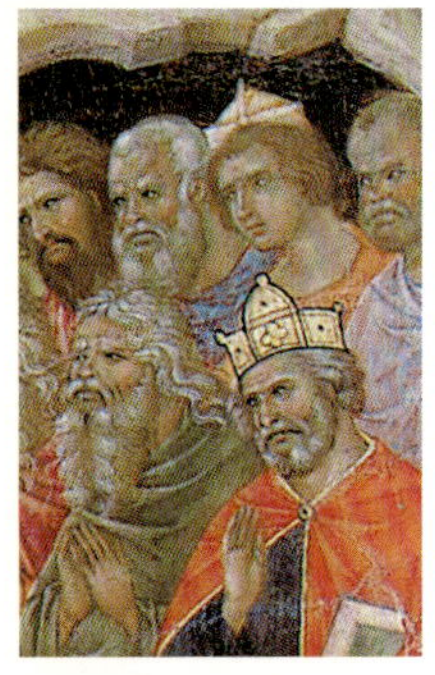

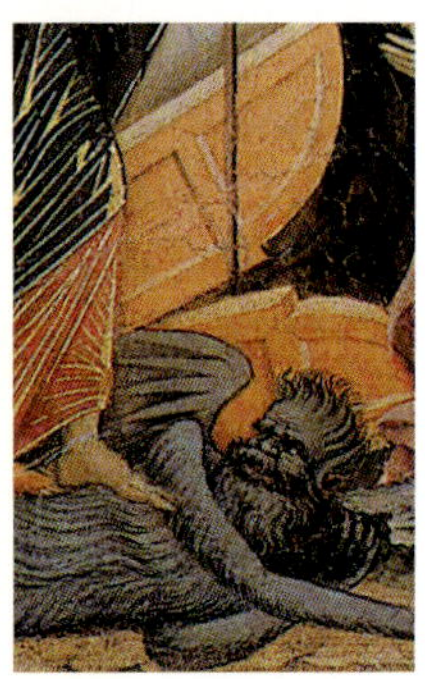

This conviction of an approaching end of the world, if not universal, was at least very general. Several charters of the period began with *Termino mundi appropinquante* – the end of the world drawing near. In spite of some exceptions, it seems difficult not to share the opinion of historians, notably of Michelet, Henry Martin,

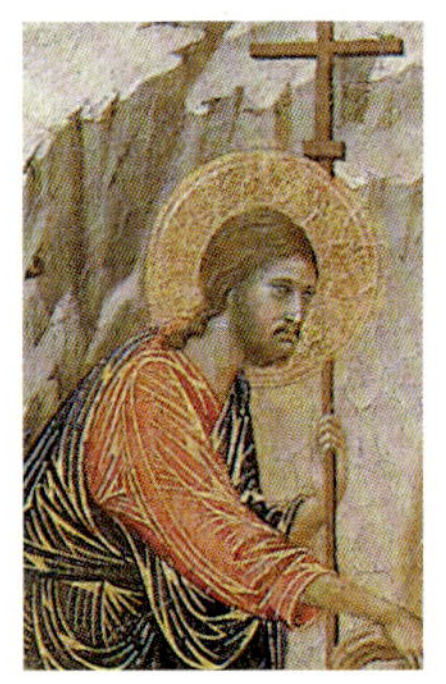

Descent to Hell, back panel of the Maestà

Duccio di Buoninsegna, 1308-1311
Tempera on wood, 51 x 53.5 cm
Museo dell'Opera Metropolitana del Duomo, Sienna

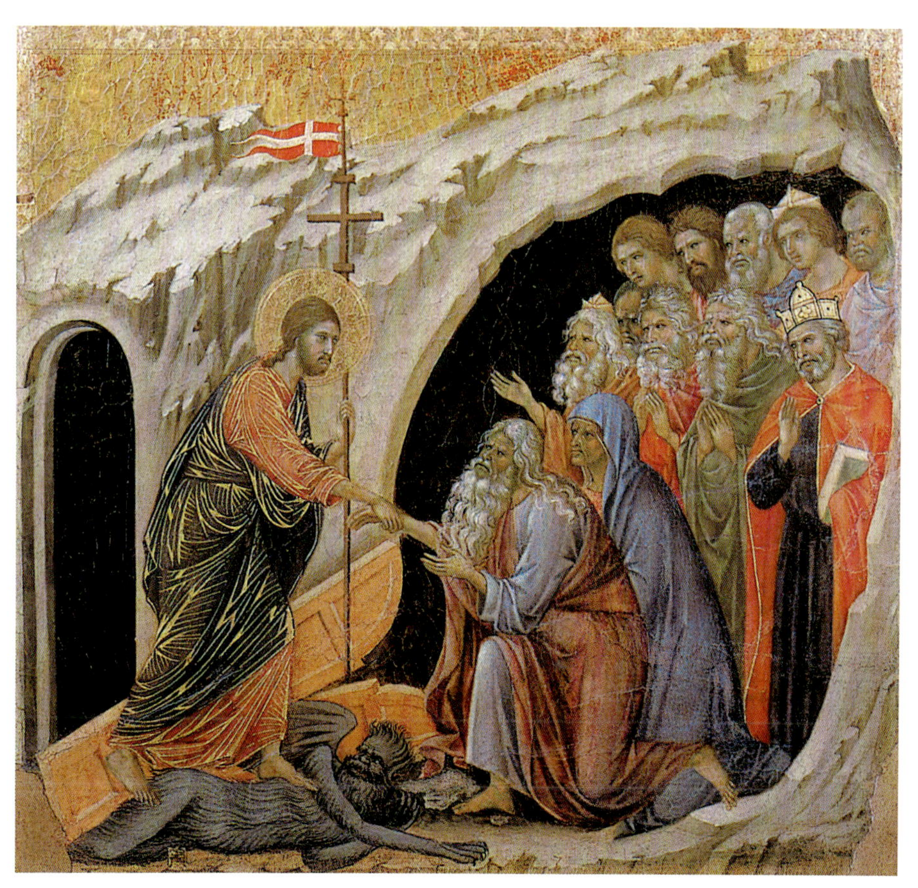

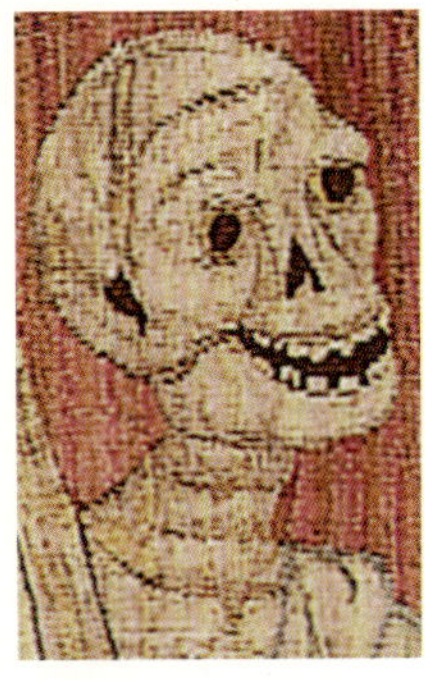

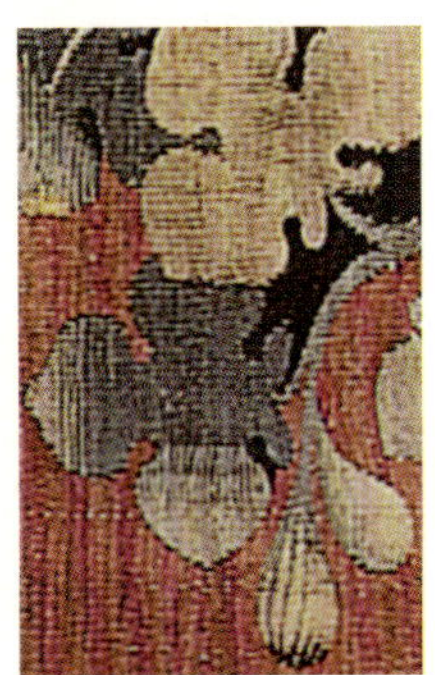

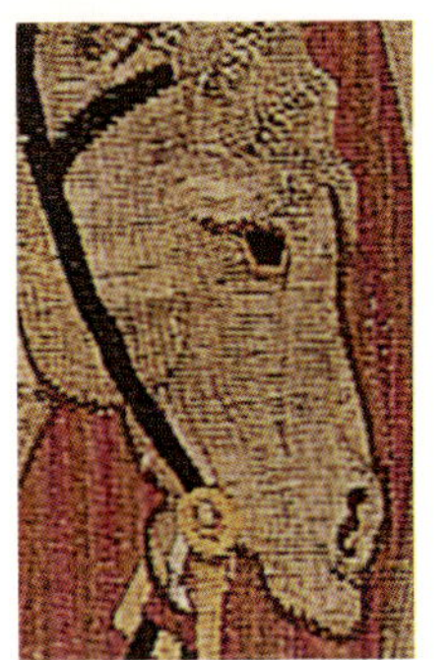

Guizot, and Duruy, regarding the prevalence of this belief throughout Christendom. Undoubtedly, neither the French monk Gerbert, at that time Pope Sylvester II, nor King Robert of France, regulated their lives by their superstition, but it, nevertheless, had penetrated the conscience of the faint-hearted, and many a sermon was preached from this text of the Apocalypse:

The Opening of the Fourth Seal (detail)

Nicolas de Bataille and Jean Bondol (design), c. 1373-1381
From The Apocalypse of Angers
Tapestry
Musée des Tapisseries, Angers

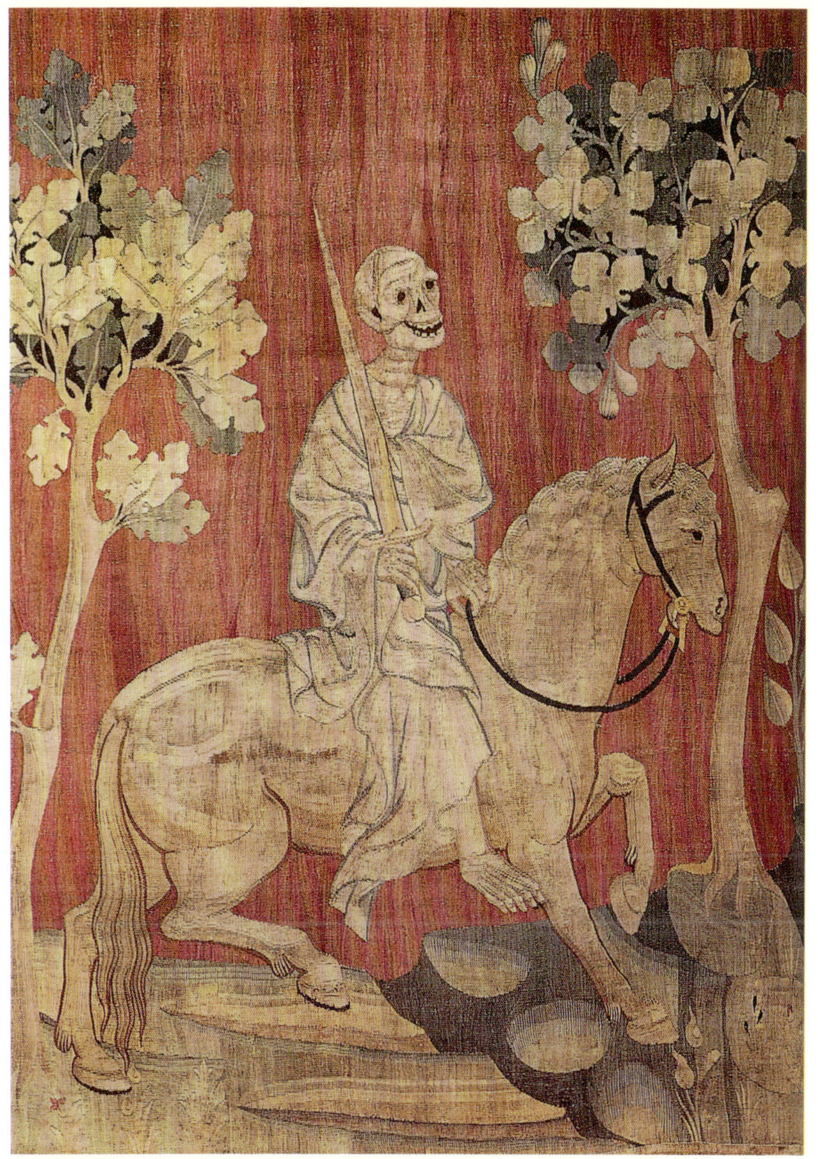

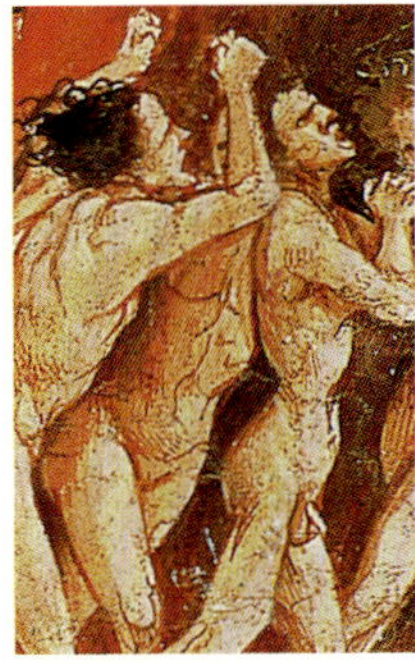

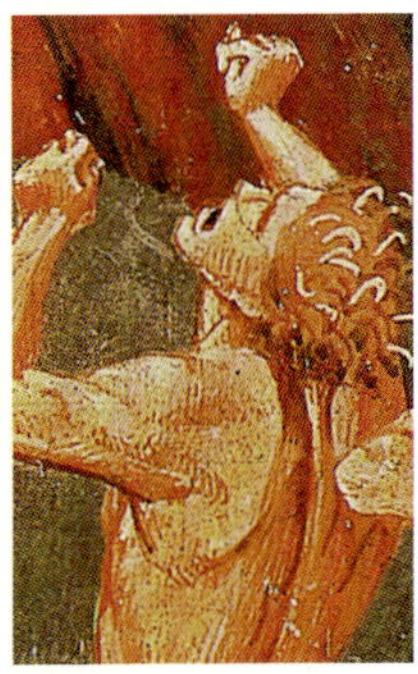

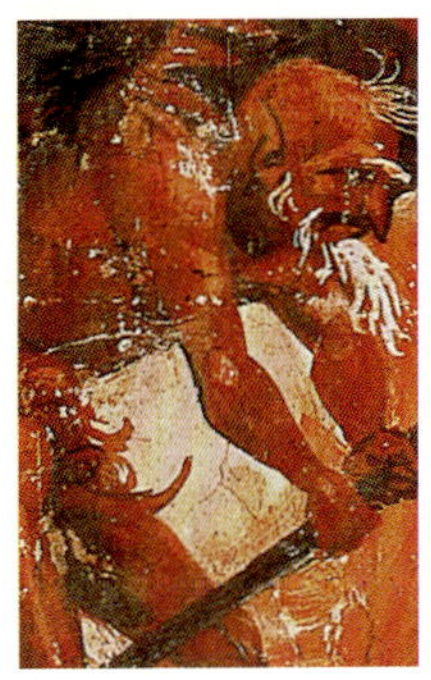

And when the thousand years are expired, Satan shall be loosed out of his prison, and shall go out to deceive the nations which are in the four quarters of the earth ... and another book was opened, which is the Book of Life ... and the sea gave up the dead which were in it:

The Orchard of Drunkenness
or The Orchard of the Consolation

12th-14th centuries
Illuminated manuscript, 44 x 30 cm
Bibliothèque Nationale de France, Paris

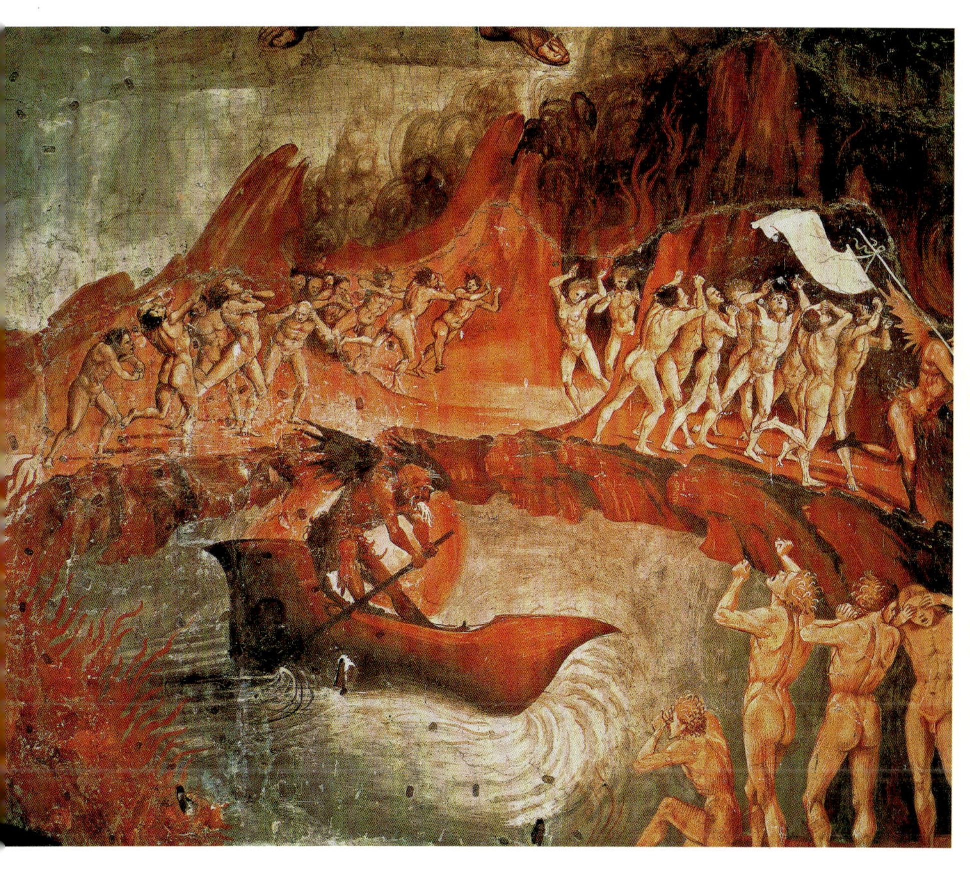

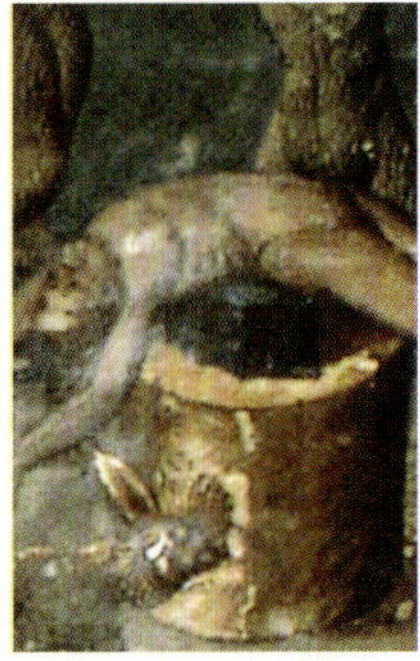

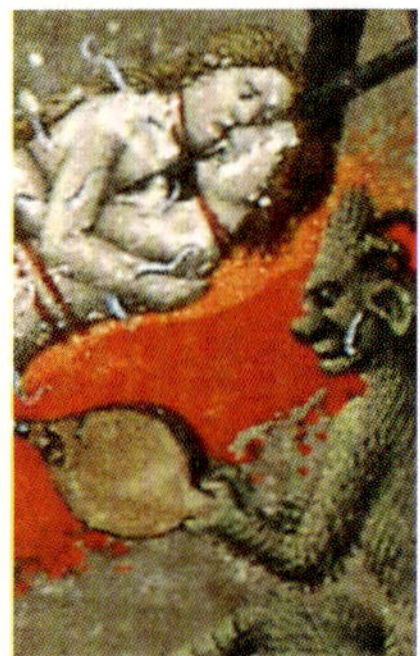

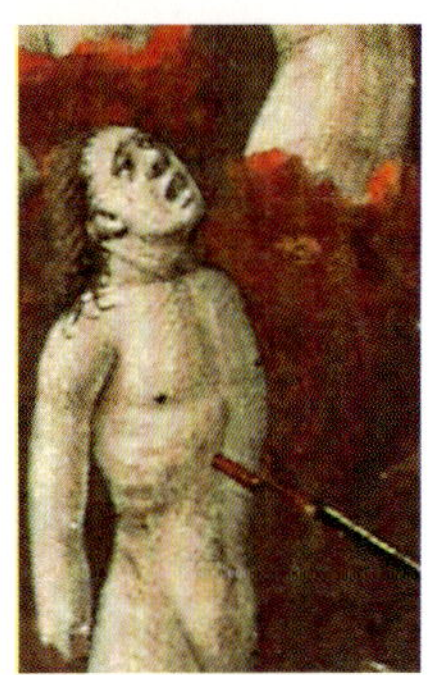

and death and hell gave up the dead
which were in them and they were judged
every man according to his works … and
I saw a new heaven and a new earth.

Bernard, a hermit of Thuringia, had taken
these very words of Revelation as the text of his
preaching, and in about the year 960 he publicly
announced that the end of the world was at hand.

The Last Judgement

End of the 14th century
Oil on wood mounted on canvas
Musée des Arts décoratifs, Paris

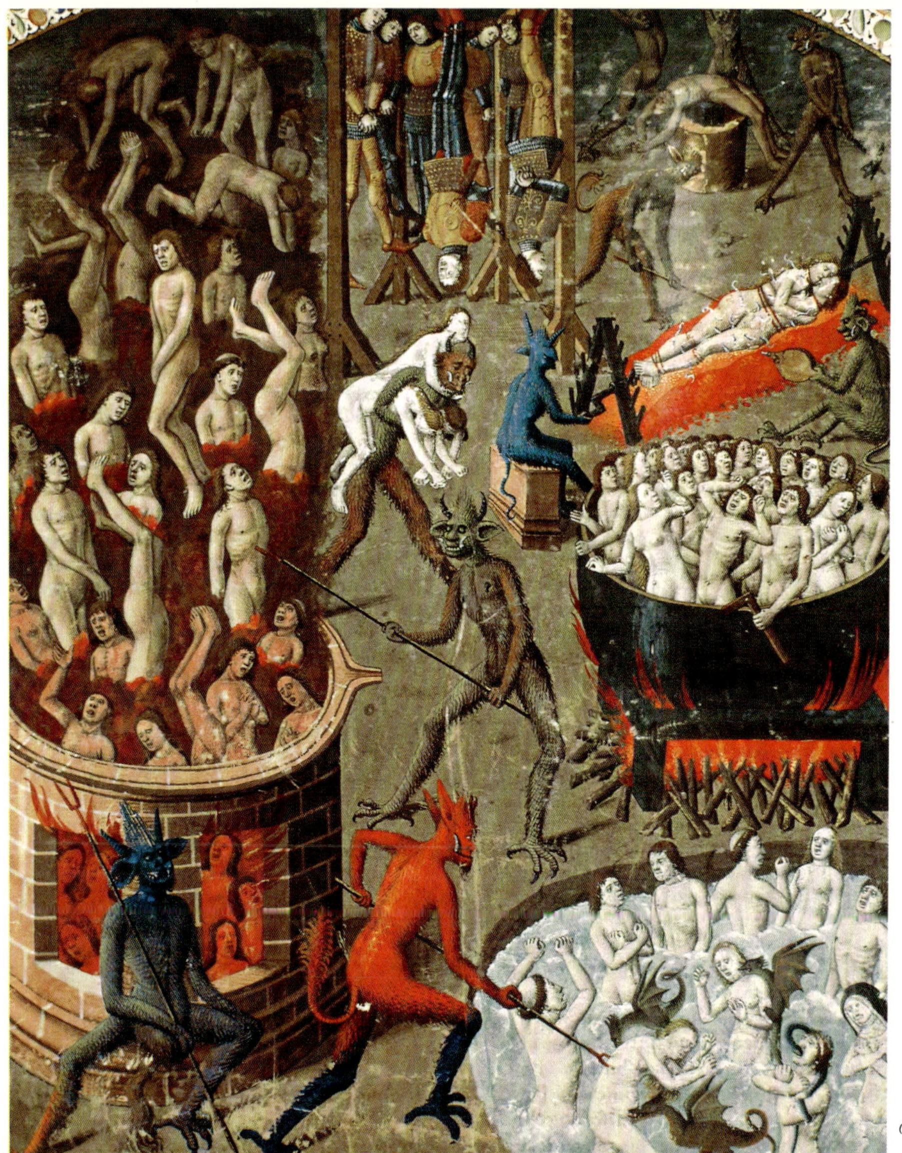

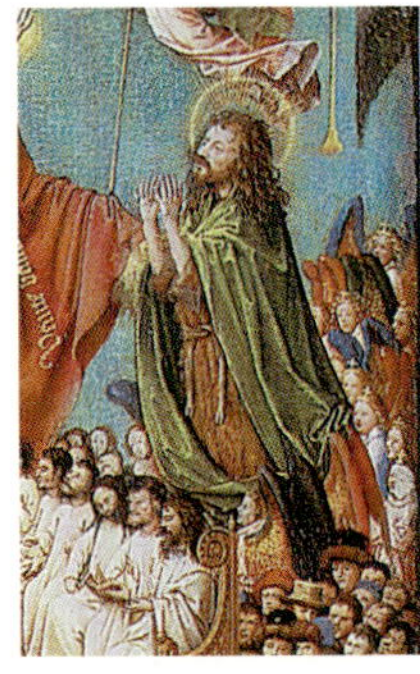

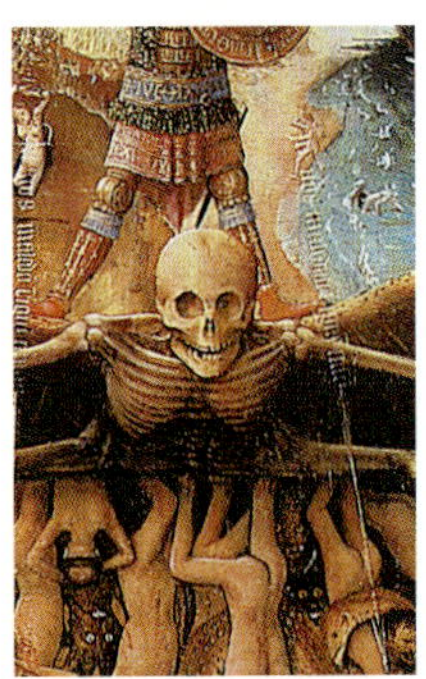

He even fixed the fatal day itself, as that on which "The Annunciation" and Holy Friday should fall on the same day, a coincidence which occurred in 992.

Druthmar, a monk of Corbie, prophesied the end of the world for 24 March 1000. In many cities, popular terror was so great on that day that people sought refuge in the churches,

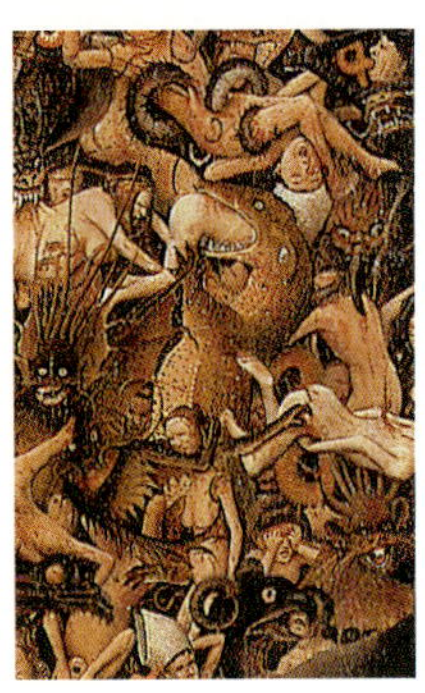

The Last Judgement (detail)

Jan Van Eyck, c. 1430
Oil on wood mounted on canvas, 56.5 x 19.7 cm
The Metropolitan Museum of Art, New York

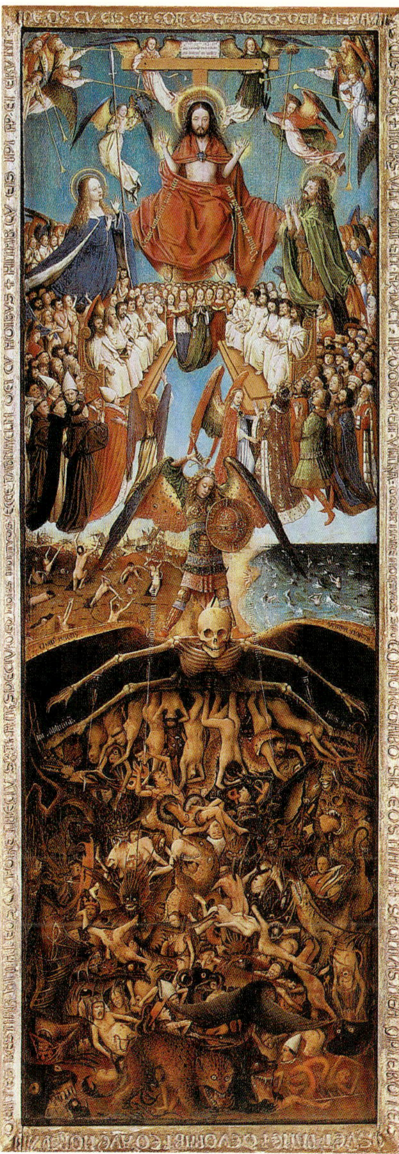

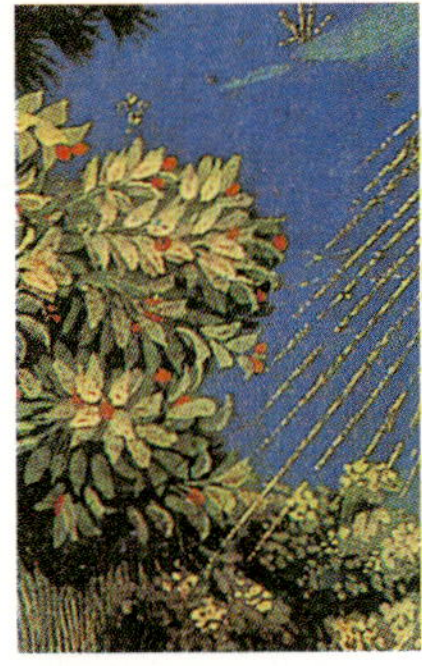

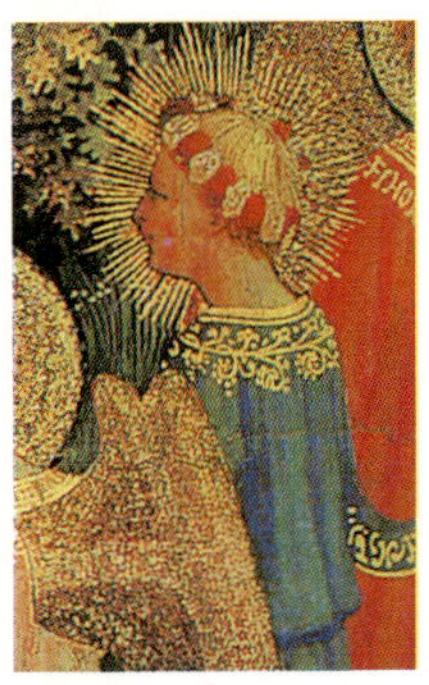

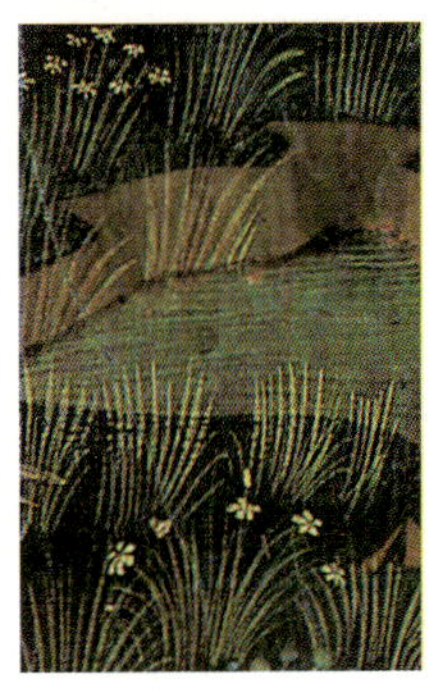

remaining until midnight, prostrate before the relics of the saints in order to await the last sing of Judgement and die at the foot of the cross.

Many gifts to the Church date to this epoch. Lands and goods were given to the monasteries. In fact, an authentic and very interesting document is preserved, written in the year 1000

The Last Judgement (detail), The Elect

Fra Angelico, c. 1431
Tempera on wood, 105 x 210 cm
Museo di San Marco, Florence

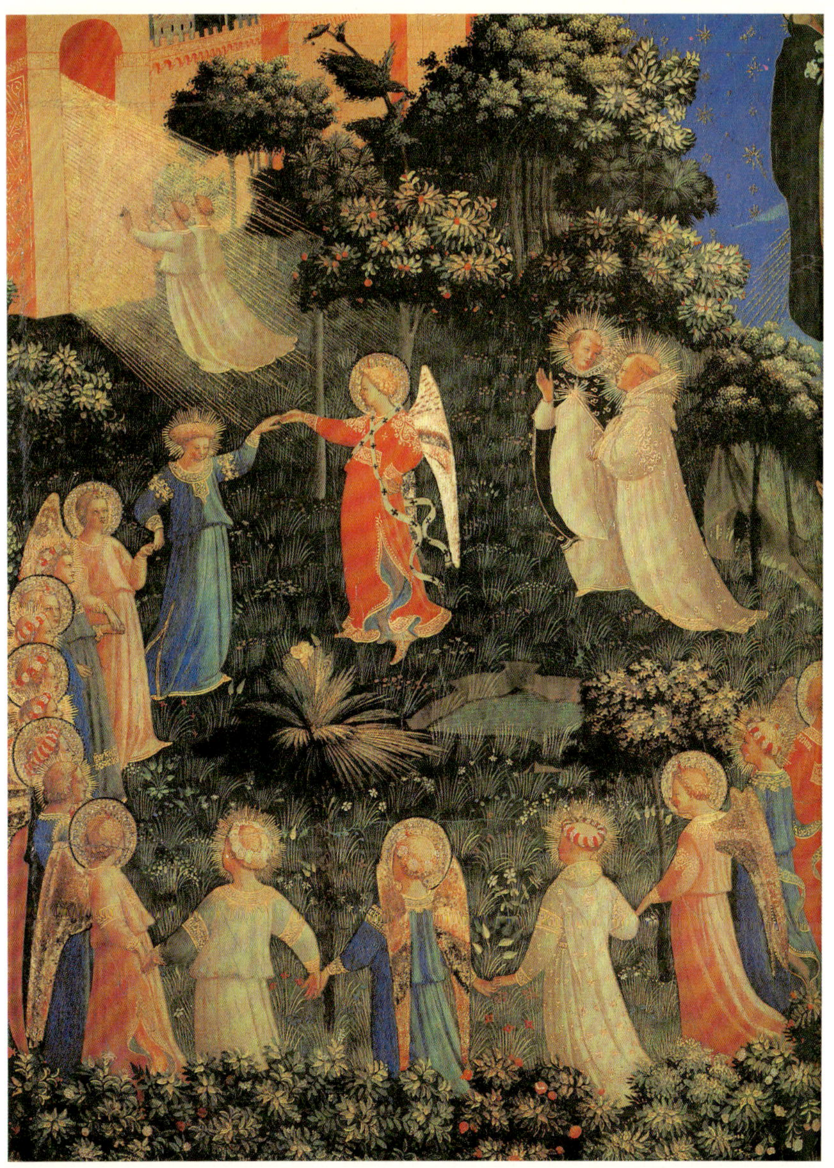

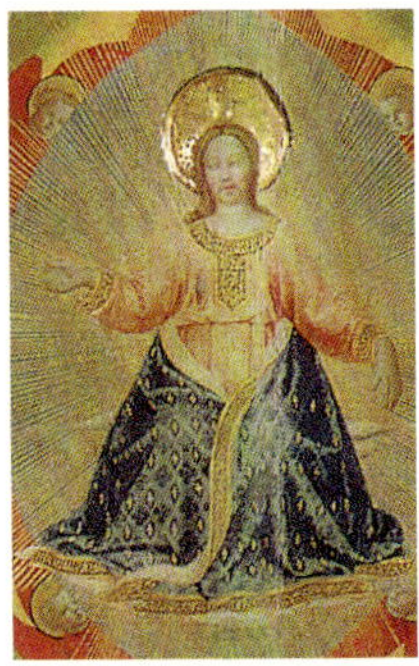

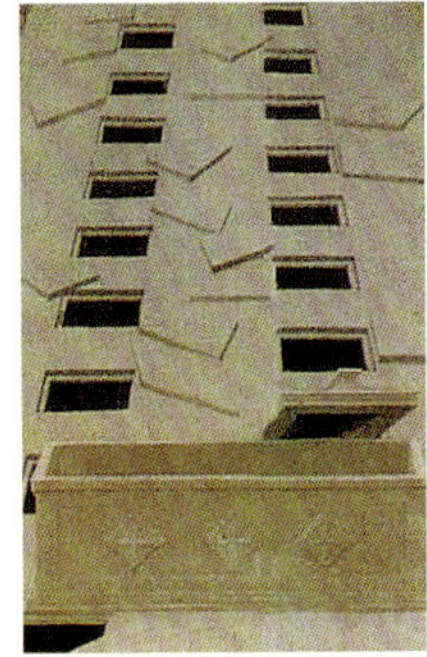

by a certain monk, Raoul Glaber, on whose first pages we find: "Satan will soon be unloosed, as prophesied by St John, the thousand years having been accomplished. It is of these years that we are to speak."

The end of the 10th century and the beginning of the 11th century was a truly strange and fearful

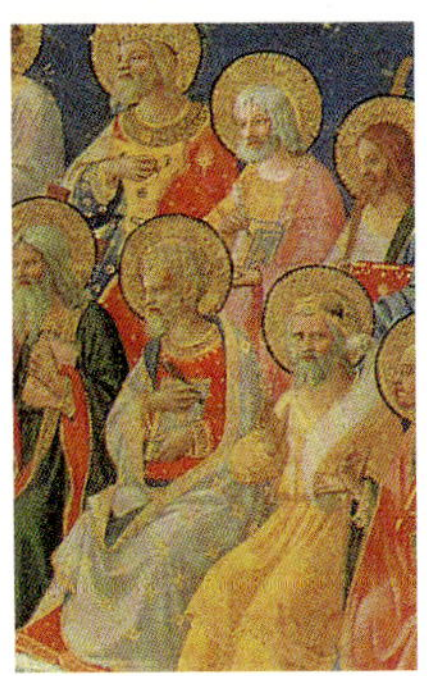

The Last Judgement

Fra Angelico, 1432-1435
Tempera and gold on wood panel, 105 x 210 cm
Museo di San Marco, Florence

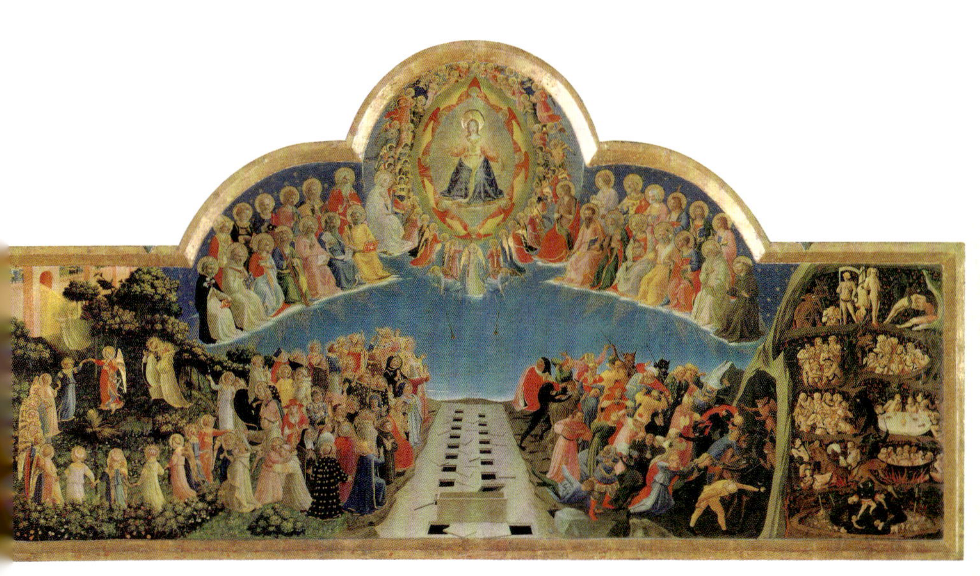

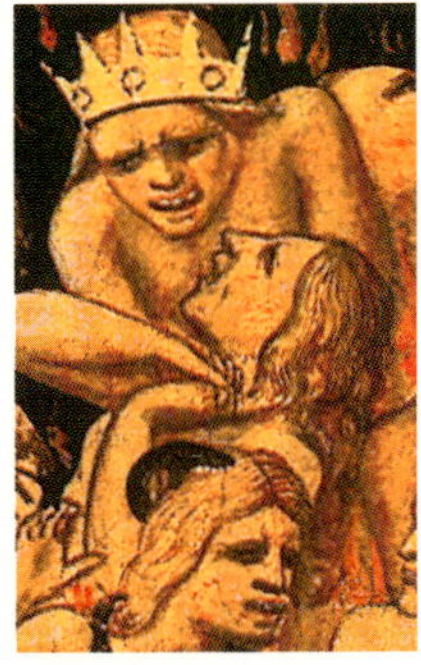

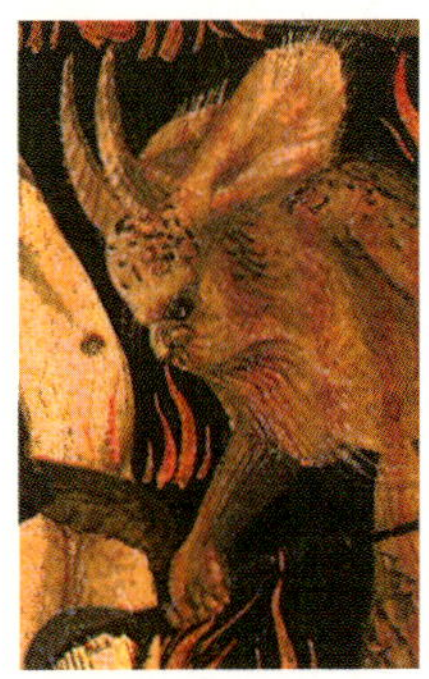

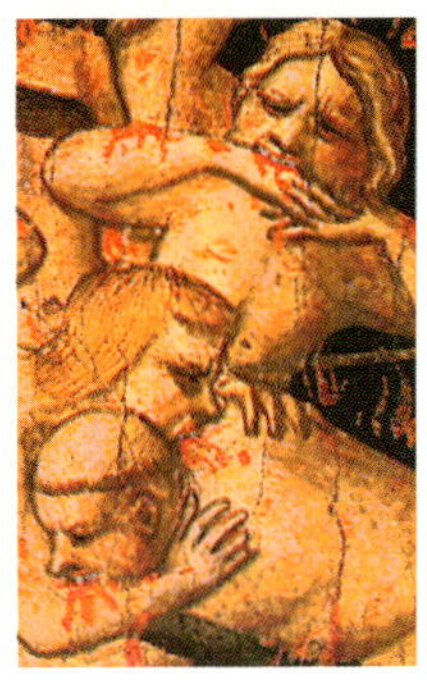

period. From 980 to 1040 it seemed as if the Angel of Death had spread his wings over the world. Famine and pestilence desolated the length and breadth of Europe. Firstly there was *Saint Anthony's fire*, or Ergotism, a gangrenous disease causing limbs to fall off its victims and flesh to decay and fall from the bones, consuming the body like fire.

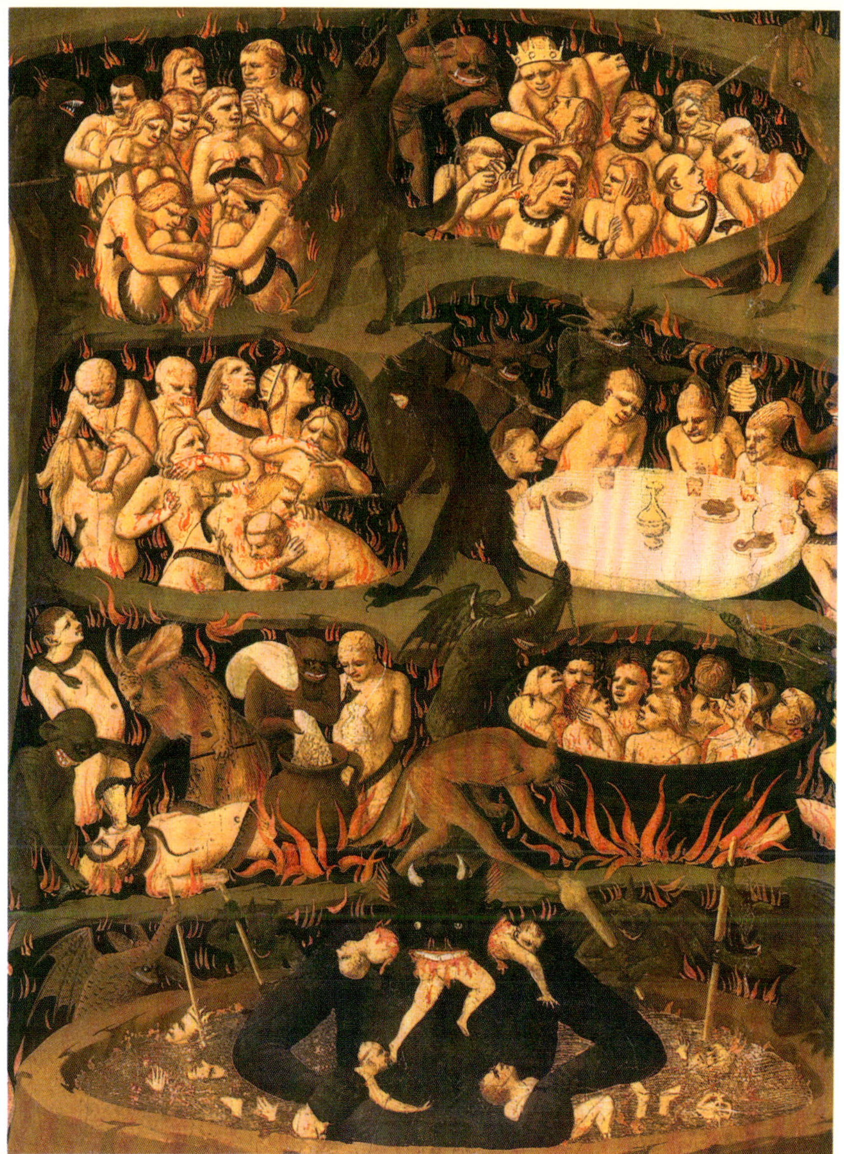

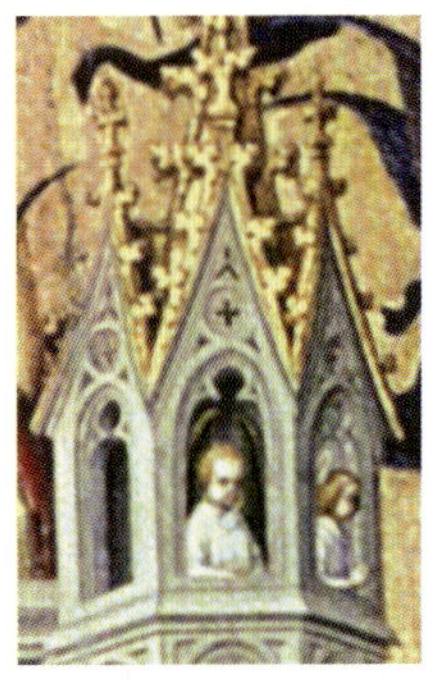

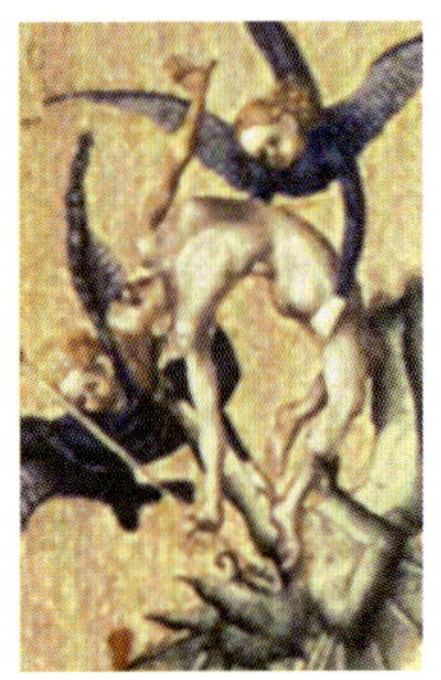

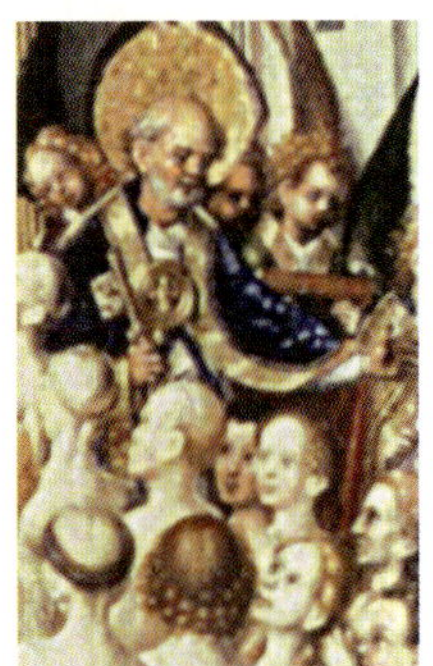

Wretches thus afflicted thronged the roads leading to the shrines and besieged the churches, filling them with terrible odours, and dying before the relics of the saints. The terrible plague reaped more than 40,000 victims in the Aquitaine region, and devastated the southern portions of France.

The Last Judgement

Stephan Lochner, 1435
Oil on wood, 124 x 172 cm
Wallraff-Richartz-Museum, Cologne

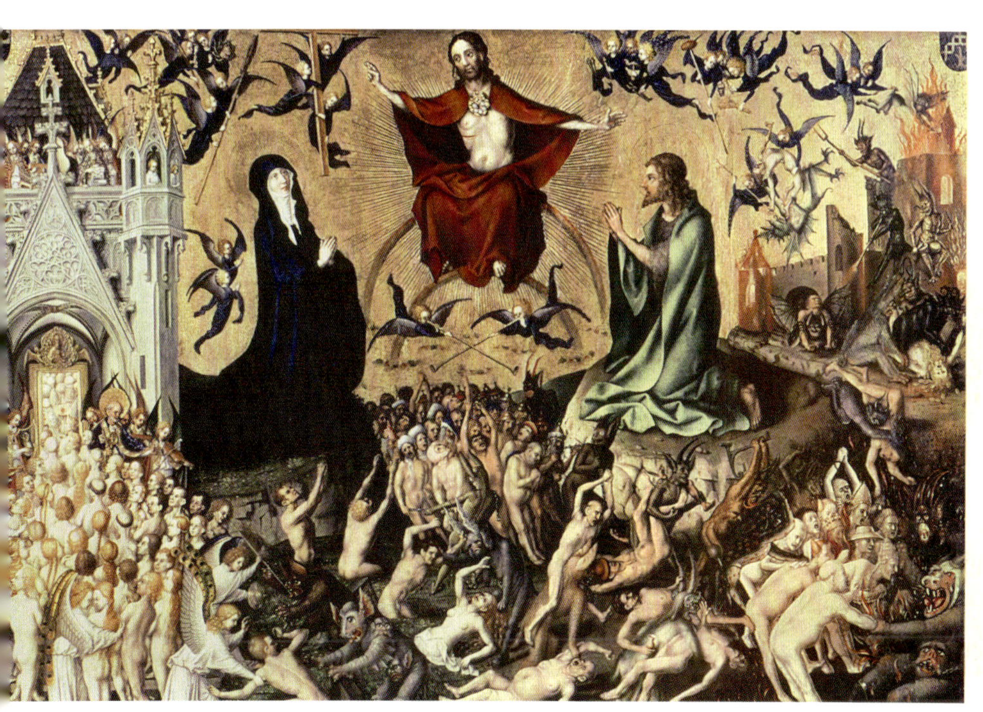

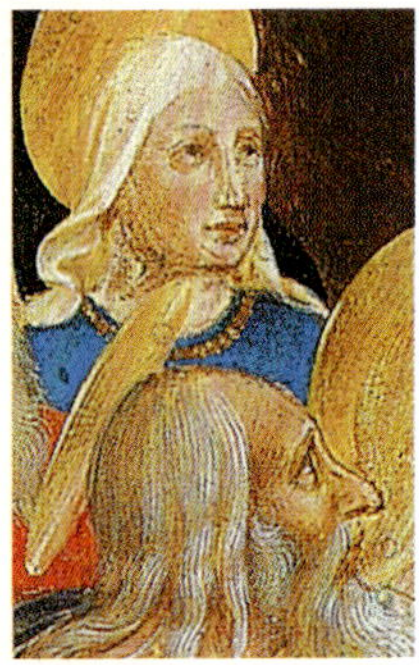

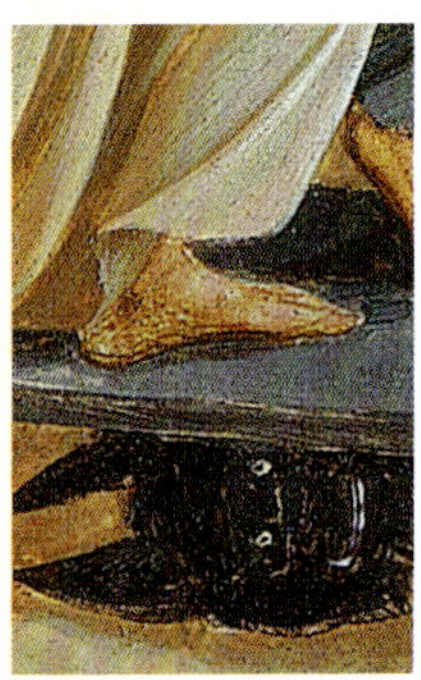

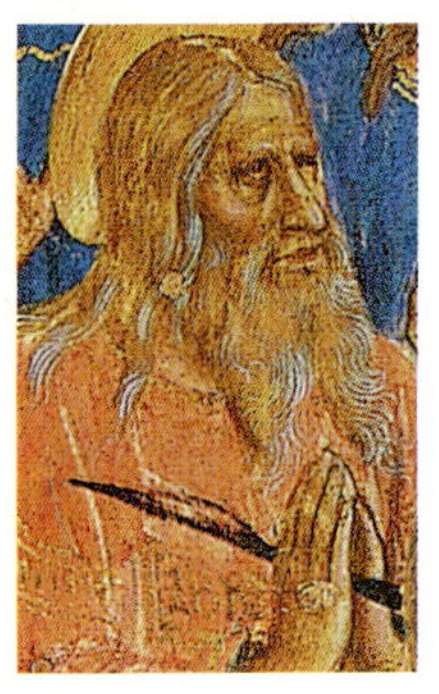

Then came famine, ravaging a large part of Christendom. Of the 73 years between 987 and 1060, 48 were years of famine and pestilence. The invasion of the Hungarians, between 910 and 945, revived the horrors of Attila, and the soil was so laid waste by wars between domains and provinces that it ceased to be cultivated.

Christ in Limbo

Fra Angelico, c. 1450
One of 35 paintings for the Silver Treasury
of Santissima Annunziata
Tempera on wood, 39 x 39 cm
Museo di San Marco, Florence

EDVXIT EOS DE TENEBRIS 7 VMBRA MORTIS 7 VINCVLA EORV DIRVPIT . PS . CVI

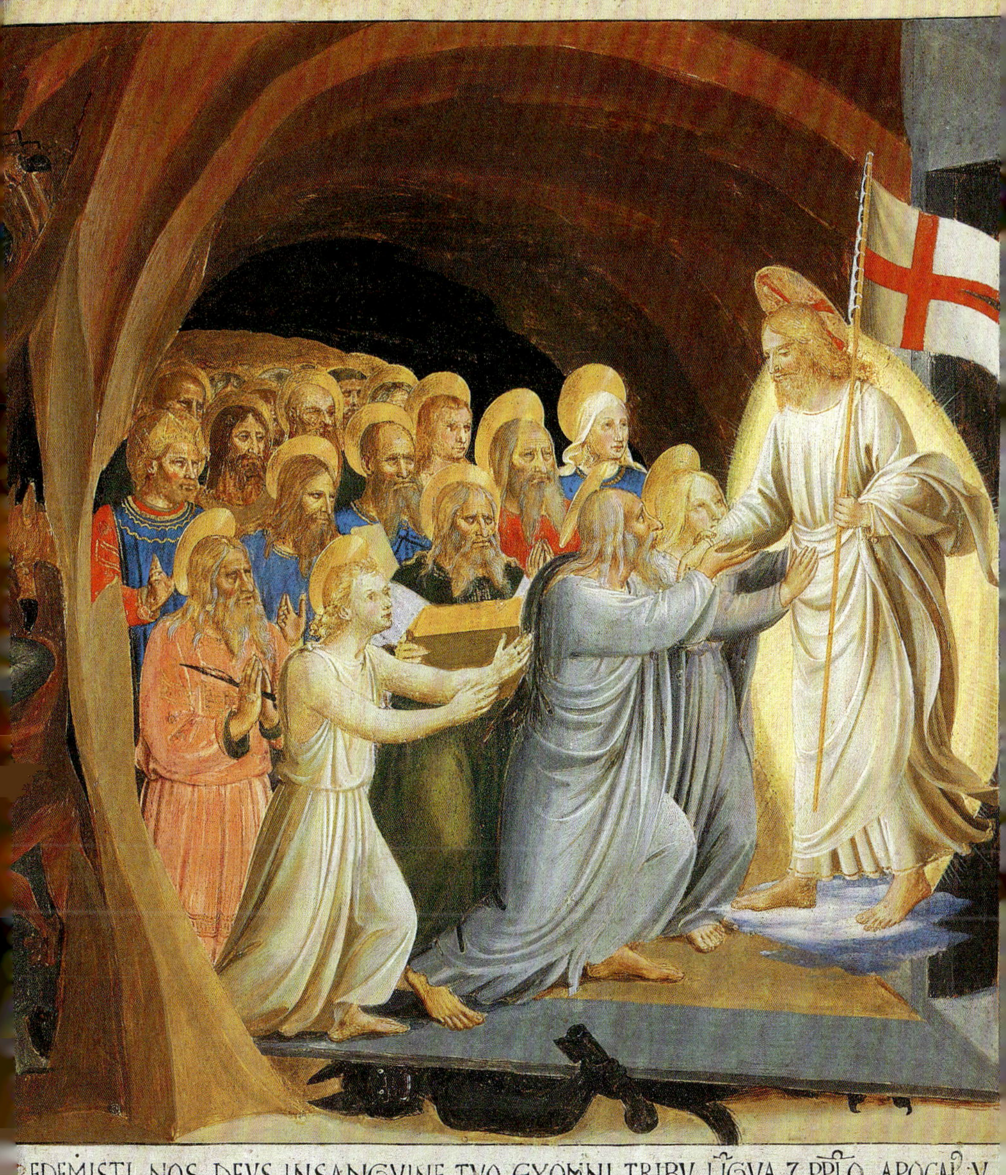

REDEMISTI NOS DEVS IN SANGVINE TVO EX OMNI TRIBV LIGVA 7 PPLO APOCA P V

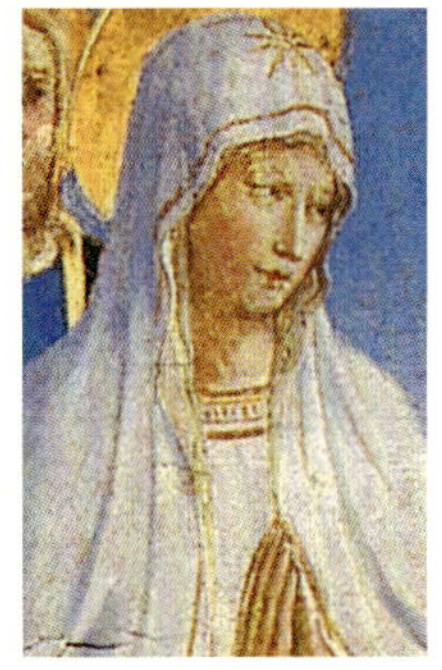

For three years rain fell continuously; it was impossible either to sow or to reap. The earth became barren and was abandoned.

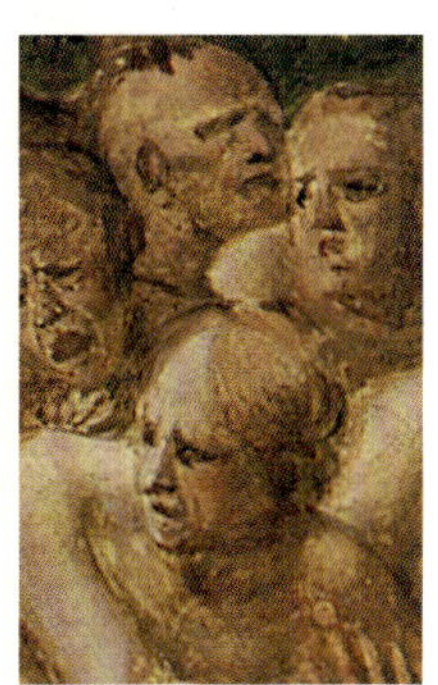

The price of a hogshead of wheat [equivalent to a quarter of a long ton] rose to sixty gold sous; the rich waxed thin and pale; the poor gnawed the roots

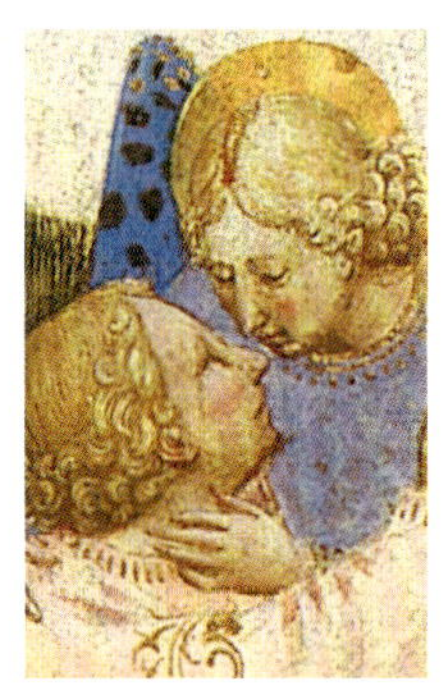

The Last Judgement

Fra Angelico, c. 1450
One of 35 paintings for the Silver Treasury
of the Santissima Annunziata
Tempera on wood panel, 39 x 78 cm
Museo di San Marco, Florence

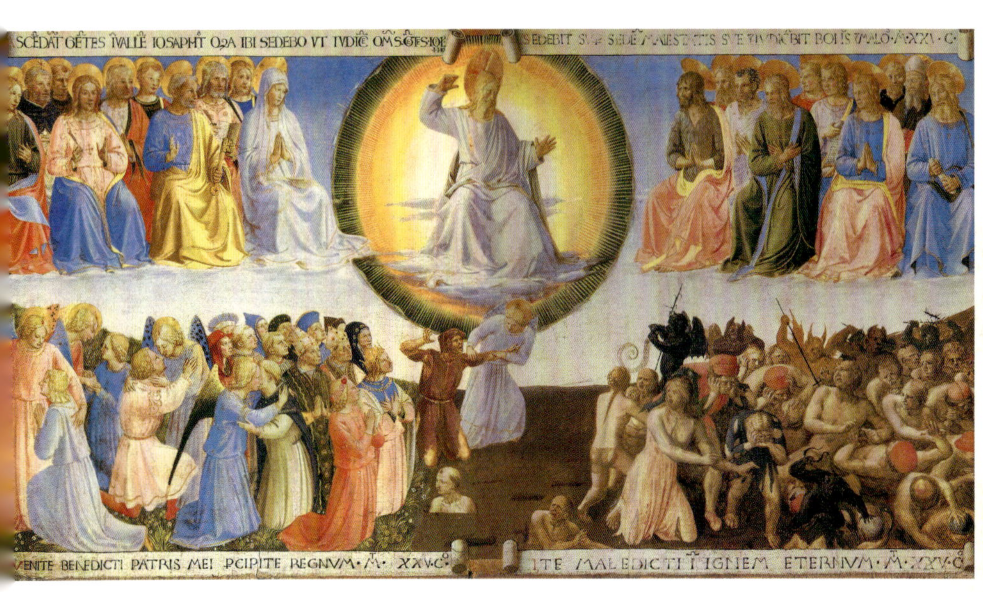

SCEDAT GÉTES ÍVALLÉ IOSAPHT QŽA IBI SEDEBO VT IVDIC OMS GTES IOE
SEDEBIT SVP SEDE MAIESTATIS SVE IVDICABIT BOLIS ÍMALO · A · XXV · C
VENITE BENEDICTI PATRIS MEI PCIPITE REGNVM · M · XXV C
ITE MALEDICTI Í IGNEM ETERNVM · M XXV C

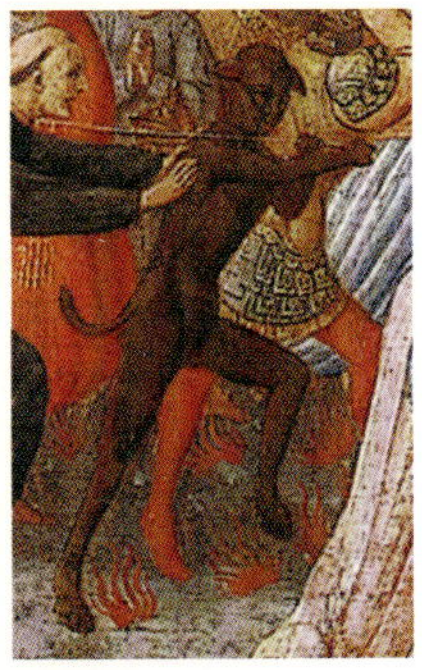

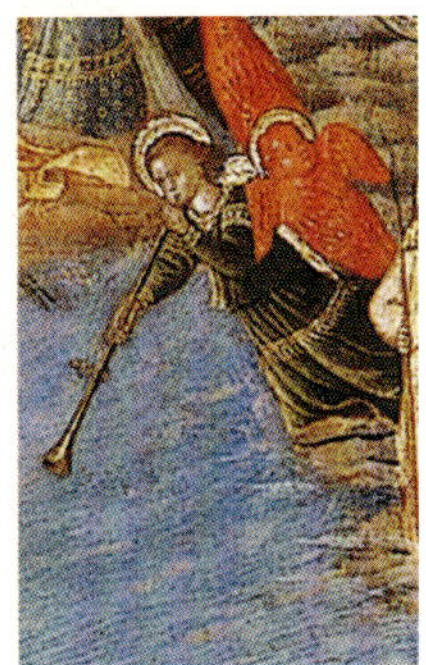

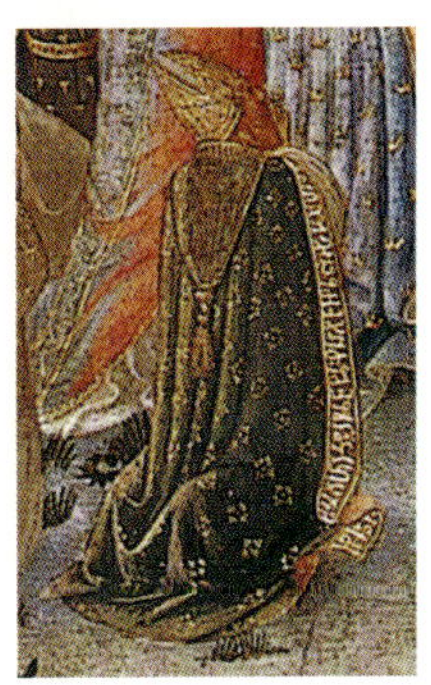

of trees, and many were in such extremity as to devour human flesh. The strong seized the weak in the public highways, tore them in pieces, and roasted them for food. Children were enticed by an egg or some fruit into alleyways, where they were then devoured by a predator.

Fra Angelico
Tempera and gold on wood panel, 106.5 x 131.5 cm
Private collection

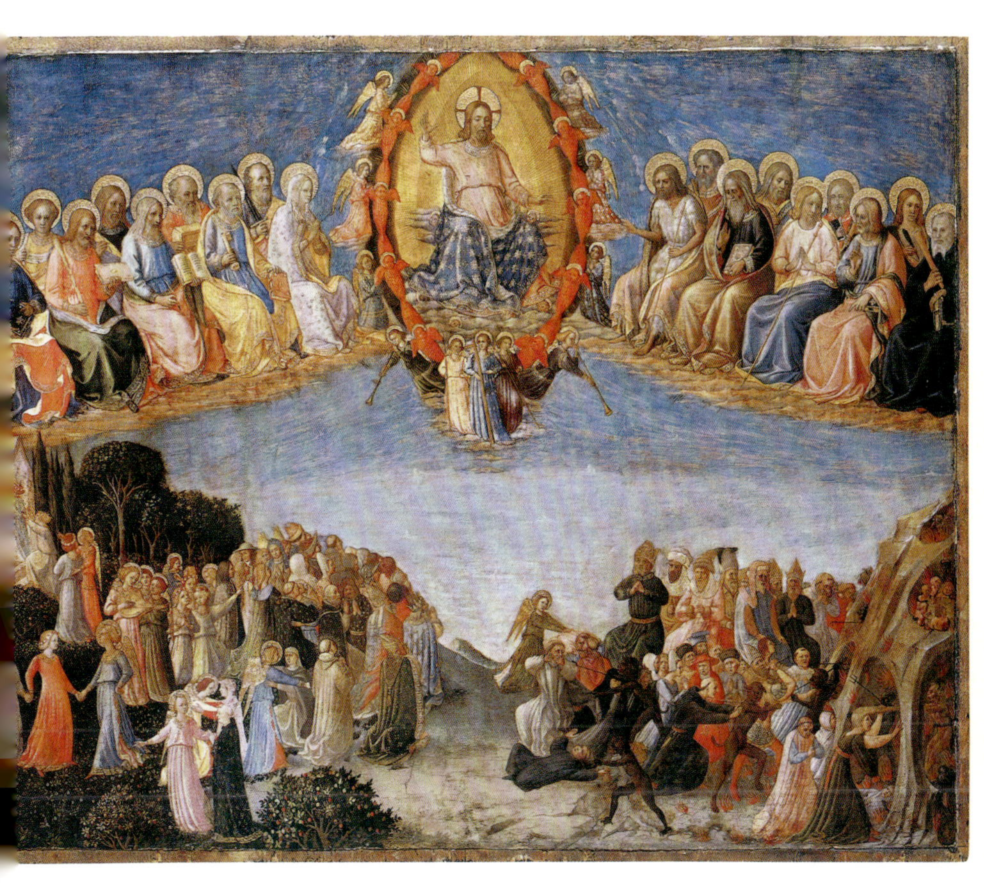

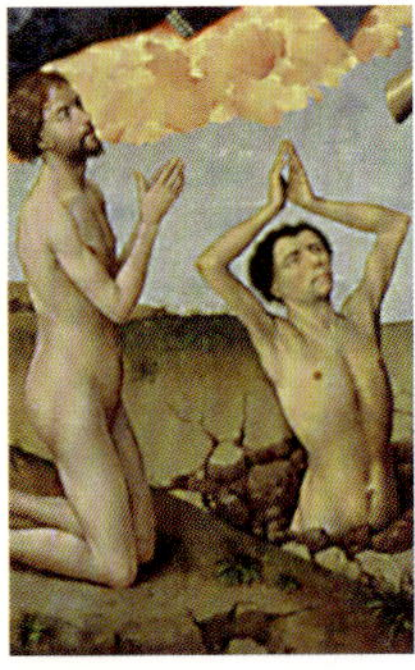

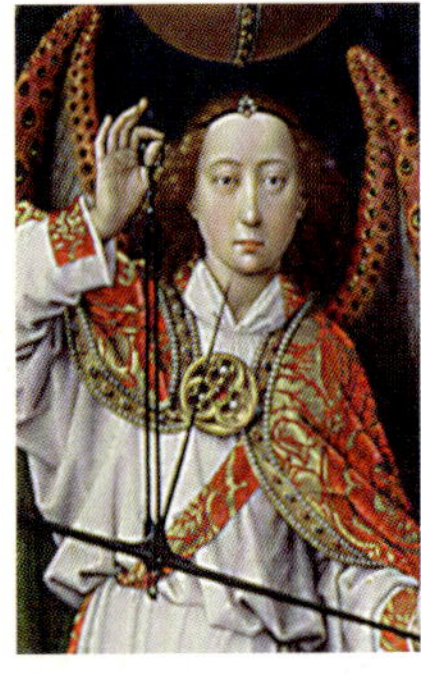

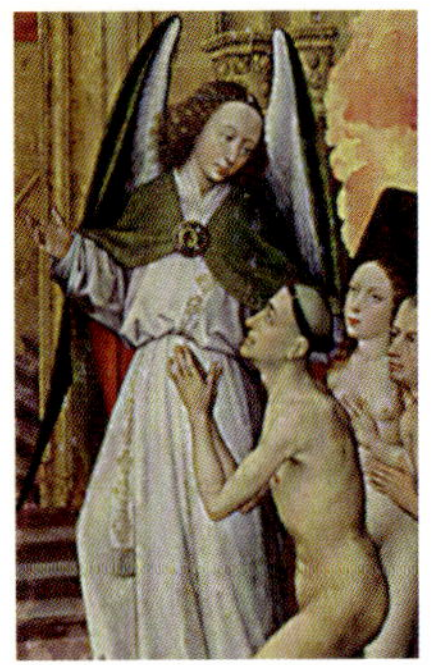

This frenzy of hunger was such that the beast was safer than man. Famished children killed their parents, and mothers feasted upon their children. One person exposed human flesh for sale in the market place of Toumus as if it were a staple article of food. He did not deny

The Last Judgement

Rogier van der Weyden, 1445-1450
Oil on oak
Musée de l'Hôtel-Dieu, Beaune

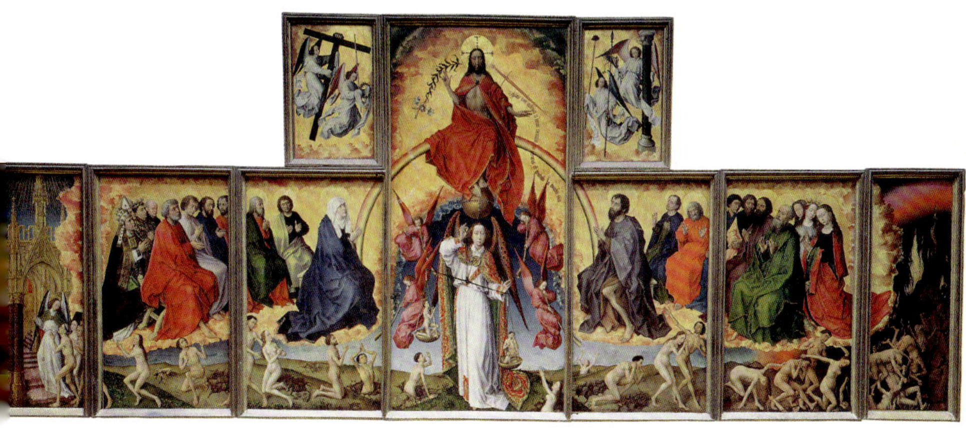

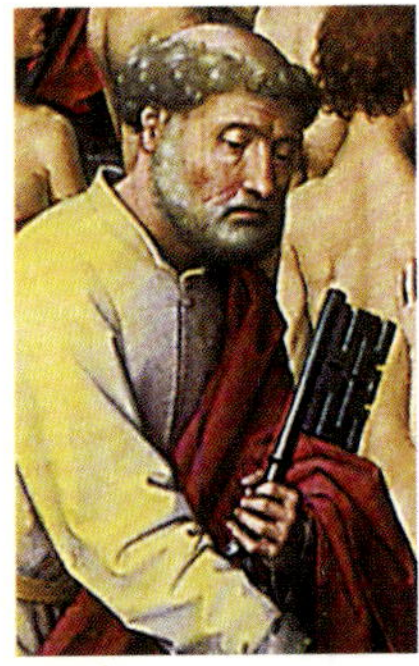

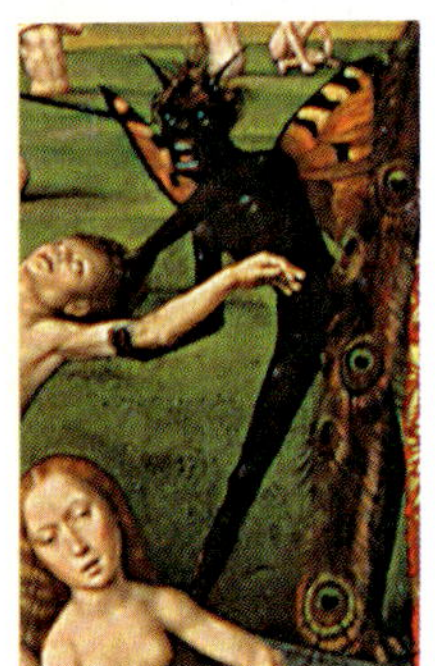

that he had done this and was burned at the stake. Another, stealing this flesh by night from the spot where it had been buried, was also burned alive.

This testimony, by Raoul Glaber, was written first hand, as he was often an eye witness to what he describes. On every side, people were

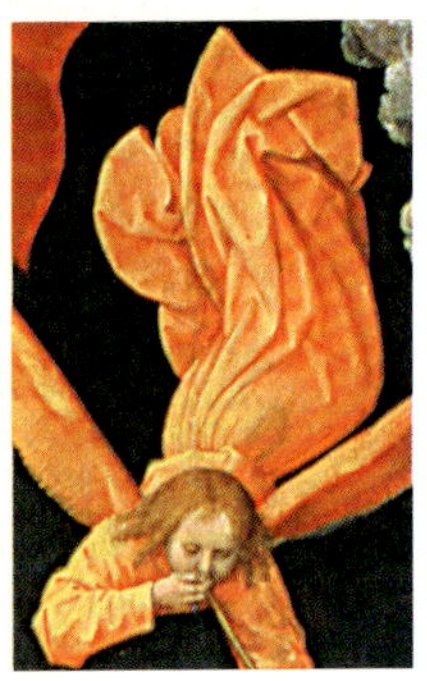

The Last Judgement (triptych)

Hans Memling, c. 1467-1471
Oil on wood, 242 x 360 cm
Muzeum Narodowe w Gdańsku, Gdansk

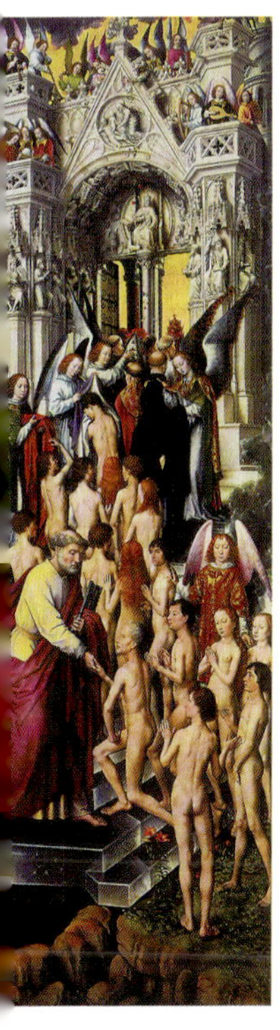

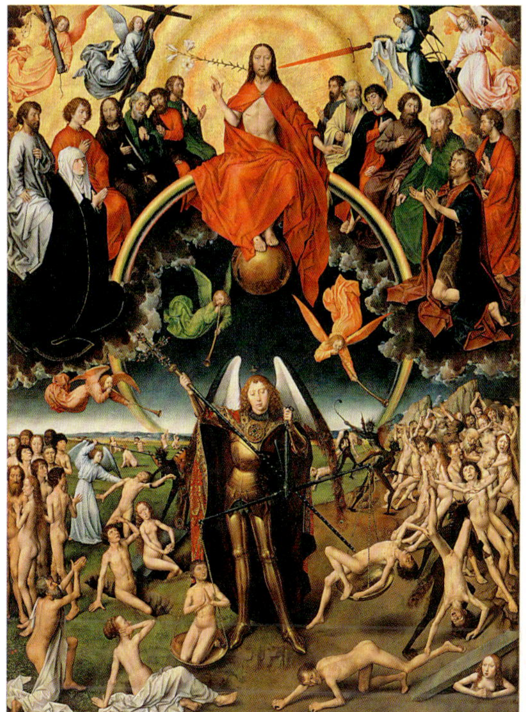

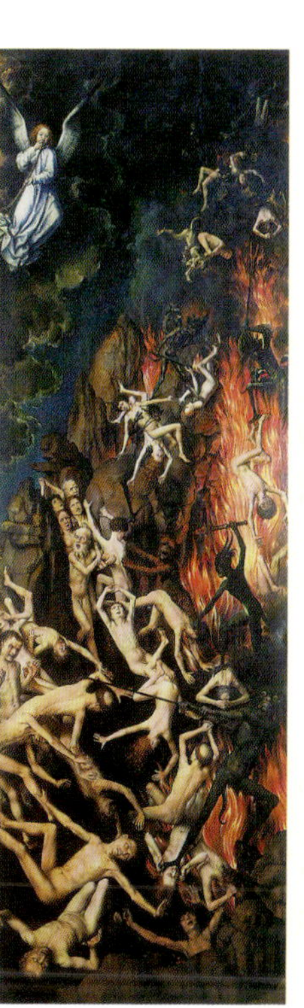

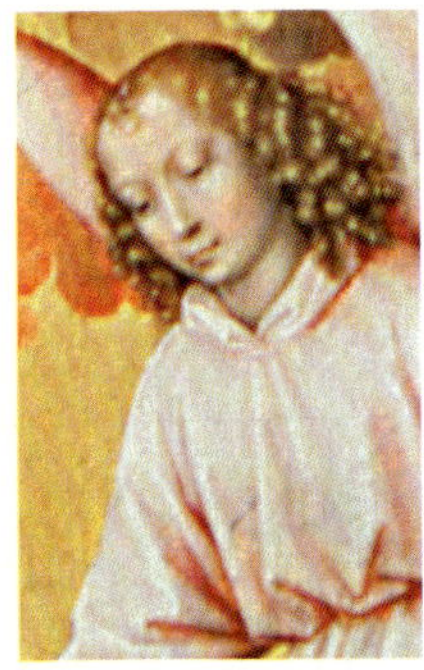

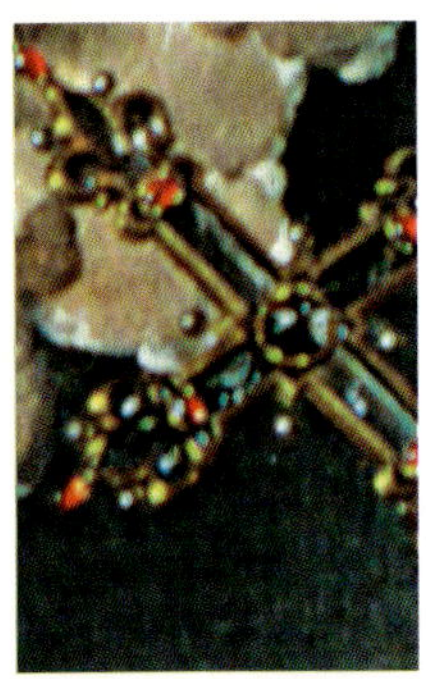

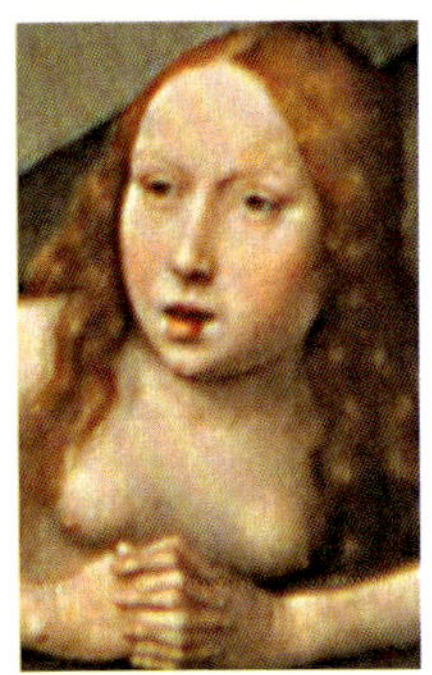

perishing of hunger and did not scruple to eat reptiles, unclean animals, and even human flesh. In the depths of the forest of Macon, in the vicinity of a church dedicated to St John, a wretch had built a hut in which he strangled pilgrims and wayfarers. One day, a traveller entering the hut with his wife to seek rest, saw the heads of men,

The Last Judgement (triptych, central panel)

Hans Memling, c. 1467-1471
Oil on wood, 242 x 360 cm
Muzeum Narodowe w Gdańsku, Gdansk

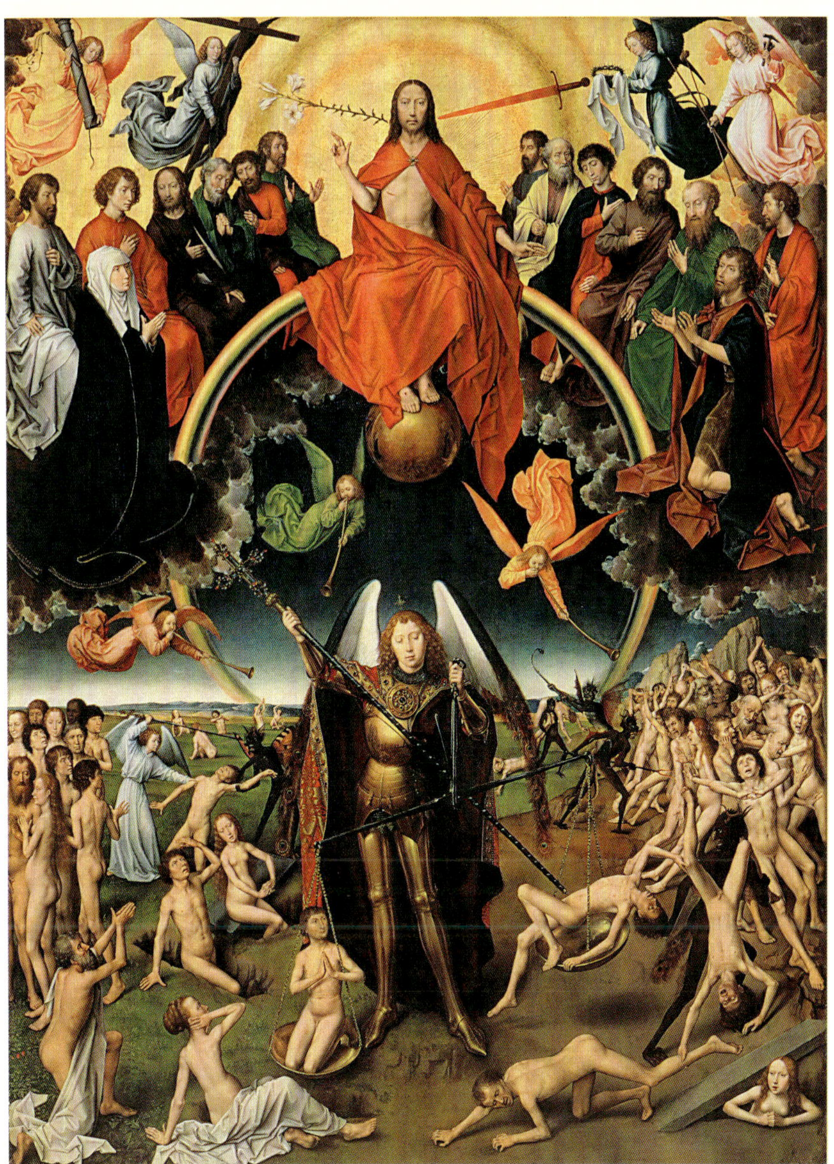

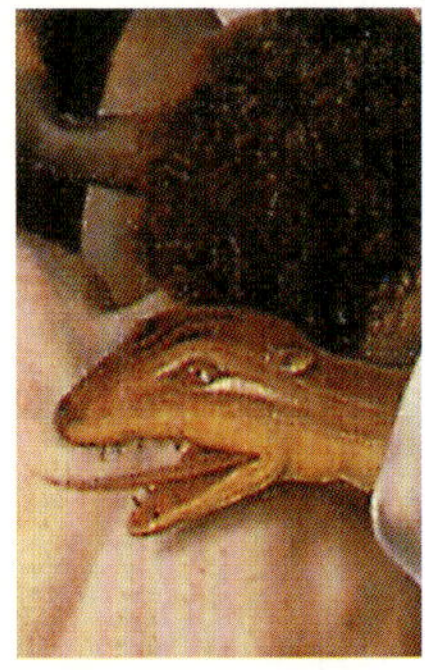

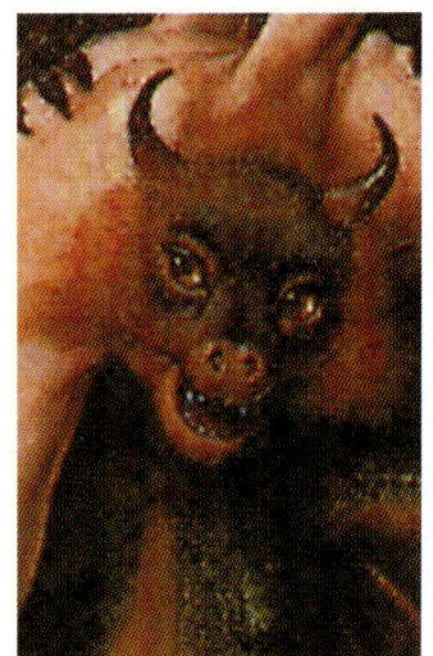

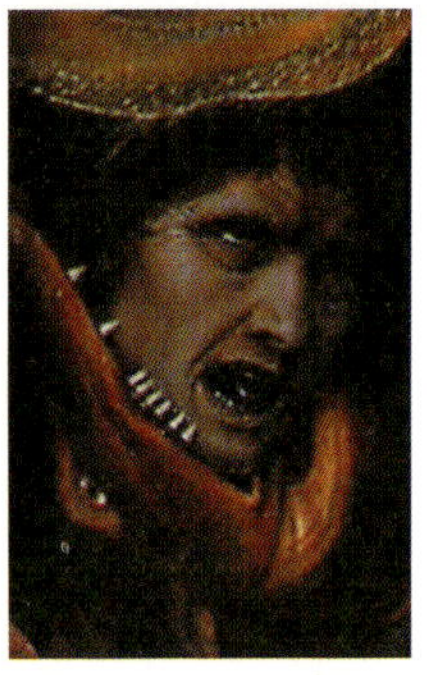

women, and children strewn about. Attempting to escape, they were detained by their host; however, they managed to escape, and on reaching Macon, explained what they had seen. Soldiers were sent to the bloody spot, where they counted forty-eight human heads. The murderer was dragged to the town and burned alive.

The Fall of the Damned
right panel of a Last Judgement triptych

Dieric Bouts the Elder, c. 1470
Oil on wood, 116 x 71 cm
Palais des Beaux Arts, Lille

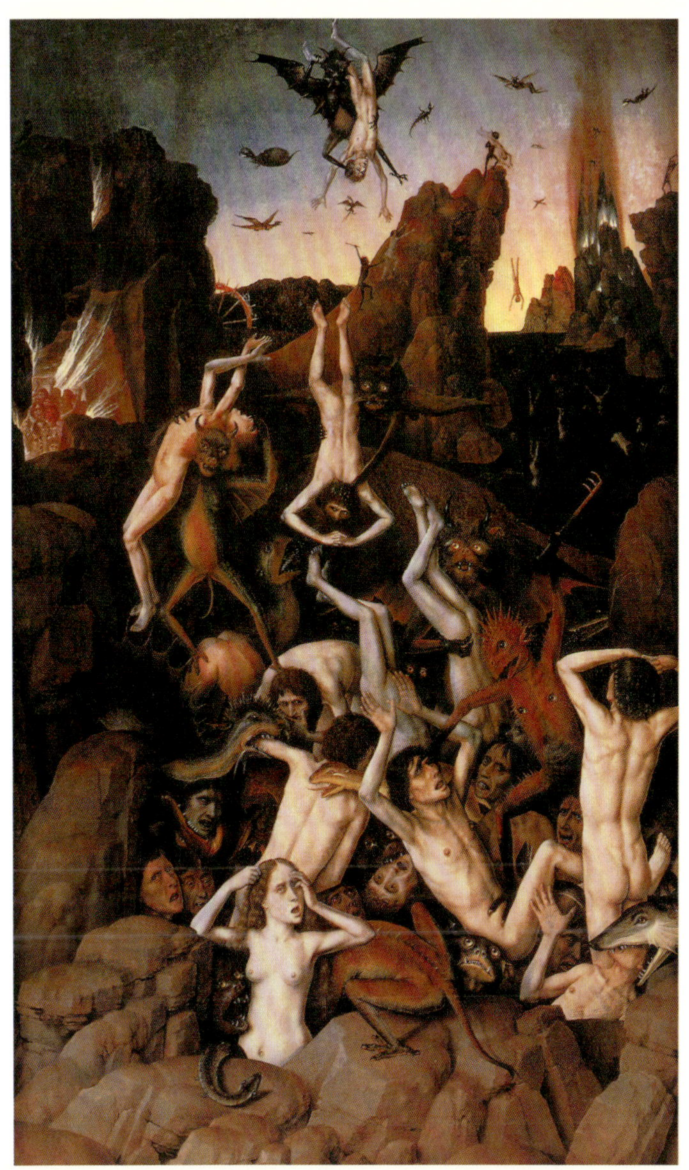

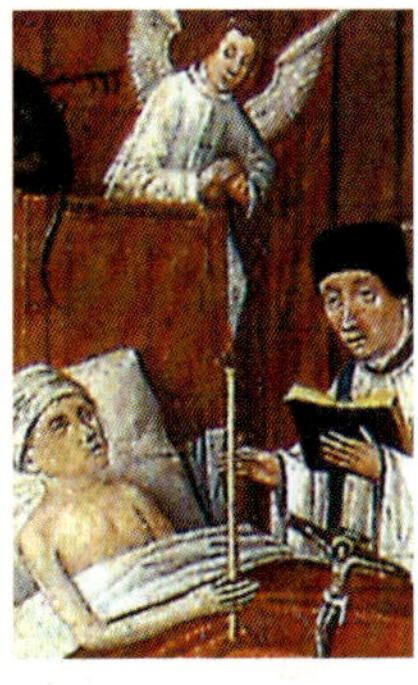

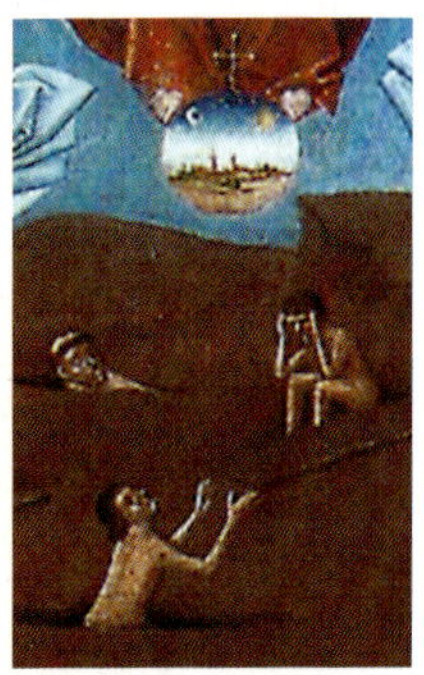

Glaber saw the hut and the ashes of the funeral pyre. Burial was impossible, as the corpses were so numerous; disease followed close upon famine. Hordes of wolves preyed upon the unburied. Never before had such misery been known.

War and pillage were the universal rule, but these plagues from heaven made men

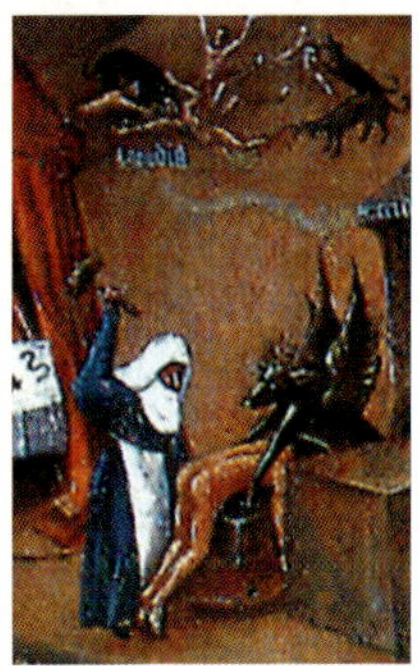

Table of the Mortal Sins

Hieromymus Bosch, 1475-1480
Oil on panel, 120 x 150 cm
Museo Nacional del Prado, Madrid

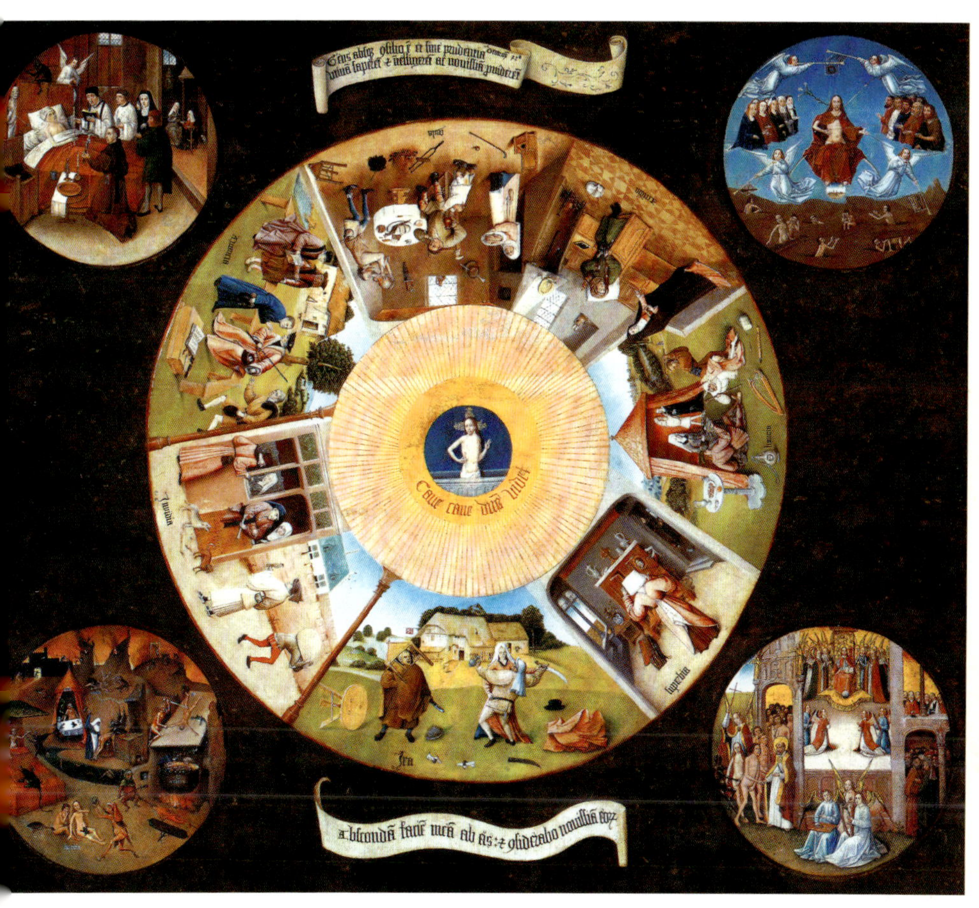

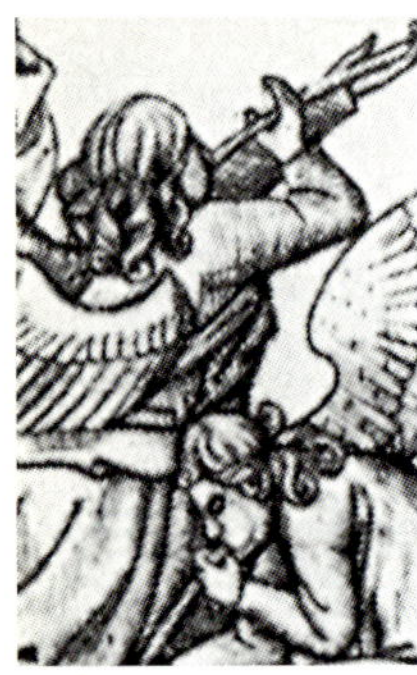

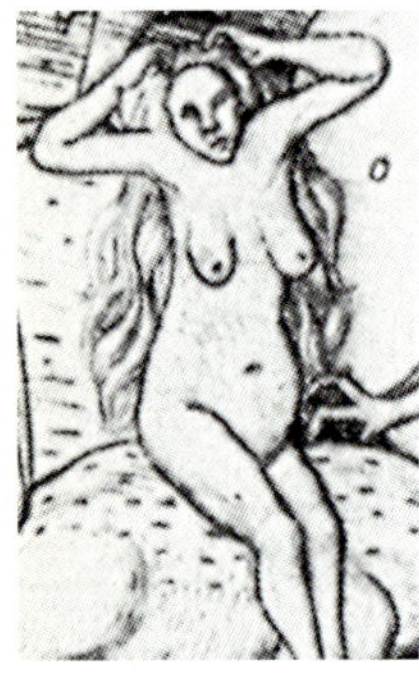

somewhat more reasonable; the bishops came together and it was agreed that a truce would be established for four days a week, from Wednesday night to Monday morning. This was known as the Truce of God.

It is not strange that the end of so miserable a world was both the hope and the terror of this terrible period.

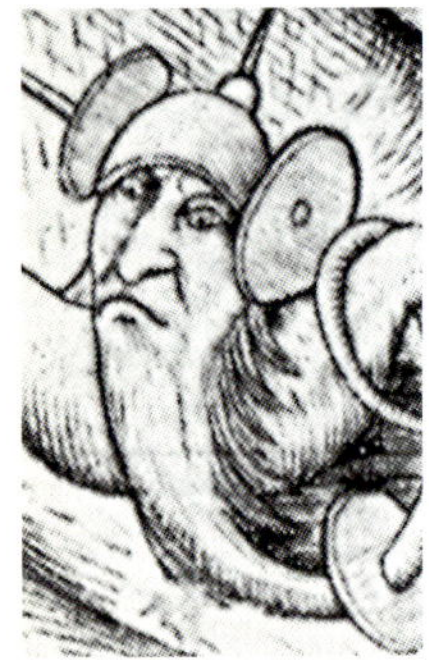

The Last Judgement

Alaert Du Hamel, 1478-1509
Engraving, 24.5 x 35.2 cm
Rijksmuseum, Amsterdam

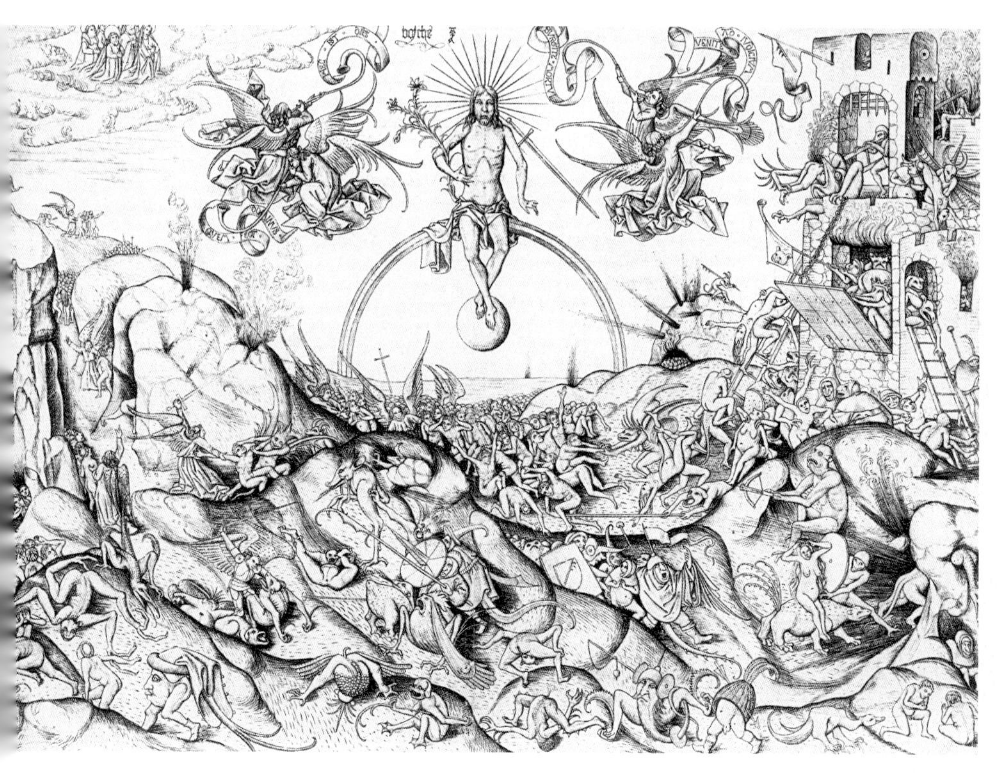

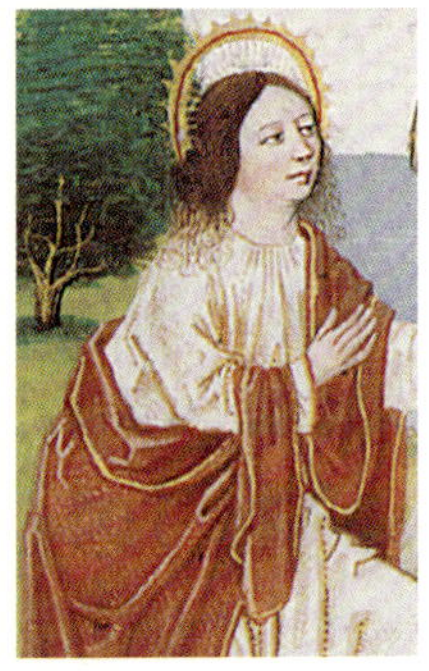

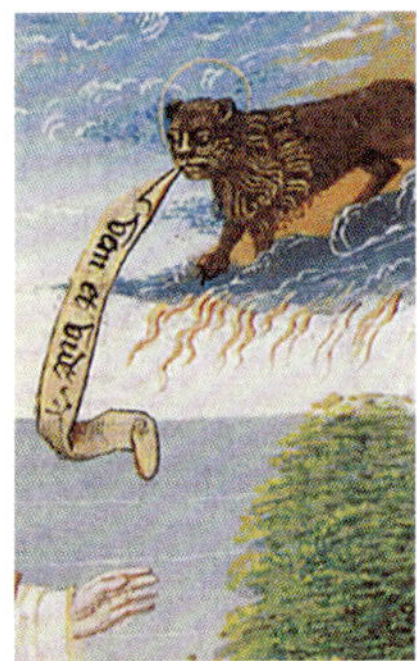

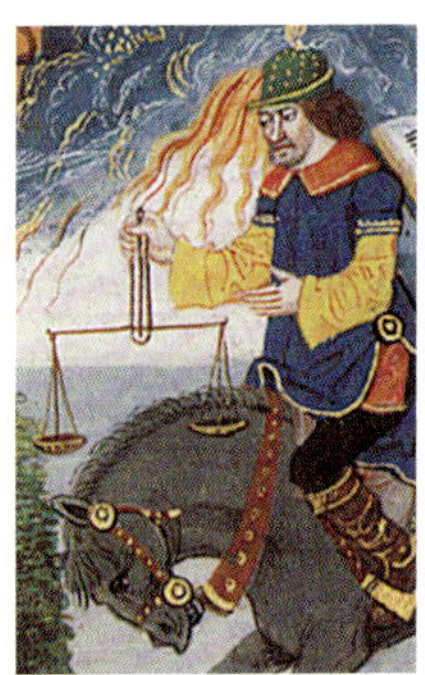

The year 1000, however, passed like its predecessors, and the world continued to exist. Were the prophets wrong again, or did the thousand years of Christendom point to the year 1033? The world waited and hoped. In that very year occurred a total eclipse of the sun; "The orb of light became saffron coloured; gazing into

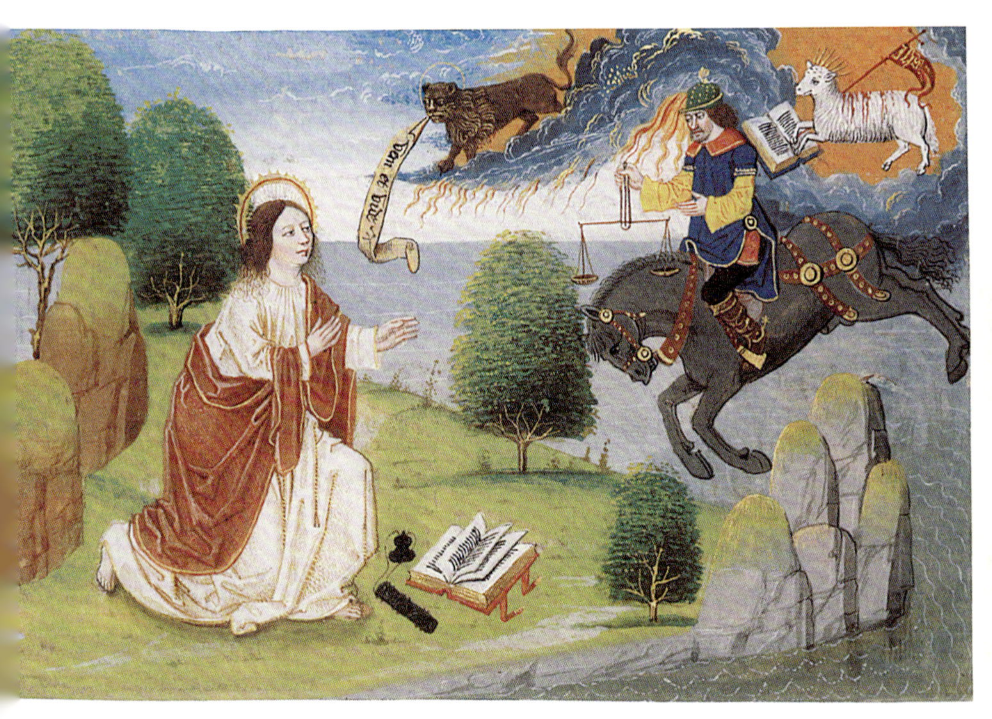

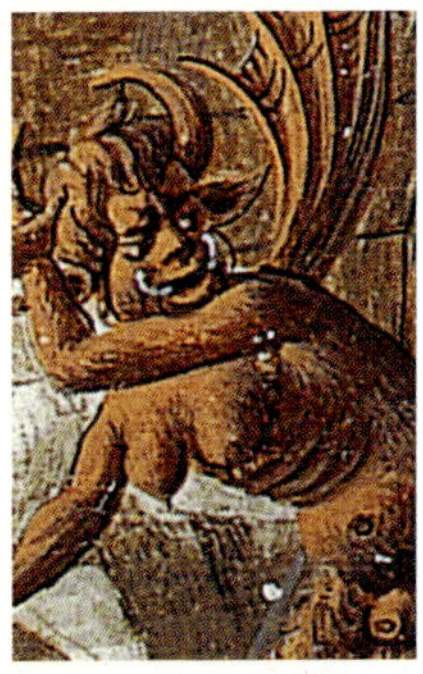

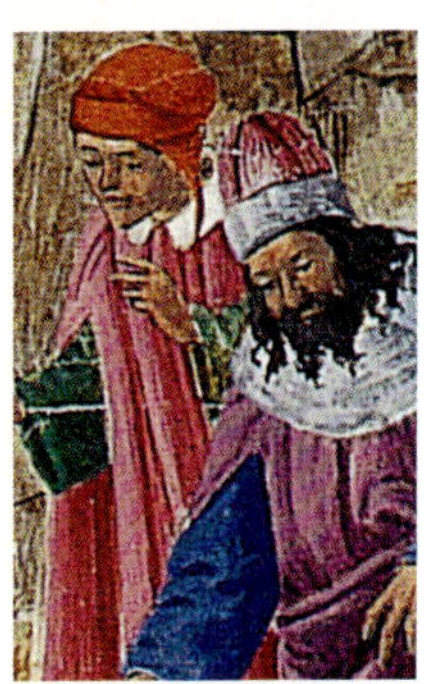

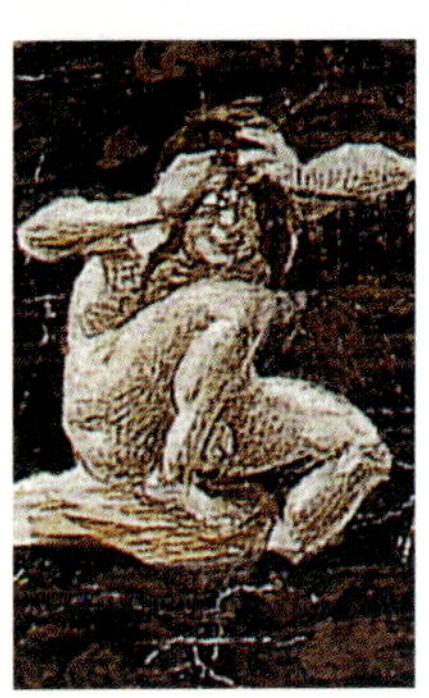

each others faces, men saw that they were pale as death; every object presented a livid hue; stupor seized upon every heart and a general catastrophe was expected." But the end of the world had not yet come to pass.

It is to this critical period that we owe the construction of the magnificent cathedrals which

Inferno: Canto XVIII – 8th Circle (Malebolge)
and the Punishment of Seducers,
Pimps and Prostitutes

c. 1480
Drawing, pen and coloured ink
on parchment, 32.3 x 47 cm
Staatliche Museen zu Berlin, Kupferstichkabinett, Berlin

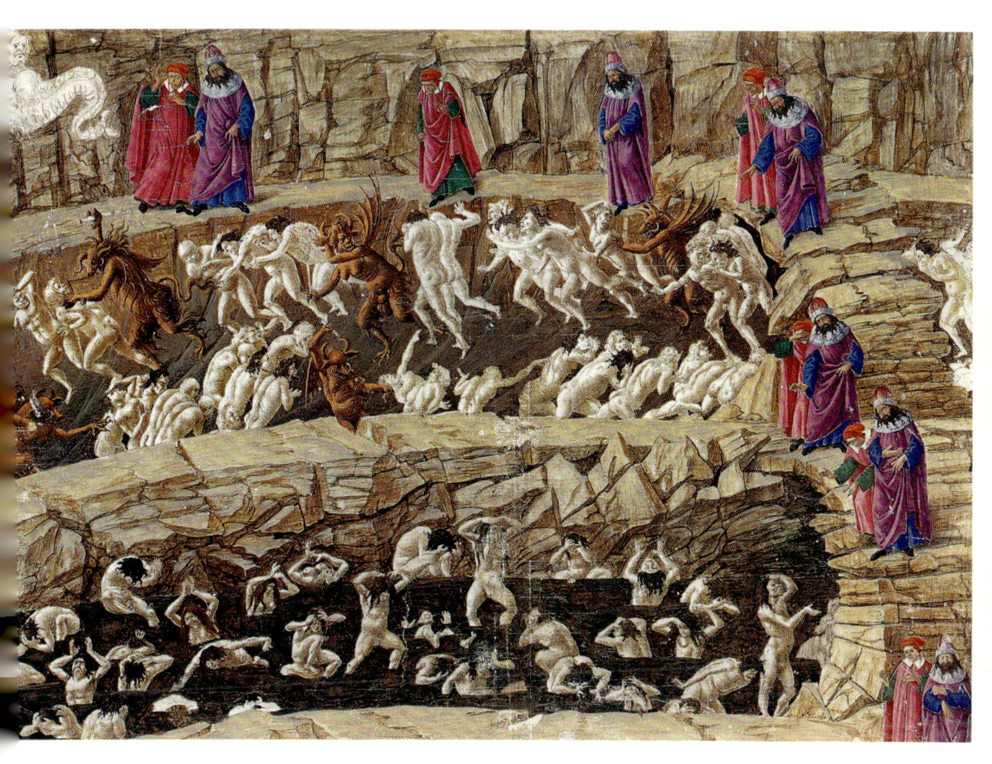

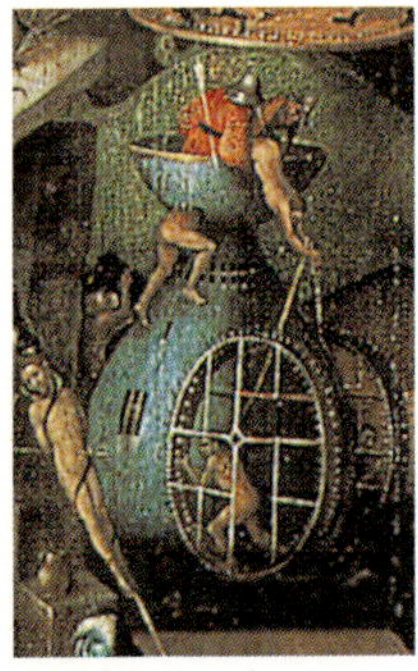

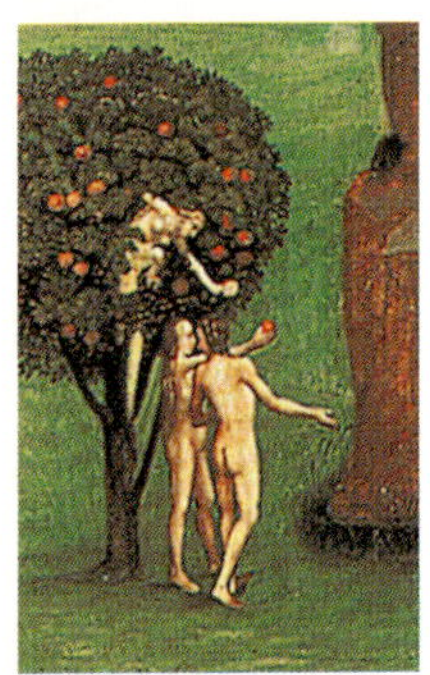

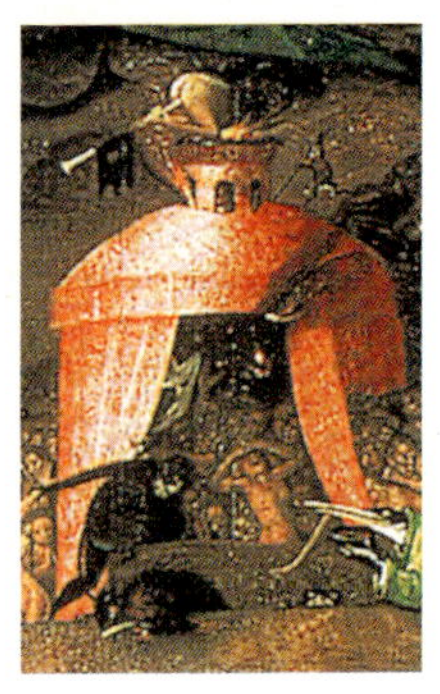

have survived the ravages of time and excited the wonder of centuries. Immense wealth had been lavished upon the clergy, and their riches increased by donations and inheritance. A new era seemed to be at hand. Raoul Glaber continues:

After the year 1000, the holy basilicas throughout the world were entirely renovated, especially in Italy and Gaul,

The Last Judgement (triptych)

Hieronymus Bosch, after 1482
Oil on wood, 163.7 x 127 cm (central panel)
163.7 x 60 cm (side panels)
Akademie der bildenden Künste, Vienna

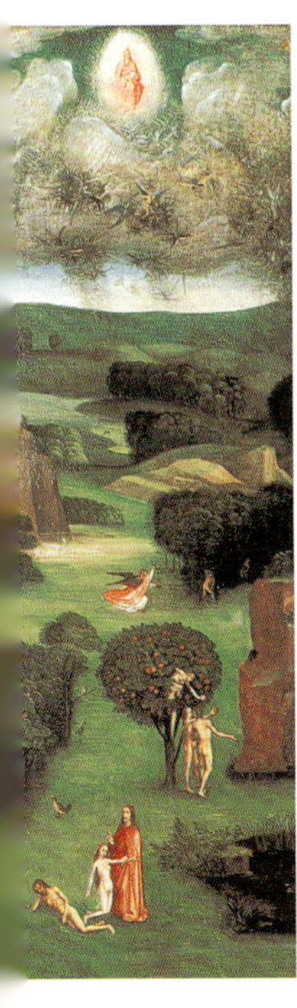
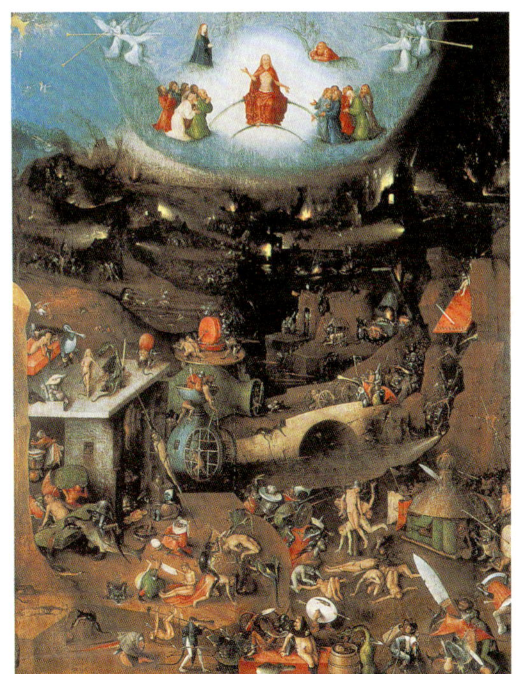
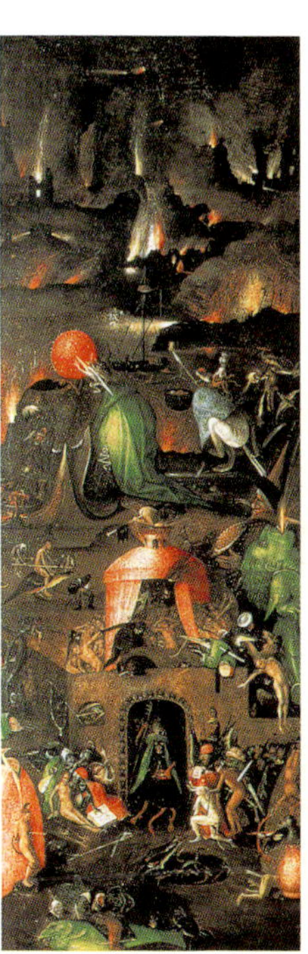

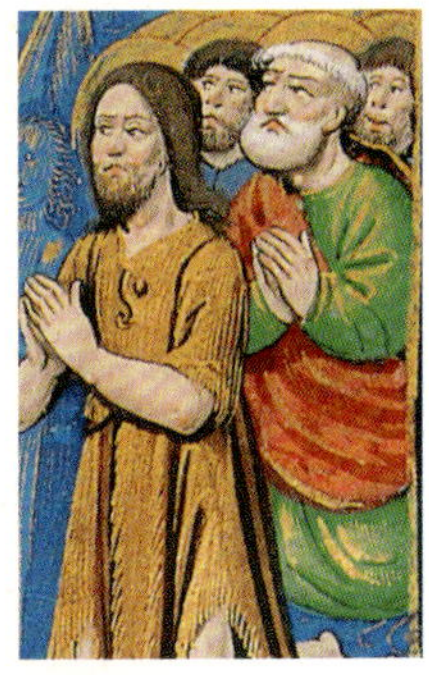

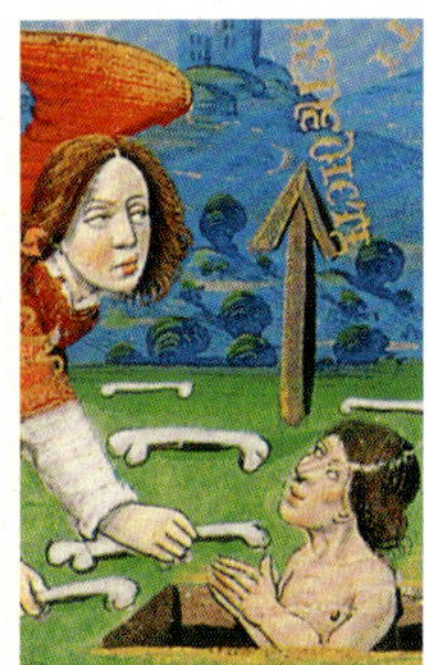

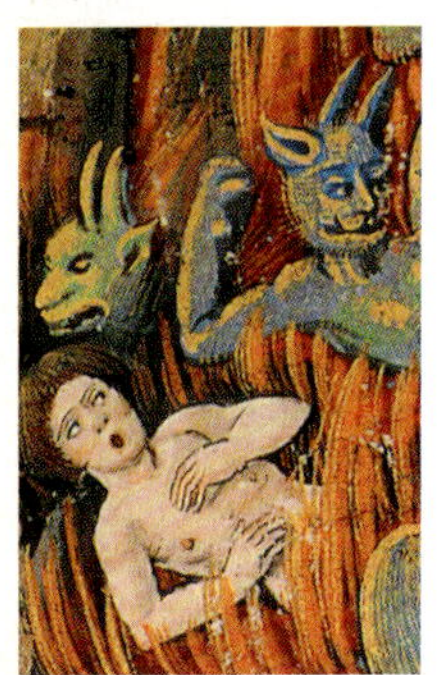

although for the most part they were in no need of repair. Christian nations vied with each other in the erection of magnificent churches. It seemed as if the entire world, animated by a common impulse, shook off the rags of the past to put on a new garment; and the faithful

15ᵗʰ Century Missal with an Illustration of the The Last Judgement

1490
Illuminated manuscript, 37.5 x 27.5 cm
Russian National Library, St Petersburg

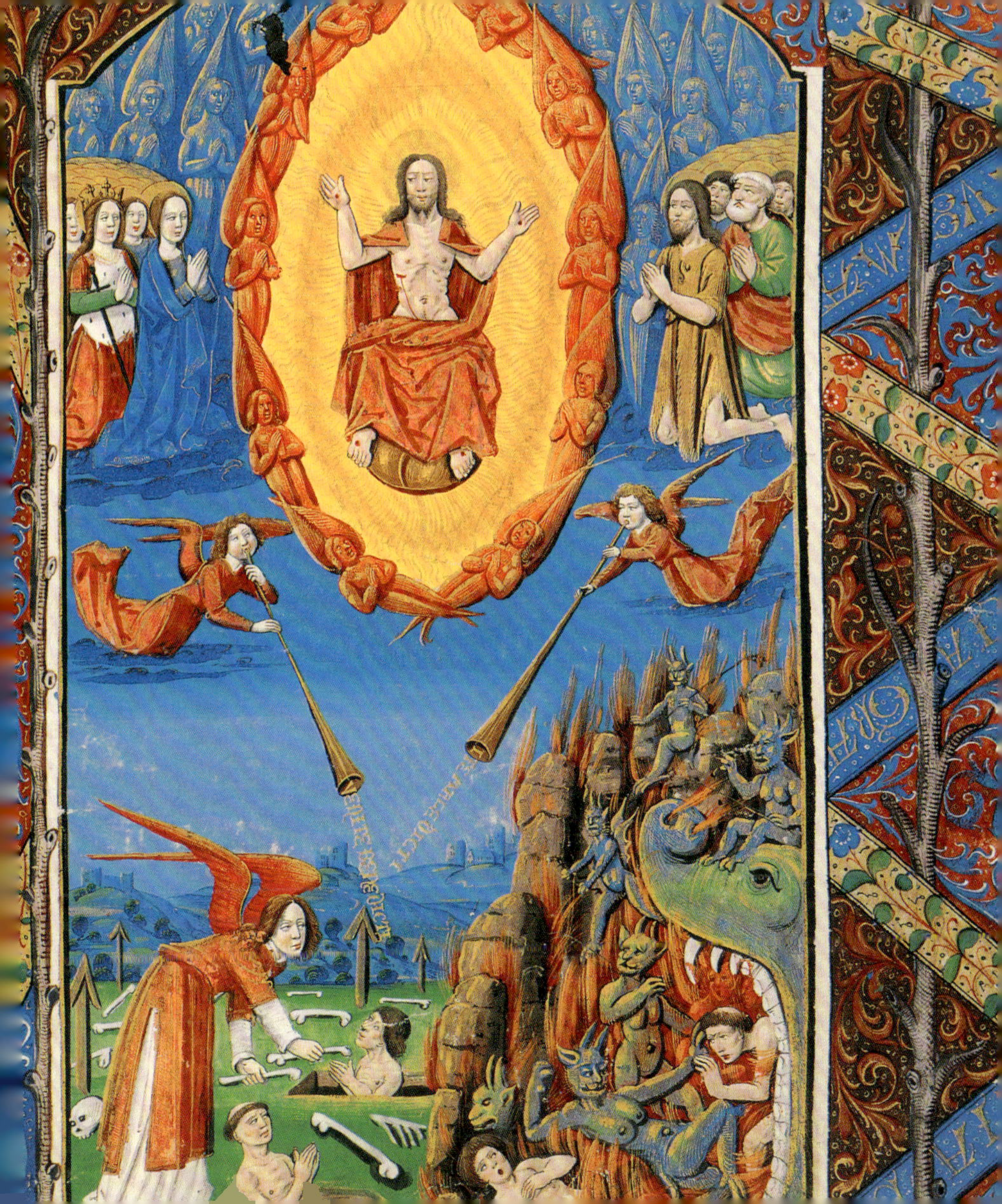
venite benedicti
ite maledicti

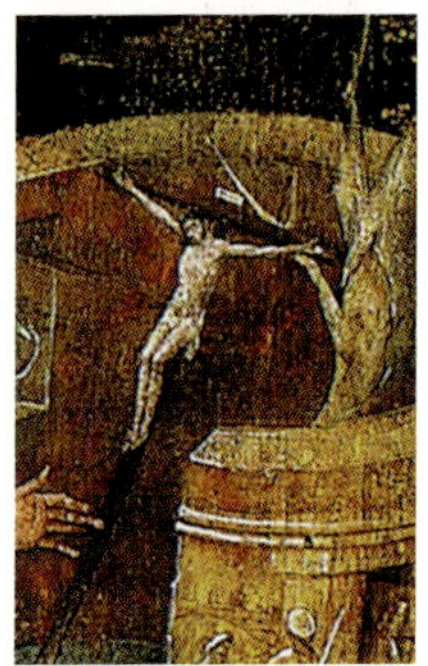

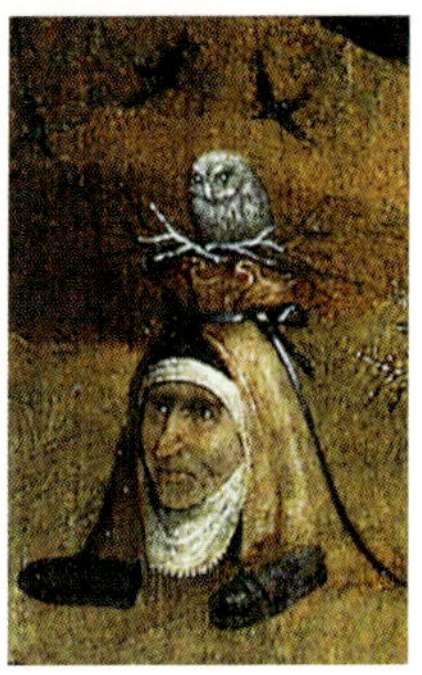

were not content to rebuild nearly all the Episcopal churches, but also embellished the monasteries dedicated to the various saints, and even the chapels in the smaller villages.

The sombre year 1000 had followed the vanished centuries into the past, but through what

Altarpiece of the Hermits

Hieronymus Bosch, c. 1490-1499
Oil on panel, 86.5 x 60 cm (central panel)
86.5 x 29 cm (side panels)
Palazzo Ducale, Venice

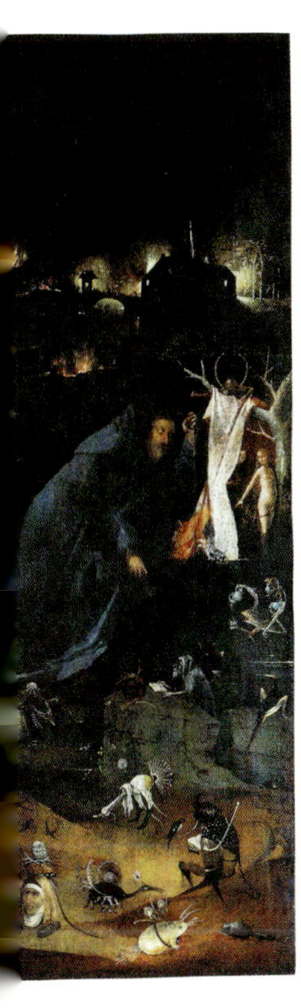
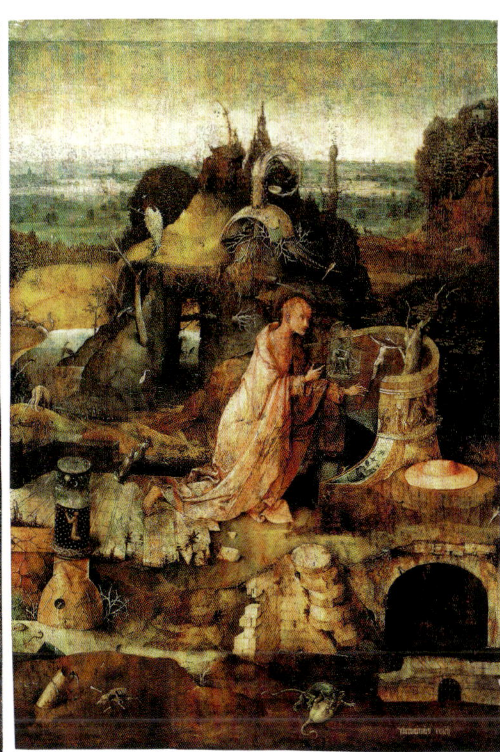
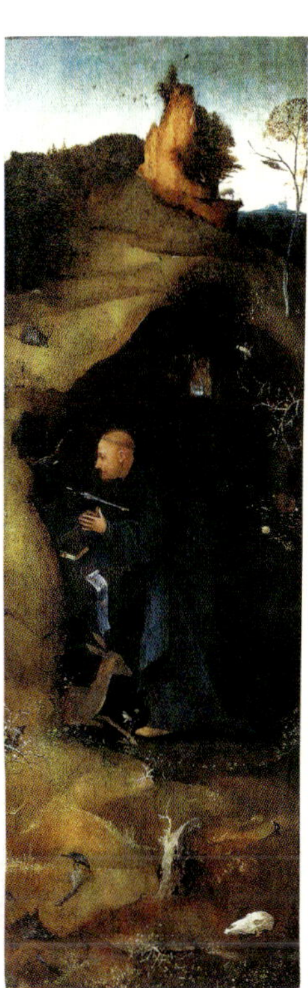

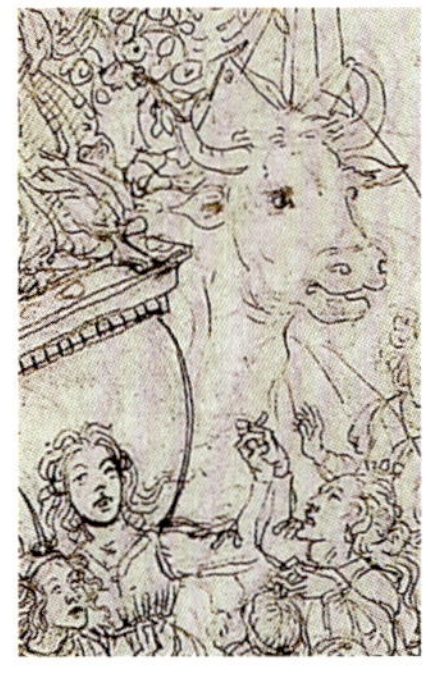

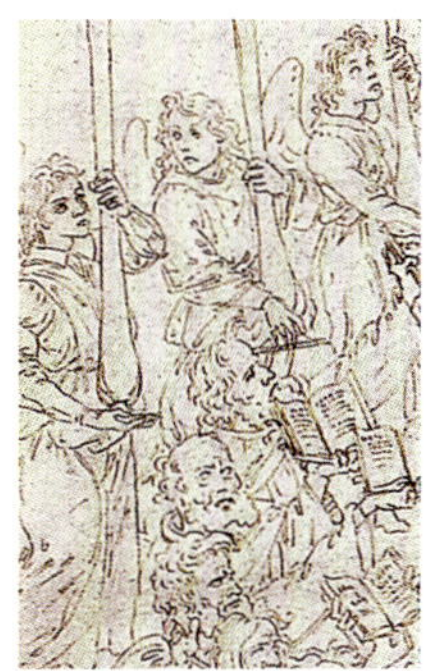

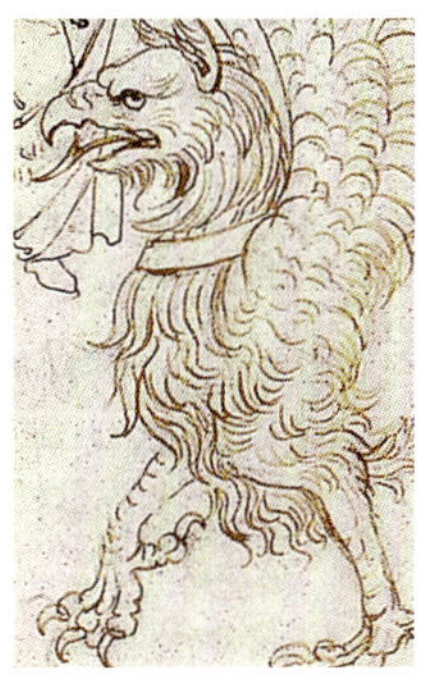

troubled times the Church had passed! The popes were the puppets of the rival Saxon emperors and the princes of Latium. All Christendom was in an indescribable mess. The crisis had passed, but the problem of the end of the world remained, and credence of this dreadful event, though uncertain and vague, was fostered by that profound belief

Purgatory: Canto XXX

Sandro Botticelli, early 1490s
Illustration for Dante's Divine Comedy
Preliminary sketch with silverpoint
on parchment, retraced in ink, 32 x 47 cm
Staatliche Museen zu Berlin, Kupferstichkabinett, Berlin

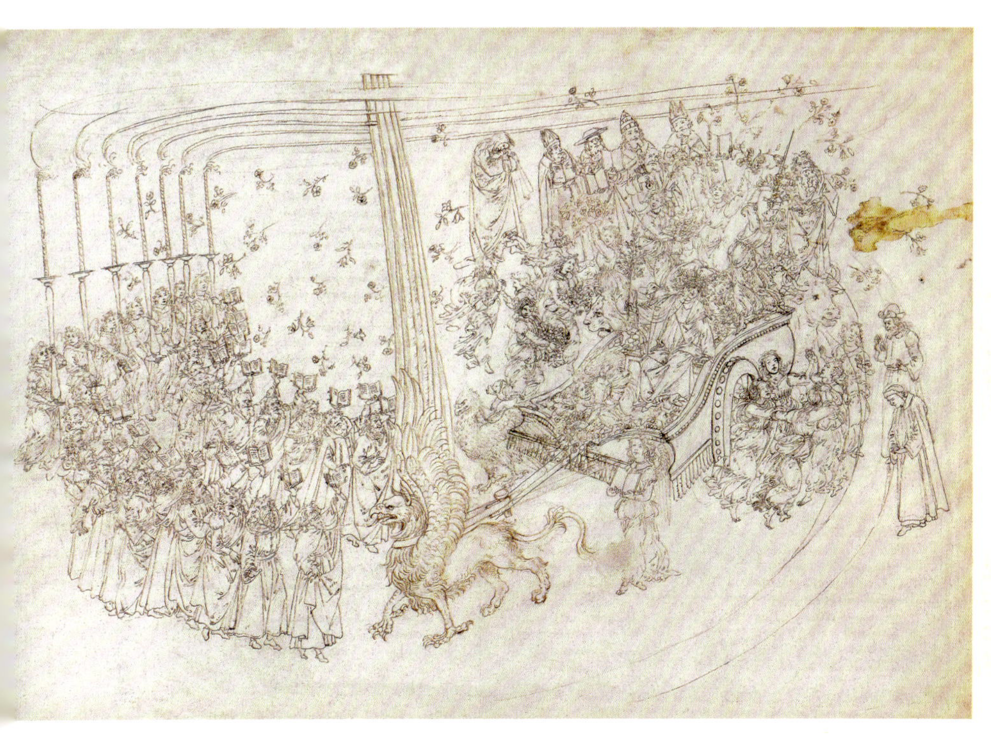

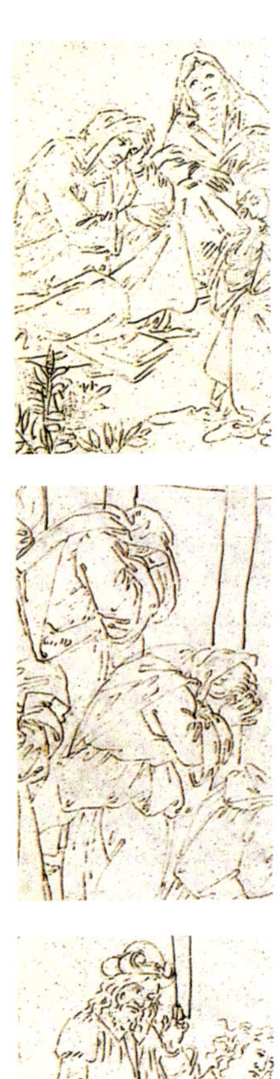

in the devil and in miracles which was yet to endure for centuries in the foundations of popular superstitions. The final scene of the Supreme Judgement was sculpted over the portals of every cathedral, and on entering the sanctuary of the church, one passed under the balance of the archangel, which, on the left, showed images of

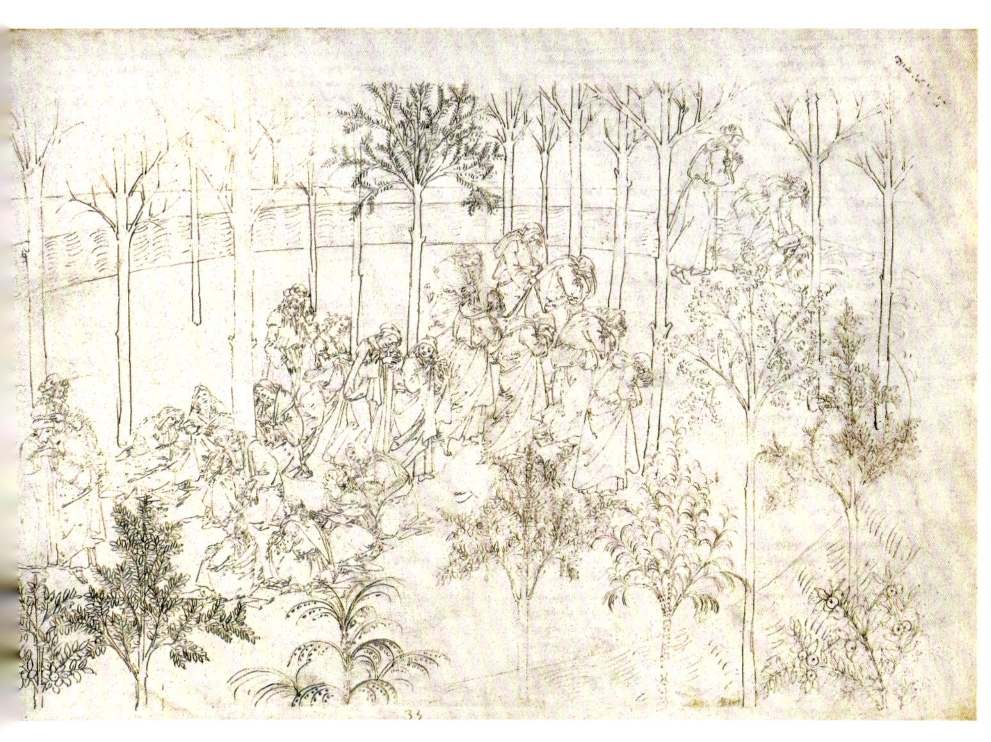

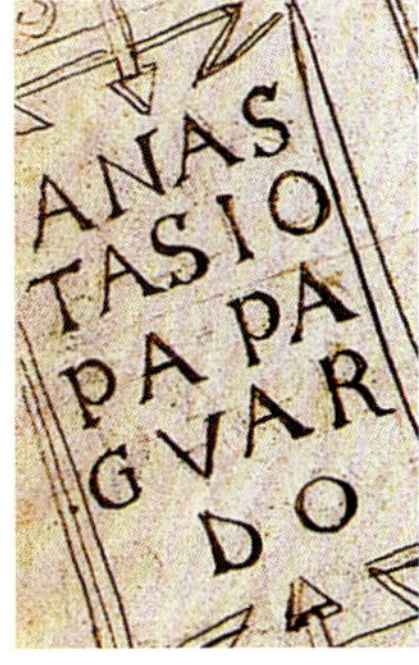

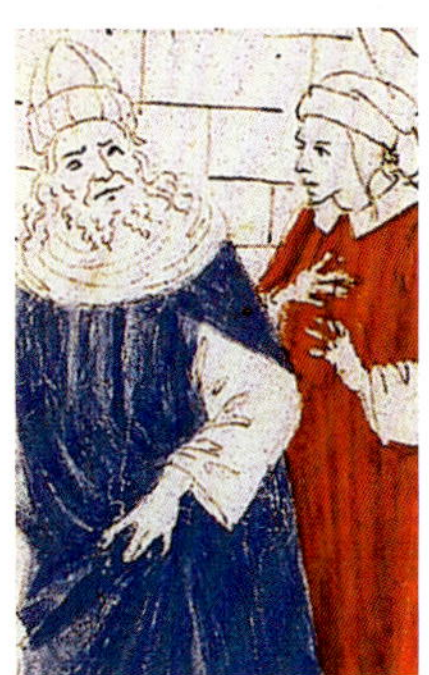

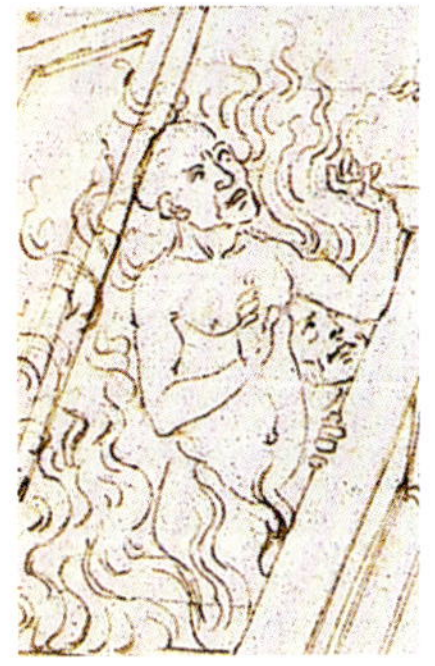

the devils and the damned writhing in strange and fantastic convulsions, being thrown into the eternal flames of hell.

But the idea that the world was to end was not confined to the Church. In the 12th century, astrologers terrified Europe with the announcement of a conjunction of all the planets in the

Inferno: Canto X

Illustration for Dante's Divine Comedy, c. 1480-1490
Preliminary sketch with silverpoint
on parchment, retraced in ink, 32 x 47 cm
Biblioteca Apostolica Vaticana, Vatican City

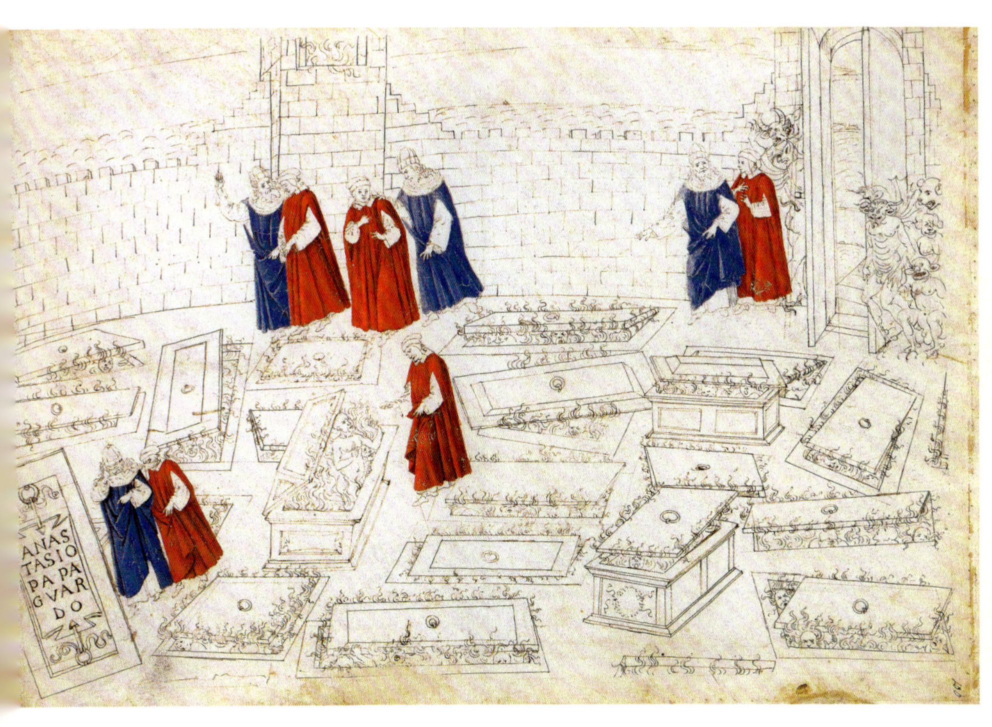
ANAS
TASIO
PAPA
GVAR
DO

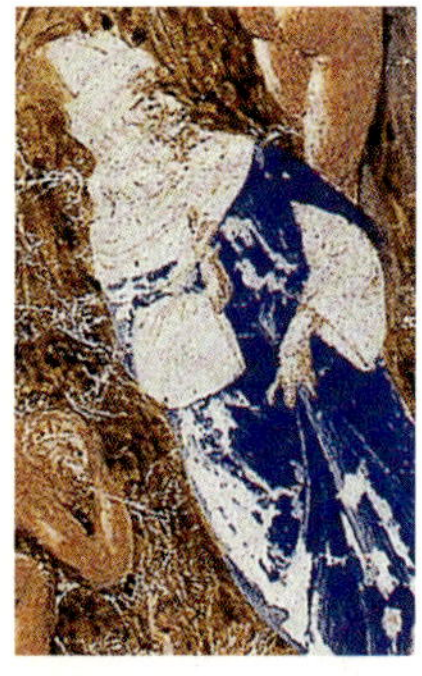

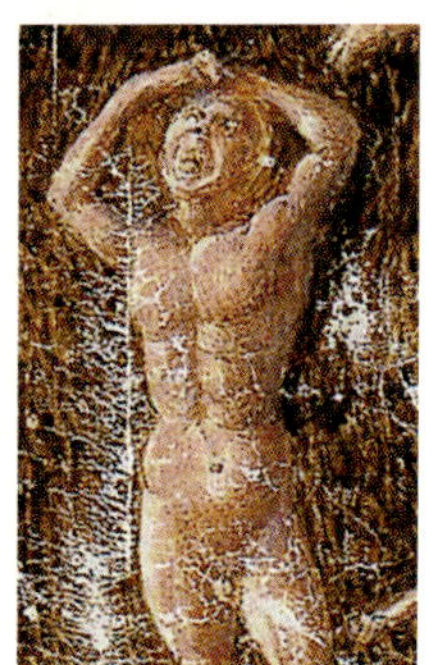

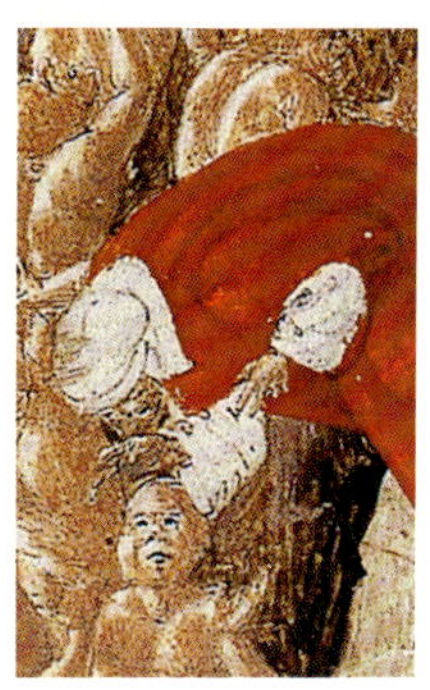

constellation of the scales. This conjunction actually occurred, for on 15 September all the planets were found between the 180th and 190th degrees of longitude. But, alas, the end of the world did not come.

The celebrated alchemist, Arnauld de Villeneuve, predicted it again for the year 1335.

Inferno: Canto XV

Illustration for Dante's Divine Comedy, c. 1480-1490
Preliminary sketch with silverpoint
on parchment, retraced in ink, 32 x 47 cm
Biblioteca Apostolica Vaticana, Vatican City

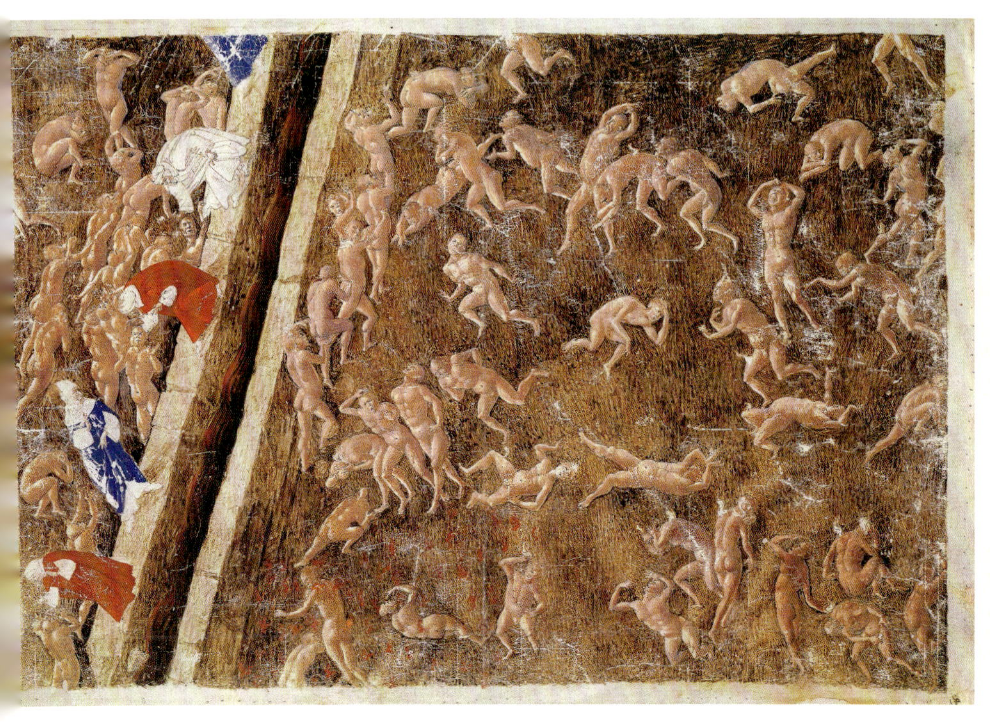

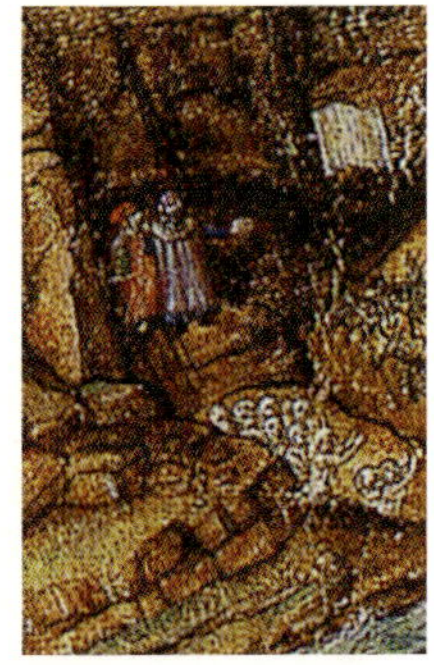

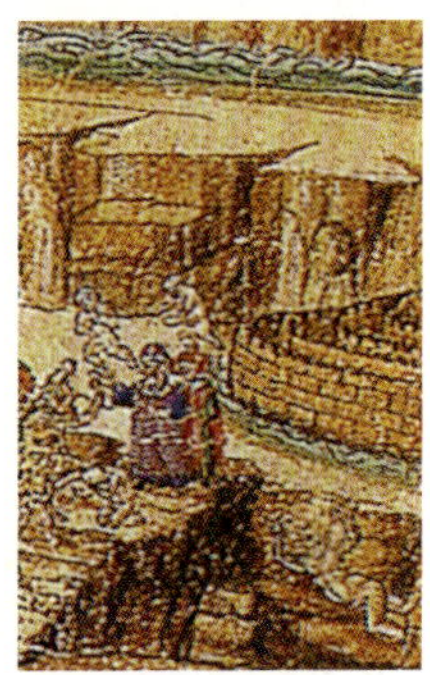

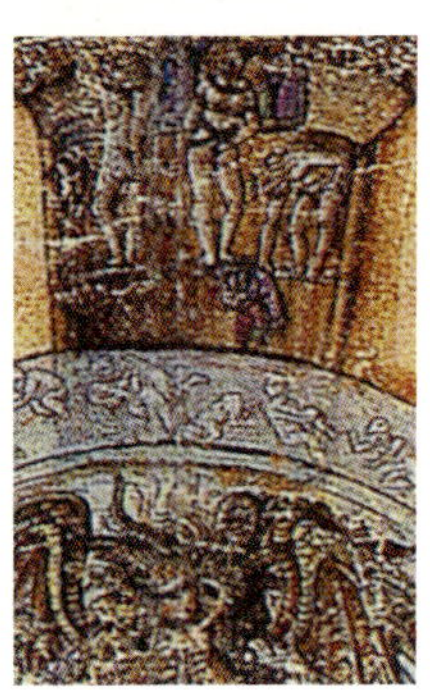

In 1406, under Charles VI, an eclipse of the sun, occurring on 16 June, produced a general panic, which was chronicled by Juvenal of the Ursuline Order: "It is a pitiable sight," he says, "to see people taking refuge in the churches as if the world were about to perish." In 1491, St Vincent Ferrier wrote a treatise entitled "De la Fin du

Illustration for Dante's Divine Comedy, c. 1490
Preliminary sketch with silverpoint on parchment
retraced in ink and coloured, 33 x 47.5 cm
Biblioteca Apostolica Vaticana, Vatican City

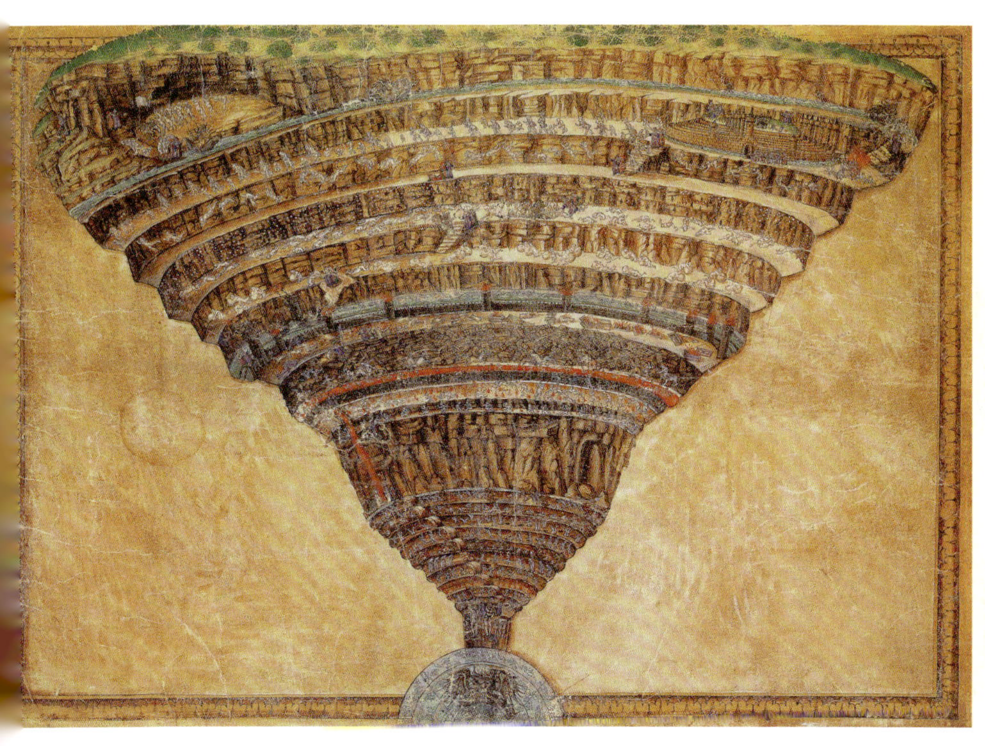

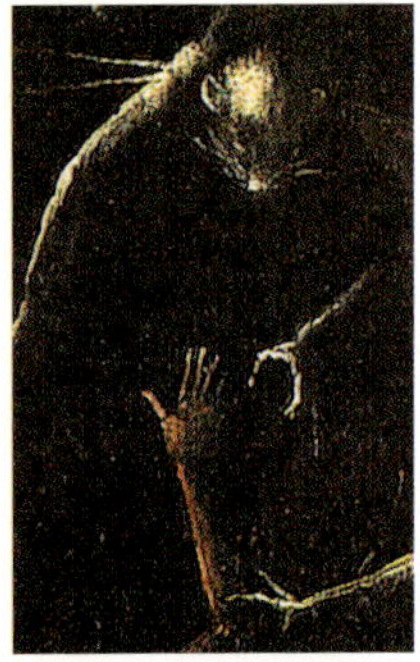

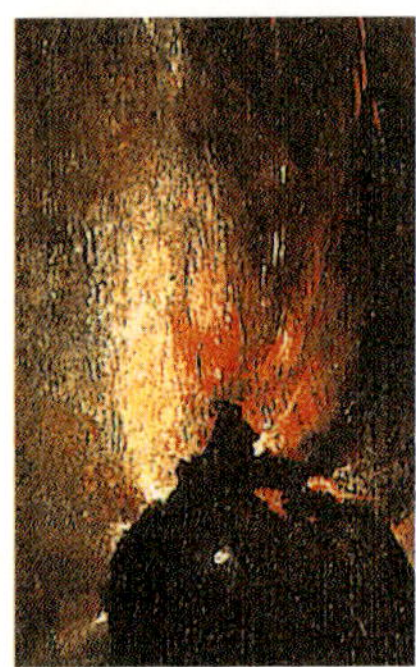

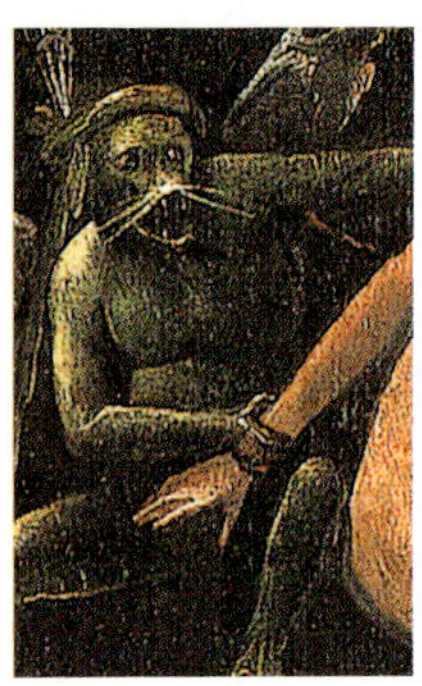

Monde et de la Science Spirituelle". He allows Christendom as many years of life as there are verses in the Psalter, namely, 2537.

Then a German astrologer by the name of Stoffler, predicted that on 20 February 1524, a general deluge would result from a conjunction of the planets. He was very widely believed, and the

The Falling of the Damned into Hell

Hieronymus Bosch, before 1490
Oil on panel, 86.5 x 39.5 cm
Palazzo Ducale, Venice

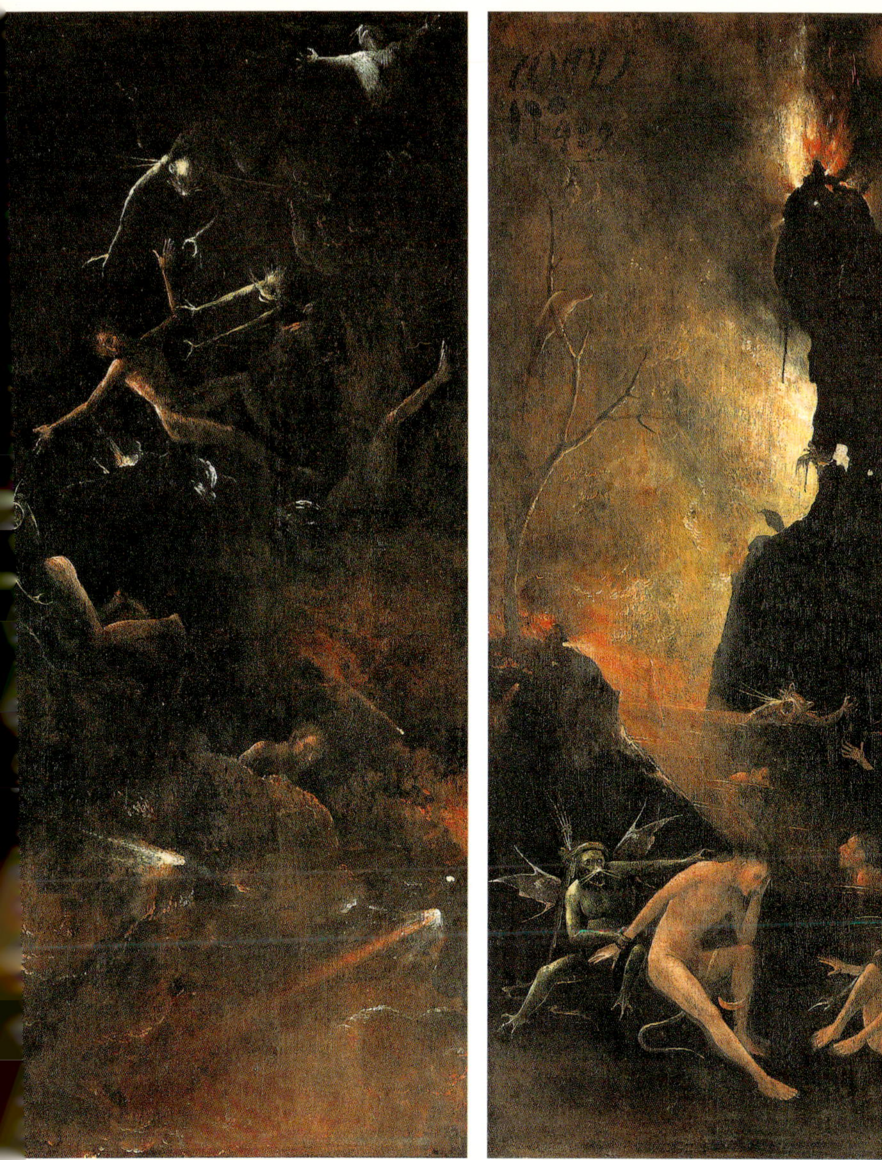

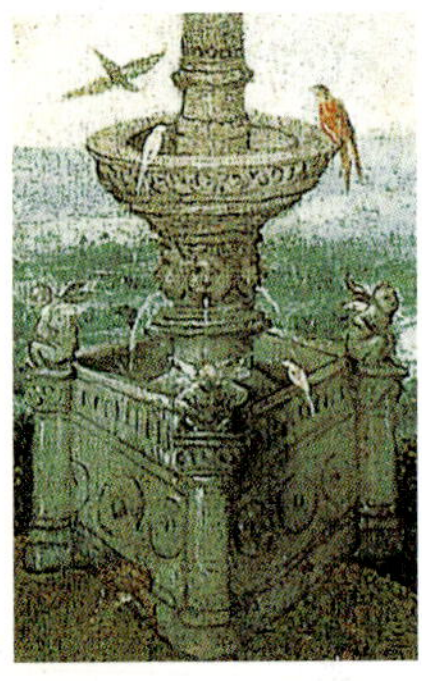

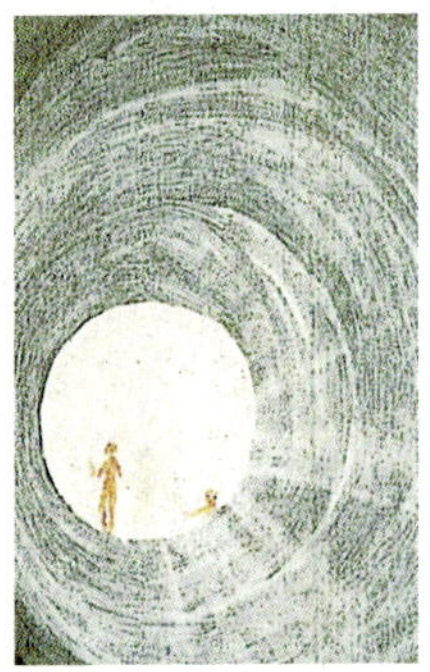

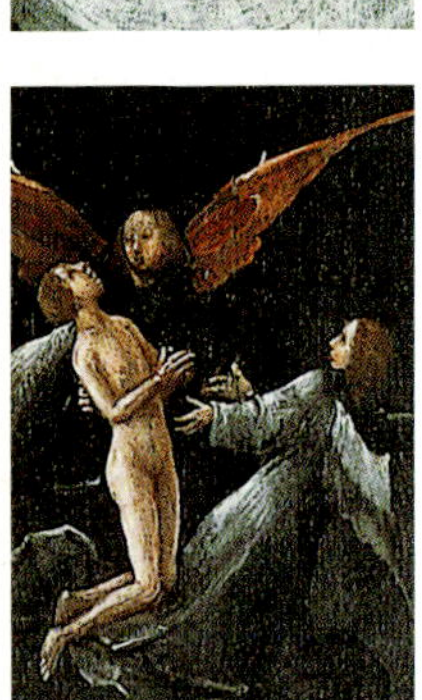

panic was extreme. Property situated in valleys, along river banks, or near the sea, was sold to the less credulous for essentially nothing. A certain doctor, Auriol of Toulouse, had an ark built for himself, his family, and his friends, and Bodin asserts that he was not the only one who took this precaution.

The Ascent into the Empyrean or Highest Heaven

Hieronymus Bosch, 15th century
Oil on panel, 86.5 x 39.5 cm
Palazzo Ducale, Venice

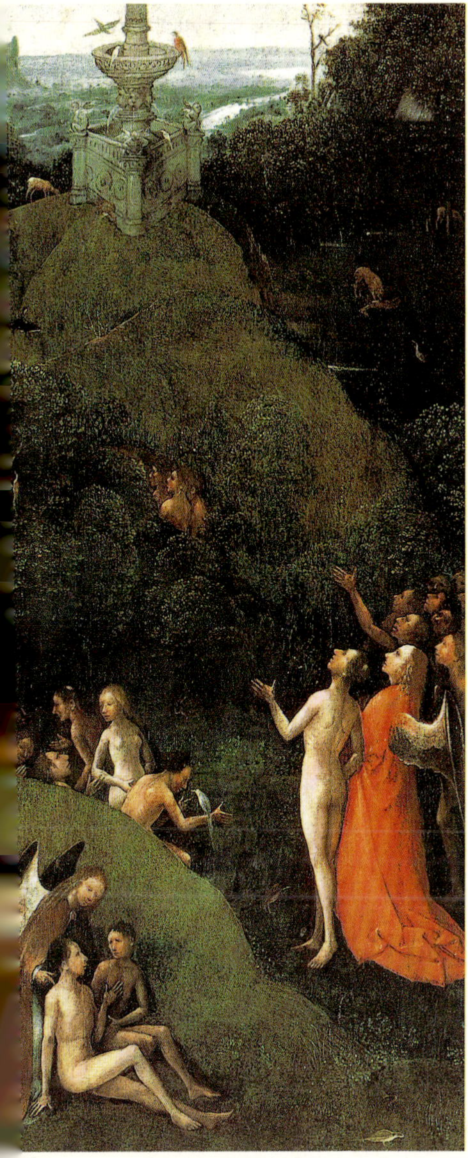

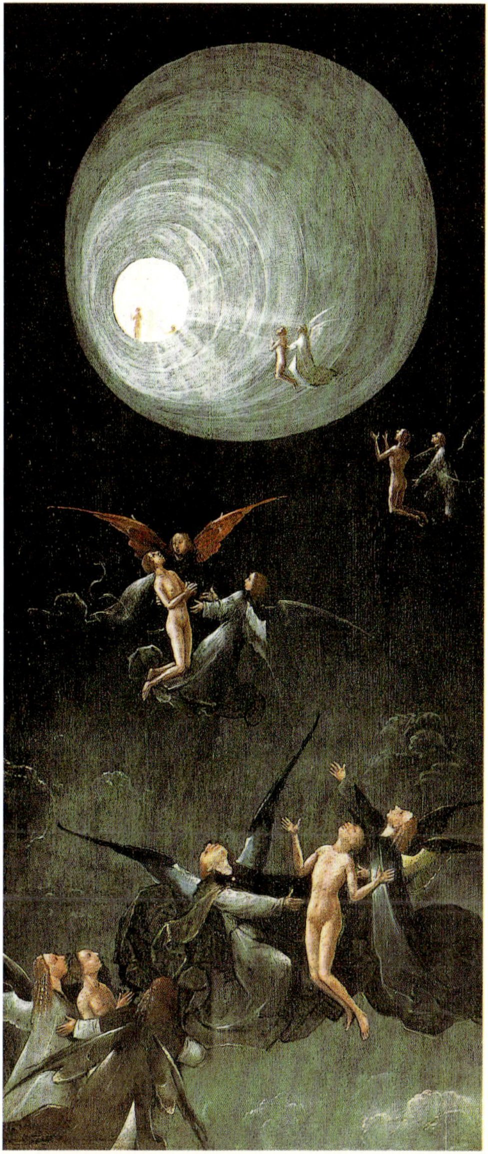

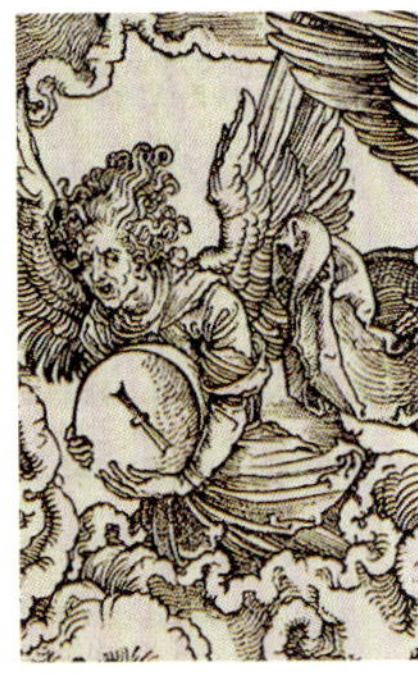

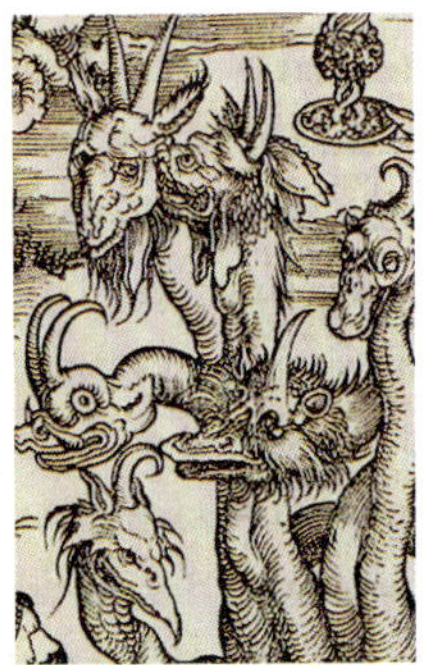

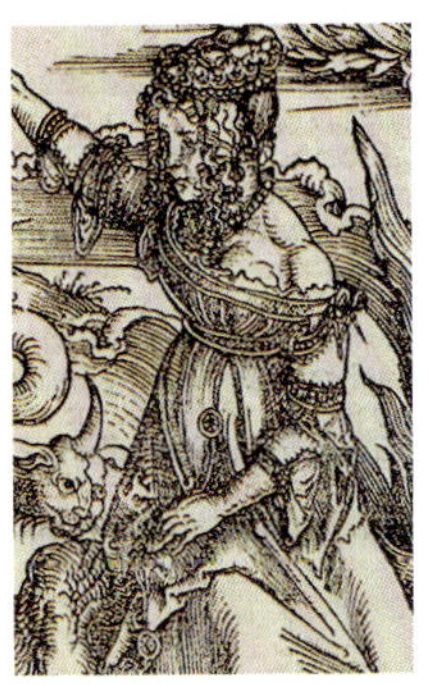

There were few sceptics. The grand chancellor of Charles V sought the advice of Pierre Martyr, who told him that the event would not be as fatal as was feared, but that the conjunction of the planets would undoubtedly occasion grave disasters. The fatal day arrived … and never had the month of February been so dry! But this did

The Whore of Babylon

Scene from the Revelation of St John
Albrecht Dürer, c. 1496-1497
Engraving, 39.2 x 28.1 cm
Musée du Petit Palais, Paris

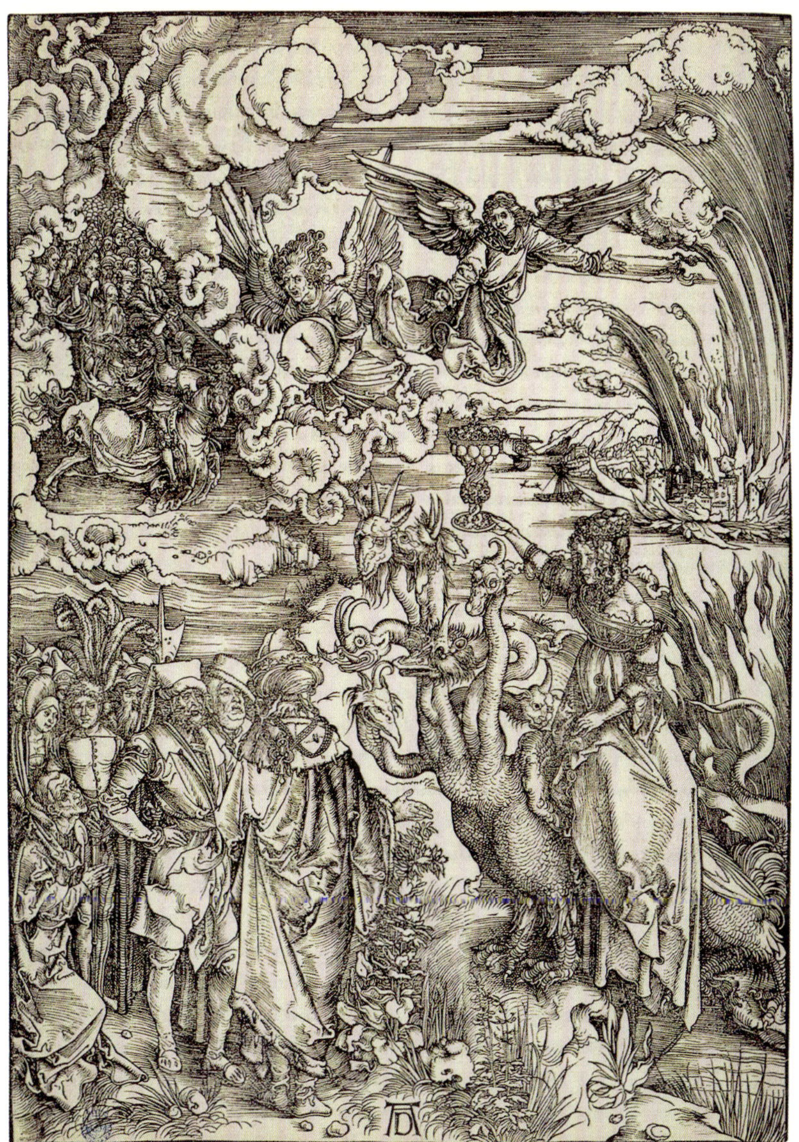

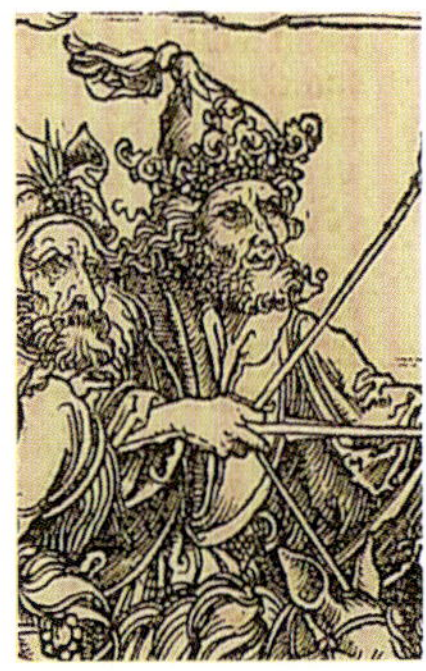

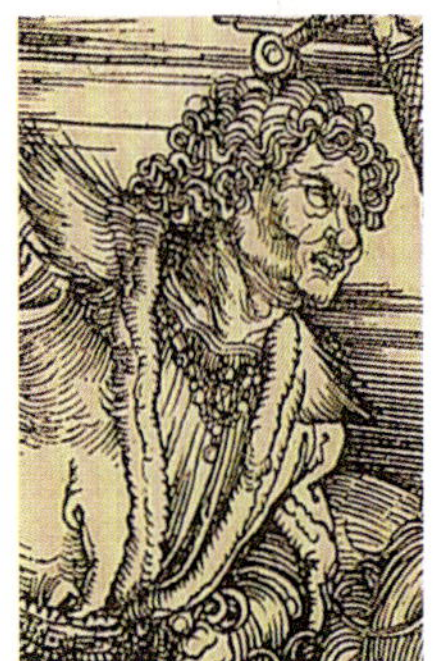

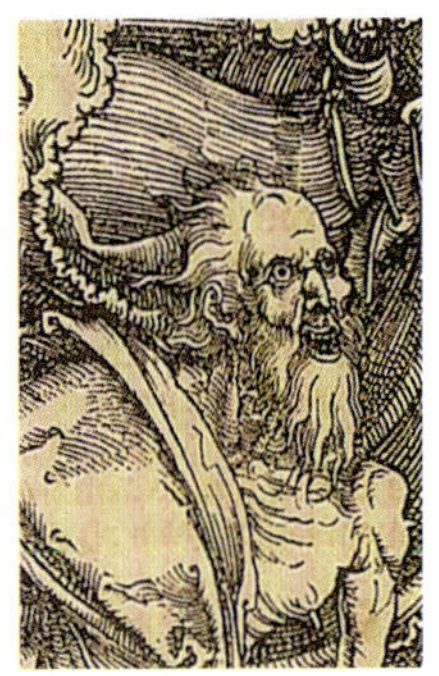

not prevent new predictions for the year 1532, by the astrologer of the elector of Brandenburg, Jean Carion; and again for the year 1584, by the astrologer Cyprian Lëowitz. It was again a question of a deluge, due to planetary conjunctions. "The terror of the populace," writes a contemporary, Louis Guyon, "was extreme,

The Four Horsemen of the Apocalypse

Albrecht Dürer, 1497-1498
Woodcut, 39.9 x 28.6 cm
Kupferstichkabinett, Staatliche Kunsthalle, Karlsruhe

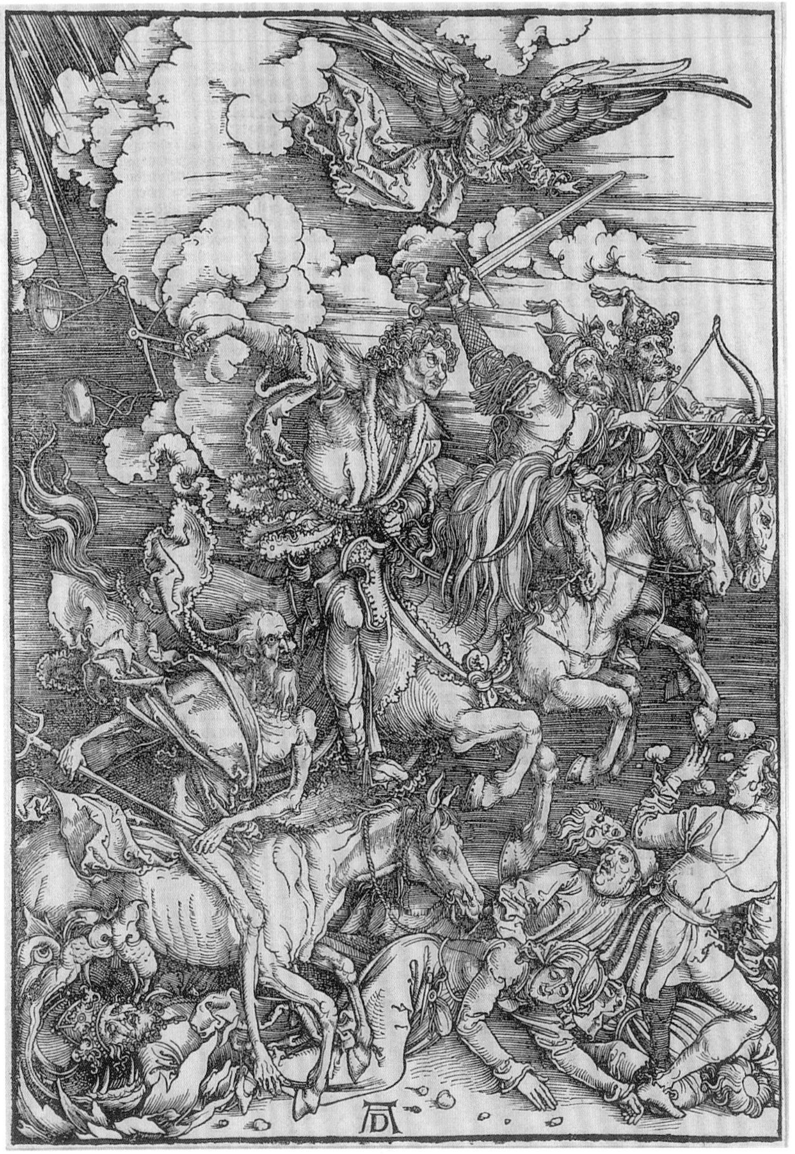

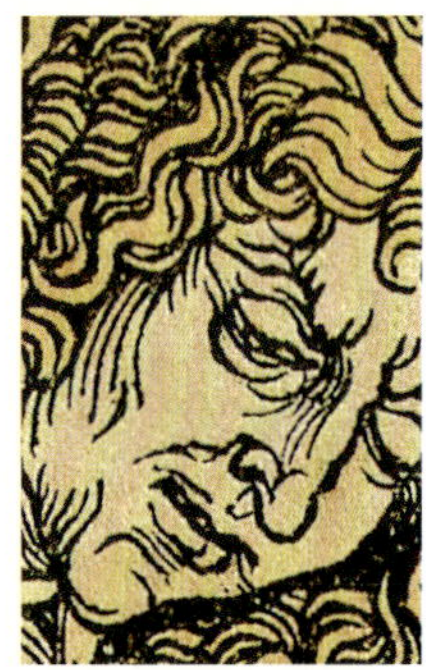

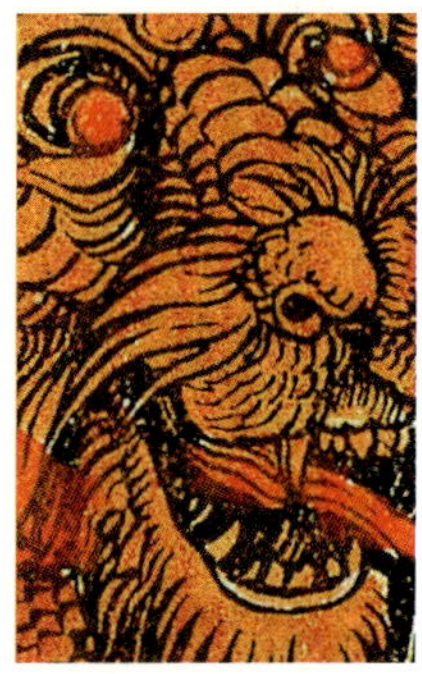

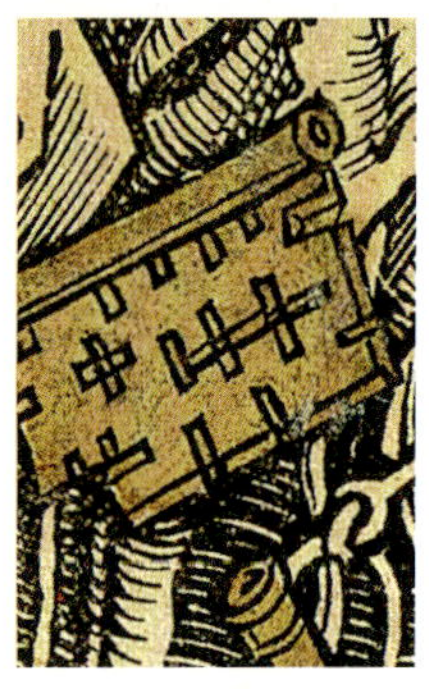

and the churches could not hold the multitudes which fled to them for refuge; many made their wills without stopping to think that this availed little if the world was really to perish; others donated their goods to the clergy, in the hope that their prayers would put off the day of judgement."

In 1588, there was another astrological prediction, couched in apocalyptic language:

The Apocalypse (detail)

Albrecht Dürer, 1498
Coloured woodcut
Library of the Museo Correr, Venice

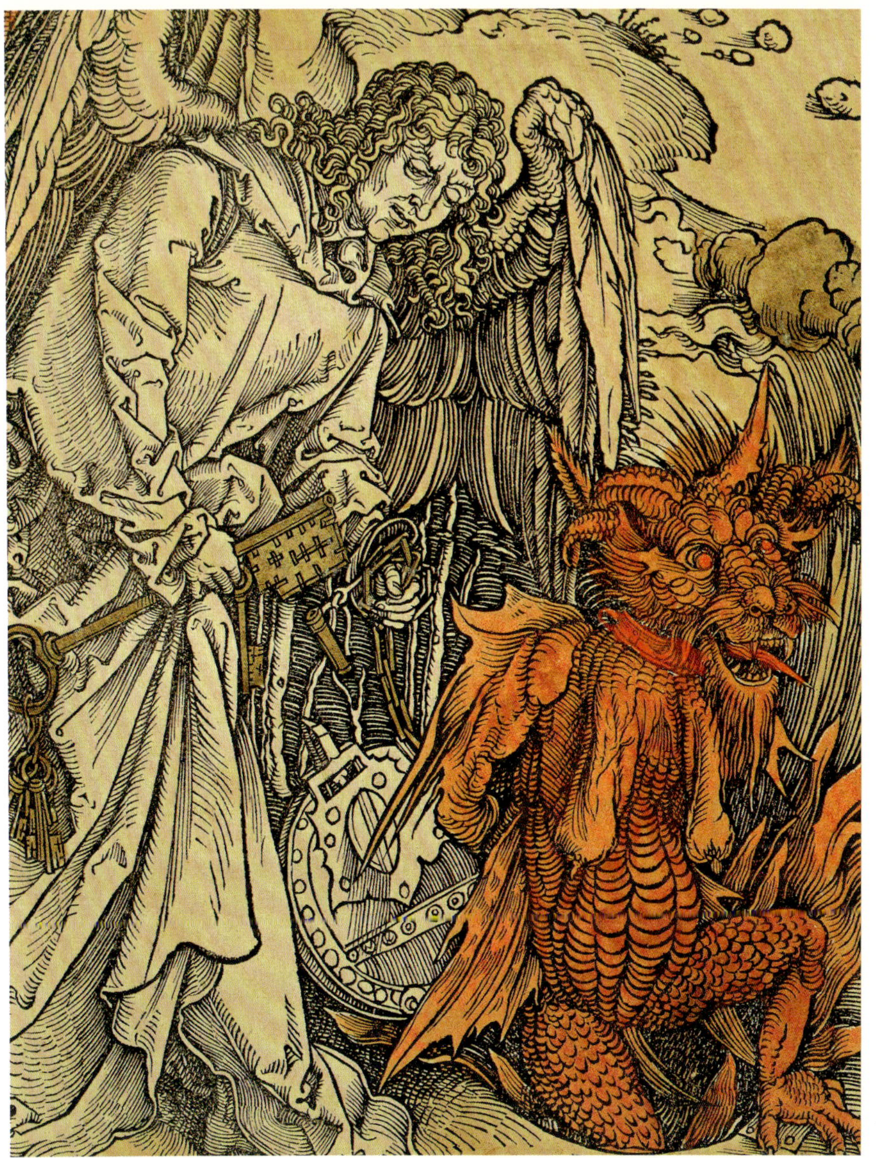

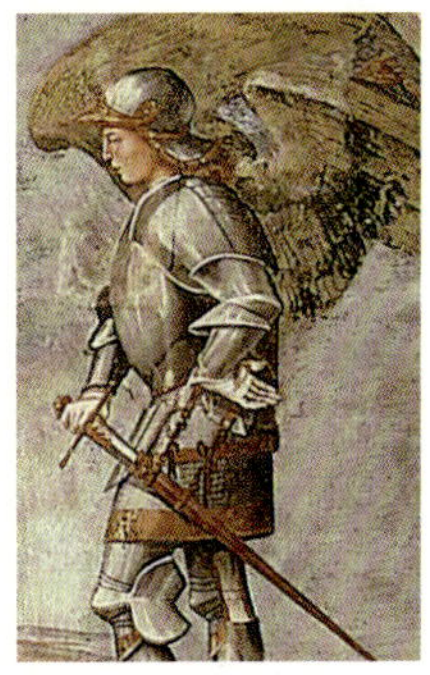

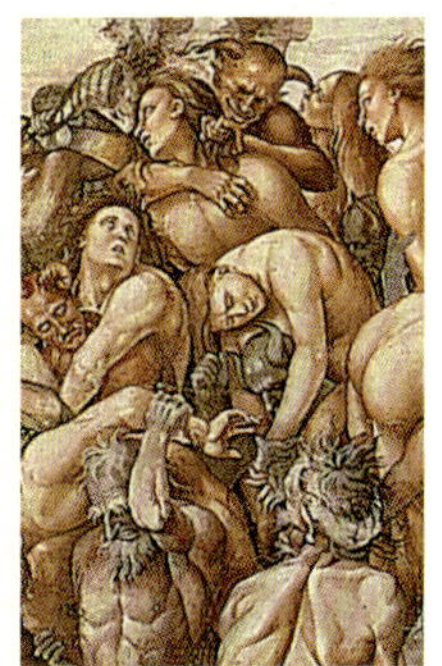

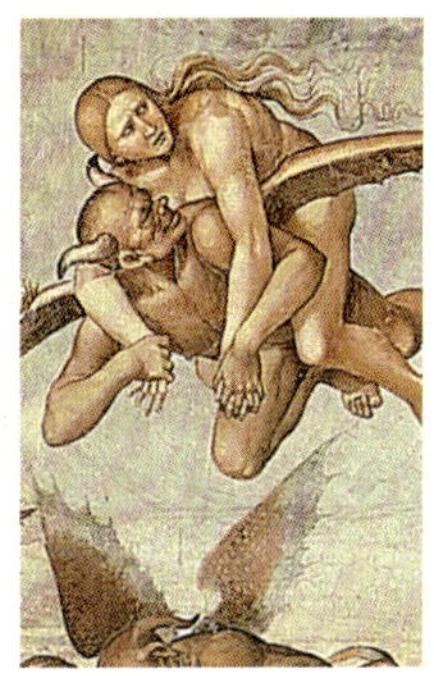

The eighth year following the fifteen hundred and eightieth anniversary of the birth of Christ will be a year of prodigies and terror. If in this terrible year the globe be not dissolved in dust, and the land and the sea be not destroyed, every kingdom will be overthrown and humanity will travail in pain.

The Last Judgement (detail),
The Damned Taken to Hell

Luca Signorelli, 1499-1502
Fresco
Duomo di Orvieto, Orvieto

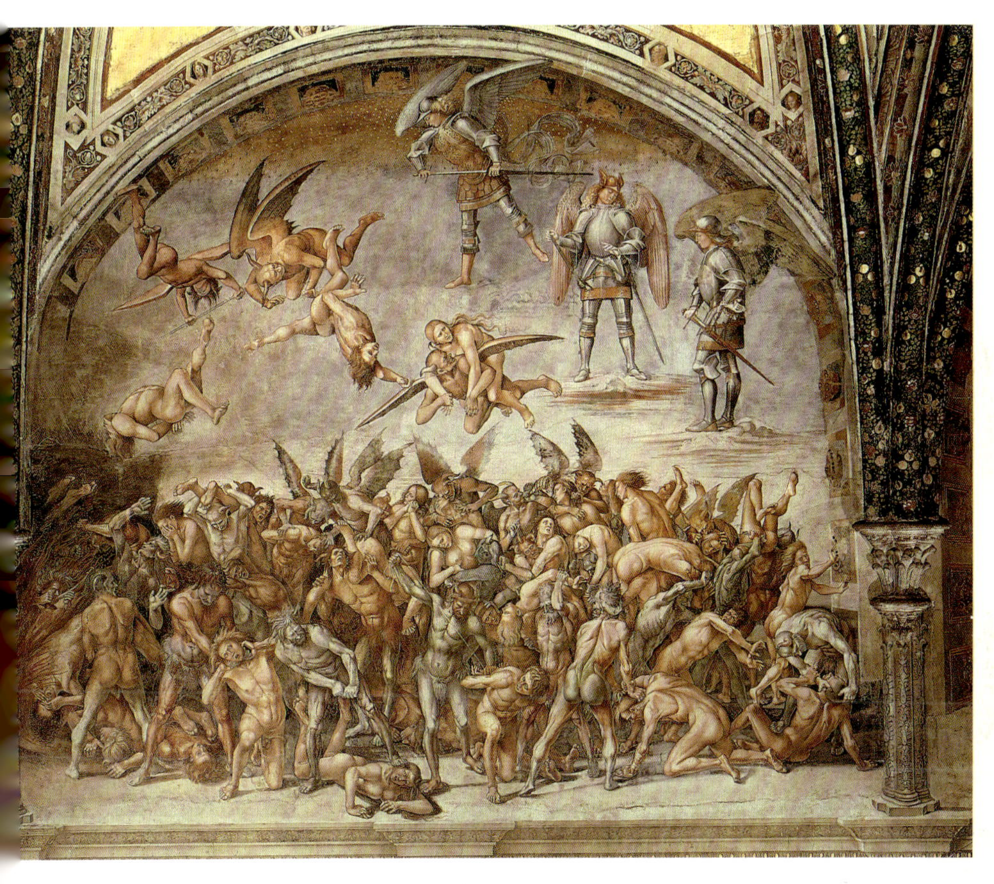

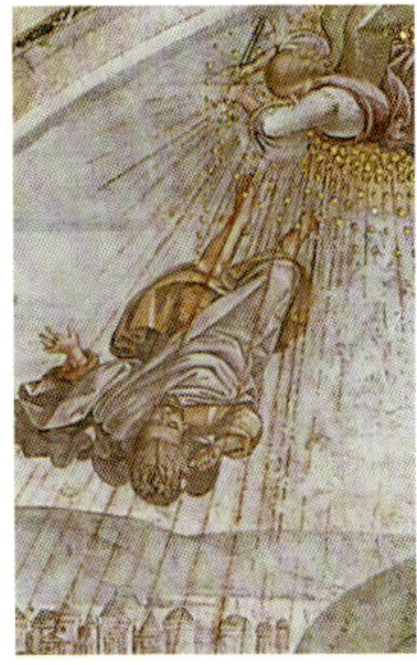

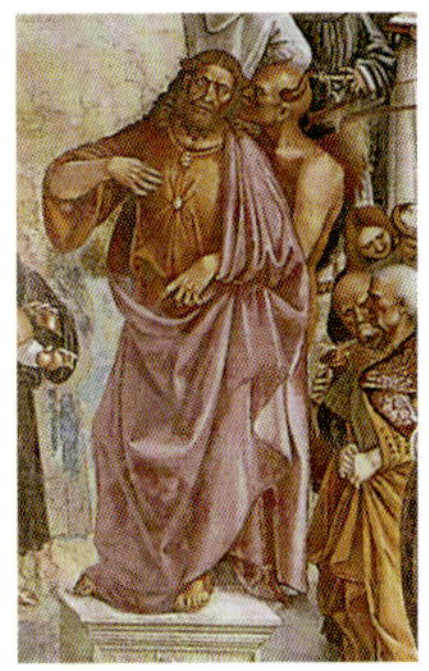

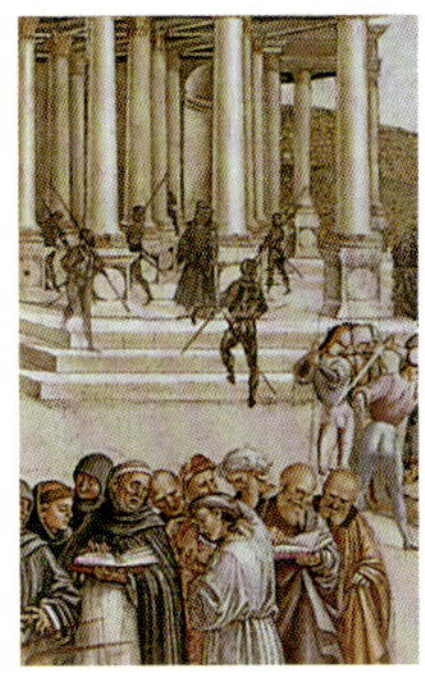

As might be expected, the celebrated soothsayer, Nostradamus, is found among these prophets of evil. In his book of rhymed prophecies, entitled *Centuries*, we find the following quatrain, which excited much speculation:

Quand Georges Dieu crucifiera,
Que Marc le ressuscitera,

The Preaching and Acts of the Anti-Christ

Luca Signorelli, 1499-1502
Fresco
San Brizio Chapel, Duomo di Orvieto, Orvieto

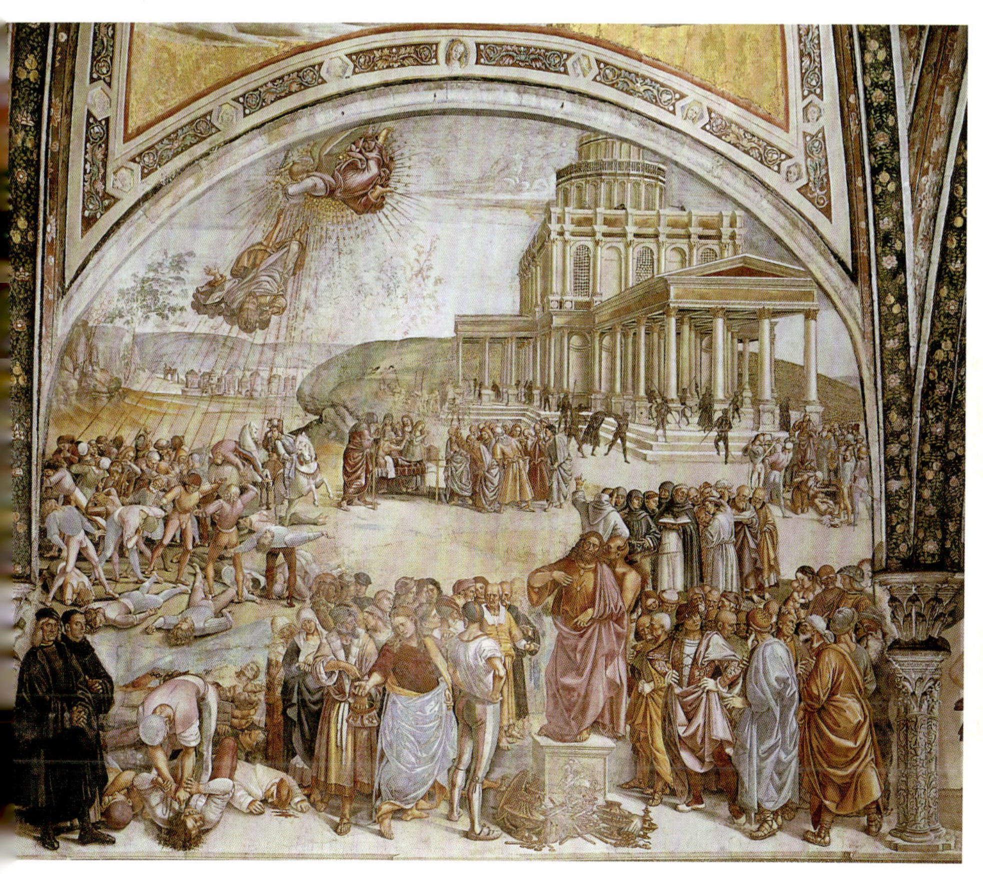

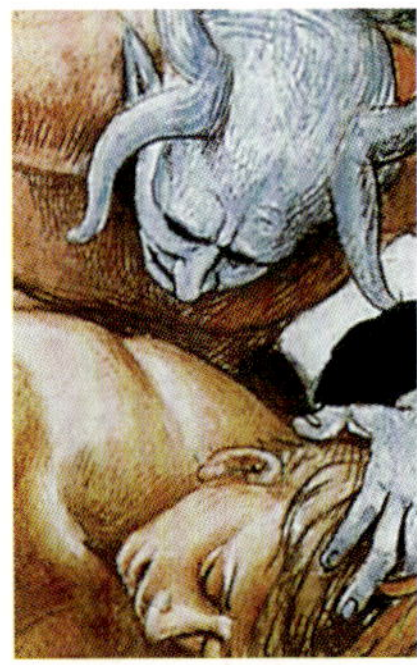

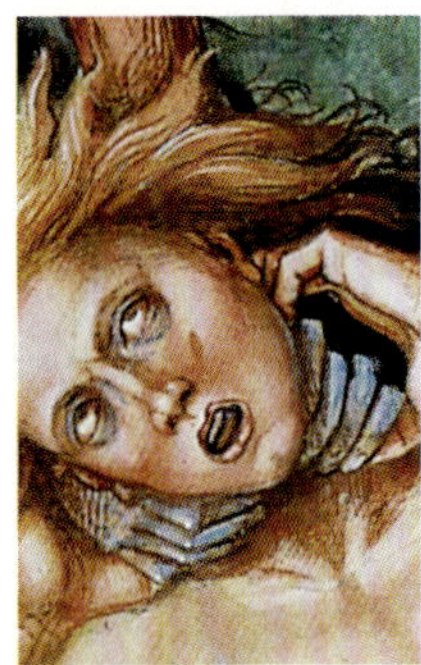

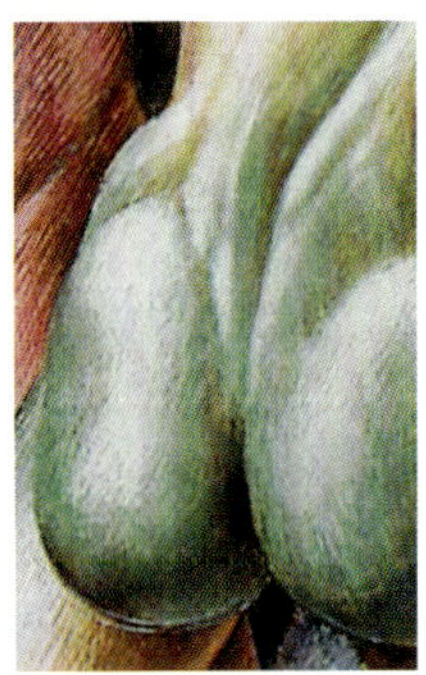

Et que St Jean le portera,
La fin du monde arrivera.

The meaning of which is, that when Easter falls on 25 April (St Mark's day). Holy Friday will fall on 23 April (St George's day), and Corpus Christi on 24 June (St John's day), and the end of the world will come. This verse was

The Damned (detail)

Luca Signorelli, 1499-1502
Fresco
Cappella di San Brizio, Duomo di Orvieto, Orvieto

124

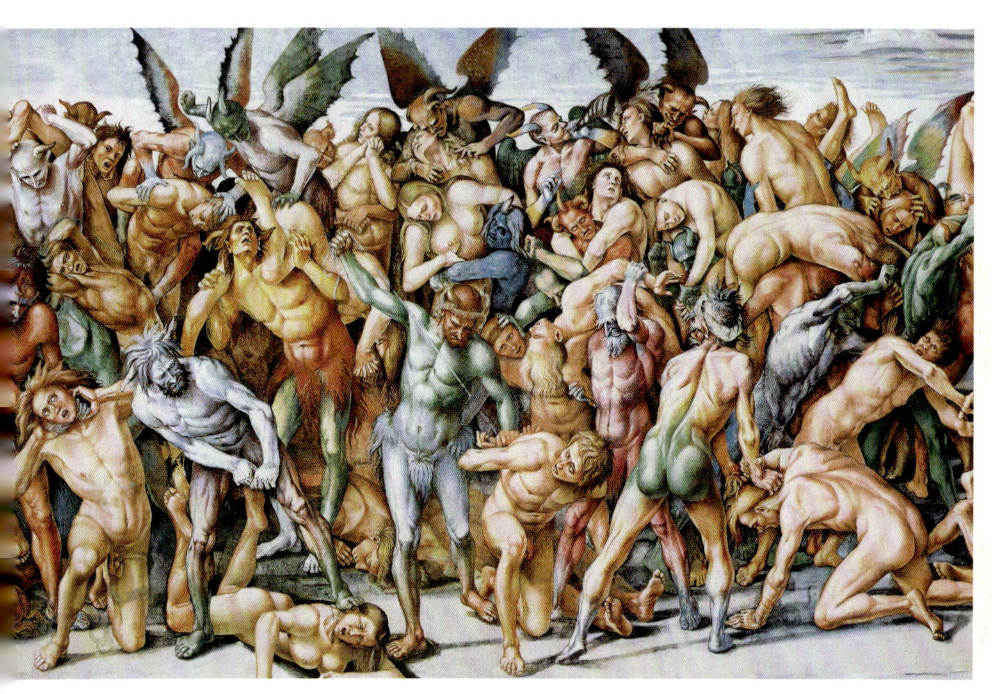

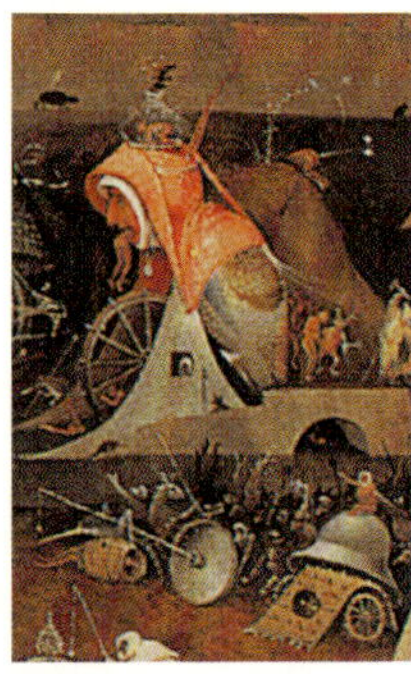

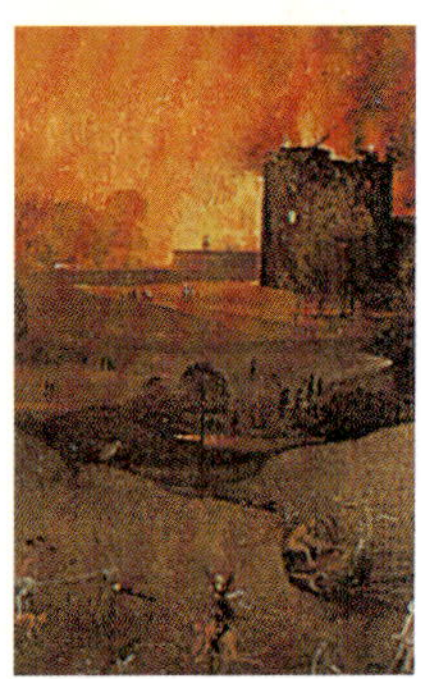

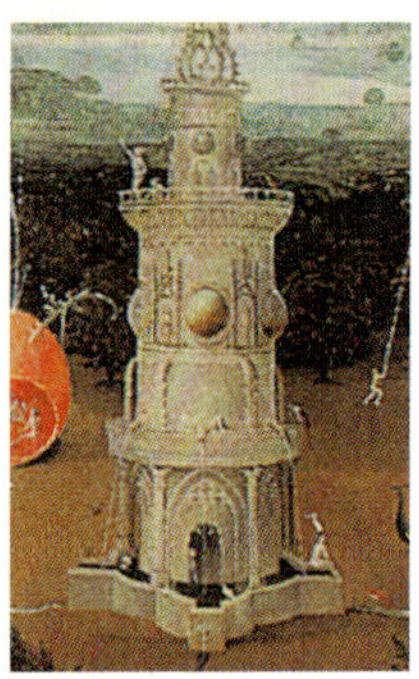

not without malice, for at this time (Nostradamus died in 1556) the calendar had not been reformed; this was not done until 1582, and it was impossible for Easter to fall on 25 April. In the 16th century, 25 April corresponded to the 15.

After the introduction of the Gregorian calendar, Easter might fall on 25 April, its latest

The Last Judgement (triptych)

Hieronymus Bosch, 1486
Oil on panel, 99.5 × 117.5 cm
Groeninge Museum, Bruges

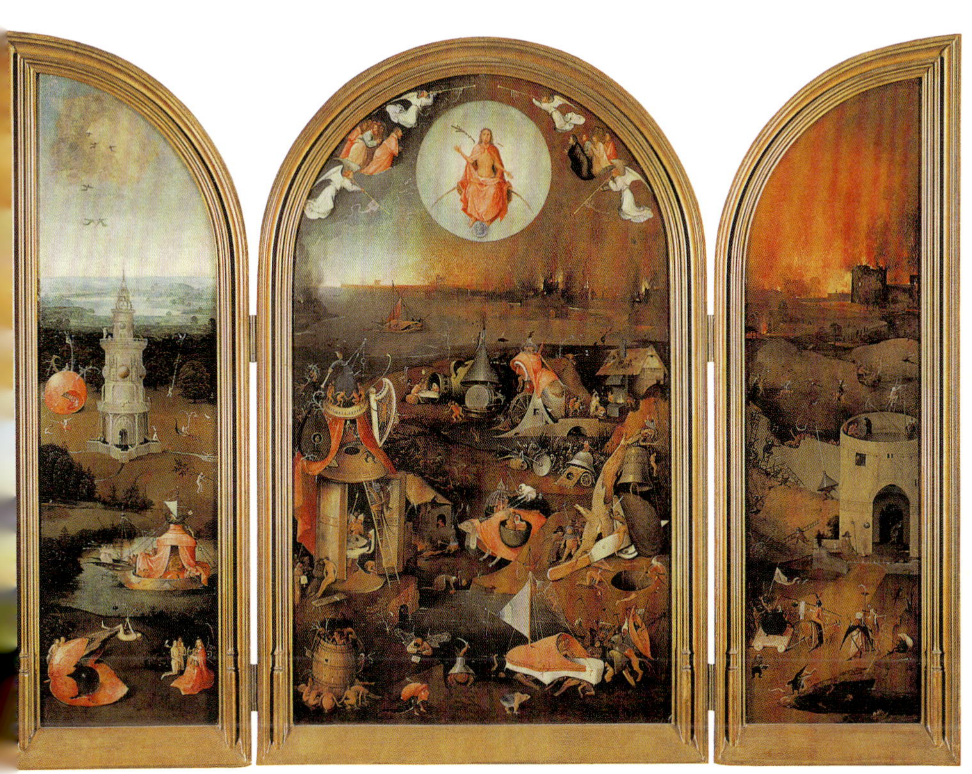

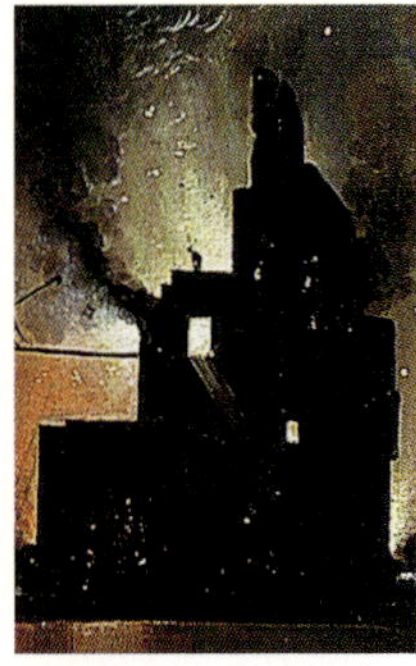

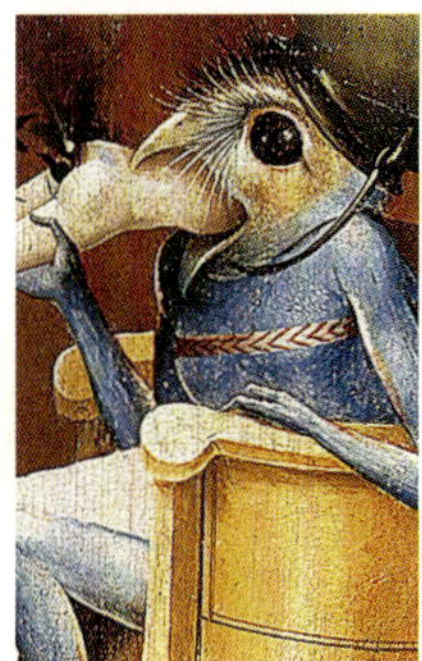

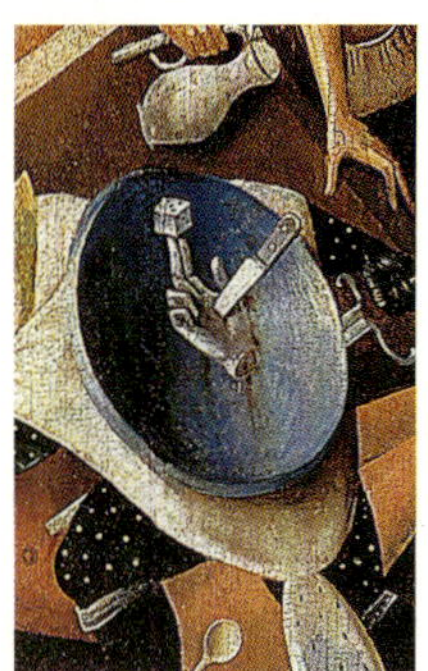

possible date, and this was or will be the case in 1666, 1734, 1886, 1942, 2038, 2190, and so on, the end of the world, however, not being a necessary consequence of this coincidence.

Planetary conjunctions, eclipses, and comets all share dire prophecies of evil. Among the most memorable historical comets in this regard,

The Garden of Delights, Hell (right panel)

Hieronymus Bosch, 1503-1504
Oil on panel, 220 x 97 cm
Museo Nacional del Prado, Madrid

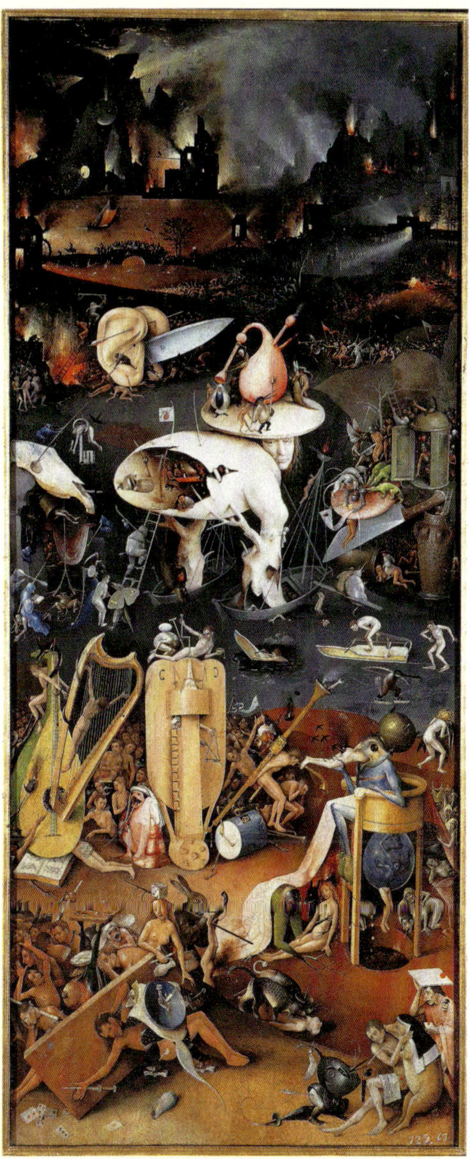

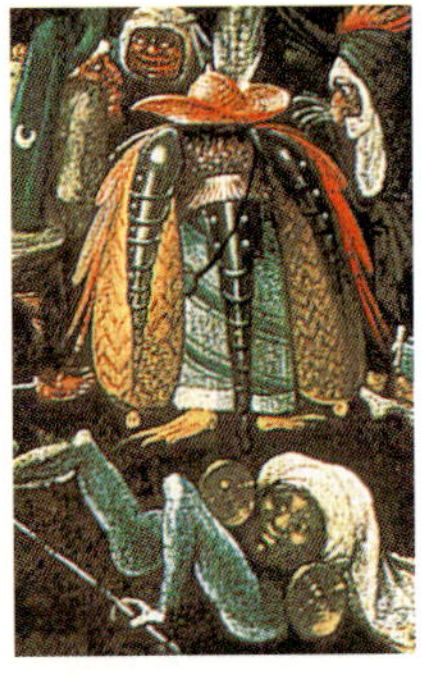

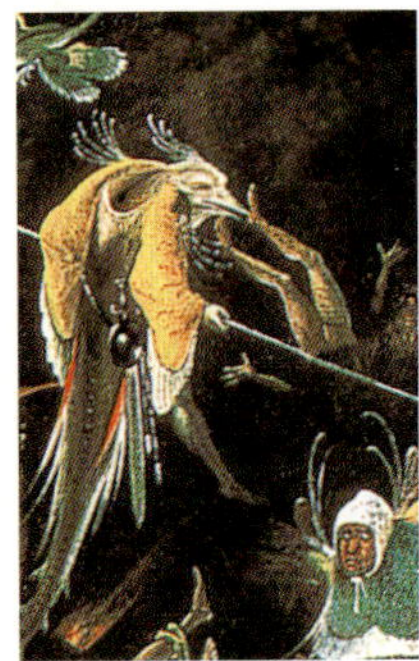

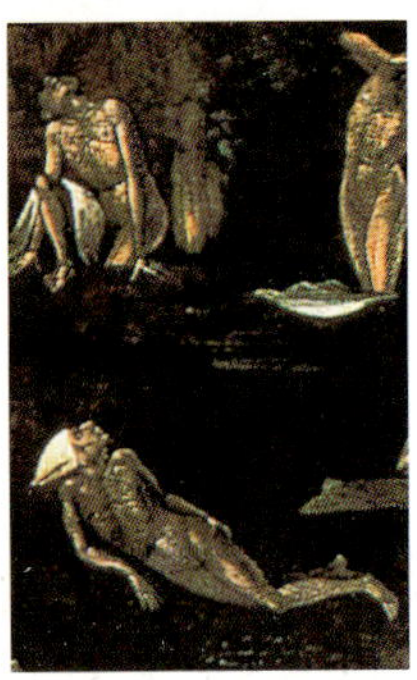

we may mention that of William the Conqueror, which appeared in 1066, and which is pictured on the tapestry of Queen Matilda of Bayeux; that of 1264, which, it is said, disappeared on the day of the death of Pope Urban IV; that of 1337, one of the largest and most imposing ever seen, which "presaged" the death of Frederick, king of

The Last Judgement (fragment)

Hieronymus Bosch, 1506-1508
Oil on oak, 59.4 x 112.9 cm
Alte Pinakothek, Munich

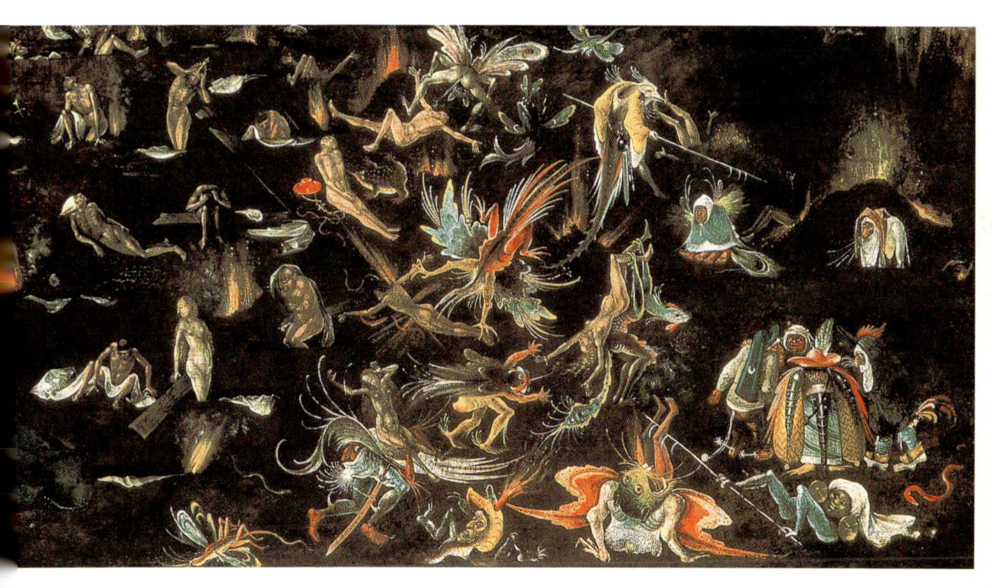

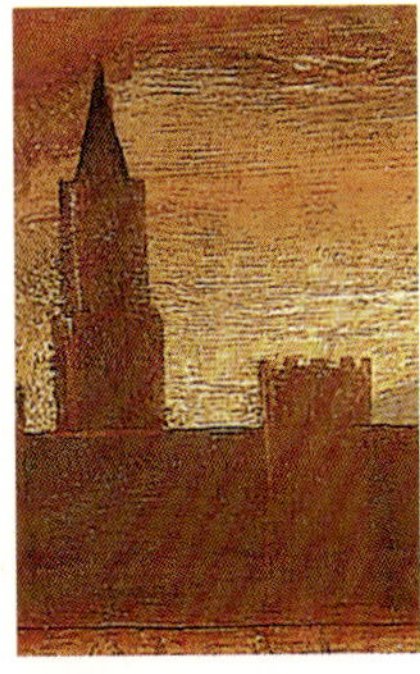

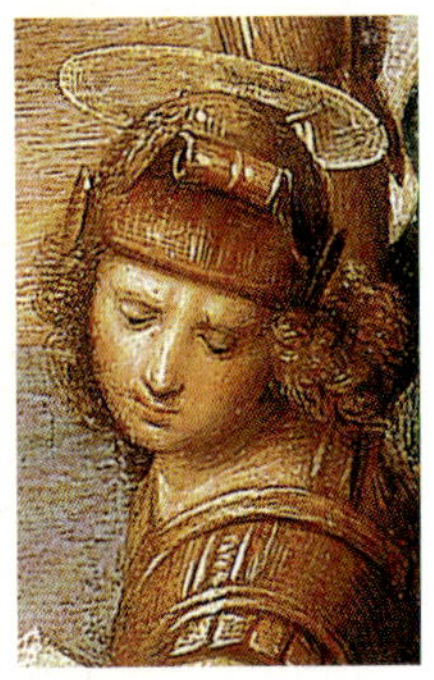

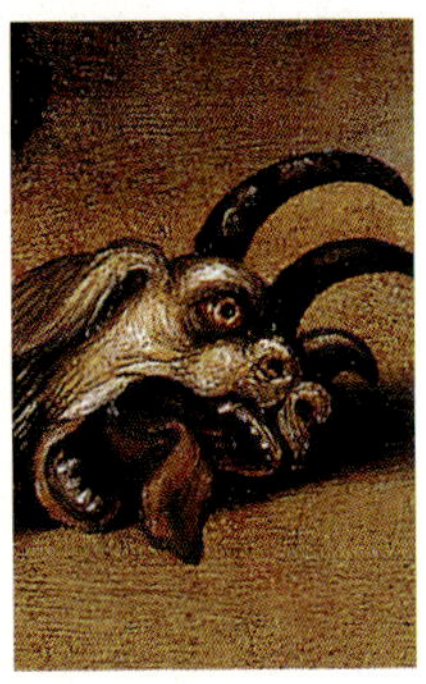

Sicily; that of 1399, which Juvenal the Ursuline, described as "the harbinger of coming evil"; that of 1402, to which was ascribed the death of Gian Galeazzo Visconti, duke of Milan; that of 1456, which filled all Christendom with terror under Pope Calixtus III, during the war with the Turks, and which is associated with the

Saint Michael and the Demon
known as The Small Saint Michael

Raffaello Sanzio (Raphael), c. 1503-1505
Oil on wood, 30 x 26 cm
Musée du Louvre, Paris

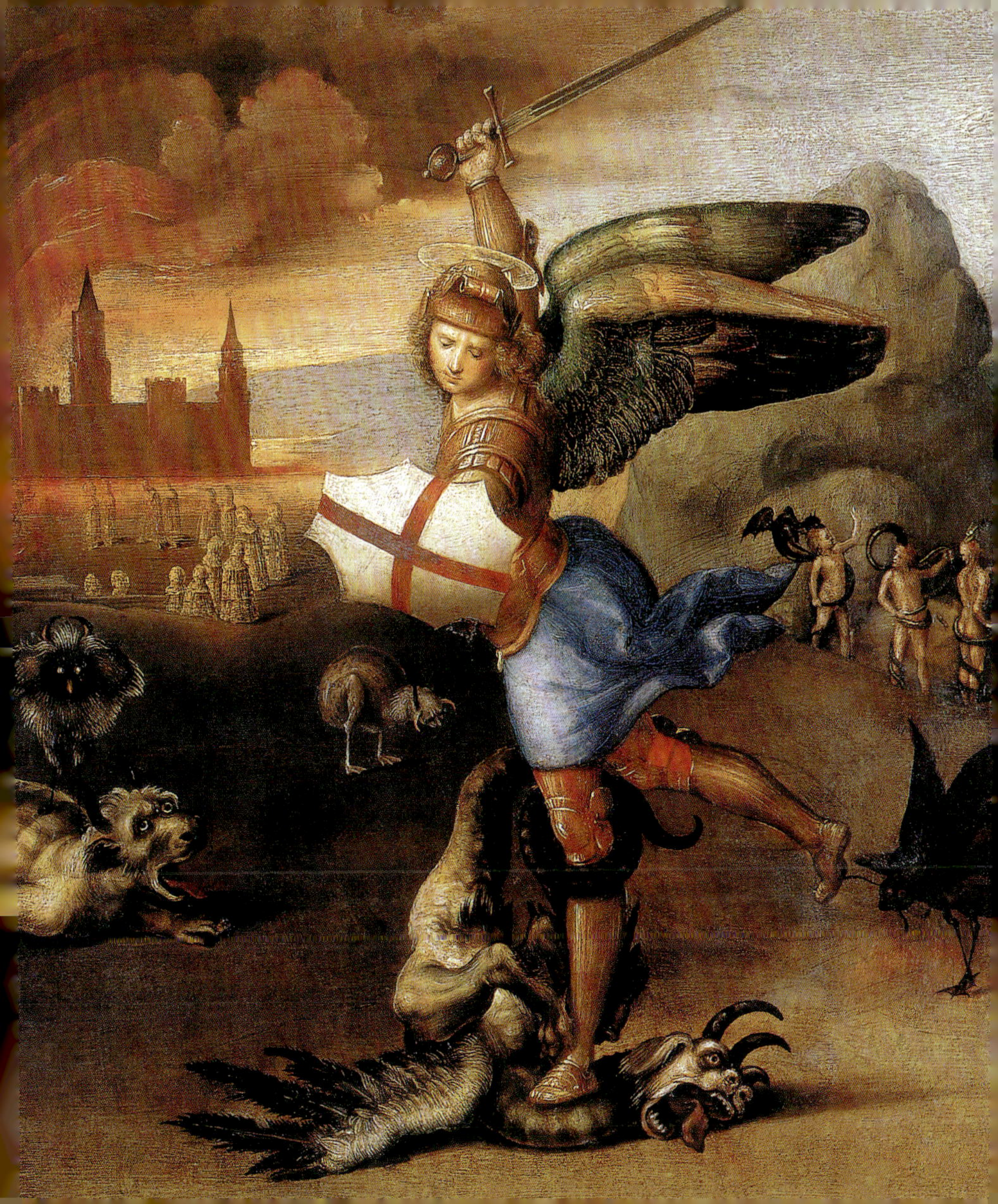

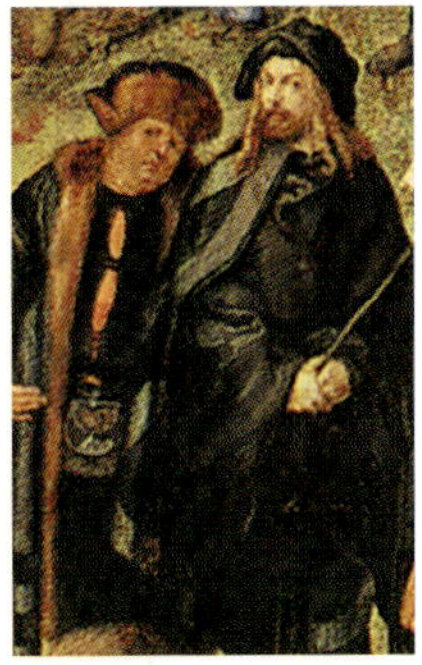

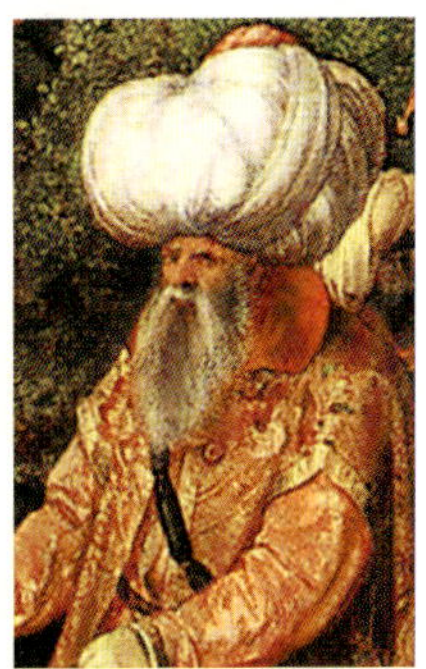

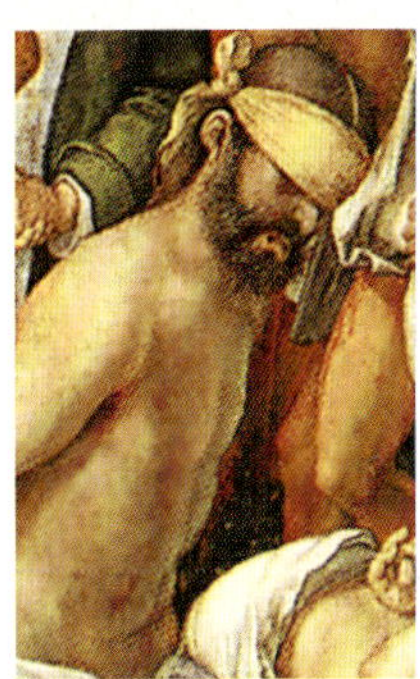

history of the Angelus; and that of 1472, which preceded the death of the brother of Louis XI. There were also others which were associated, like the ones before, with catastrophes and wars, and especially with the dreaded last hours of the human race. That of 1527 is described by Ambroise Paré and Simon Goulart, as consisting

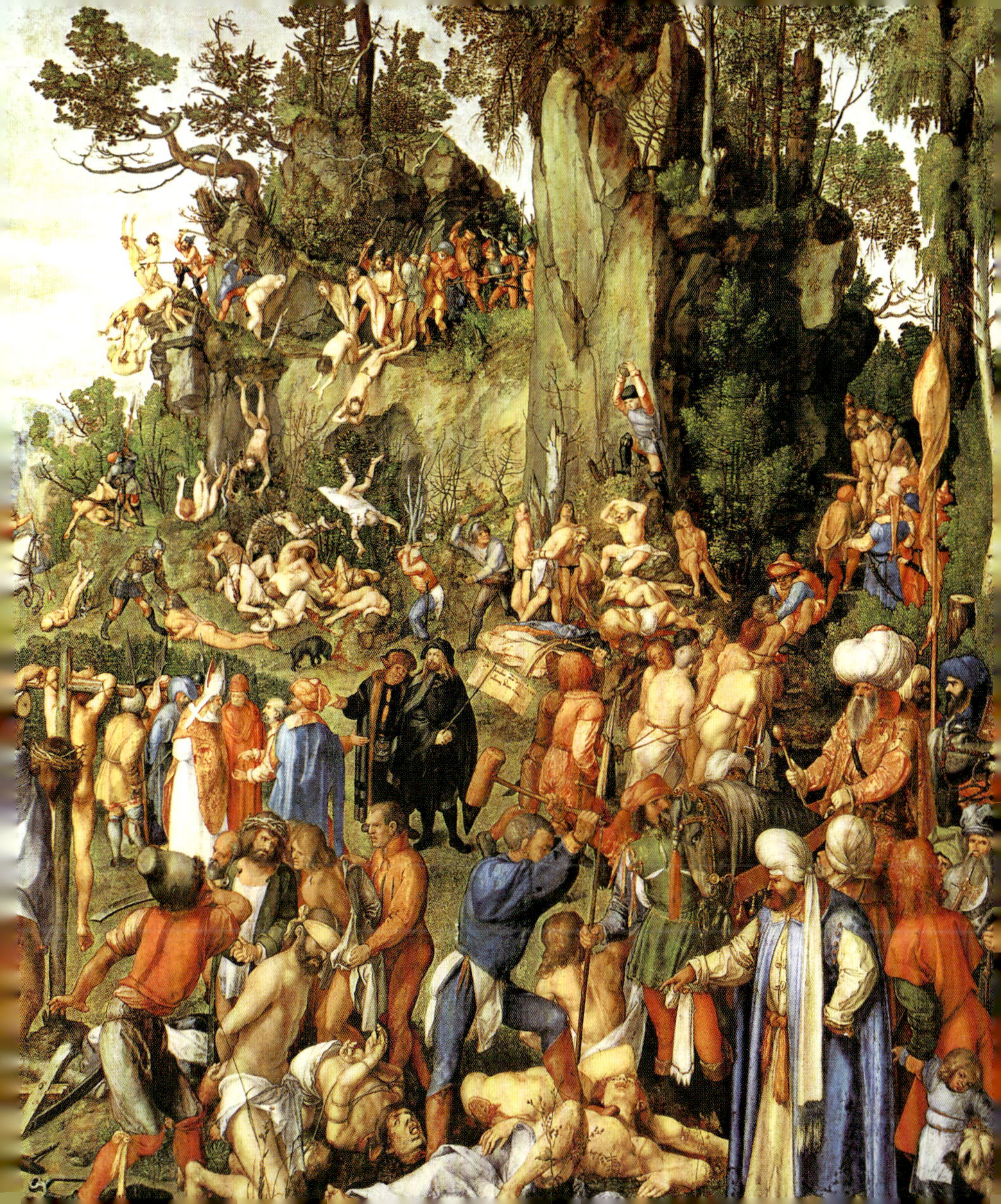

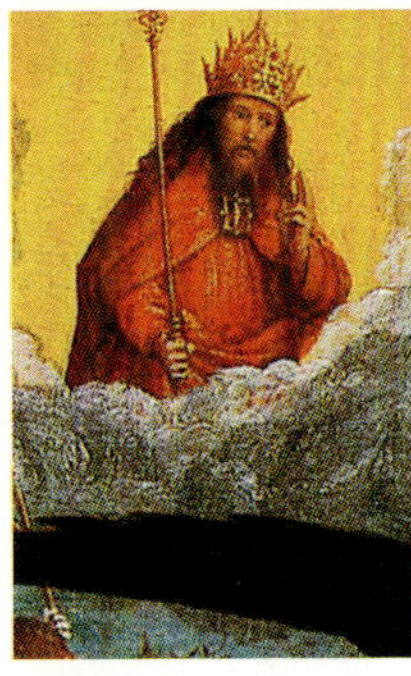

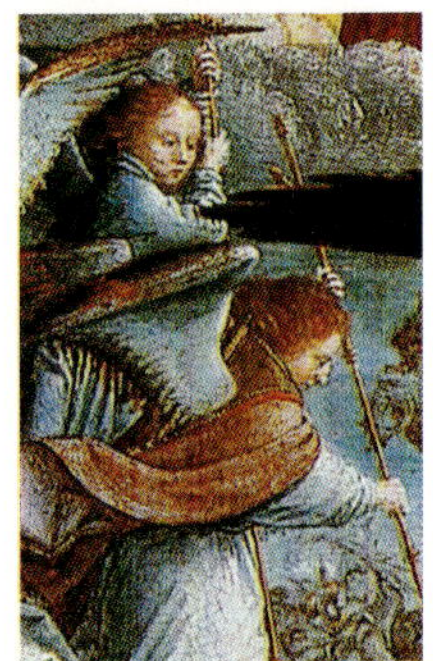

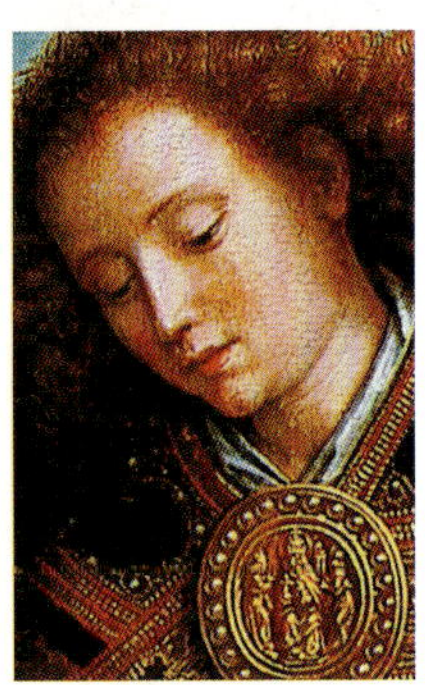

of severed heads, daggars, and bloody clouds. The comet of 1531 was thought to herald the death of Princess Louise of Savoy, mother of Francis I, who shared the popular superstition in reference to evil stars: "Behold!" she exclaimed from her bed, on perceiving the comet through the window, "behold an omen which is not

The Archangel St Michael
(central panel of the Michael Altar)

Gérard David, c. 1510
Oil on oak, 66 x 53 cm
Kunsthistorisches Museum, Vienna

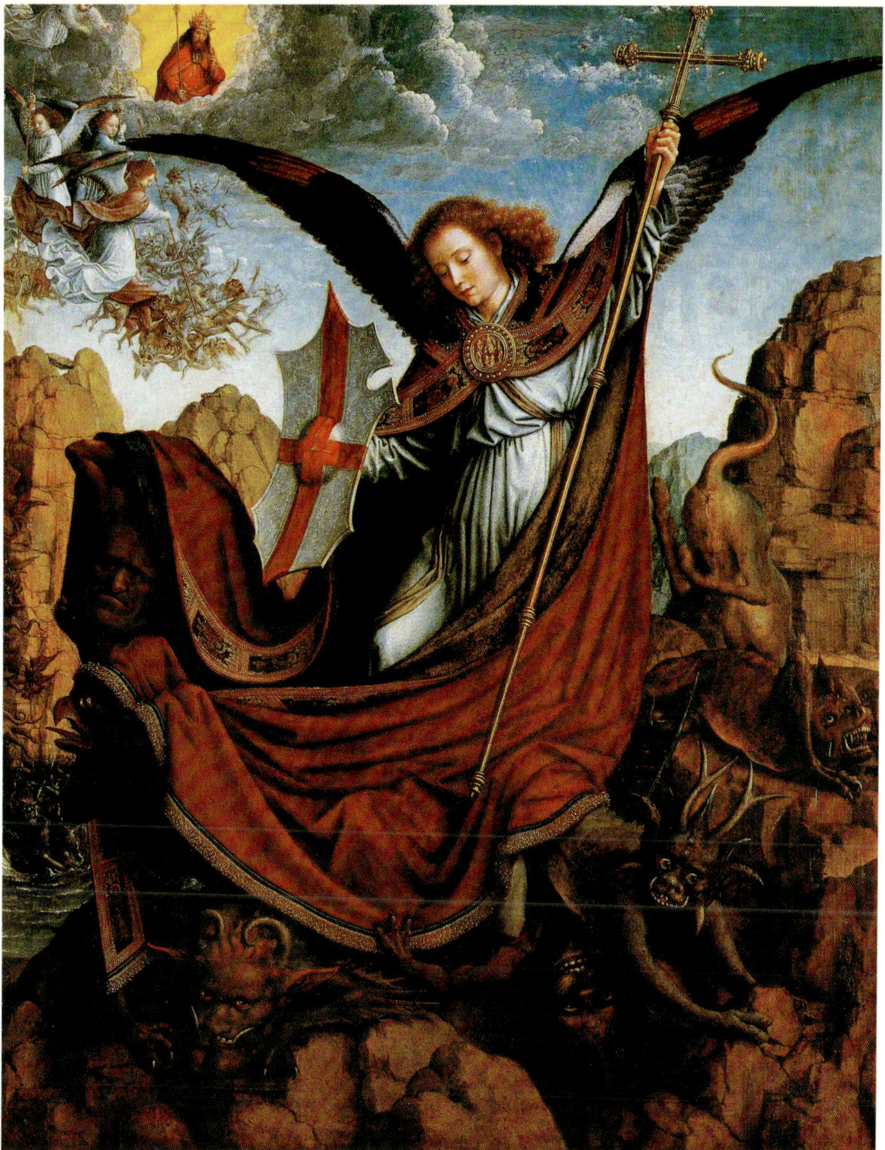

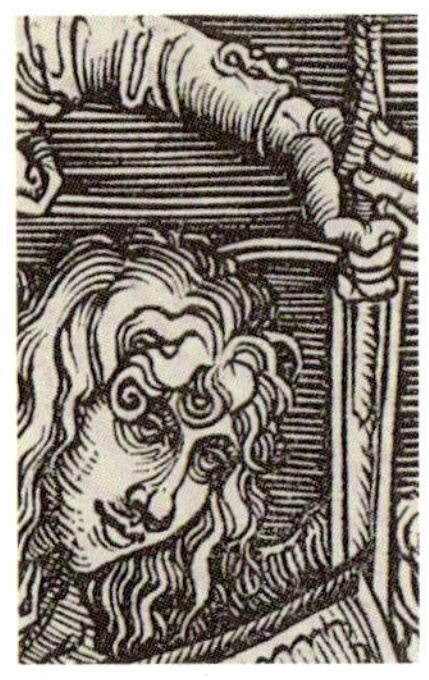

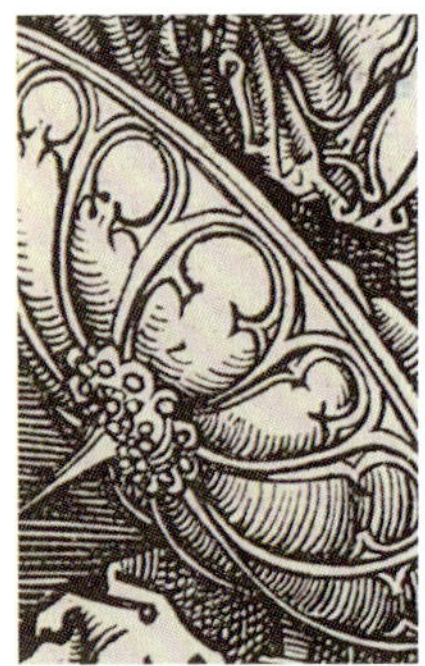

given to one of low degree. God sends it as a warning to us. Let us prepare to meet death." Three days later, she died. But the famous comet of Charles V, appearing in 1556, was perhaps the most memorable of all. It had been identified as the comet of 1264, and its return was announced for 1848. But it did not reappear.

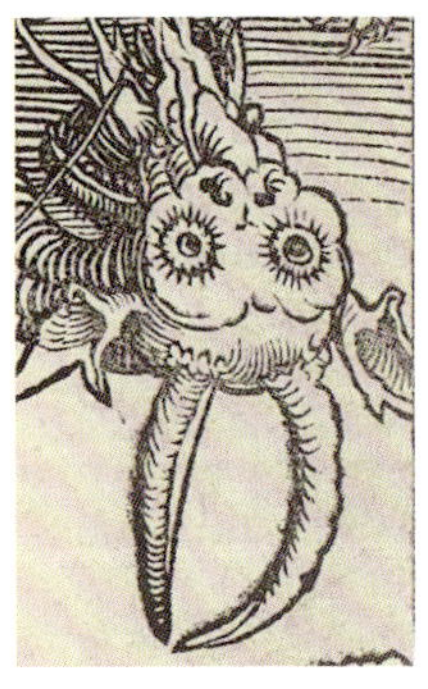

St Michael Fighting the Dragon

Albrecht Dürer, 1498
Woodcut, 39.5 x 28.6 cm
Library of Congress Prints and Photographs Division
Washington, D.C.

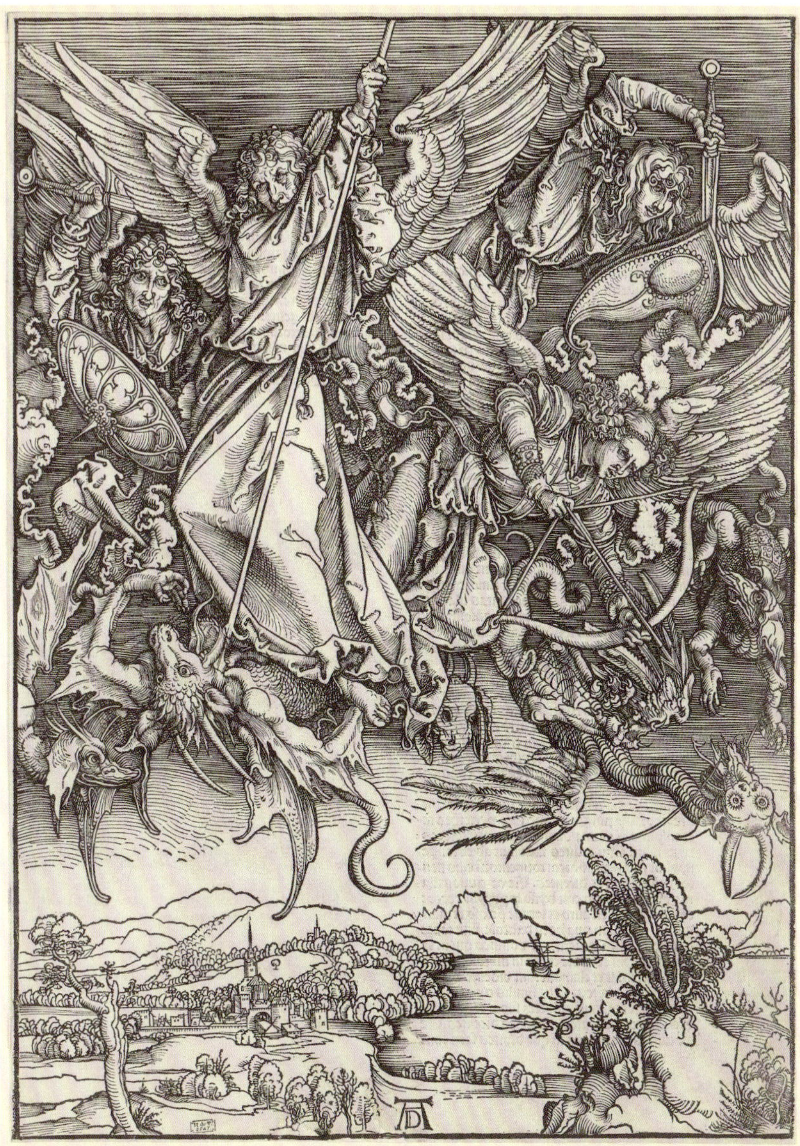

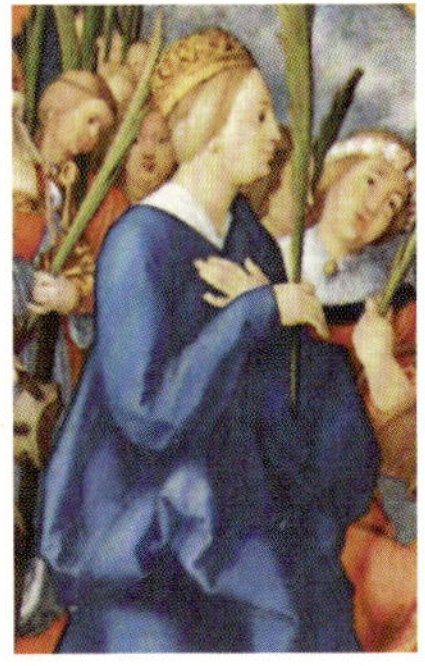

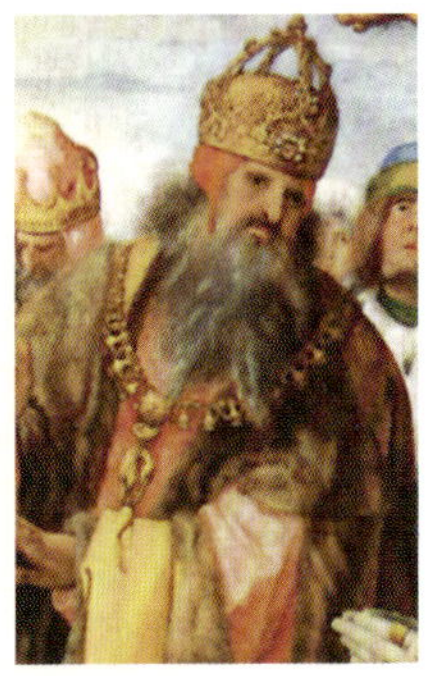

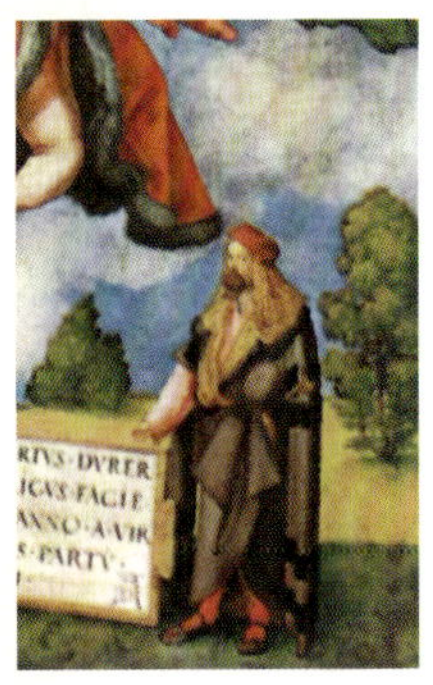

The comets of 1577, 1607, 1652, and 1665 were the subjects of endless commentaries, forming a library by themselves. At the last of these, King Alphonso VI of Portugal, angrily discharged his pistol with the most grotesque defiance. Pierre Petit, by order of Louis XIV, published a work designed to counteract the foolish

All Saints Day

Albrecht Dürer, 1511
Oil on panel, 135 x 123.4 cm
Kunsthistorisches Museum, Vienna

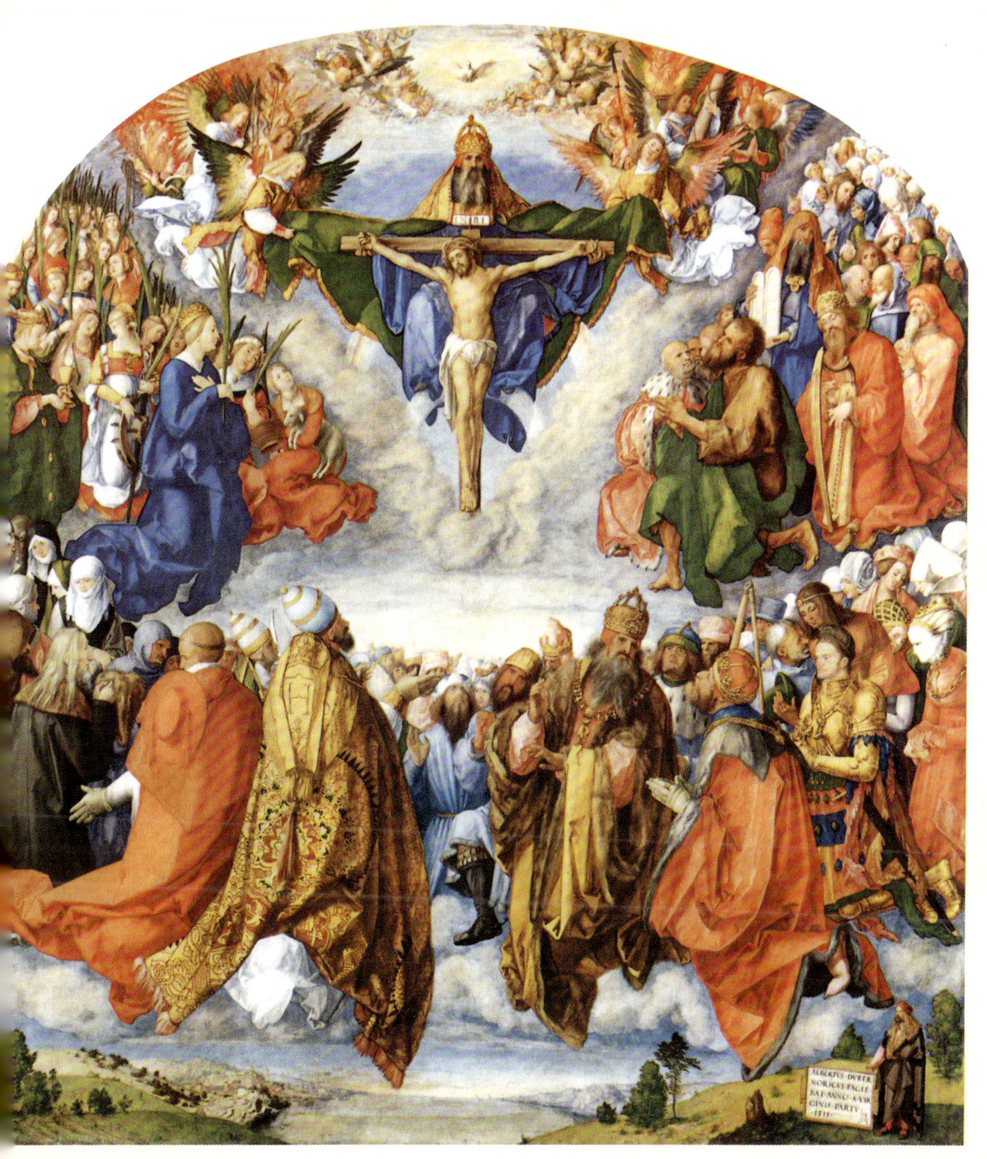

ALBERTVS · DVRER
NORICVS · FACIE
BAT · ANNO · A · VIR
GINIS · PARTV
1511

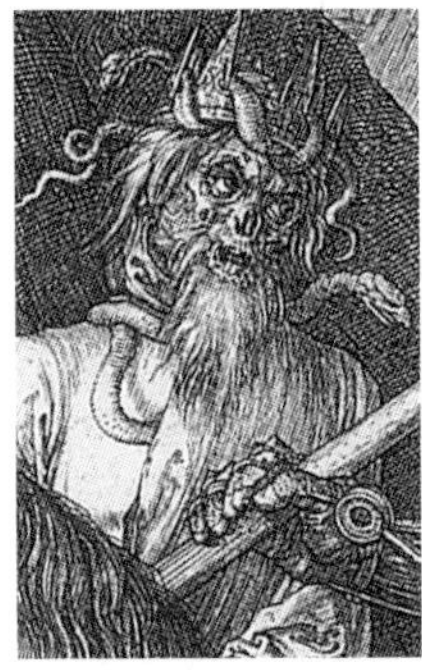

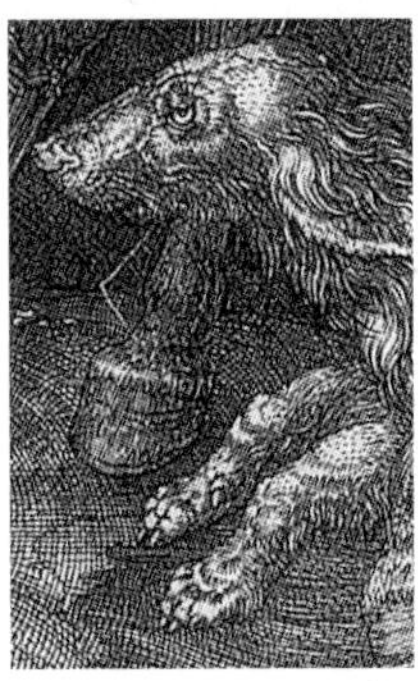

and political apprehensions excited by comets. This illustrious king desired to be without a rival, only the sun, *nec pluribus impar!*, and would not admit the supposition that the glory of France could be imperilled even by a celestial phenomenon.

One of the greatest comets which ever struck the imagination of men was assuredly the famous

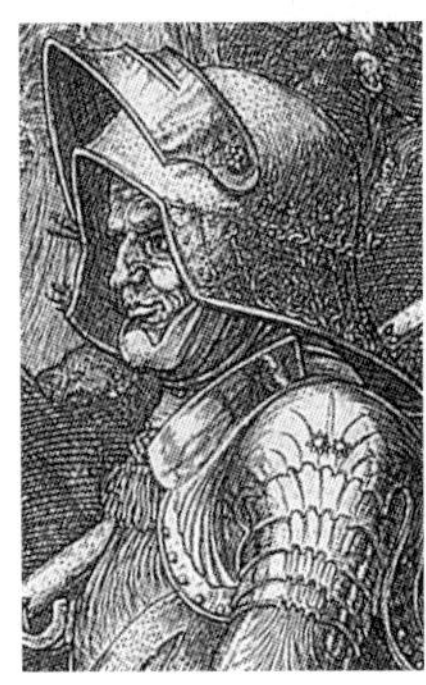

The Knight, Death, and the Devil

Albrecht Dürer, 1513
Engraving, 25 x 19.6 cm
The Metropolitan Museum of Art, New York

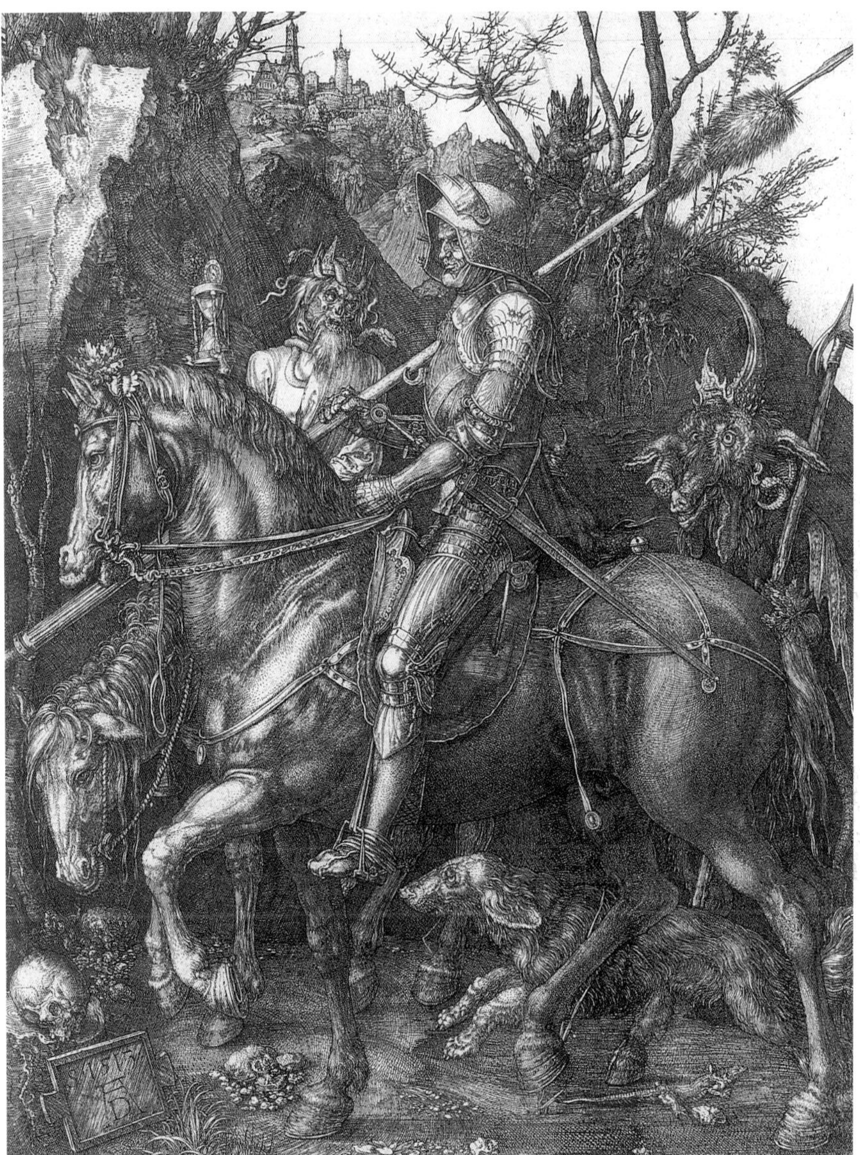

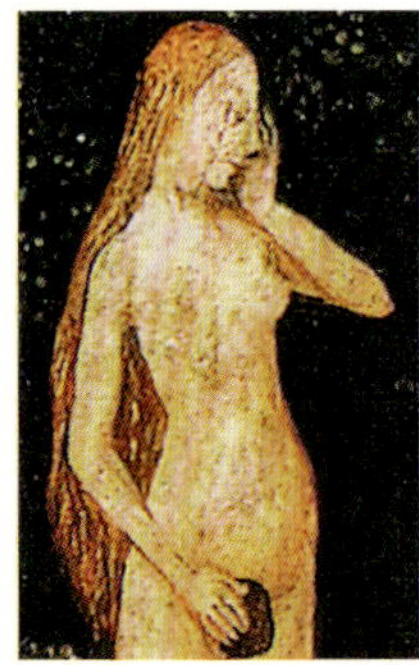

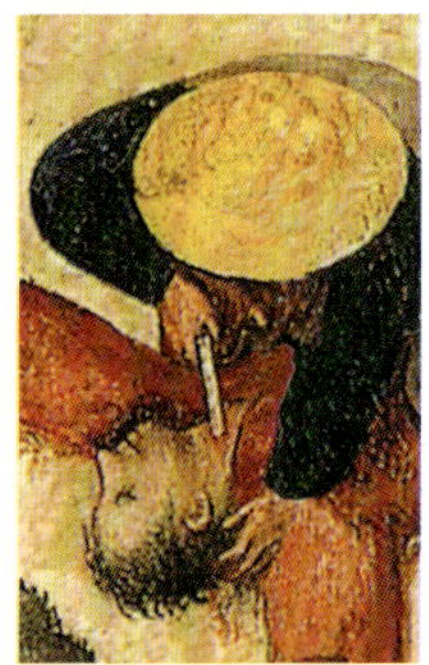

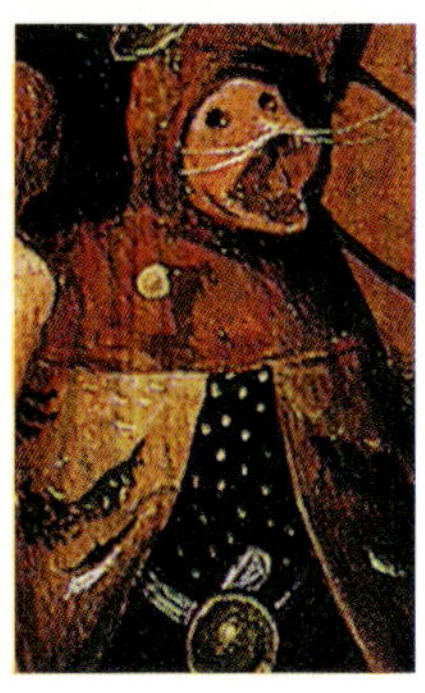

comet of 1680, to which Newton devoted so much attention. Lemonier attests:

> It issued with a frightful velocity from the depths of space and seemed falling directly into the sun and was seen to vanish with an equal velocity. It was visible for four months. It approached quite near to the earth, and Whiston ascribed the flood to its former appearance.

Hieronymus Bosch, 1515
Oil on panel, 140 x 232 cm
Museo Nacional del Prado, Madrid

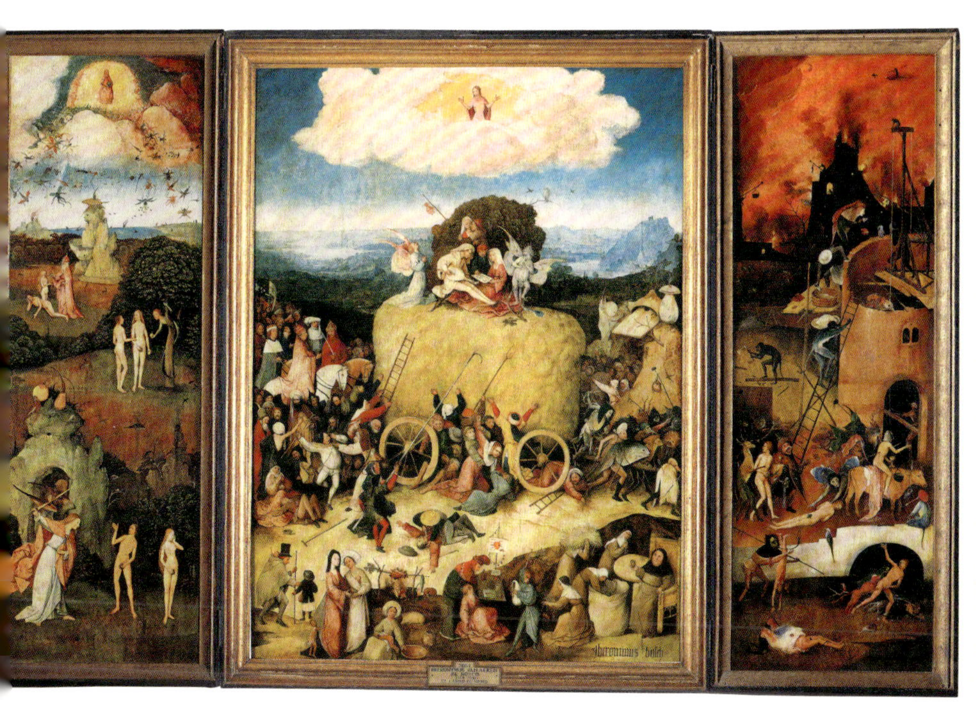

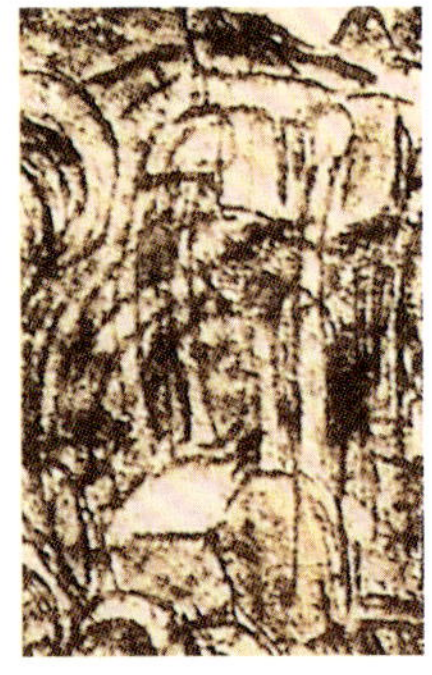

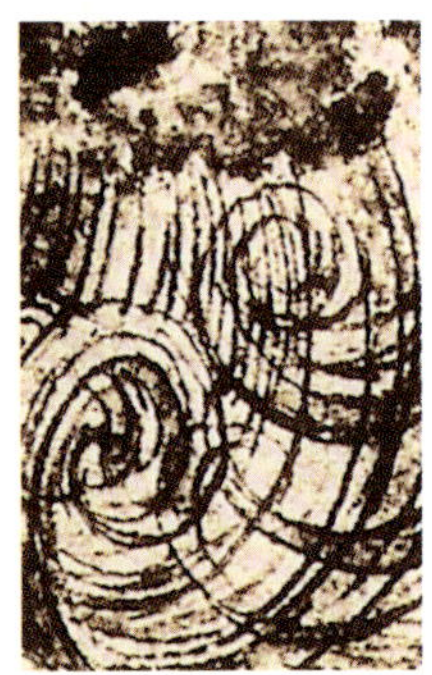

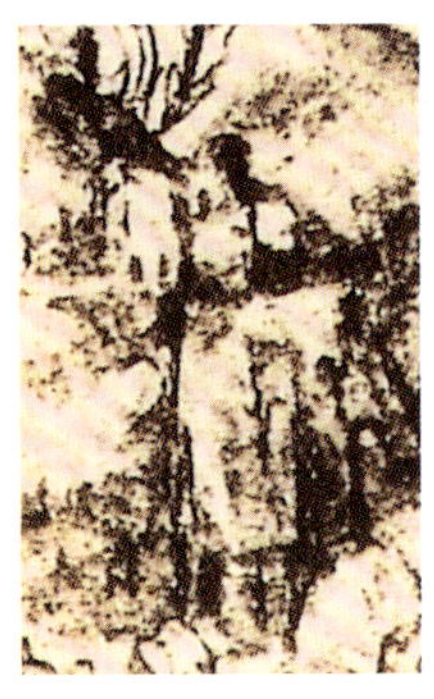

Bayle wrote a treatise to prove the absurdity of beliefs founded on these portents. Madame de Sévigné writing to her cousin, Count de Bussy-Rabutin, says:

We have a comet of enormous size; its tail is the most beautiful object conceivable. Every person of note is alarmed and believes that heaven, interested in their fate,

A Deluge

Leonardo da Vinci, 1517-1518
Black chalk, 16.2 x 20.3 cm
Royal Library, Windsor Castle

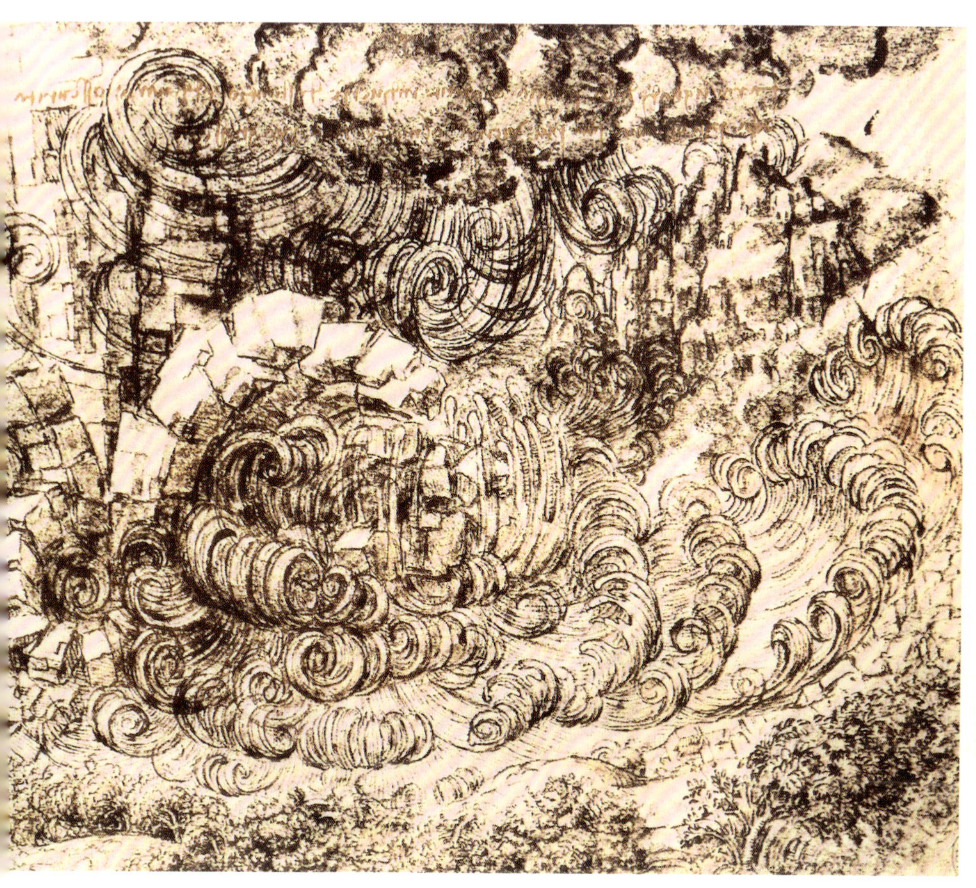

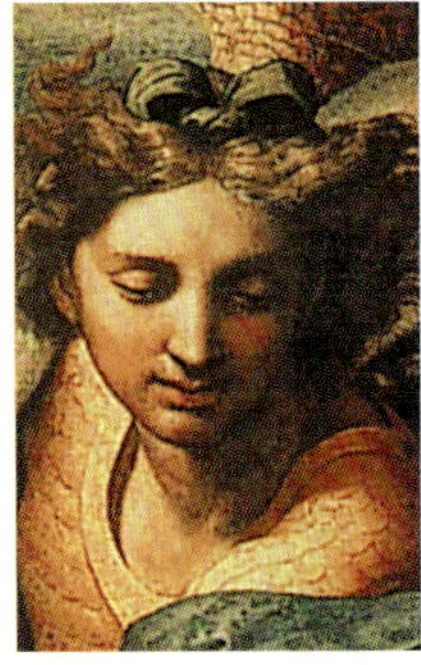

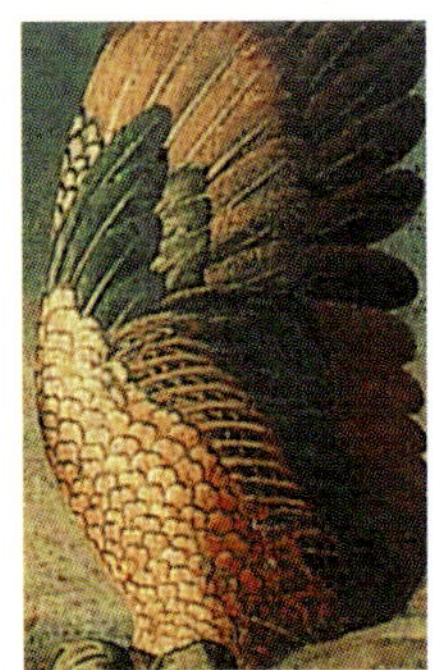

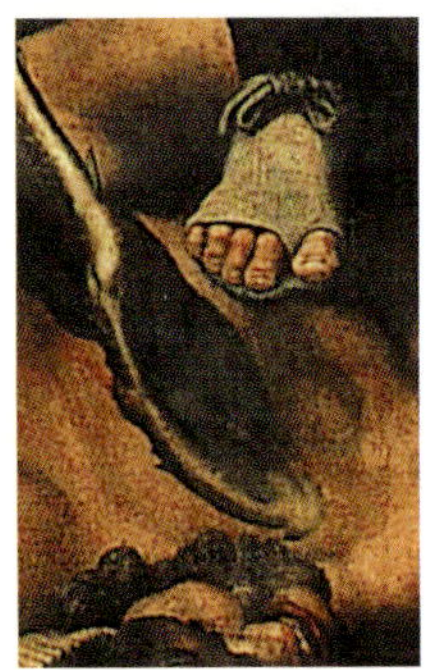

sends them a warning in this comet. They say that the courtiers of Cardinal Mazarin, who is despaired of by his physicians believe this prodigy is in honour of his passing away, and tell him of the terror with which it has inspired them. He had the sense to laugh at them, and to reply facetiously that the comet did him too much

St Michael Slaying the Devil

Raffaelo Sanzio (Raphael), c. 1518
Oil on wood transferred onto canvas, 268 x 160 cm
Musée du Louvre, Paris

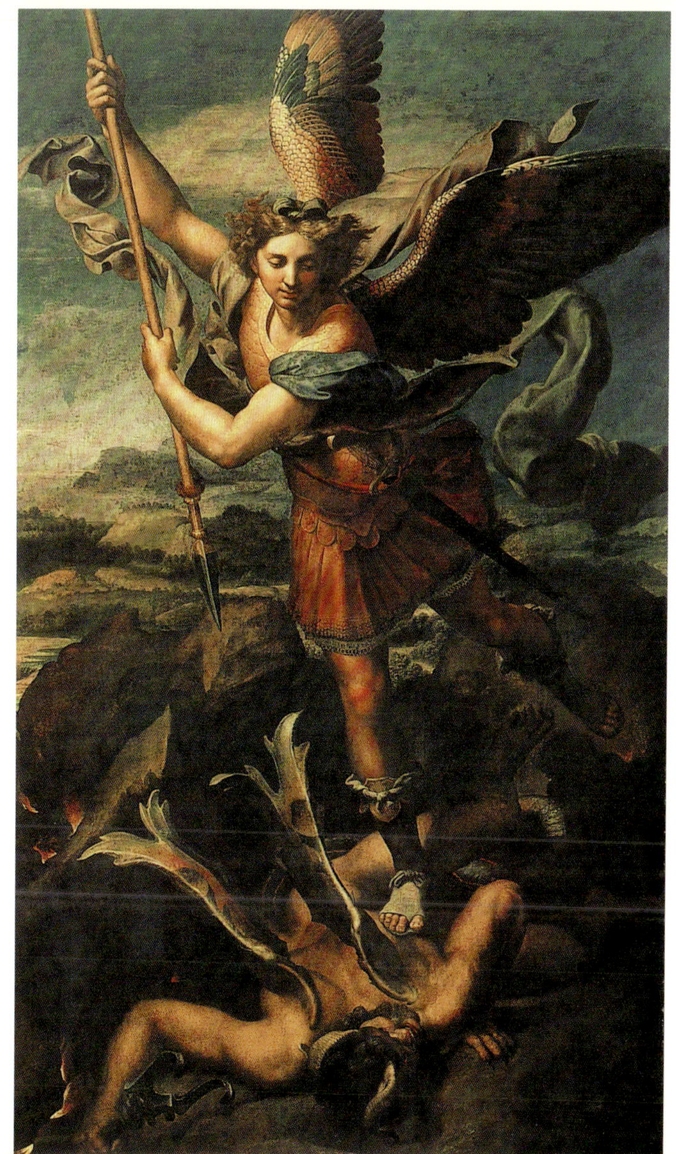

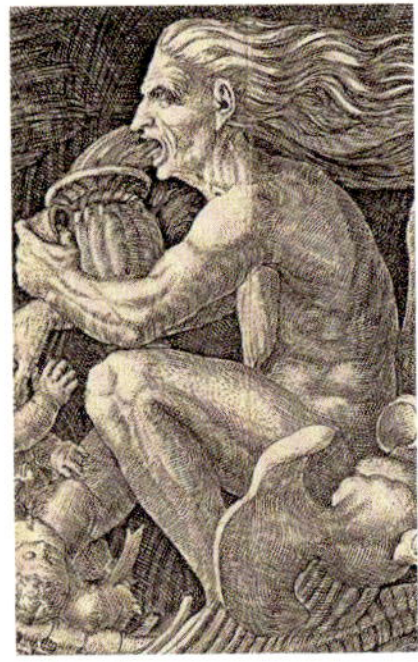

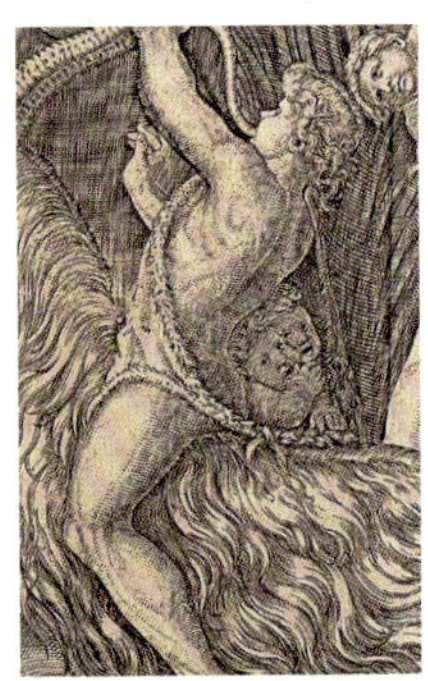

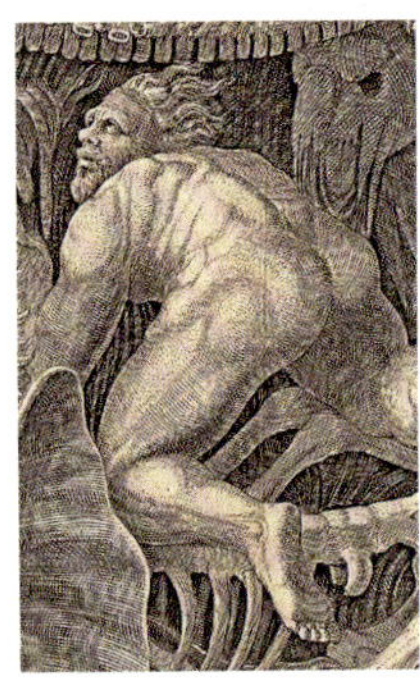

honour. In truth we ought all to agree with him, for human pride assumes too much when it believes that death is attended by such signs from heaven.

We see that comets were gradually losing their prestige. Yet we read in a treatise of the astronomer Bemouilli this singular remark: "If the head of the comet be not a visible sign of the anger of God, the tail may well be."

The Witches' Procession (Lo Stregozzo)

Marcantonio Raimondi, Agostino Veneziano
after 1520
Copper engraving on ivory-coloured paper
31.4 x 65.2 cm
Staatsgalerie, Stuttgart

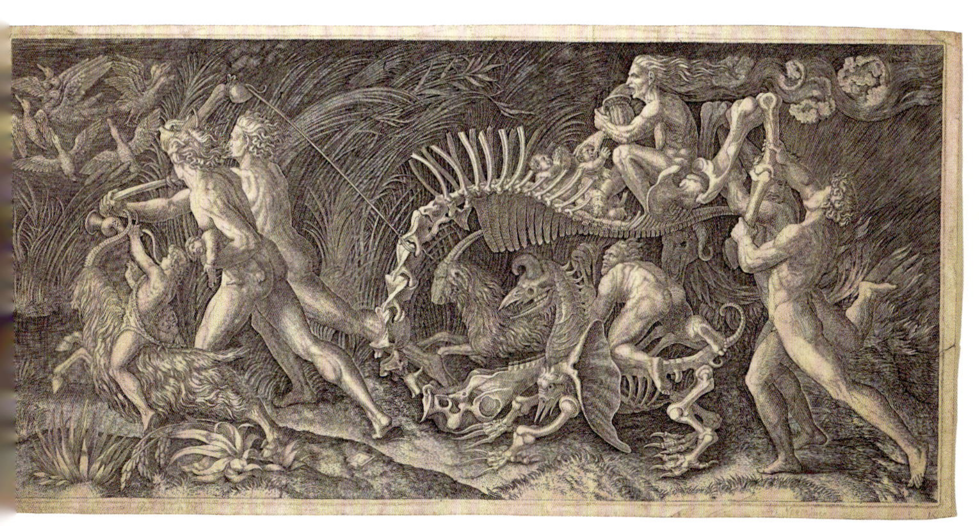

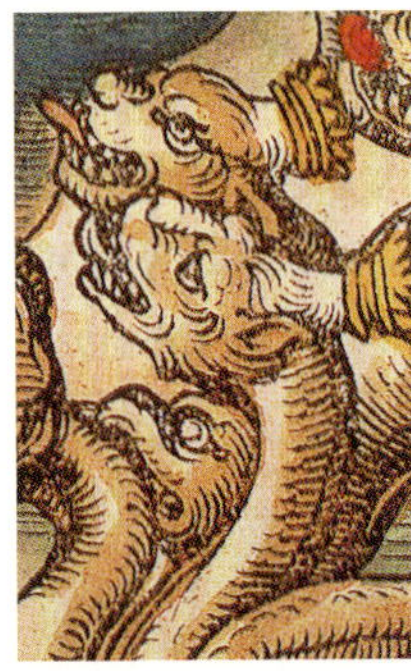

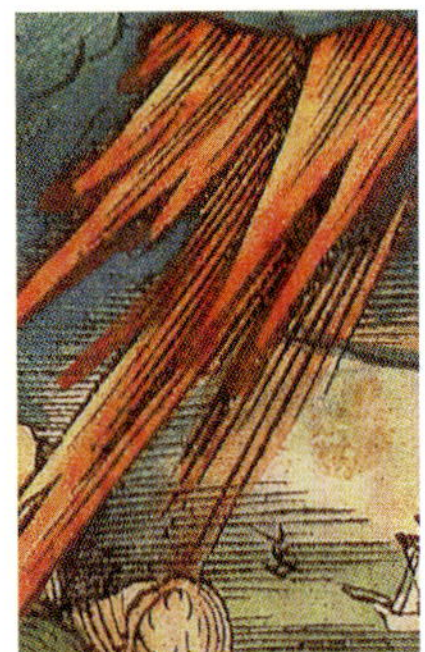

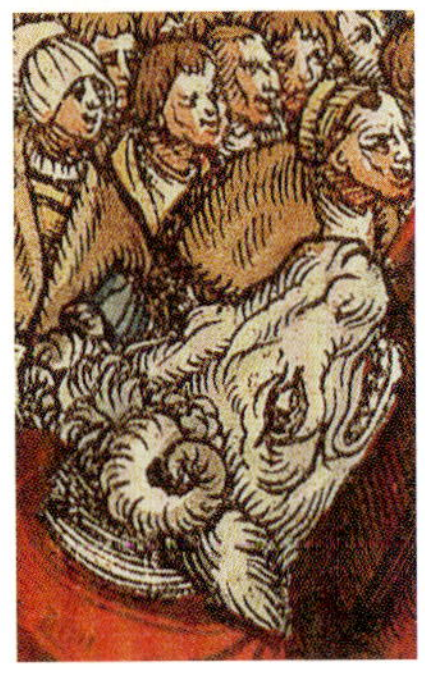

Fear of the end of the world was reawakened by the appearance of comets in 1773; a great panic spread throughout Europe, and Paris itself was alarmed. Here is an extract from the memoirs of Bachaumont, accessible to every reader:

6 May 1773. In the last public meeting of the Academy of Sciences, M. de Lalande

From the 16th century Luther Bible, c. 1530
Coloured woodcut
Bible Society, London

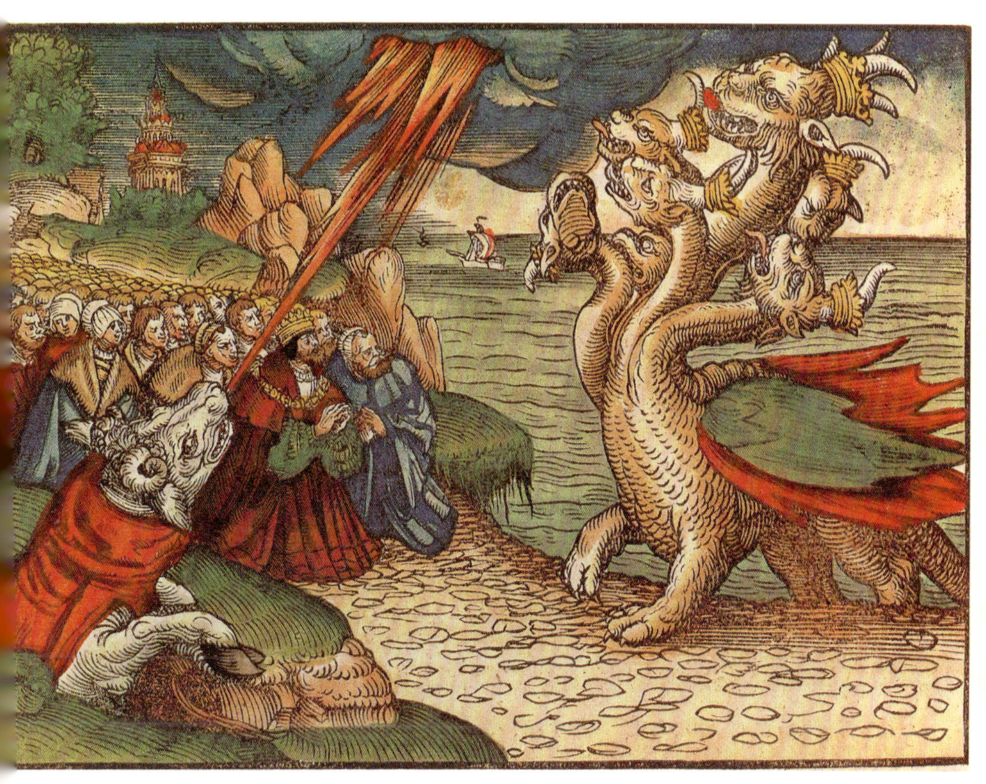

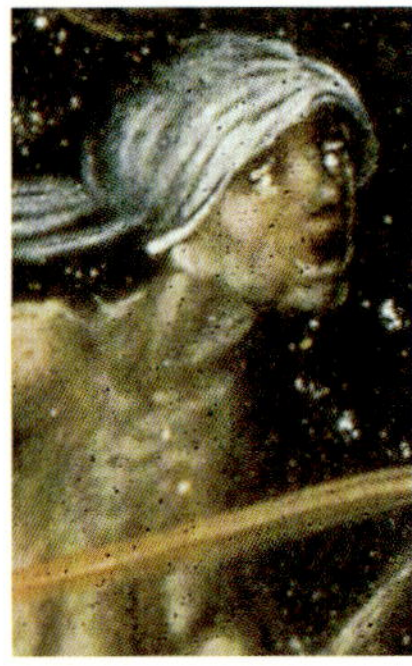

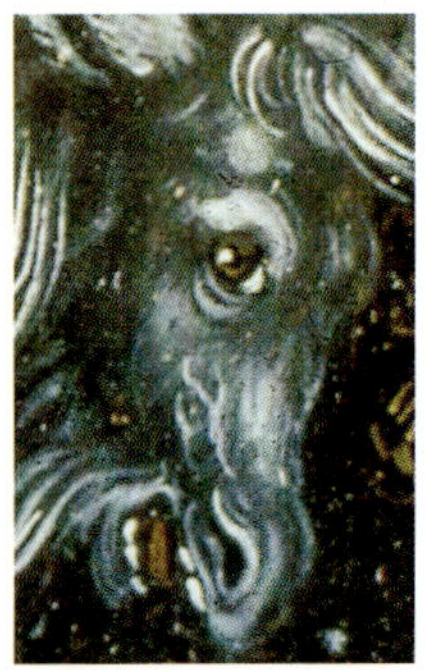

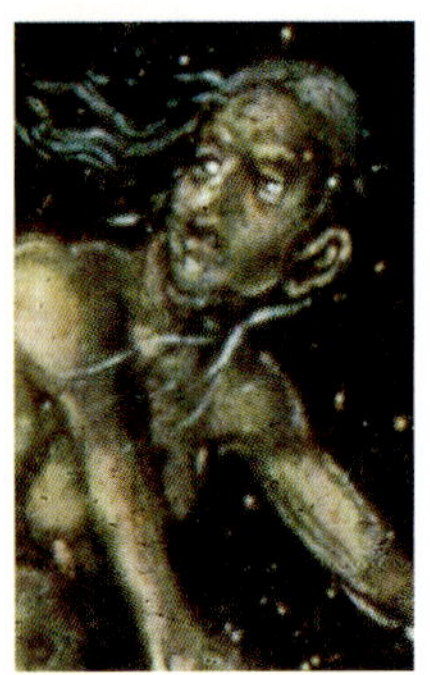

was to read by far the most interesting paper of all; this, however, he was not able to do, for lack of time. It concerned the comets which, by approaching the earth, may cause revolutions, and dealt especially with that one whose return is expected in eighteen years. But although

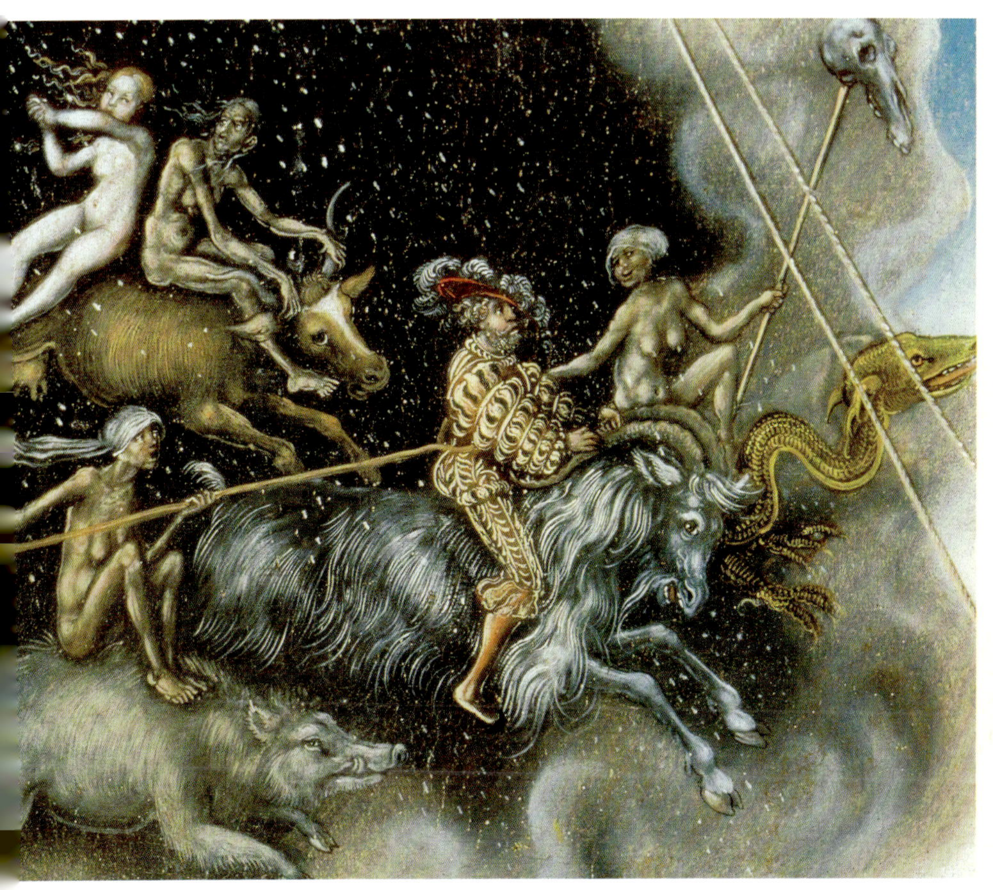

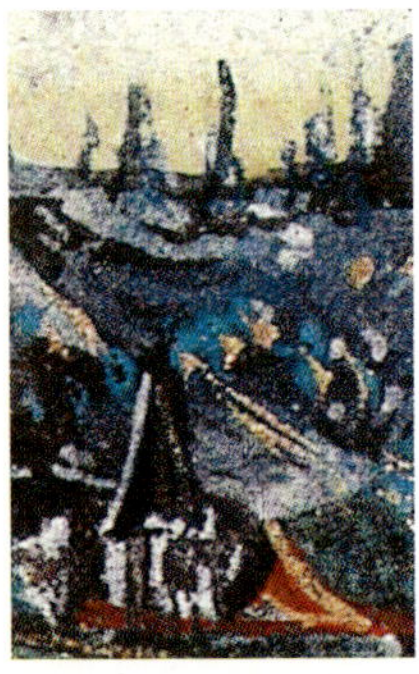

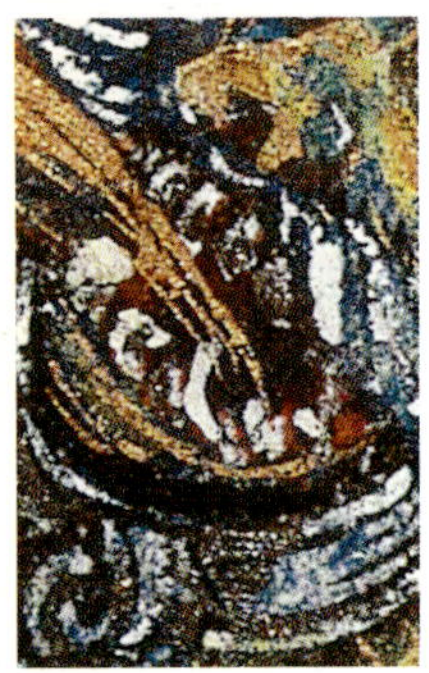

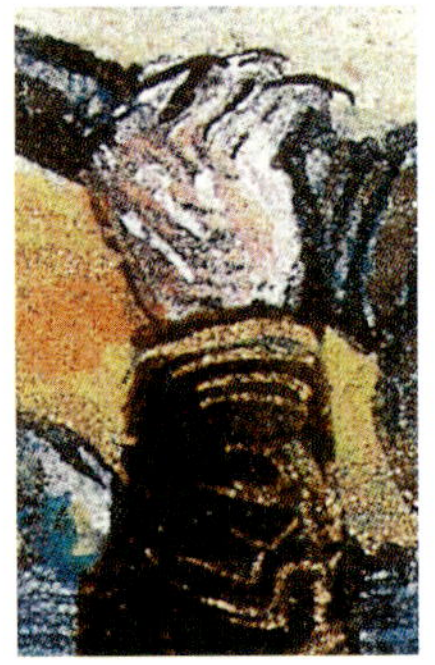

he affirmed that it was not one of those which would harm the earth, and that, moreover, he had observed that one could not fix, with any exactness, the order of such occurrences, there exists, nevertheless, a very general anxiety.

9 May. The cabinet of M. de Lalande is filled with the curious who come to

The Key of the Abyss, from Luther's Bible

Workshop of Lucas Cranach the Elder, c. 1534
Coloured woodcut
Stadtarchiv, Zerbst

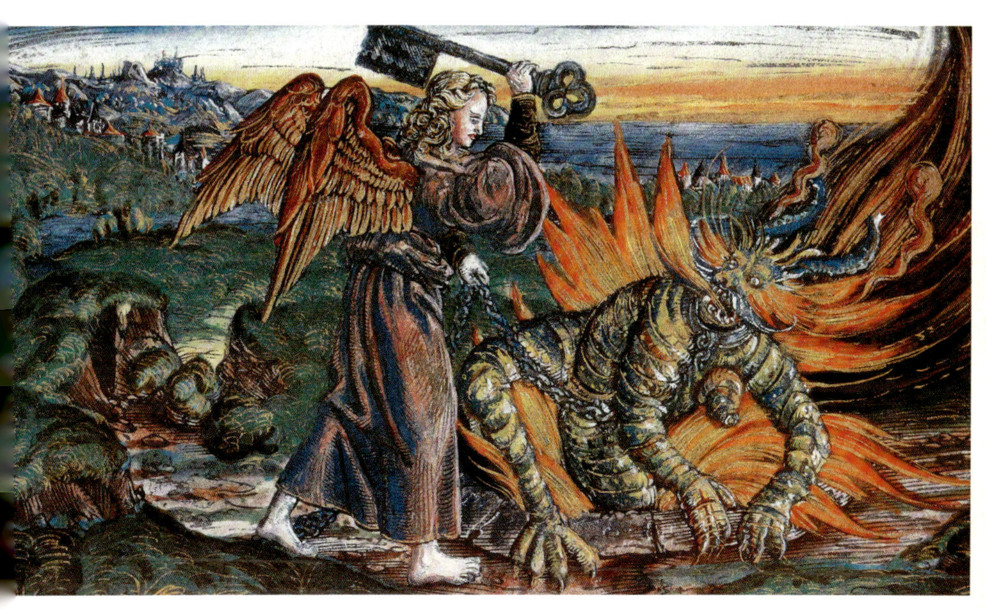

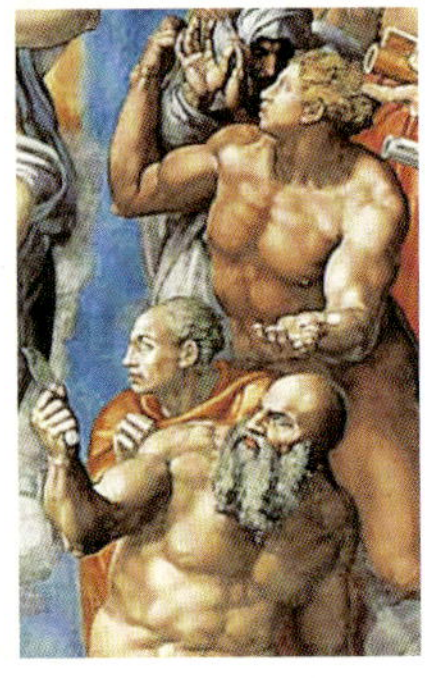

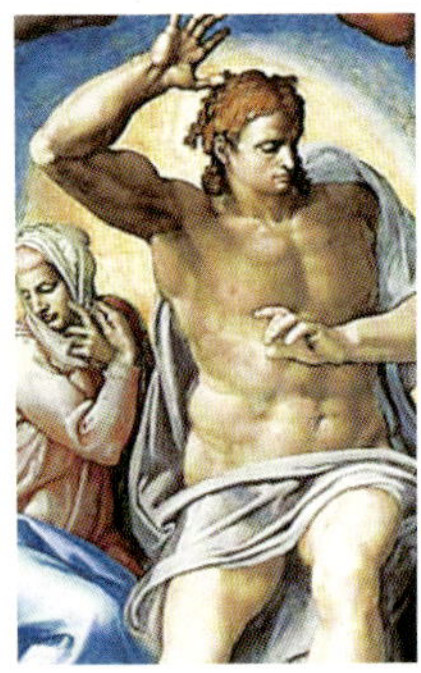

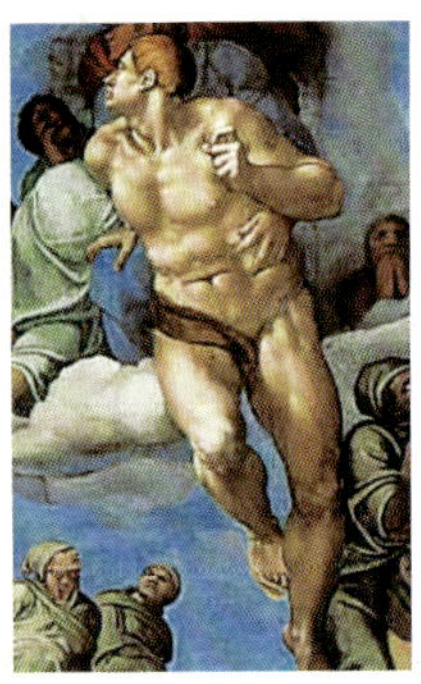

question him concerning the above memoir, and, in order to reassure those who have been alarmed by the exaggerated rumours circulated about it, he will undoubtedly be forced to make it public. The excitement has been so great that some ignorant fanatics have besought

The Last Judgement (full view)

Michelangelo, 1536-1541
Fresco after restoration, 1.37 x 1.22 m
Sistine Chapel, Vatican City

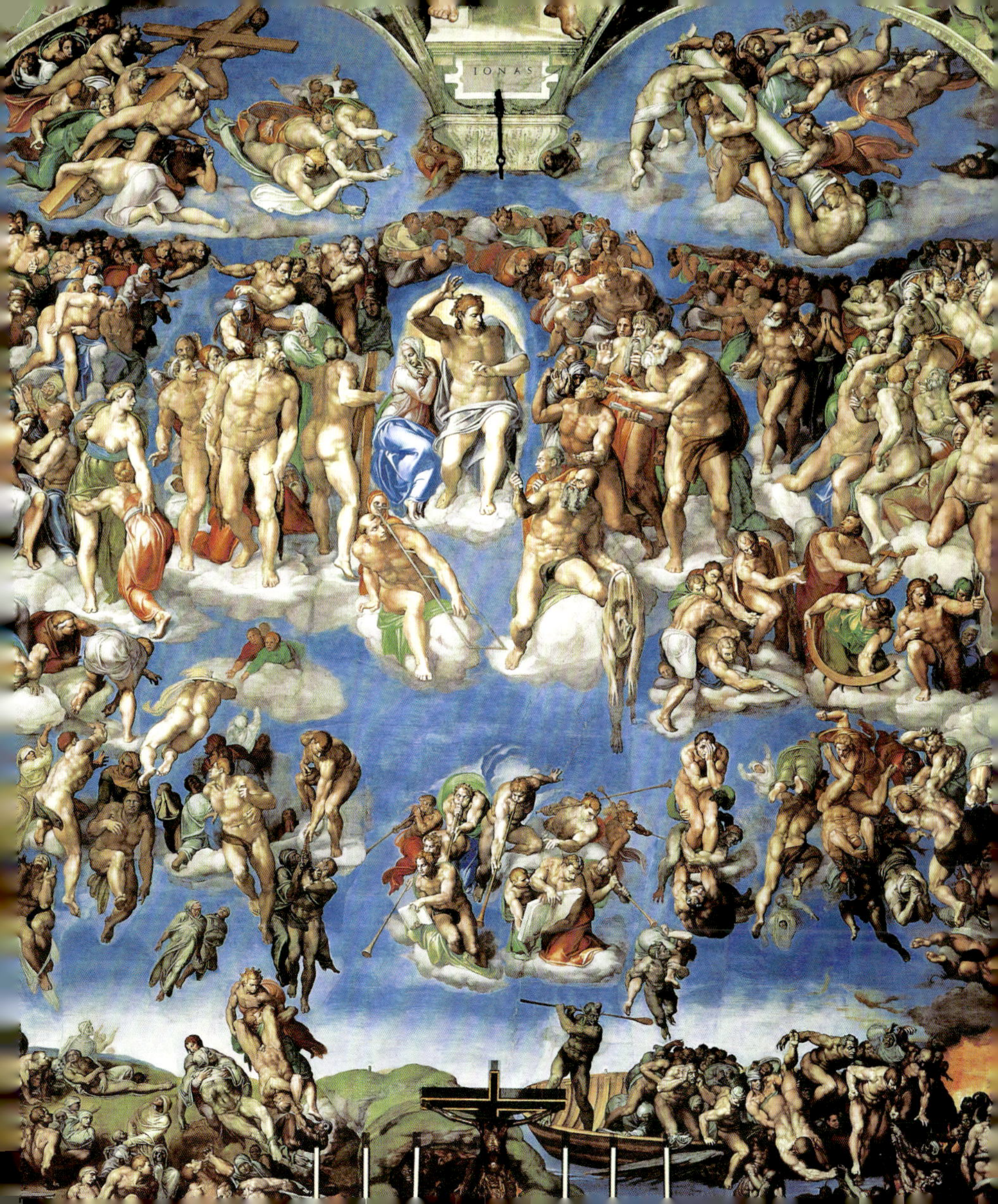

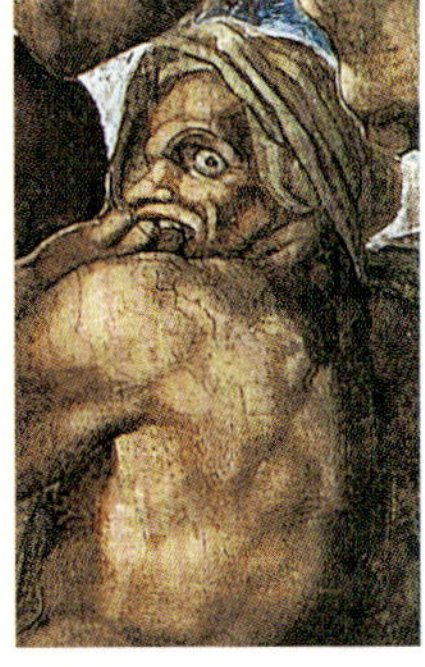

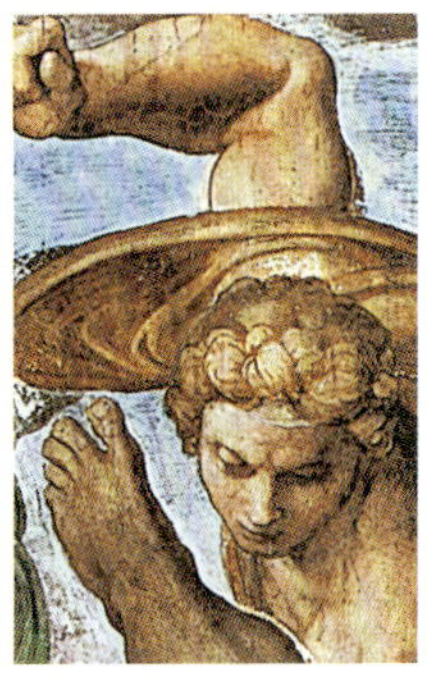

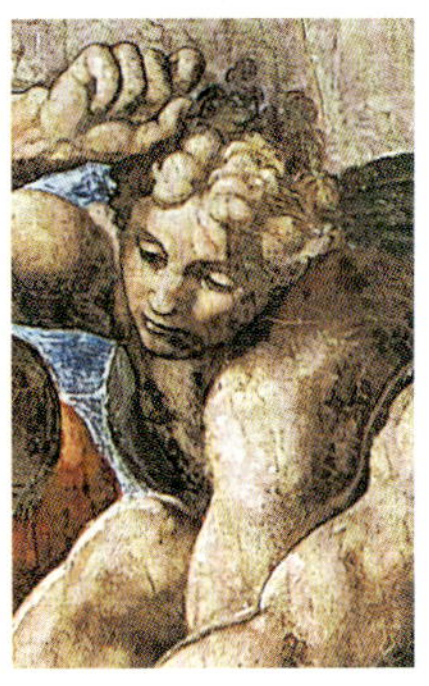

the archbishop to institute prayers for forty hours, in order to avert the deluge which menaces us; and this prelate would have authorised these prayers, had not the Academy shown him the ridicule which such a step would produce.

14 May. The memoir of M. de Lalande has appeared. He says that it is

Michelangelo, 1534-1541
Fresco after restoration, 13.7 x 12.2 m
Sistine Chapel, Vatican City

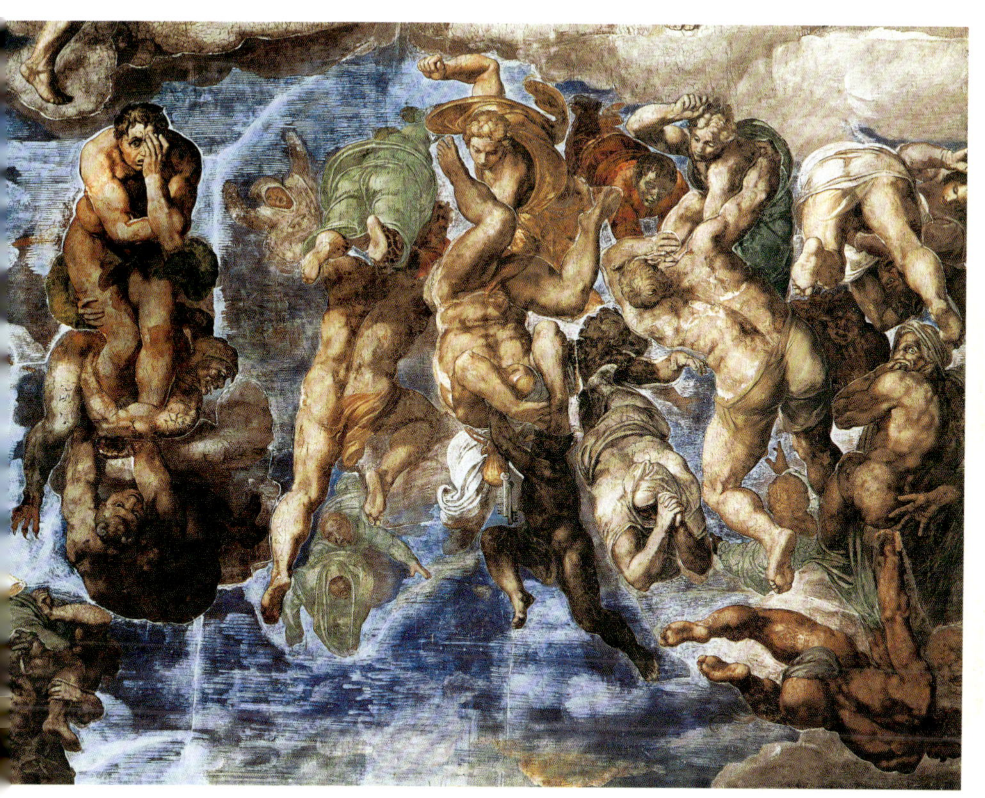

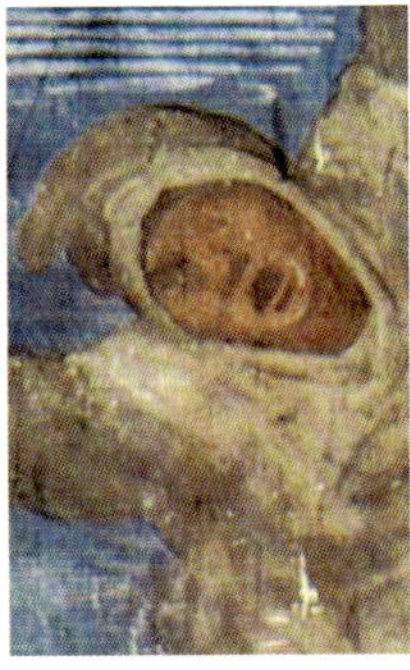

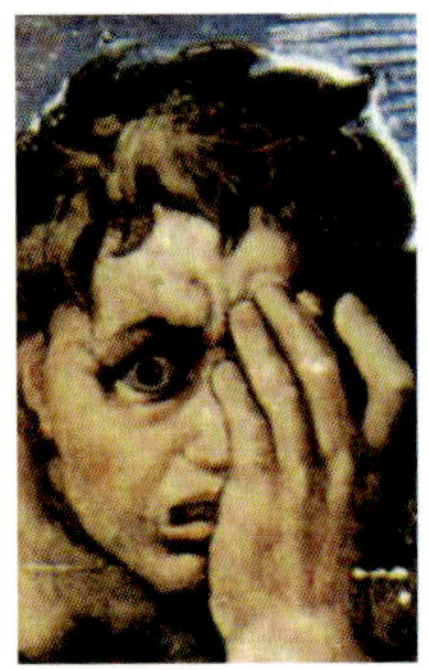

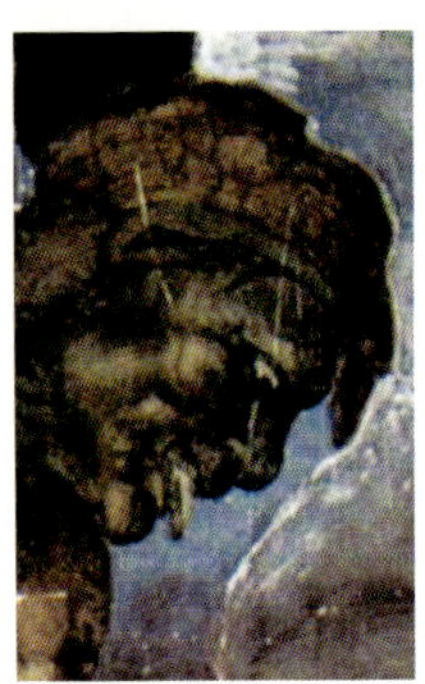

his opinion that, of the sixty known comets, eight, by their near approach to the earth, might produce a pressure such that the sea would leave its bed and cover a part of the world.

In time, the excitement died away. The fear of comets assumed a new form. They were no longer

The Last Judgement (detail)
Damned with Figures of the Underworld

Michelangelo, 1534-1541
Fresco after restoration, 13.7 x 12.2 m
Sistine Chapel, Vatican City

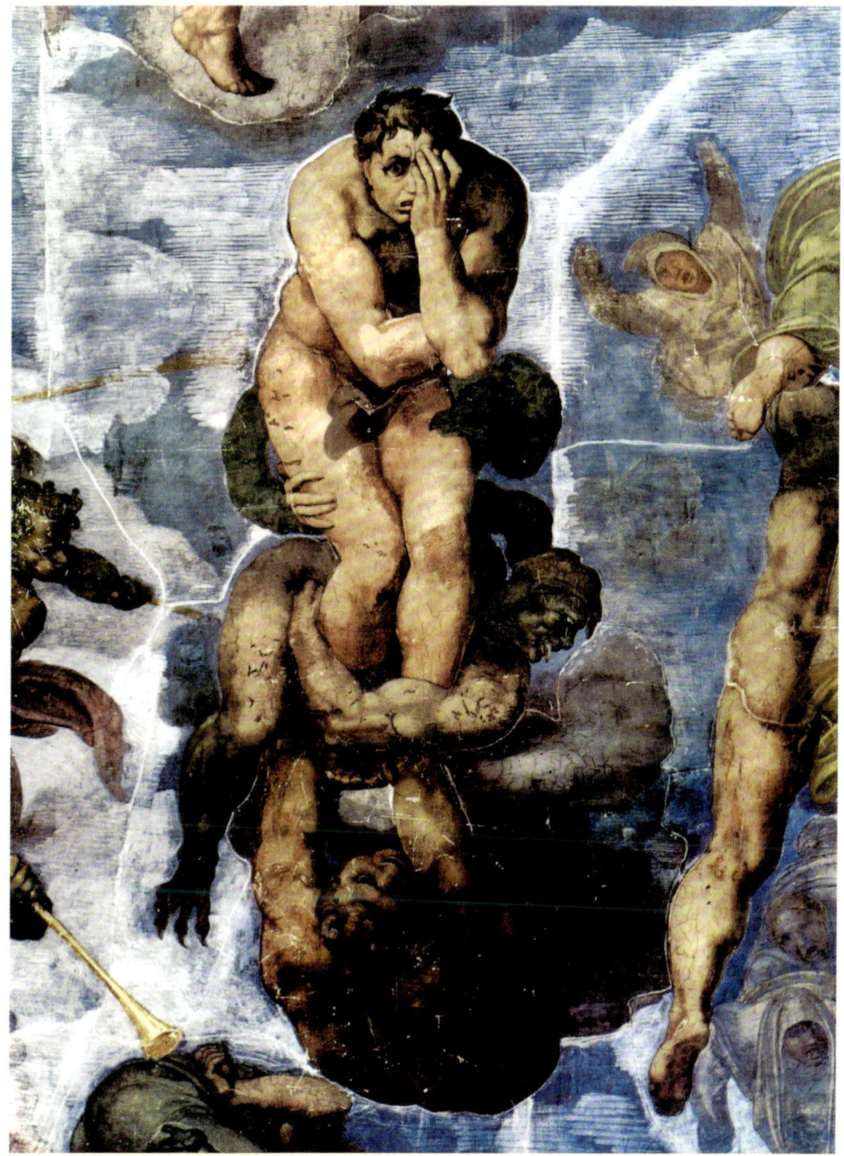

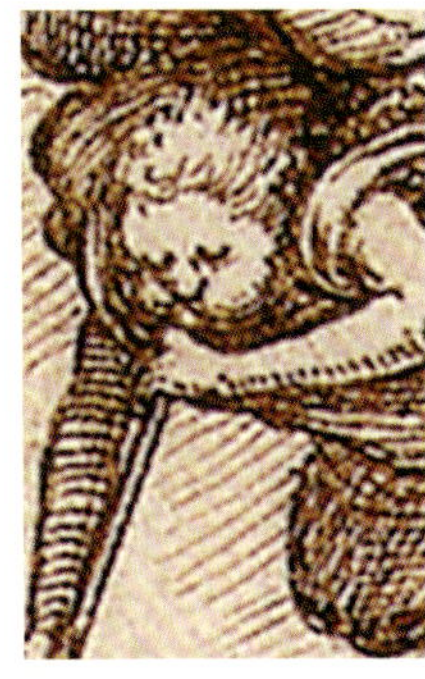

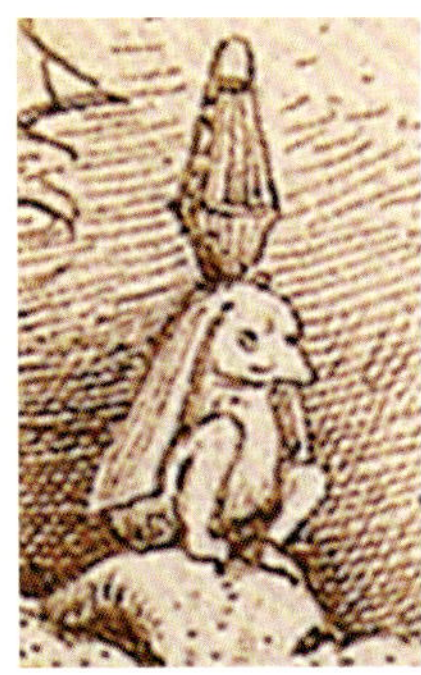

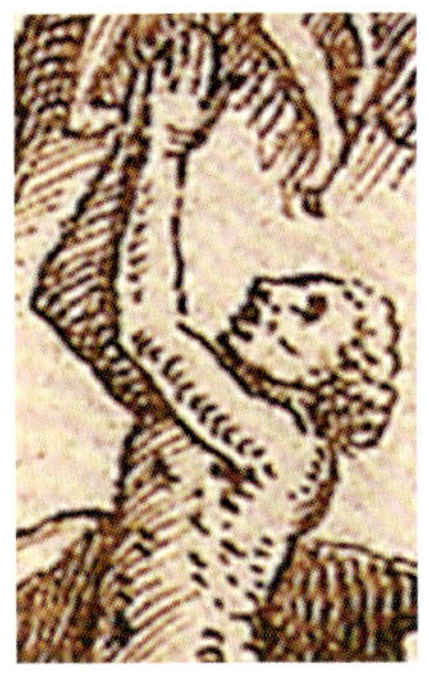

regarded as indications of the anger of God, but their collision with the earth was discussed from a scientific point of view, and these collisions were not considered free of danger.

In the 19th century, predictions concerning the end of the world were associated with the appearance of comets several times over. It was announced that the comet of Biela, for example,

Pieter Bruegel the Elder, 1558
Pen and brown ink, 23 x 30 cm
Graphische Sammlung, Albertina, Vienna

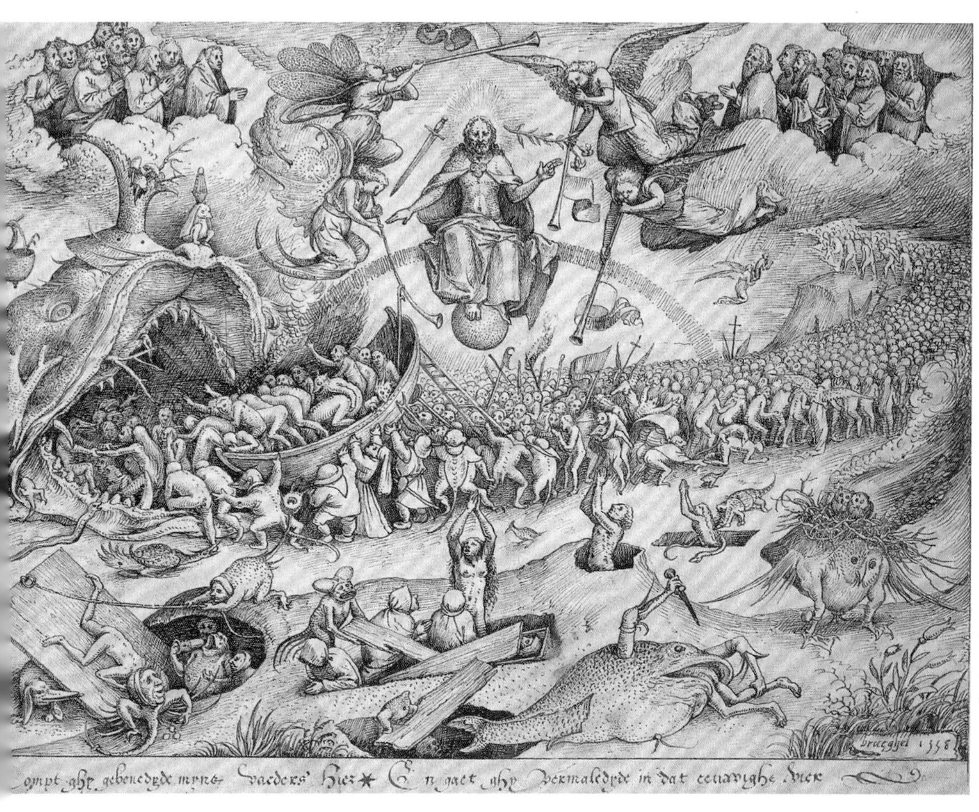

brueghel · 1558
ompt ghy gebenedyde myns vaeders Hier ✳ En gaet ghy vermaledyde in dat eeuwyghe vier

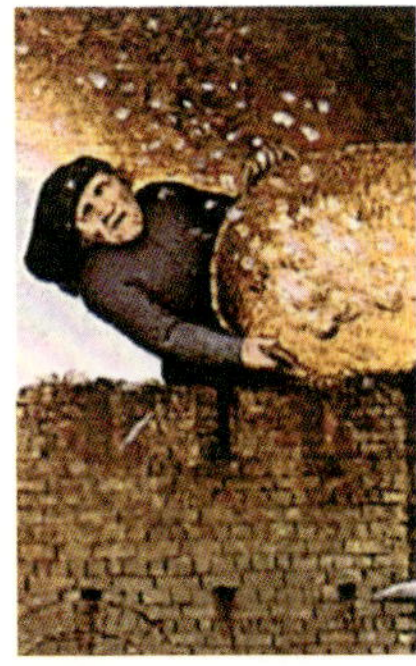

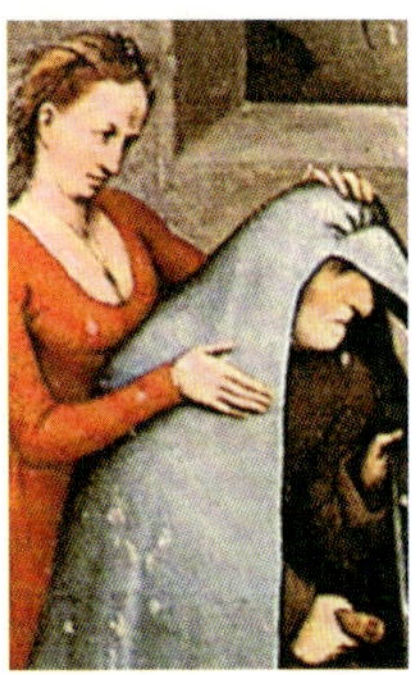

would intersect the earth's orbit on 29 October 1832, which it did, as predicted. There was great excitement. Once more the end of things was declared at hand. Humanity was threatened. What was going to happen?

The orbit, that is to say the path, of the earth was confused with the earth itself. The latter was

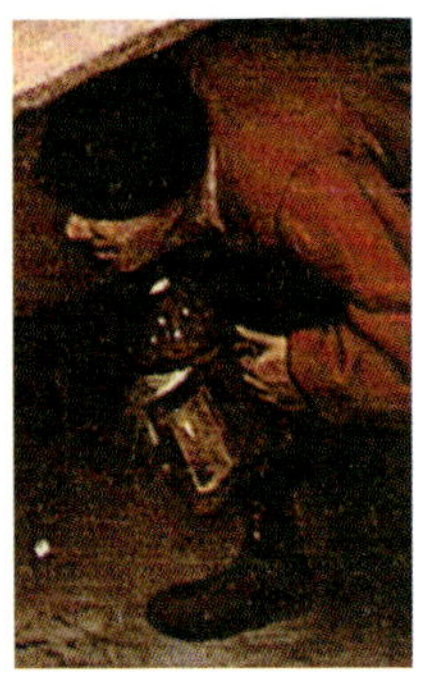

Netherlandish Proverbs

Pieter Bruegel the Elder, 1559
Oil on oak, 117 x 163.5 cm
Staatliche Museen, Gemäldegalerie, Berlin

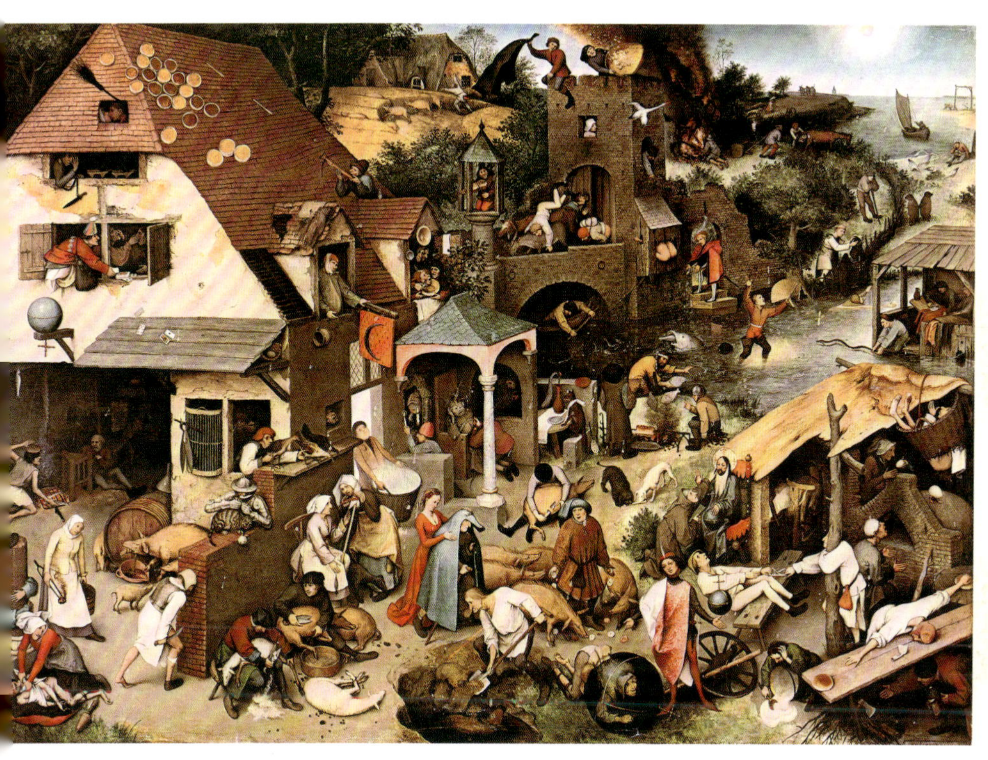

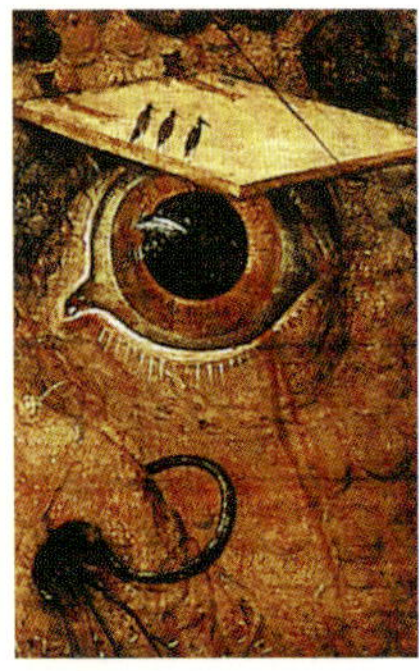

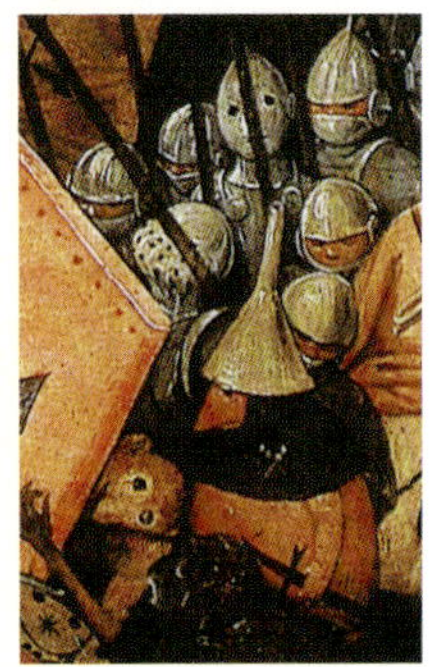

not to reach that point of its orbit traversed by the comet until 30 November, more than a month after the comet's passage, and the comet was at no time to be within 20,000,000 leagues of us. Once more we got off with a fright.

It was the same in 1857. Some prophet of doom had declared that the famous comet of

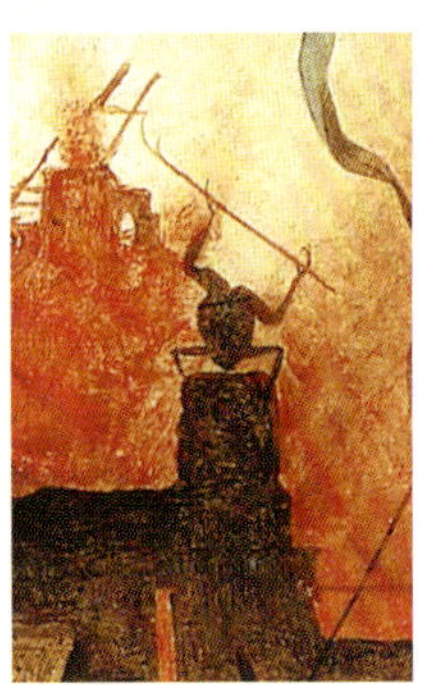

Dulle Griet or Mad Meg

Pieter Bruegel the Elder, 1561
Oil on wood, 117.4 x 162 cm
Museum Mayer van den Bergh, Antwerp

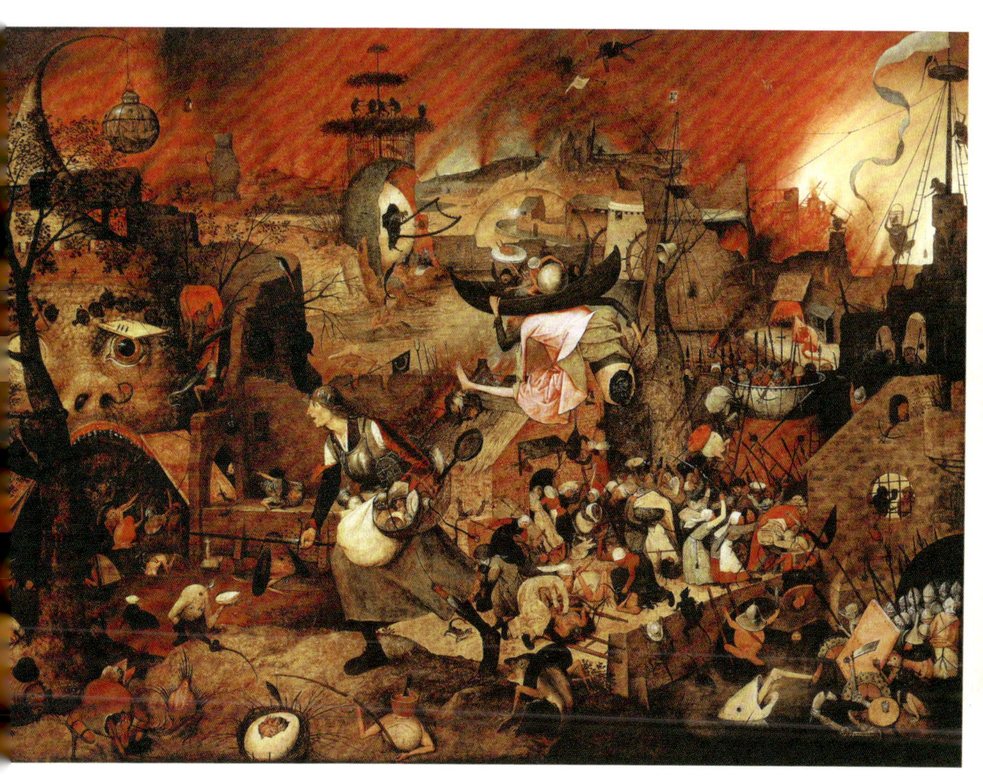

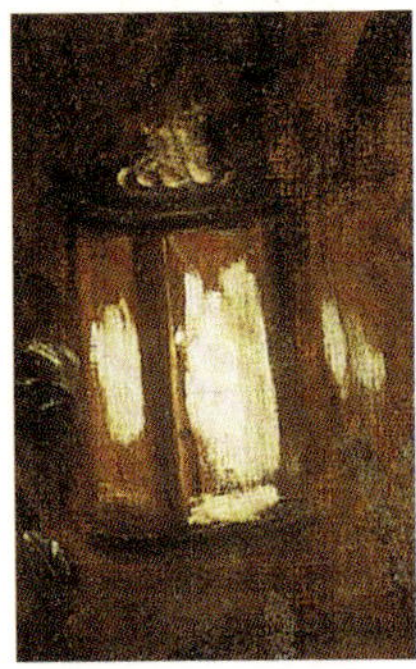

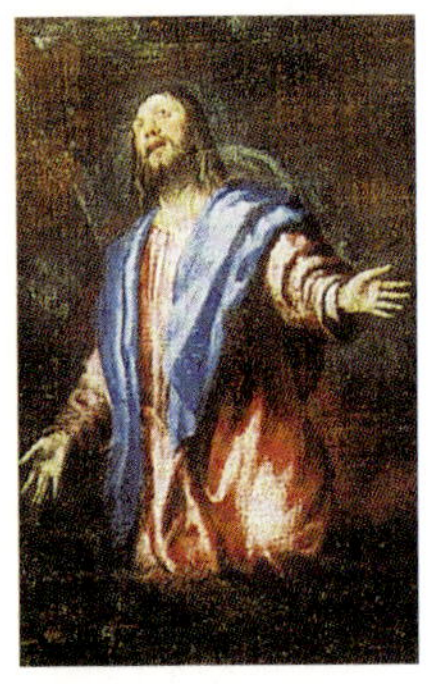

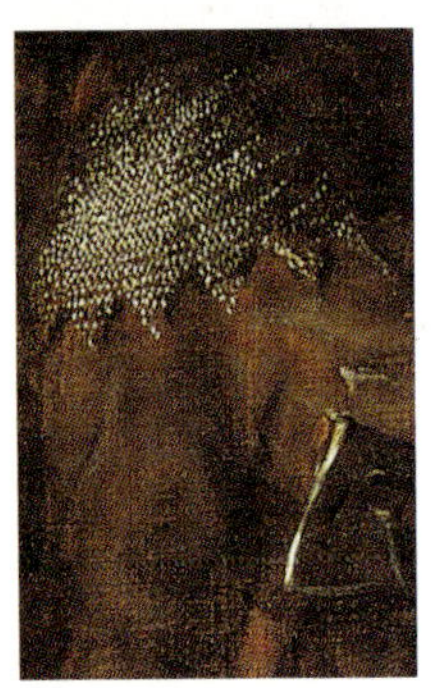

Charles V, whose periodic time was thought to be three centuries, would return on 13 June of that year. More than one timid soul was rendered anxious, and the confessionals of Paris were more than usually crowded with penitents. Another prediction was made public in 1872, in the name of an astronomer,

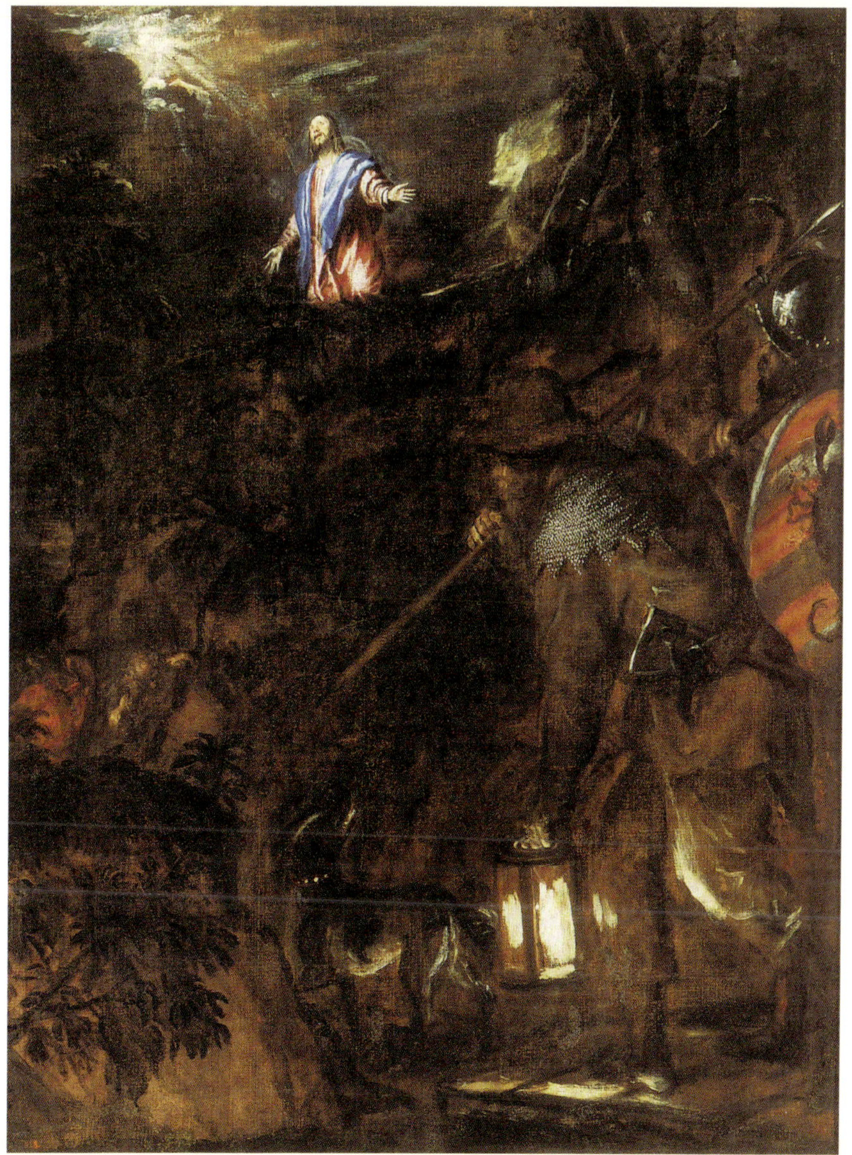

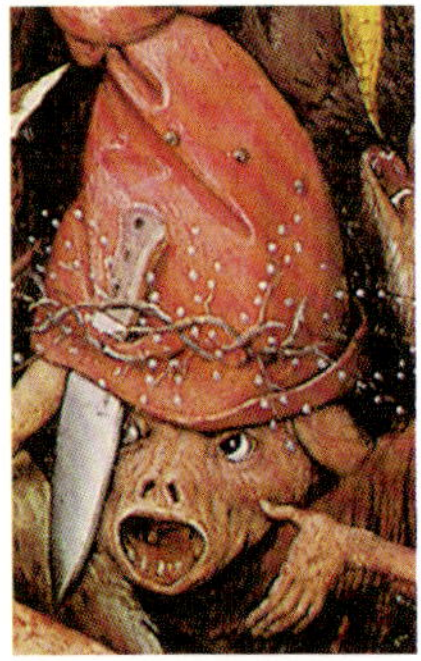

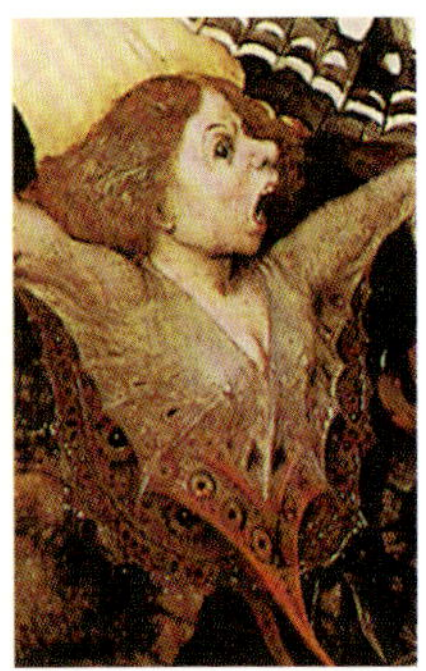

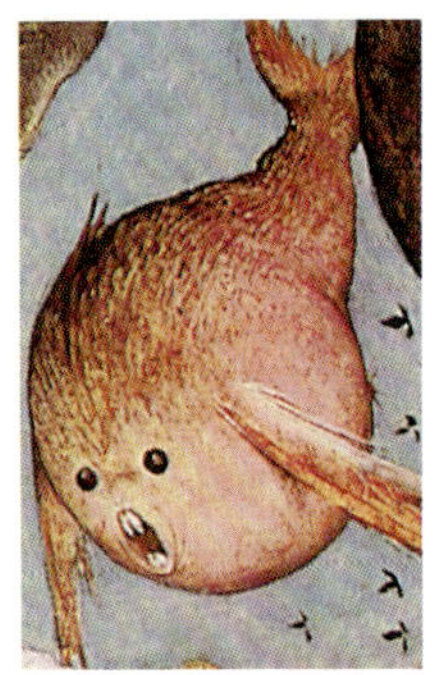

M. Plantamour, director of the Geneva observator, who was not, however, responsible for it.

As in the case of comets, so with other unusual phenomena, such as total solar eclipses, mysterious suns appearing suddenly in the skies, showers of shooting stars, great volcanic eruptions accompanied with the darkness of night and

The Fall of the Rebel Angels

Pieter Bruegel the Elder, 1562
Oil on wood, 118.5 x 162.5 cm
Koninklijke Musea voor Schone Kunsten van België
Brussels

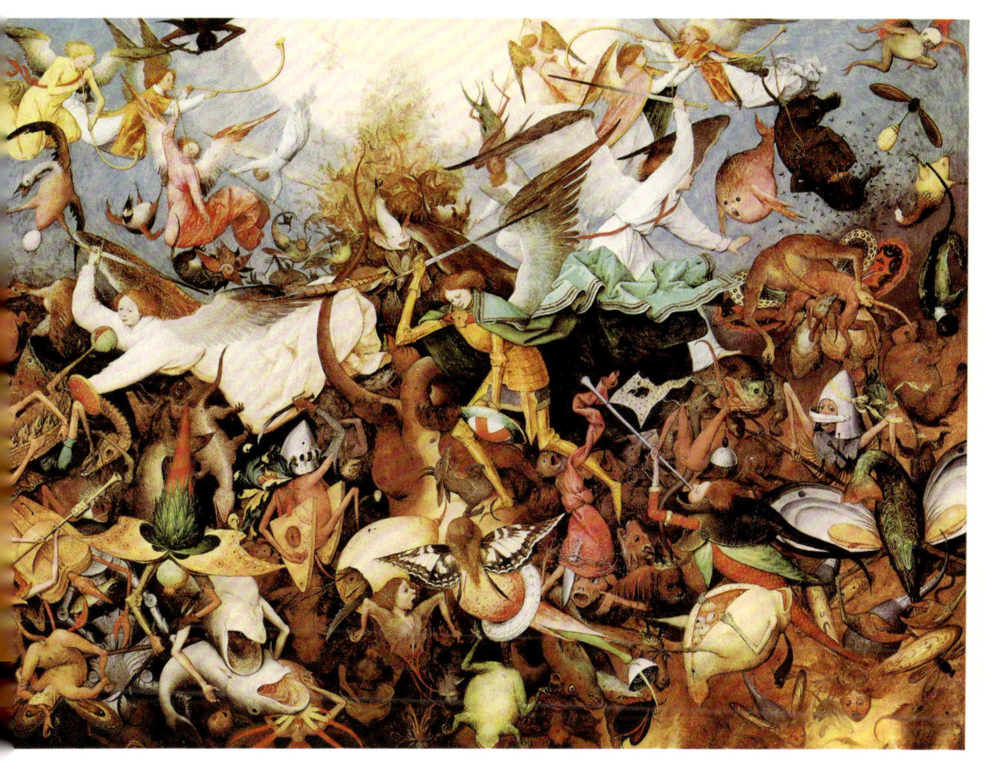

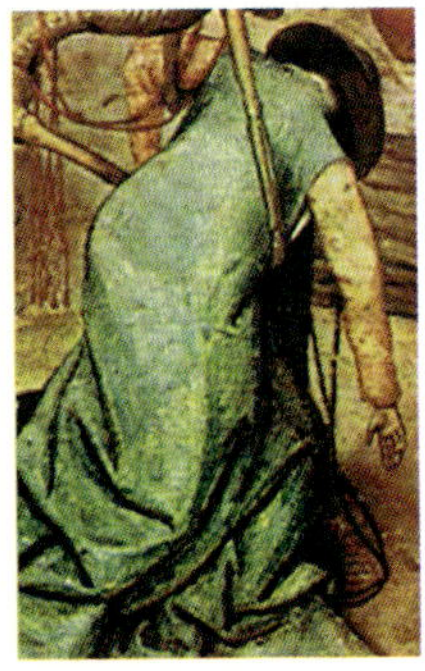

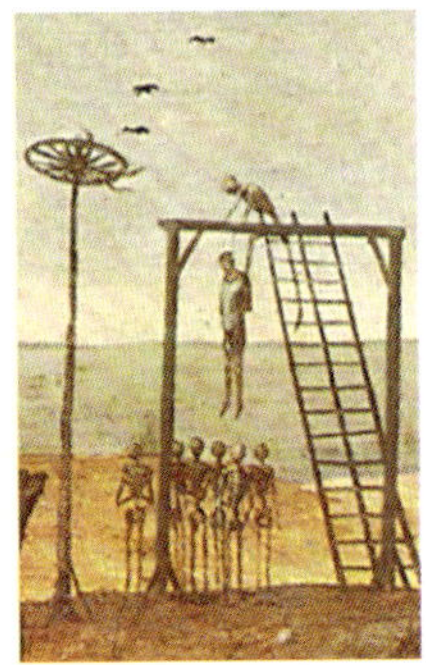

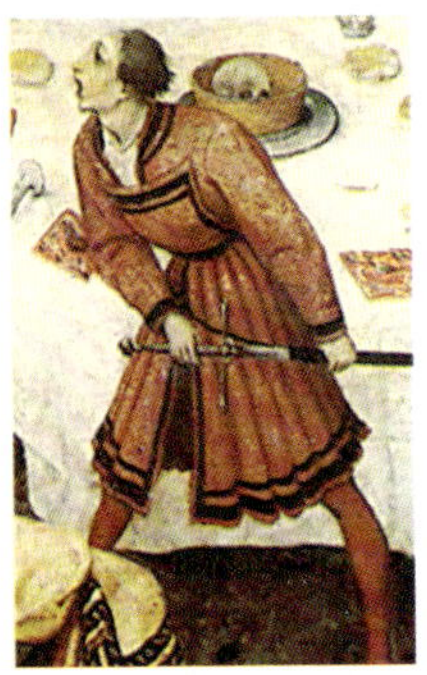

seeming to threaten the burial of the world in ashes, earthquakes overthrowing and engulfing houses and cities – all these grand and terrible events have been connected with the fear of an immediate and universal end of men and things.

The history of eclipses alone would suffice to fill a volume no less interesting than the history

The Triumph of Death

Pieter Bruegel the Elder, c. 1562
Oil on wood, 117 x 162 cm
Museo Nacional del Prado, Madrid

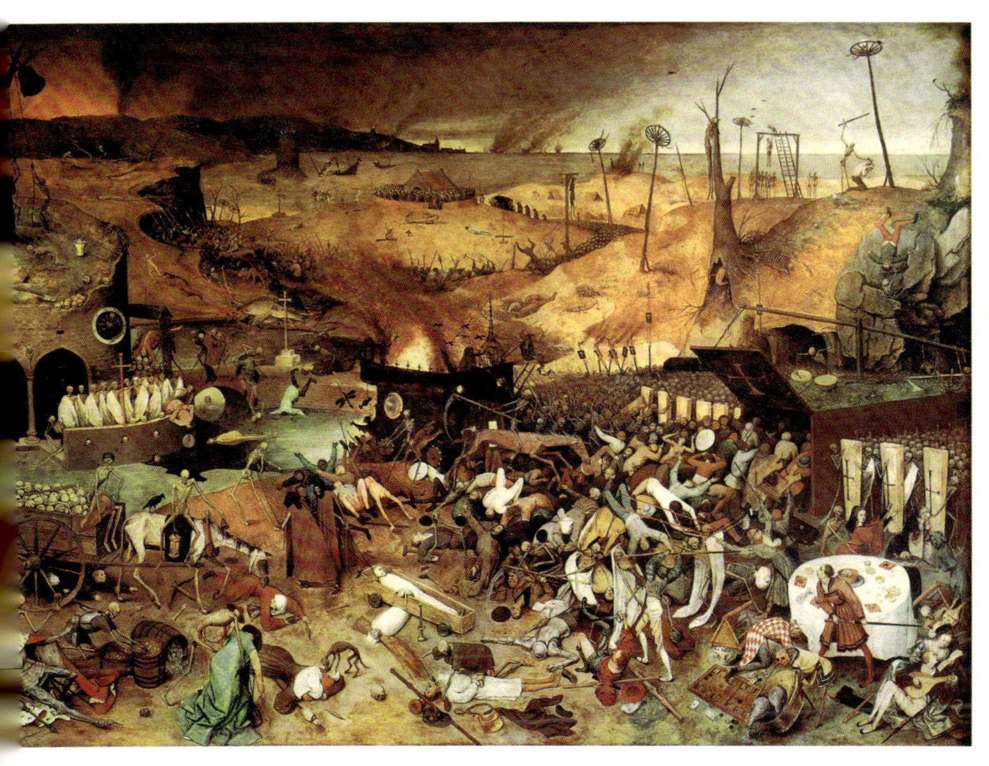

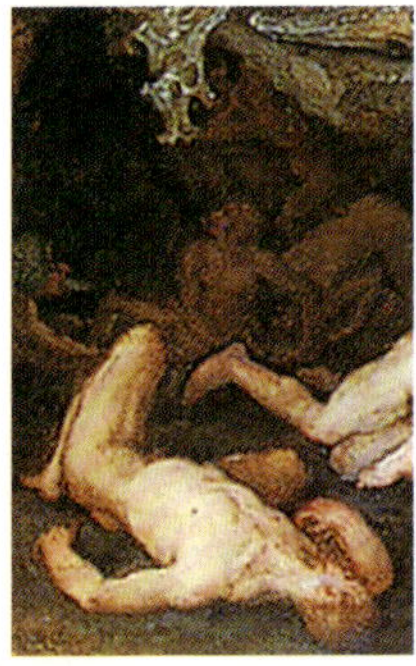

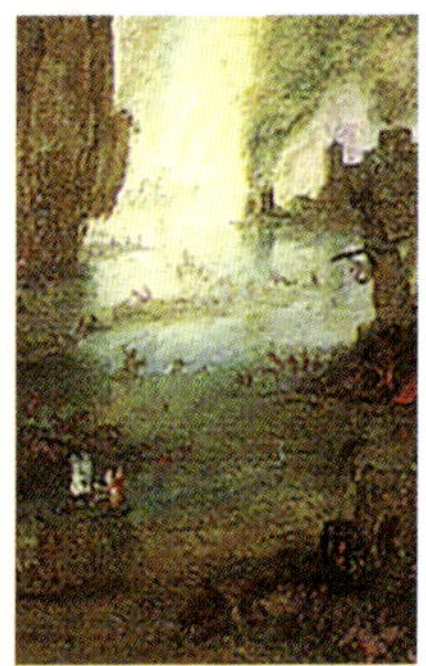

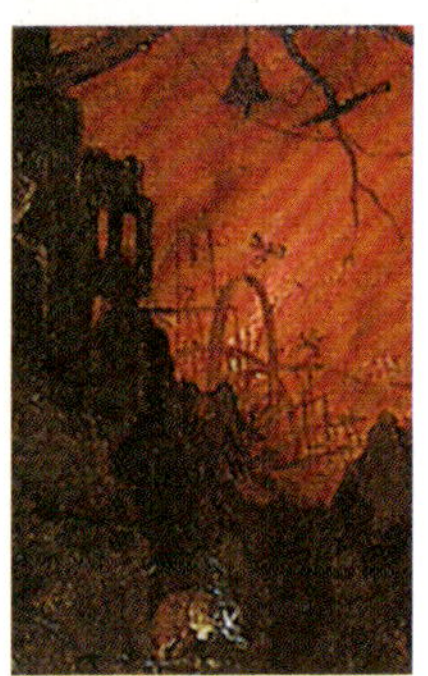

of comets. Let us now confine our attention to a total eclipse of the 17th century that was visible in France on 12 August 1654, which was predicted by astronomers and whose announcement produced great alarm. For some it meant the overthrow of states and the fall of Rome; for others it signified a new deluge; there were those who believed that

Juno in the Underworld

Jan Brueghel the Elder, c. 1598
Oil on copper, 25.5 x 35.5 cm
Staatliche Kunstsammlungen
Gemäldegalerie Alte Meister, Dresden

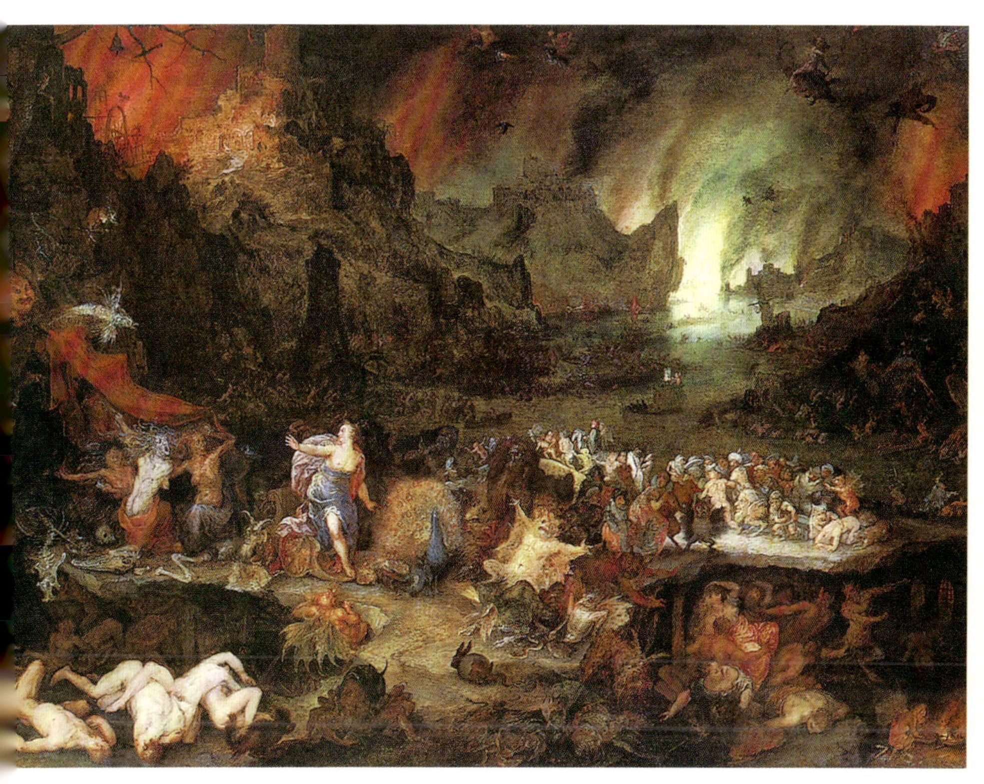

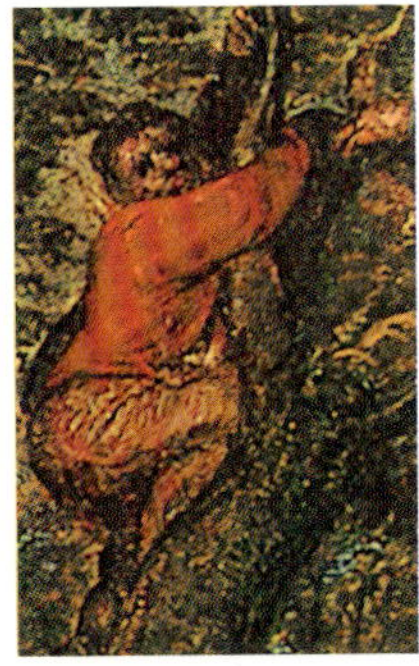

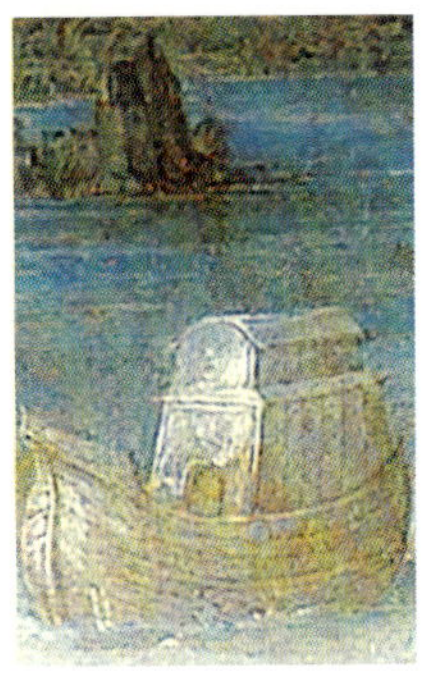

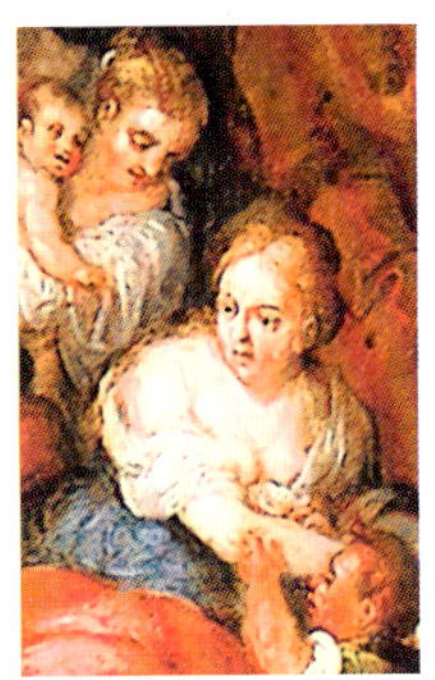

nothing less than the destruction of the world by fire was inevitable; while the more collected anticipated the poisoning of the atmosphere. Belief in these dreaded results was so widespread, that, in order to escape them, and by the express order of physicians, many terrified people shut themselves up in closed cellars,

The Flood with Noah's Ark

Jan Brueghel the Elder, 1601
Oil on copper, 26.5 x 36 cm
Gift of Betty and David M. Koetser, Kunsthaus, Zurich

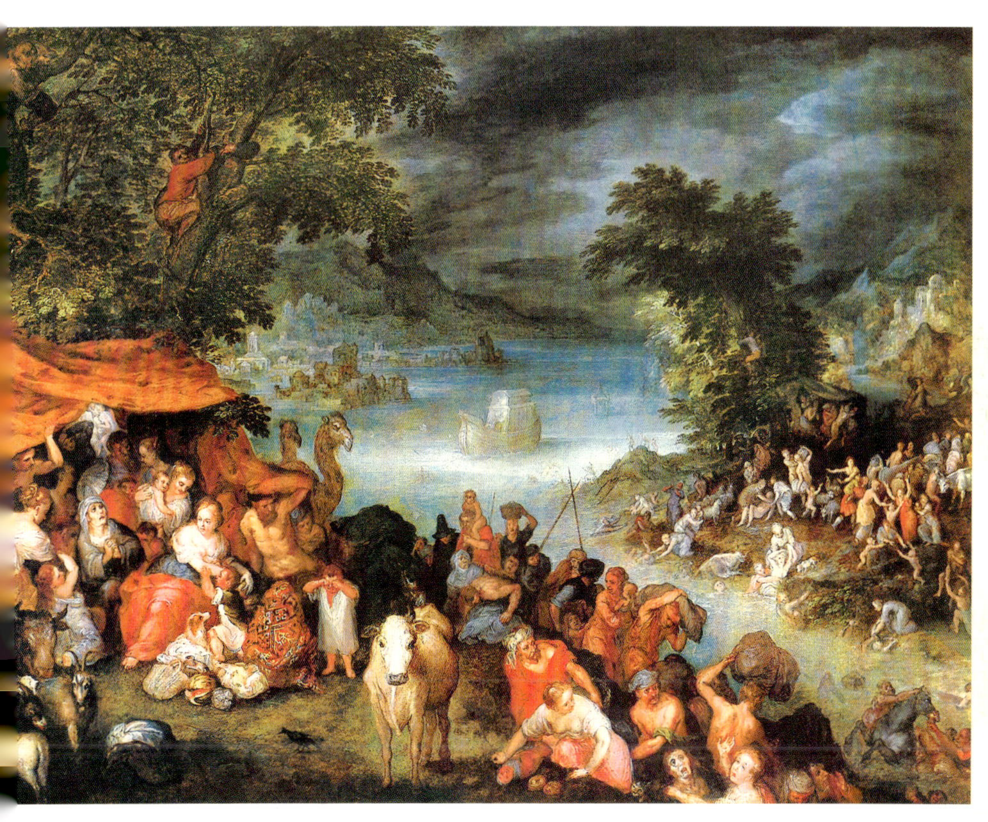

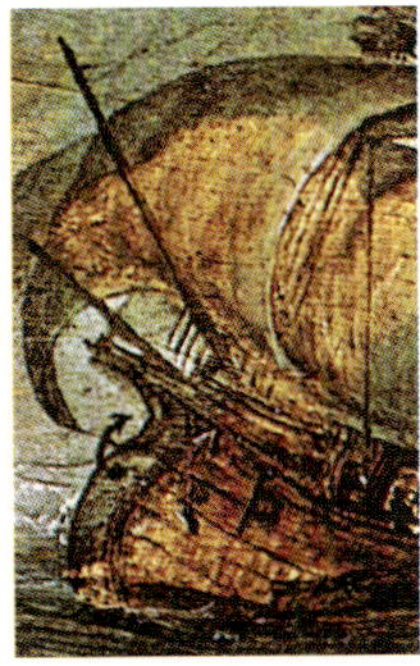

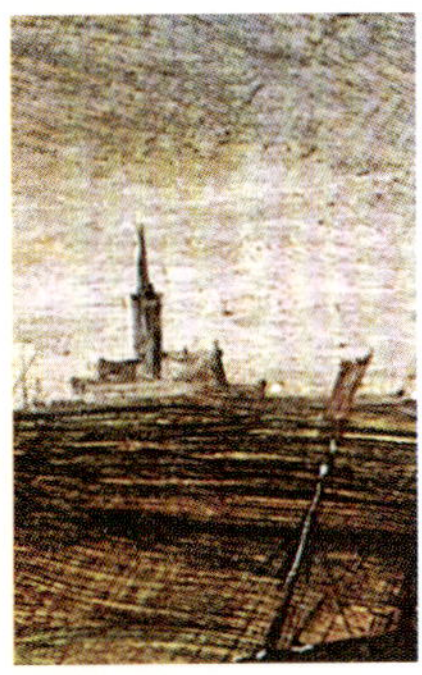

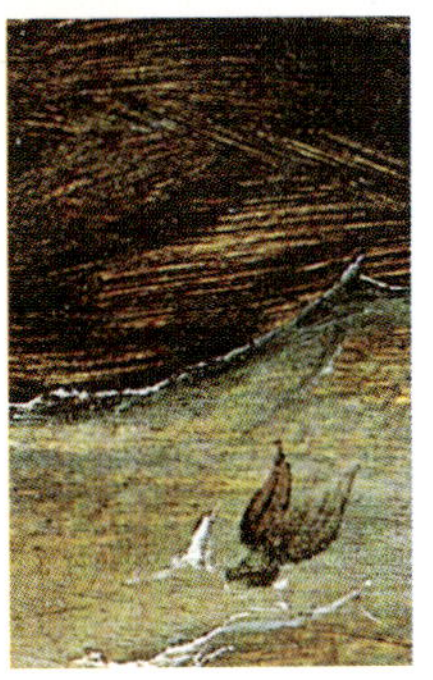

warmed and perfumed. We refer the reader, especially to the second evening, of *Les Mondes* of Fontenelle.

Another writer of the same century, Petit, wrote in his *Dissertation on the Nature of Comets* that the consternation steadily increased up to the fatal day, and that a country priest, unable to hear

The Tempest

Pieter Bruegel the Elder
or Joos de Momper the Younger, 1610-1615
Oil on wood, 70.5 x 97 cm
Kunsthistorisches Museum, Vienna

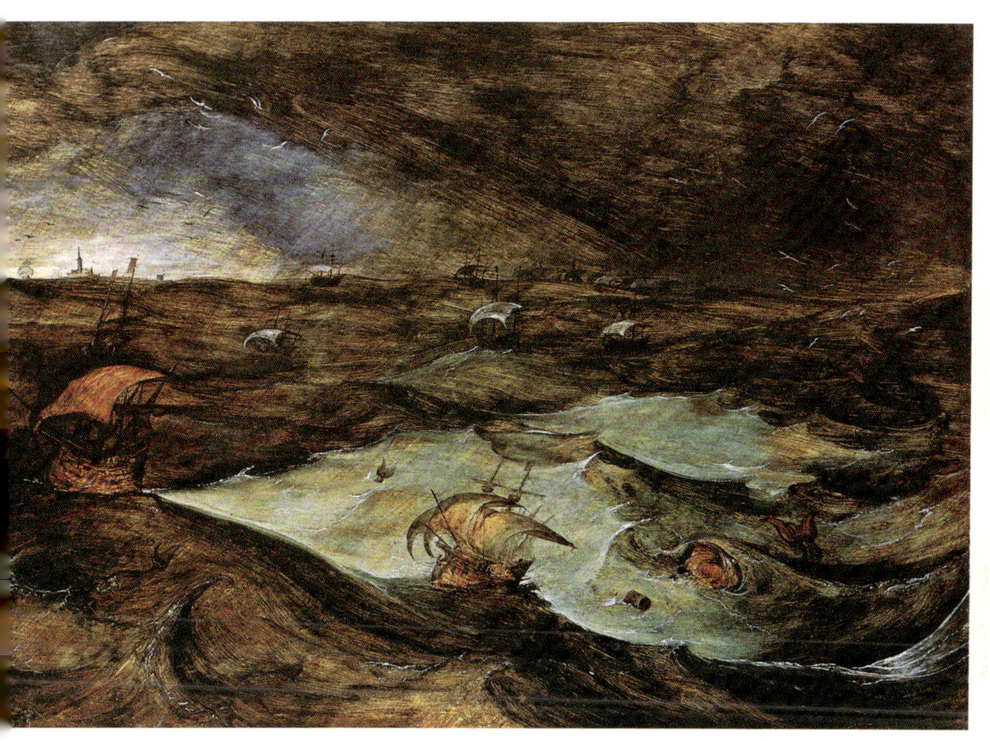

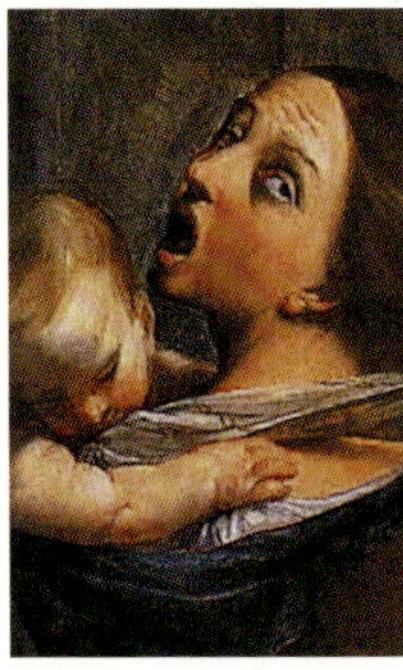

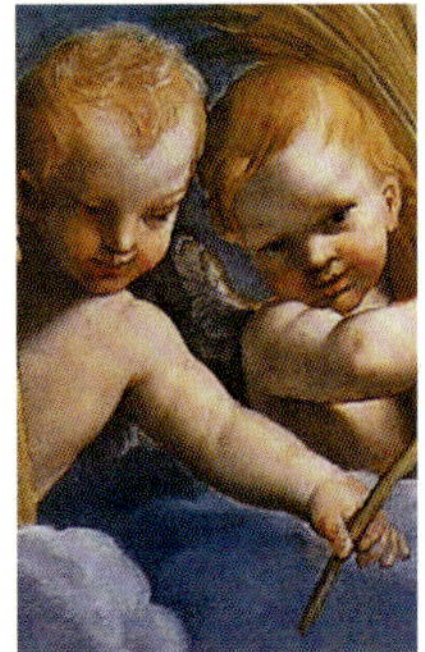

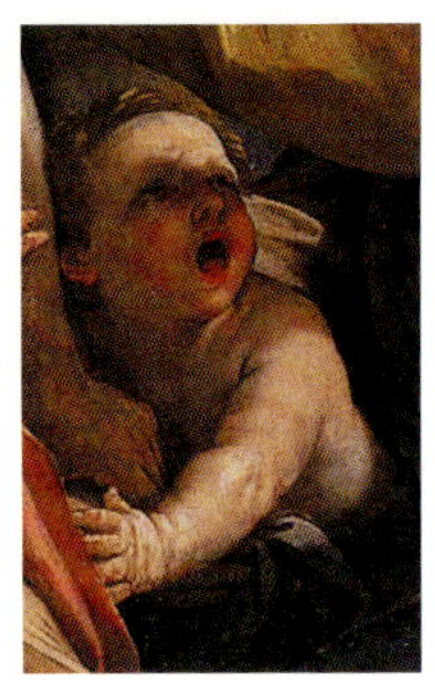

the confessions of all who believed their last hour was at hand, told his parishioners during his sermon not to be in such haste, for the eclipse had been put off for a fortnight; and these good people were as ready to believe in the postponement of the eclipse as they had been to believe in its malign influence.

The Massacre of the Innocents

Guido Reni, 1611
Oil on canvas, 268 x 170 cm
Pinacoteca Nazionale di Bologna, Bologna

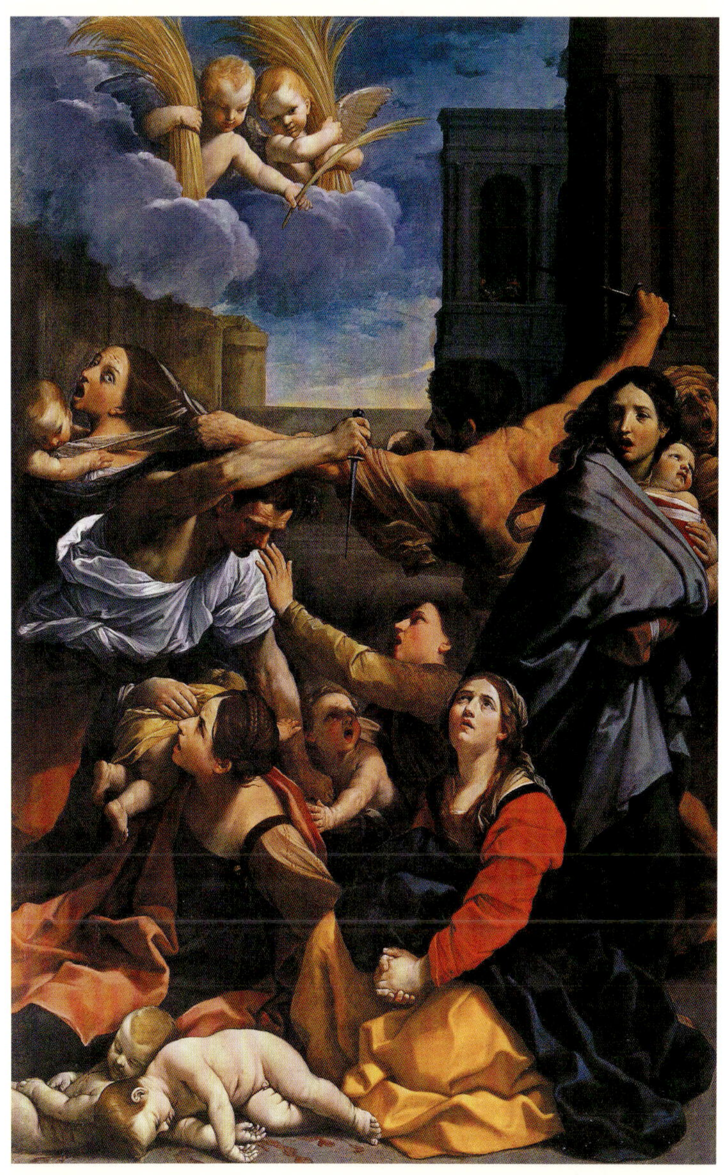

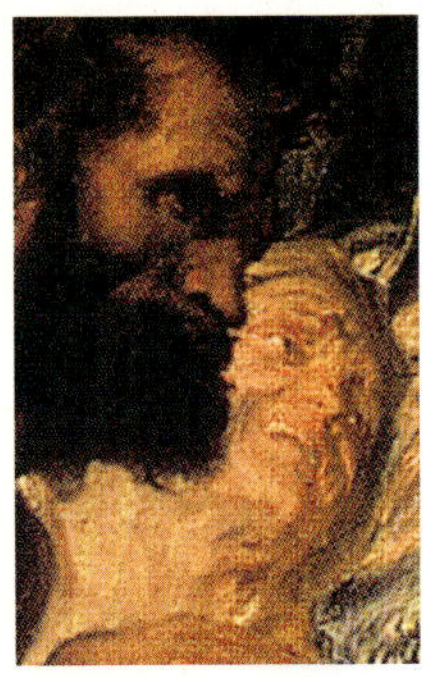

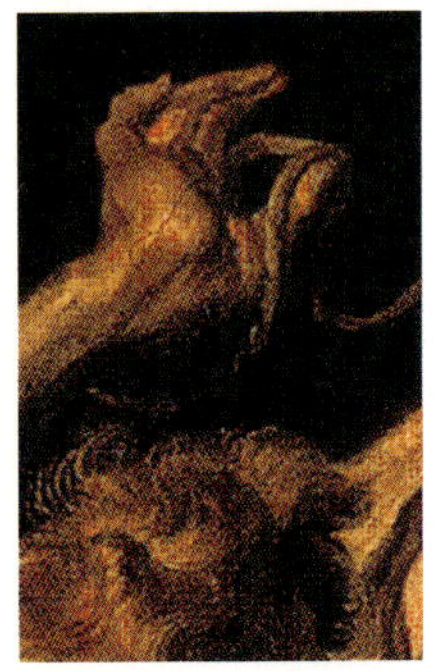

At the time of the total solar eclipses visible in France, namely those of 12 May 1706; 22 May 1724, and 8 July 1842, as also of the partial ones of 9 October 1847; 28 July 1851; 15 March 1858; 18 July 1860, and 22 December 1870, there was more or less apprehension on the part of the timid. At least,

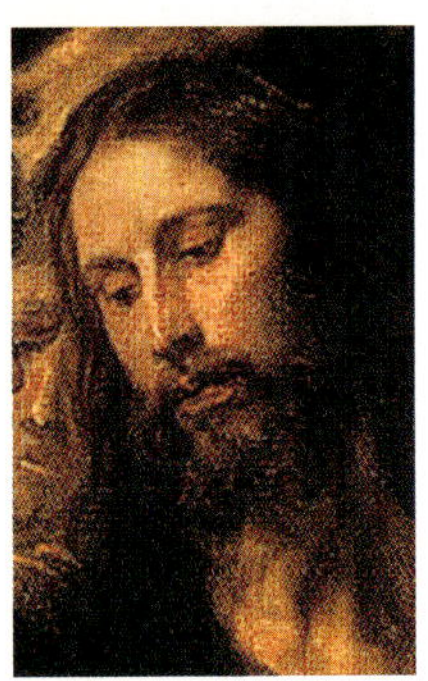

Anthony Van Dyck, c. 1621
Oil on canvas, 344 x 249 cm
Museo Nacional del Prado, Madrid

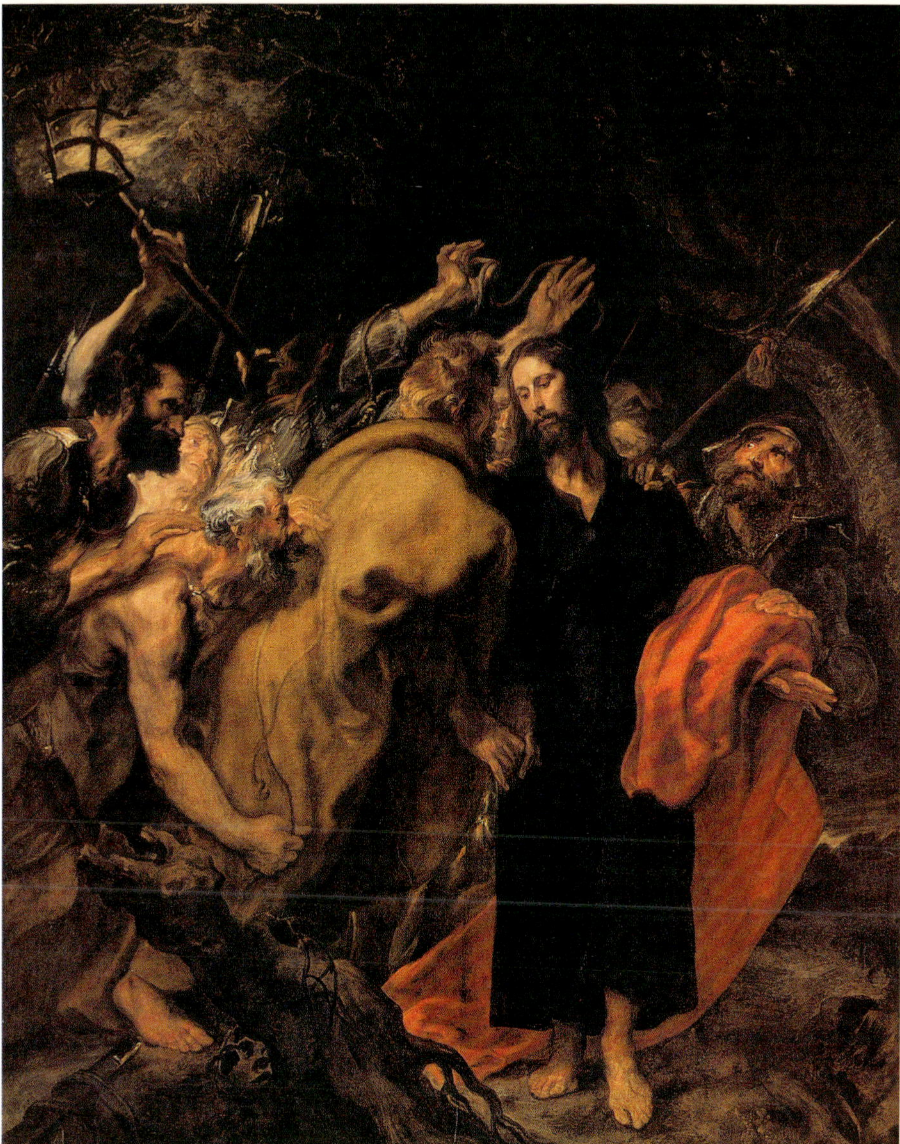

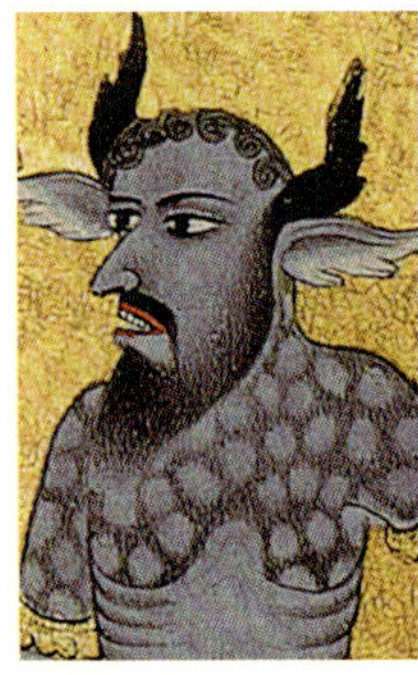

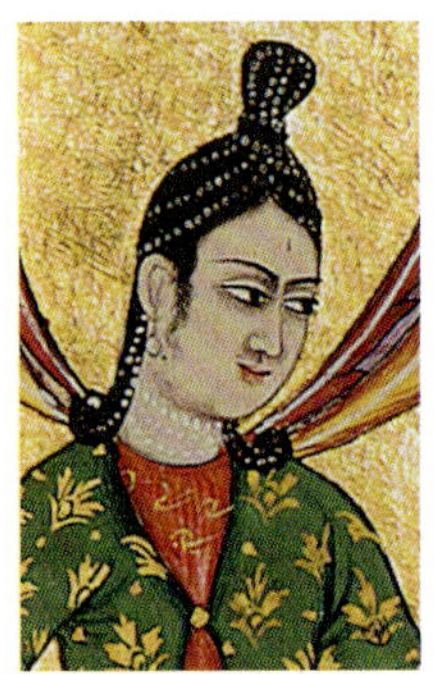

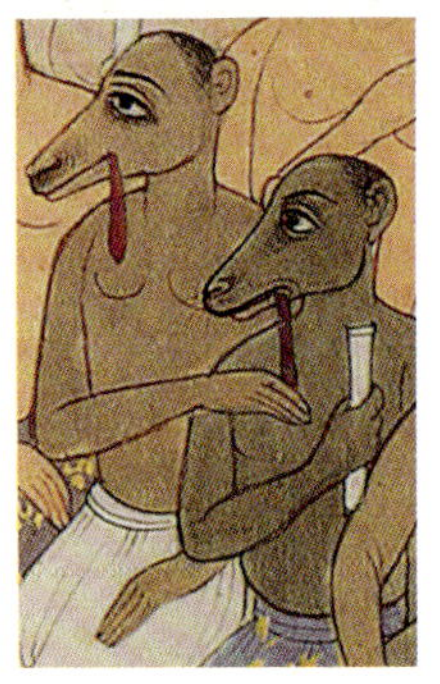

we know, from trustworthy sources, that in each of these cases these natural phenomena were interpreted by a certain class in Europe as possible signs of divine wrath, and in several religious educational establishments the pupils were requested to offer up prayers as the time of the eclipse drew near. This mystical interpretation

The Last Judgement

Illumination from a Falnama
(ancient Islamic book of omens), c. 1610-1630
Ink, gouache, gold, and silver on paper, 41 x 28.4 cm
Topkapi Palace Museum, Istanbul

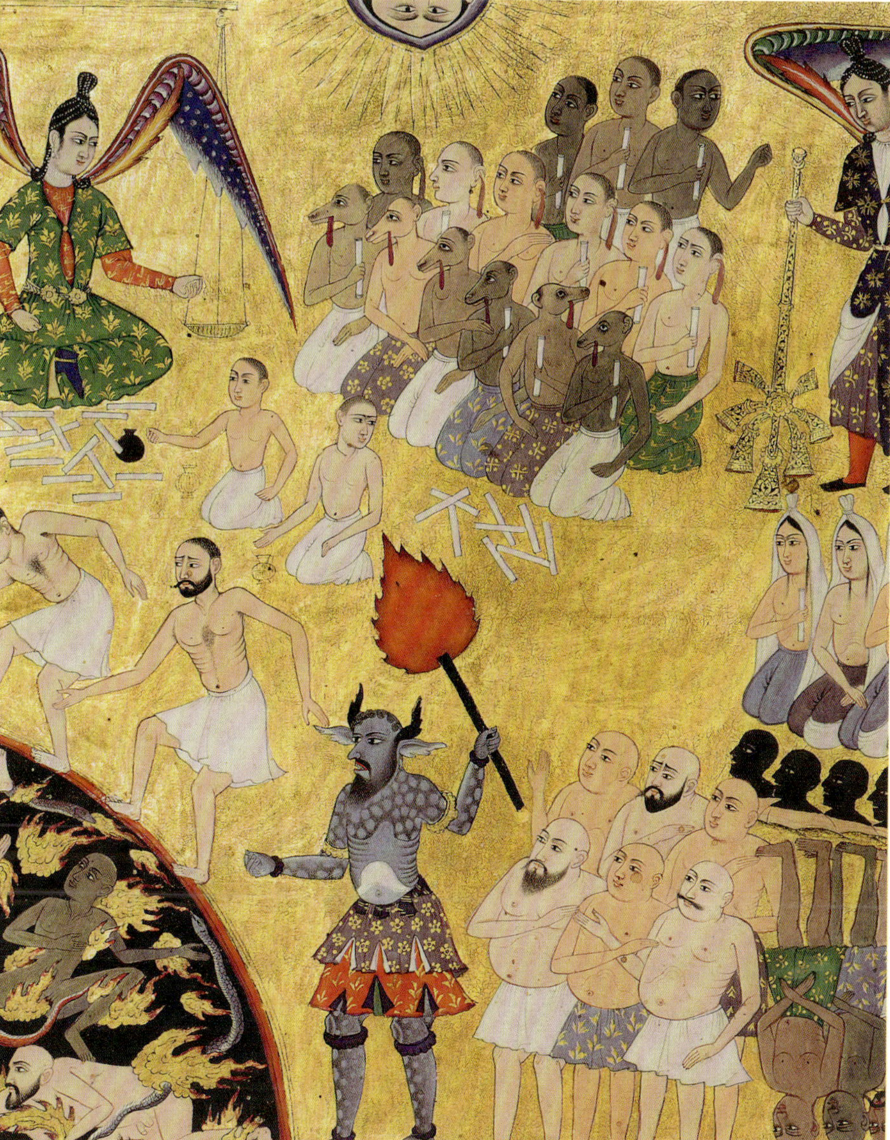

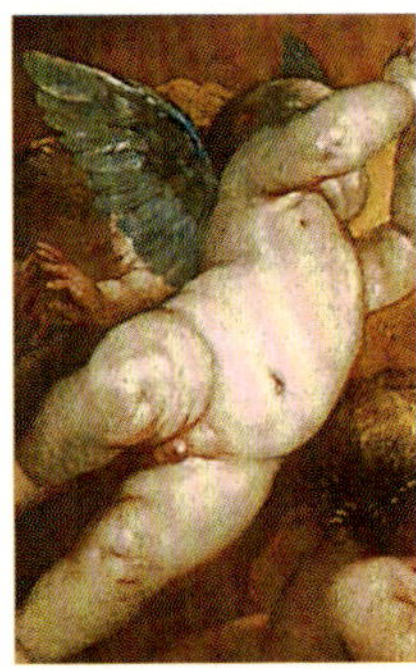

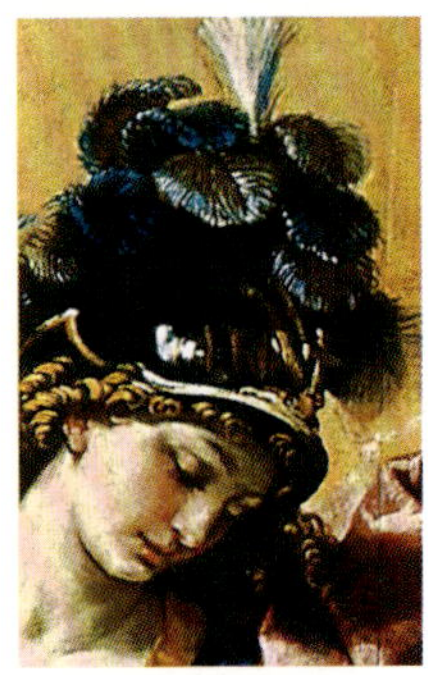

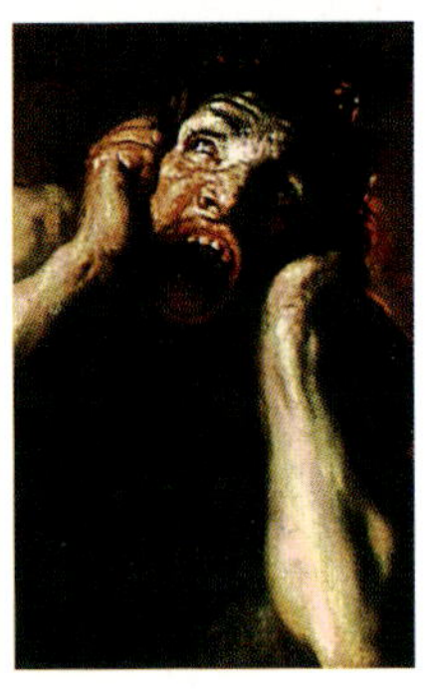

of the order of nature is slowly disappearing among enlightened nations.

Among less civilised people, these phenomena still excited the same terror which was once more prevalent around the world. This fact was frequently attested by travellers, especially in Africa. During the eclipse of 18 July 1860, in Algeria, men and

Luca Giordano, 1660-1665
Oil on canvas, 419 x 283 cm
Kunsthistorisches Museum, Vienna

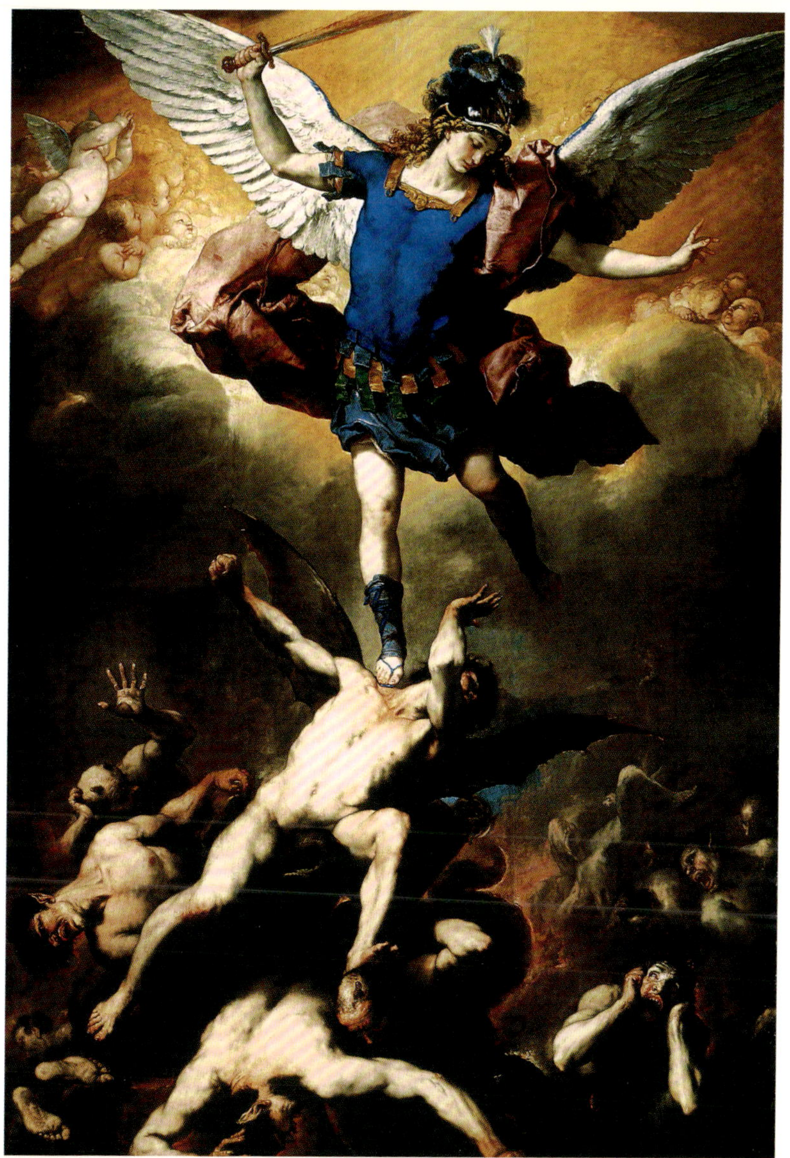

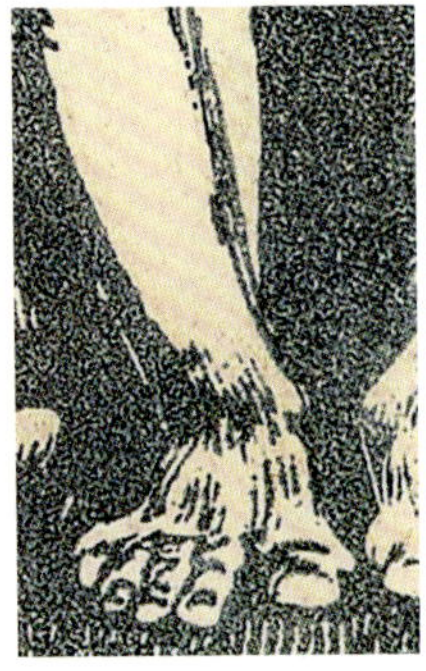

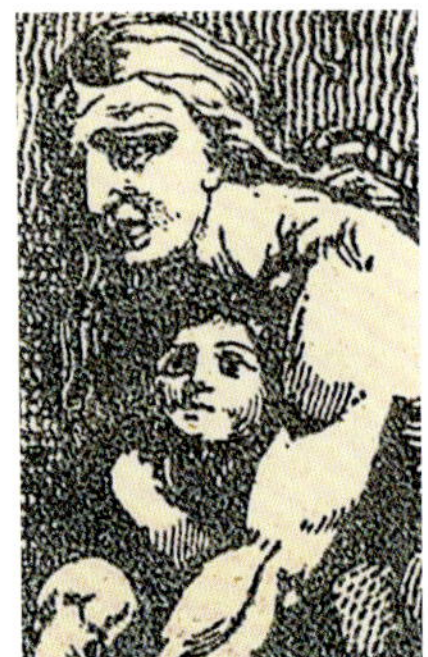

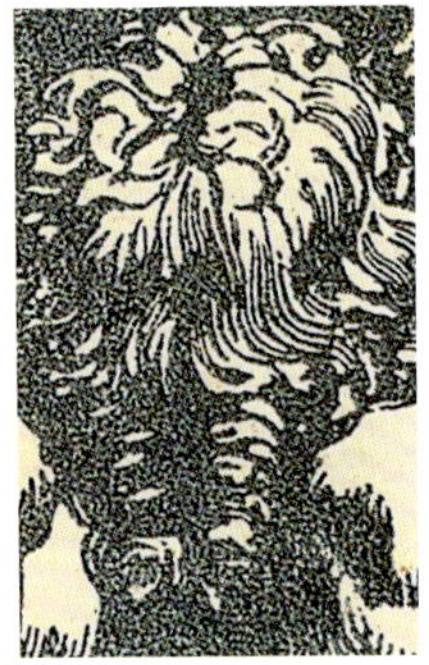

women resorted to prayer or fled, frightened, to their homes. During the eclipse of 29 July 1878, which was a totality in the United States, a black man, suddenly crazed with terror, and persuaded that the end of the world was coming, cut the throats of his wife and children.

It must be admitted that such phenomena are well calculated to overwhelm the imagination.

America, a Prophecy (frontispiece)

William Blake, 1793
Relief etching, with some wash, 23.4 x 16.9 cm
Fitzwilliam Museum, Cambridge

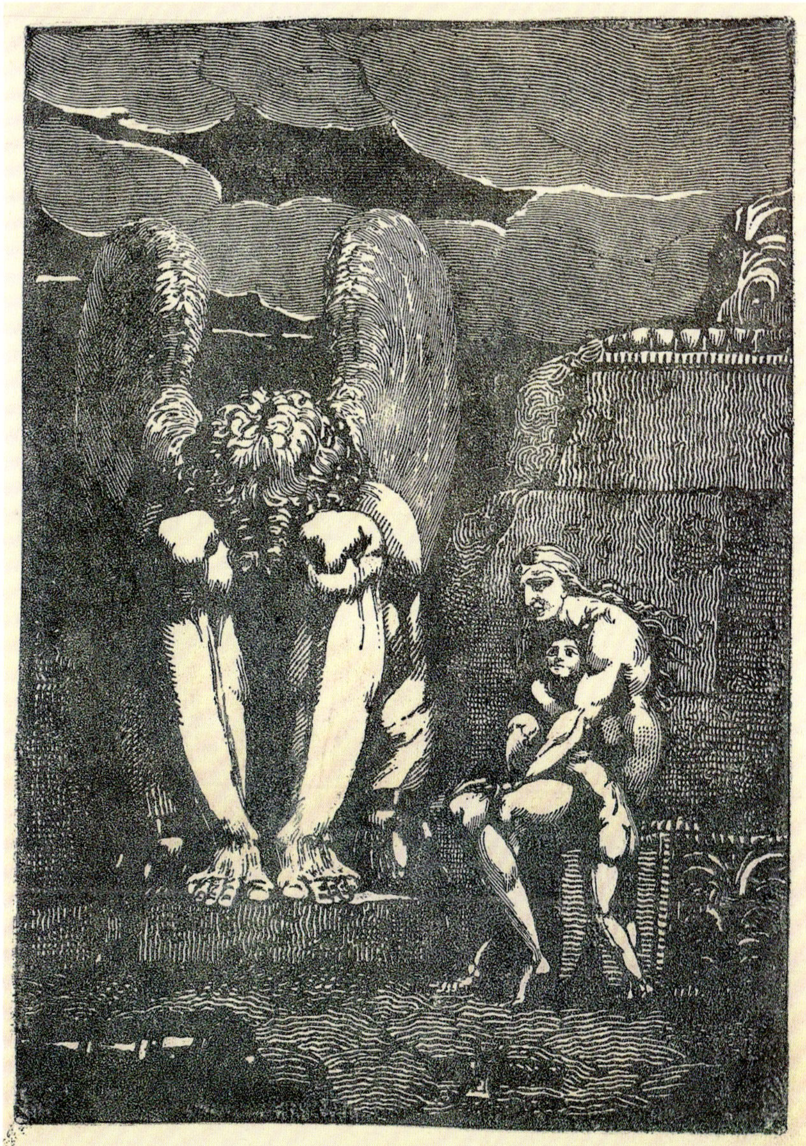

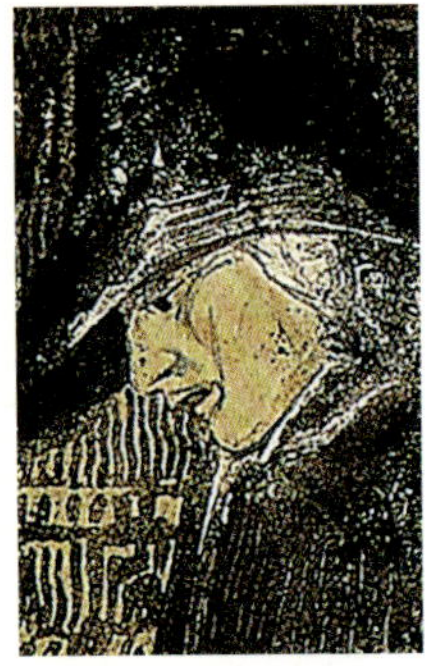

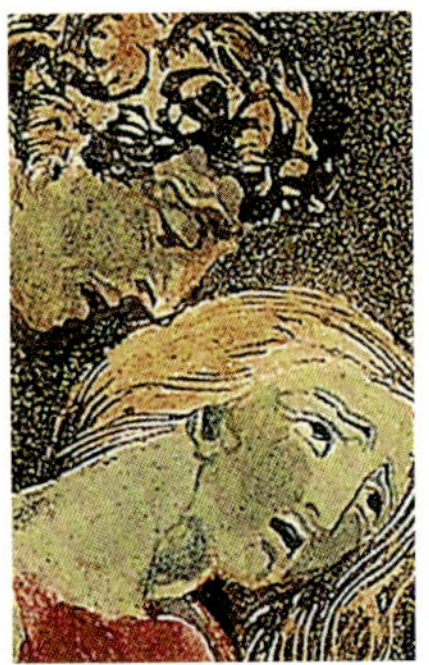

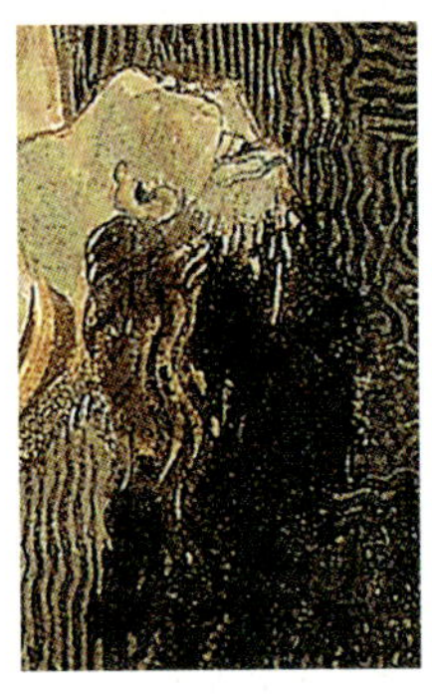

The sun, the god of day, the star upon whose light we are dependent, grows dim and, just before it becomes extinguished, takes on a sickly and mournful hue. The light of the sky pales, the animal creation is stricken with terror, the beast of burden falters at his task, the dog flees to its master, the hen retreats with her brood to the coop,

William Blake, 1794
Relief and white-line etching with colour printing
and hand colouring, 37.3 x 26.7 cm
University of Glasgow Library, Glasgow

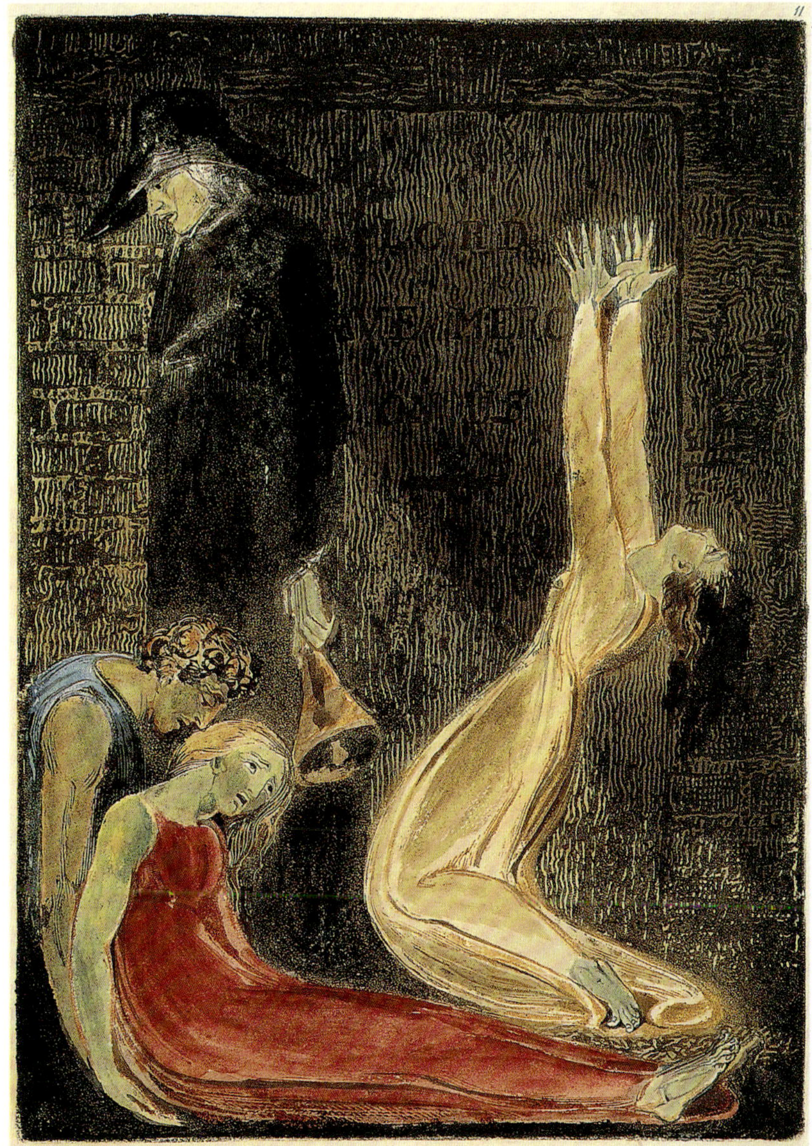

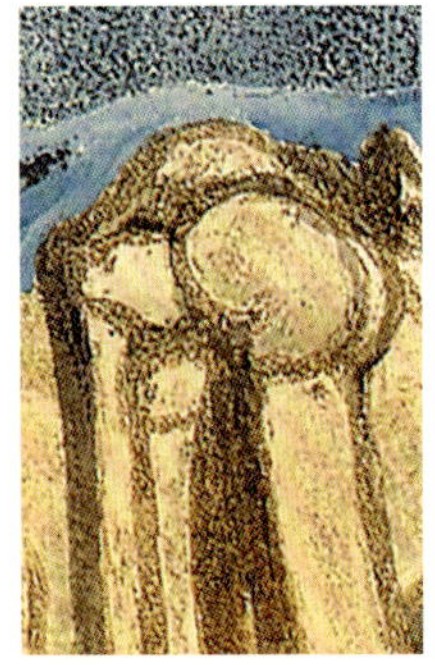

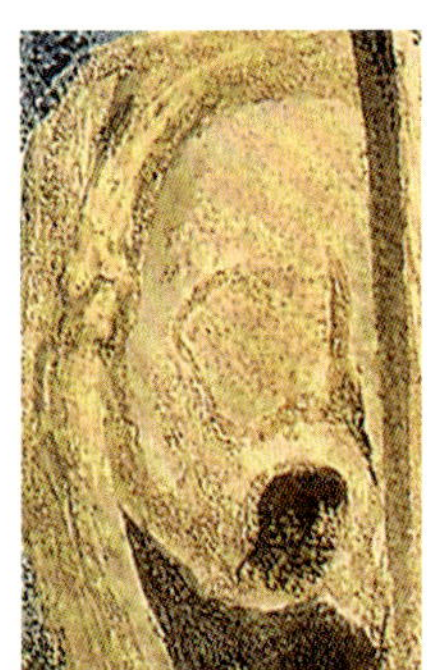

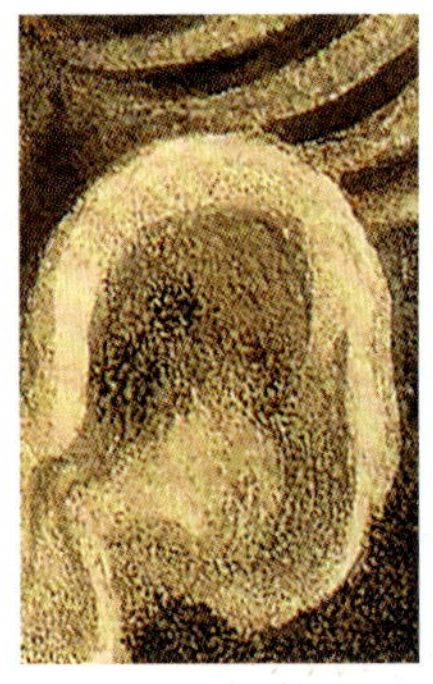

the birds cease their songs, and have even been seen to drop dead with fright. Arago relates that during the total eclipse of the sun at Perpignan, on 8 July 1842, 20,000 spectators were assembled, forming an impressive spectacle.

When the solar disc was nearly obscured, an irresistible anxiety took possession of everybody; each felt the need of sharing his impressions with his neighbour.

Illustration from The First Book of Urizen

William Blake, 1794
Colour relief etching, with added hand colouring
15.1 x 10 cm
British Museum, London

Chap: IV

1. Los smitten with astonish-ment
Frightend at the hurtling bones

2 And at the surging sulphure-
ous
Perturbed Immortal mad raging

3: In whirlwinds & pitch & nitre
Round the furious limbs of Los

4 And Los formed nets & gins
And threw the nets round about

5. He watchd in shuddring fear
The dark changes & bound every
change
With rivets of iron & brass

6. And these were the changes
of Urizen

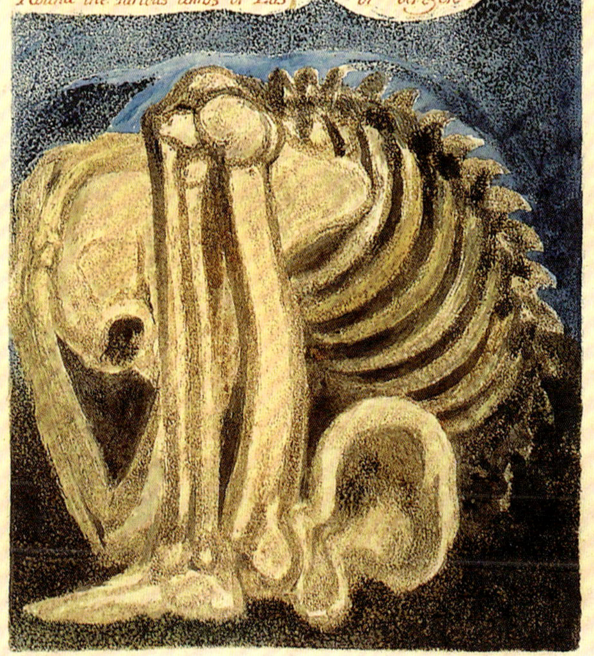

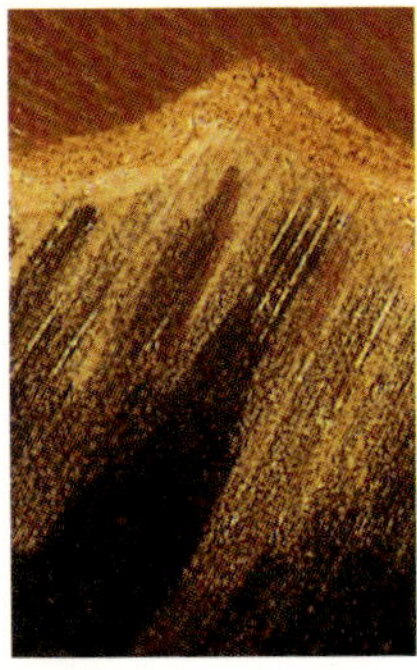

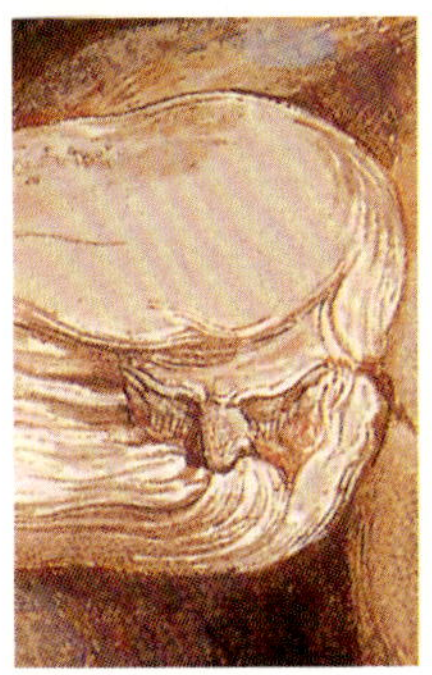

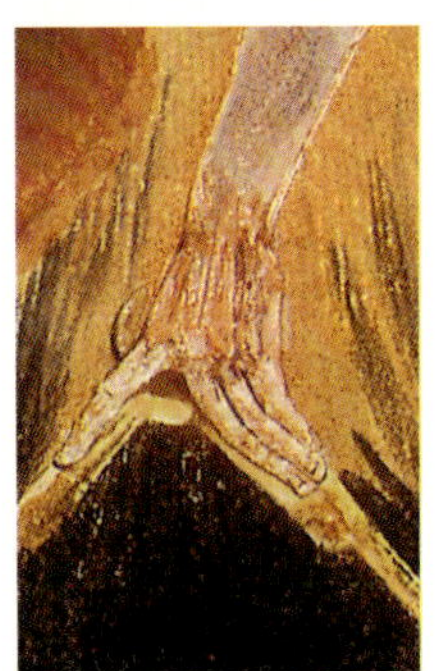

A deep murmur arose, like that of the far-away sea after a storm. This murmur deepened as the crescent of light grew less, and when it had disappeared and sudden darkness had supervened, the silence which ensued marked this phase of the eclipse as accurately as the pendulum of our astronomical clock.

Illustration from Europe, a Prophecy (frontispiece)

William Blake, 1794
Etching, 37.5 x 27 cm
University of Glasgow Library, Glasgow

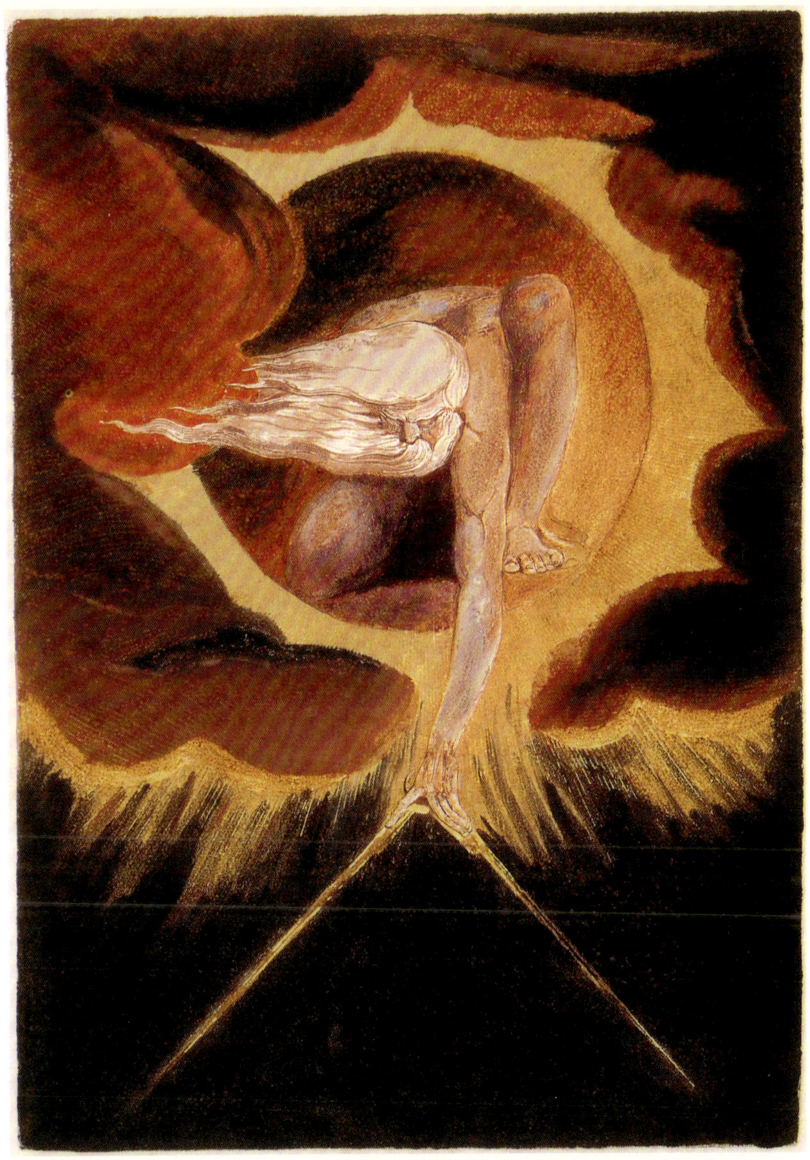

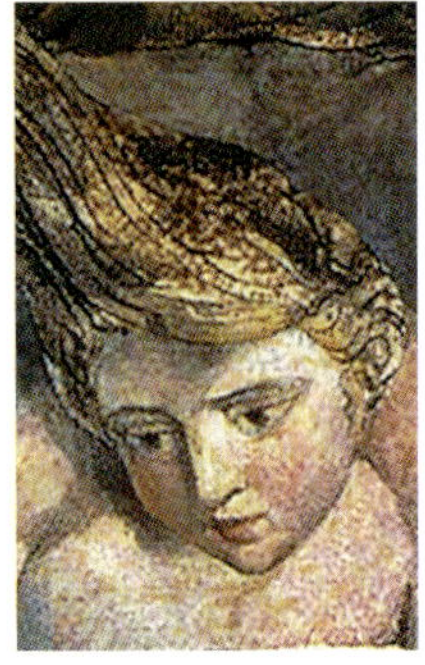

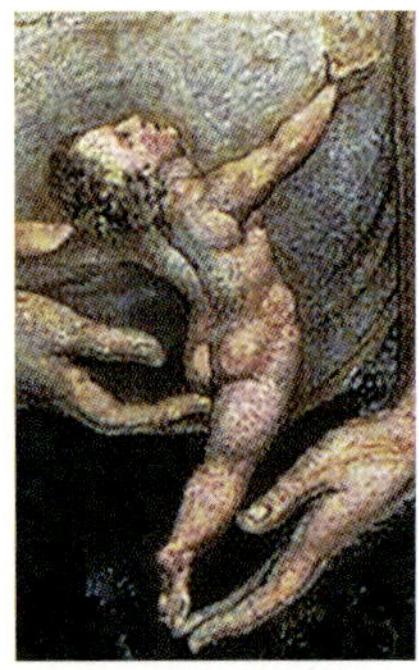

The magnificence of the spectacle triumphed over the petulance of youth, over the frivolity which some people mistake for a sign of superiority, over the indifference which the soldier frequently assumes. A profound silence reigned also in the sky: the birds had ceased their songs. After a solemn interval of

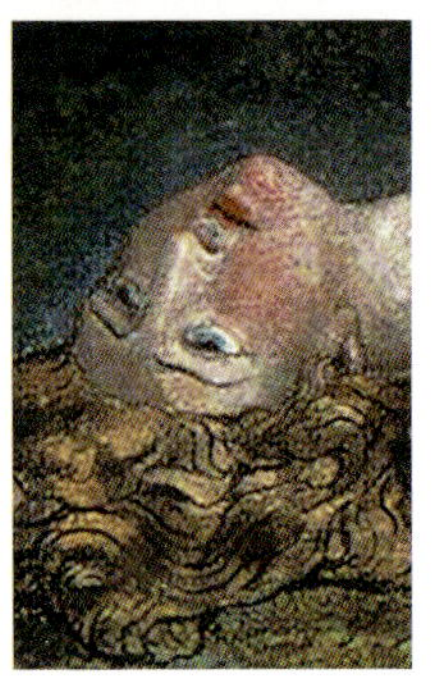

Pity

—

William Blake, c. 1795
Colour print finished in ink and watercolour on paper
42.5 x 53.9 cm
Tate Gallery, London

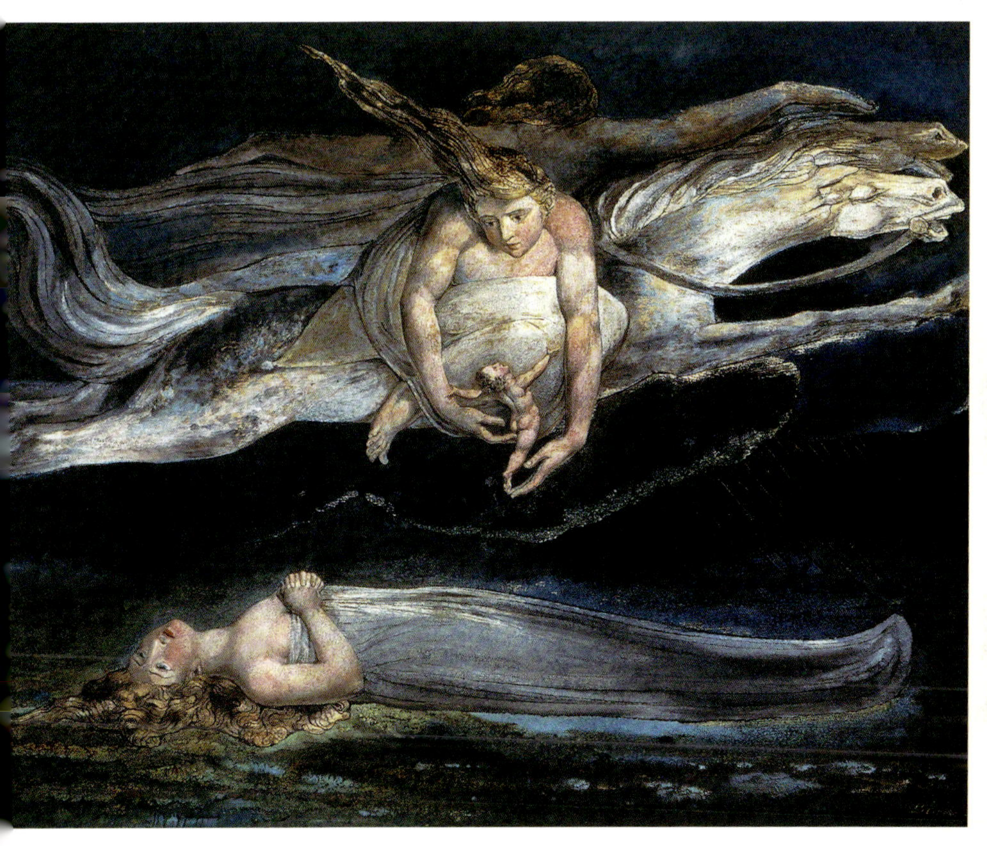

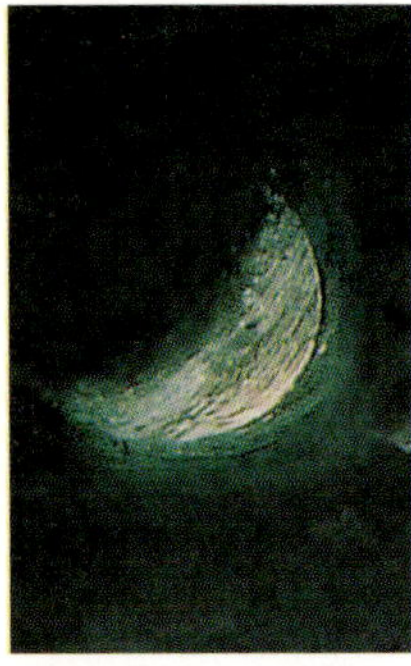

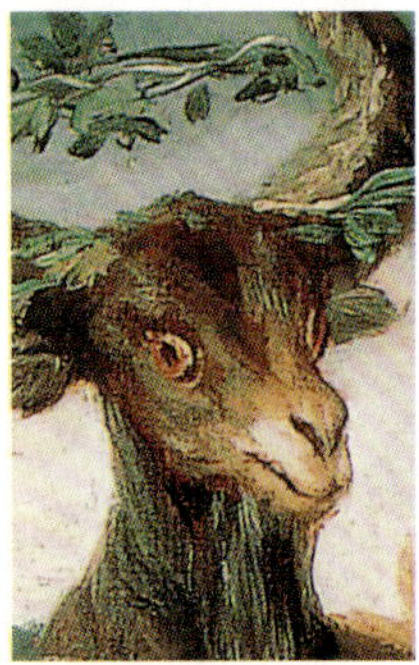

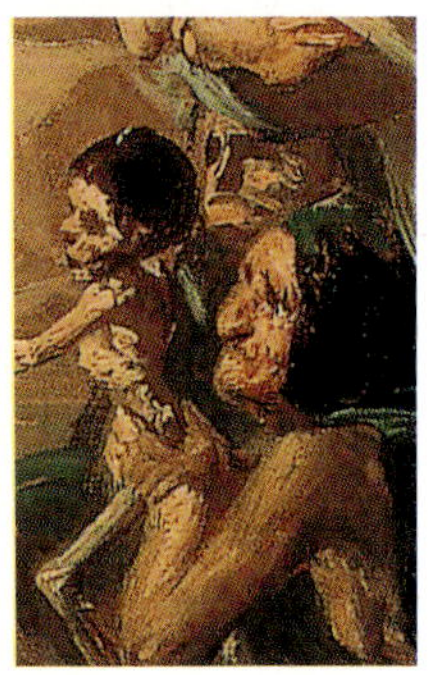

about two minutes, joyous transports and frantic applause greeted with the same spontaneity the first reappearance of the solar rays, and the melancholy and indefinable sense of depression gave way to a deep and unfeigned exultation which no one sought to moderate or repress.

El Aquelarre (The Witches Sabbath)

Francisco Goya, 1797-1798
Oil on canvas, 43.3 x 30.5 cm
Museo Lazaro Galdiano, Madrid

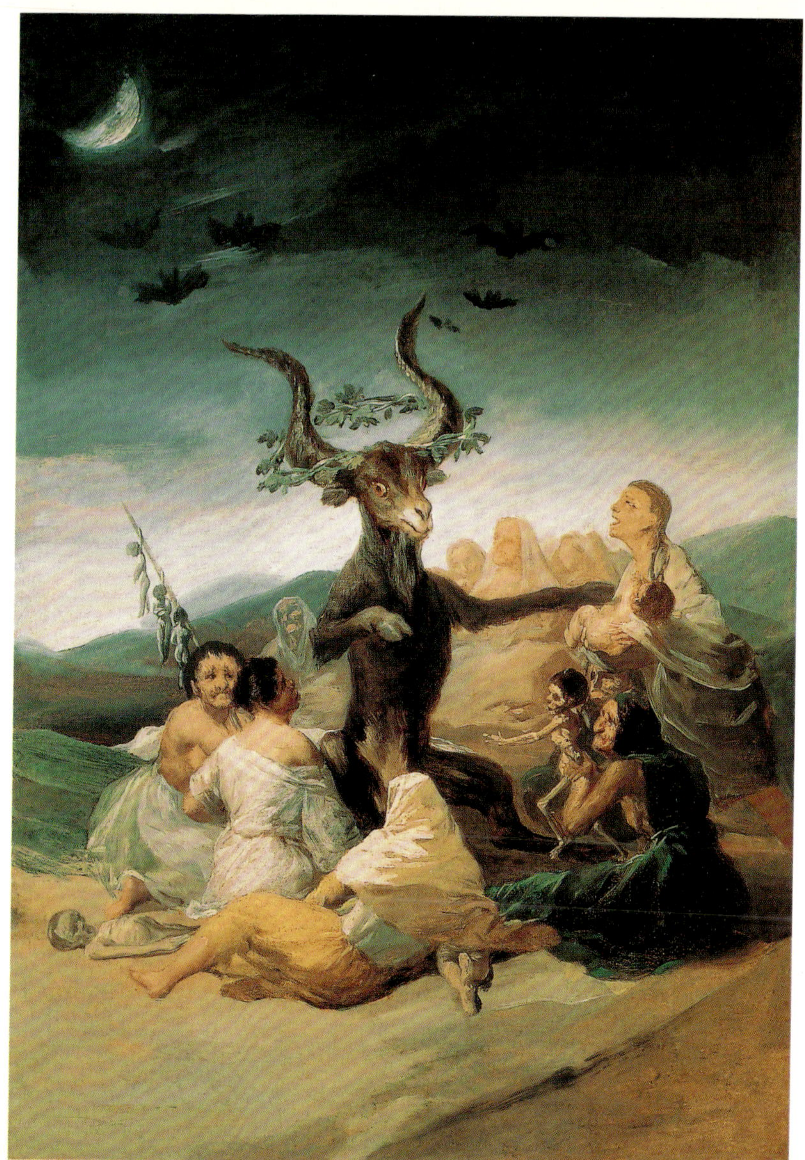

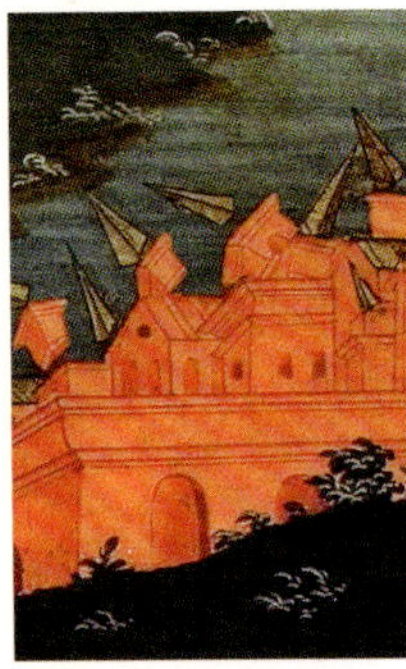

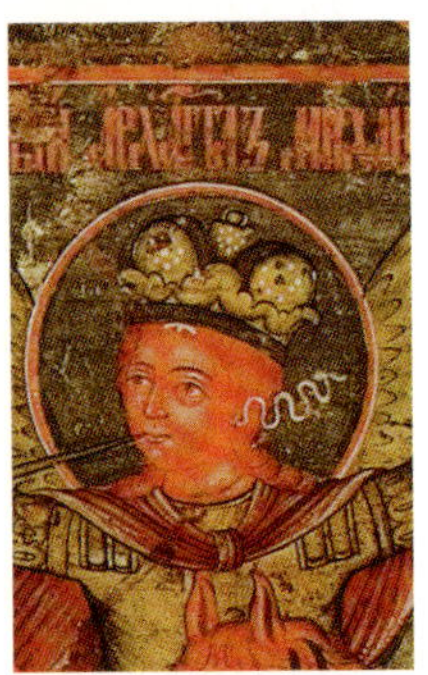

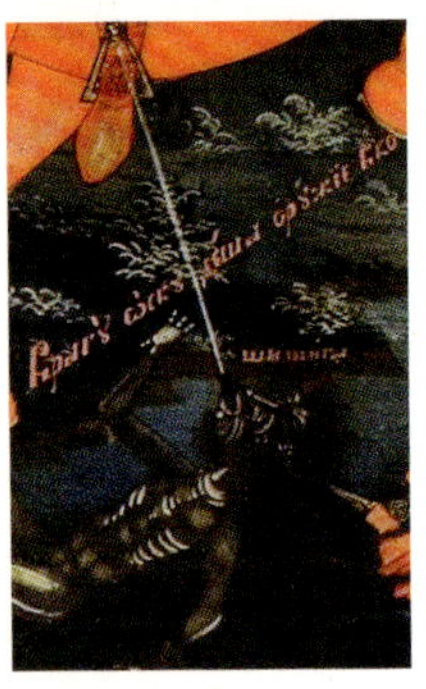

Everyone who witnessed this phenomenon, one of the most sublime which nature offers, was profoundly moved, and took away with him an impression never to be forgotten. The peasants were especially terrified by the darkness, as they believed that they were losing their sight. A poor child, tending his flock, completely ignorant of

Icon: Archangel Michael
Leader of the Heavenly Host

End of 18th century
Distemper and paint on lime, 44.5 x 36.5 x 3.5 cm
State Historical Museum, Moscow

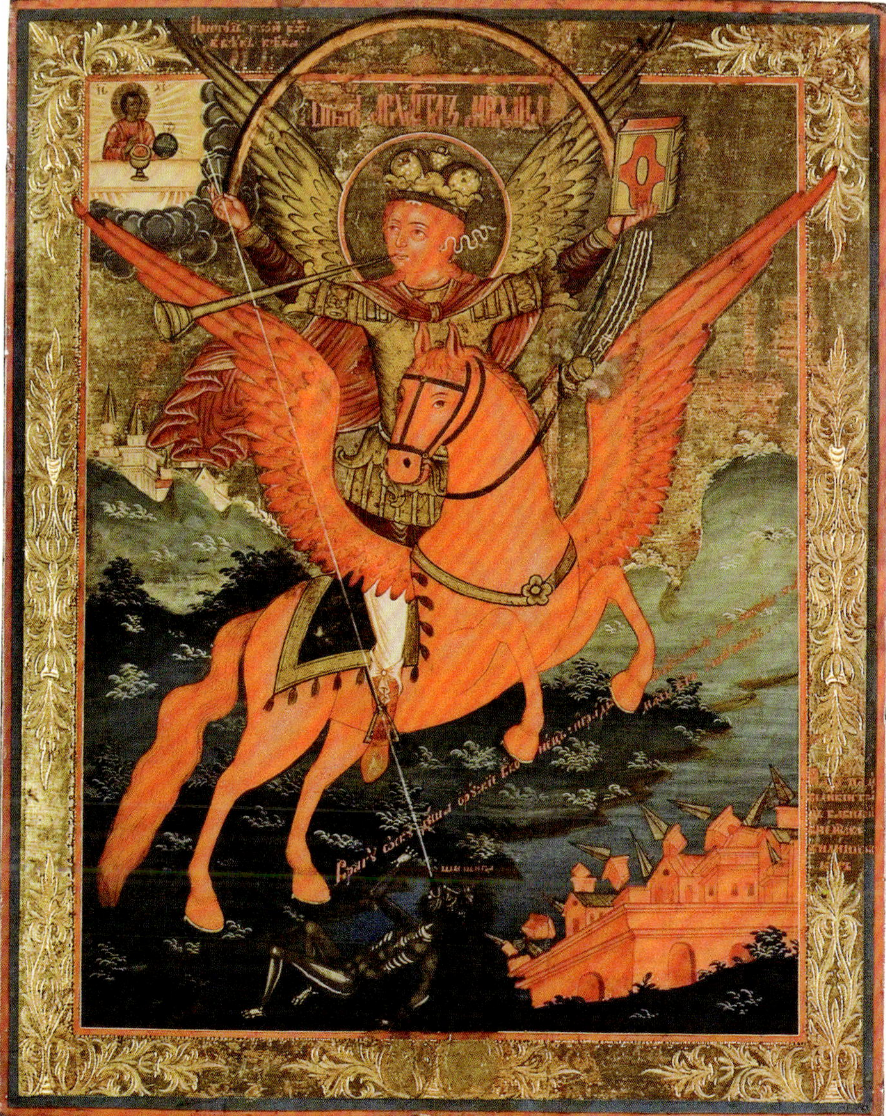

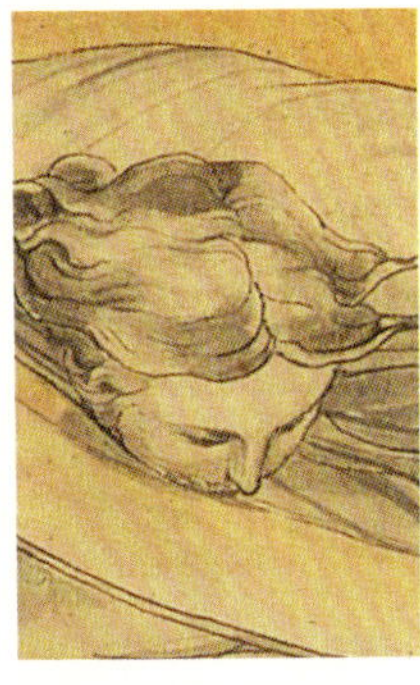

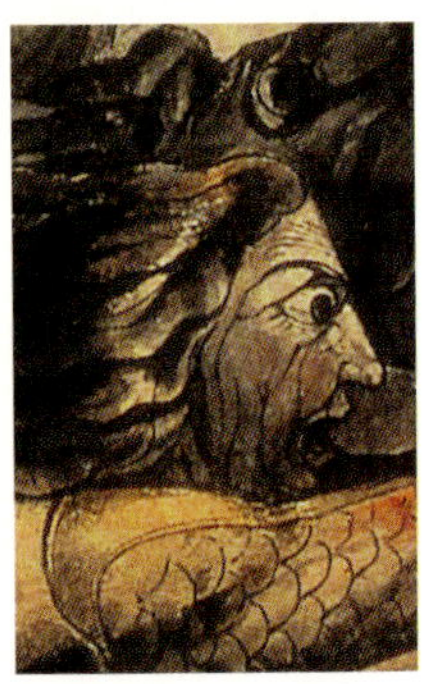

what was coming, saw the sun slowly growing dim in a cloudless sky. When its light disappeared entirely, the poor child, completely carried away by terror, began to cry and call for help. His tears flowed again when the first ray of light reappeared. Reassured, he clasped his hands, crying, "O, beautiful sun!"

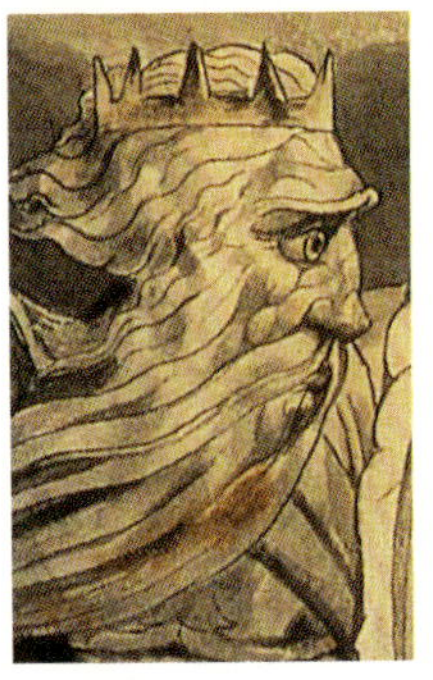

Death on a Pale Horse

William Blake, 1800
Watercolour with pen and ink over pencil on paper
39.5 x 31.1 cm
Fitzwilliam Museum, Cambridge

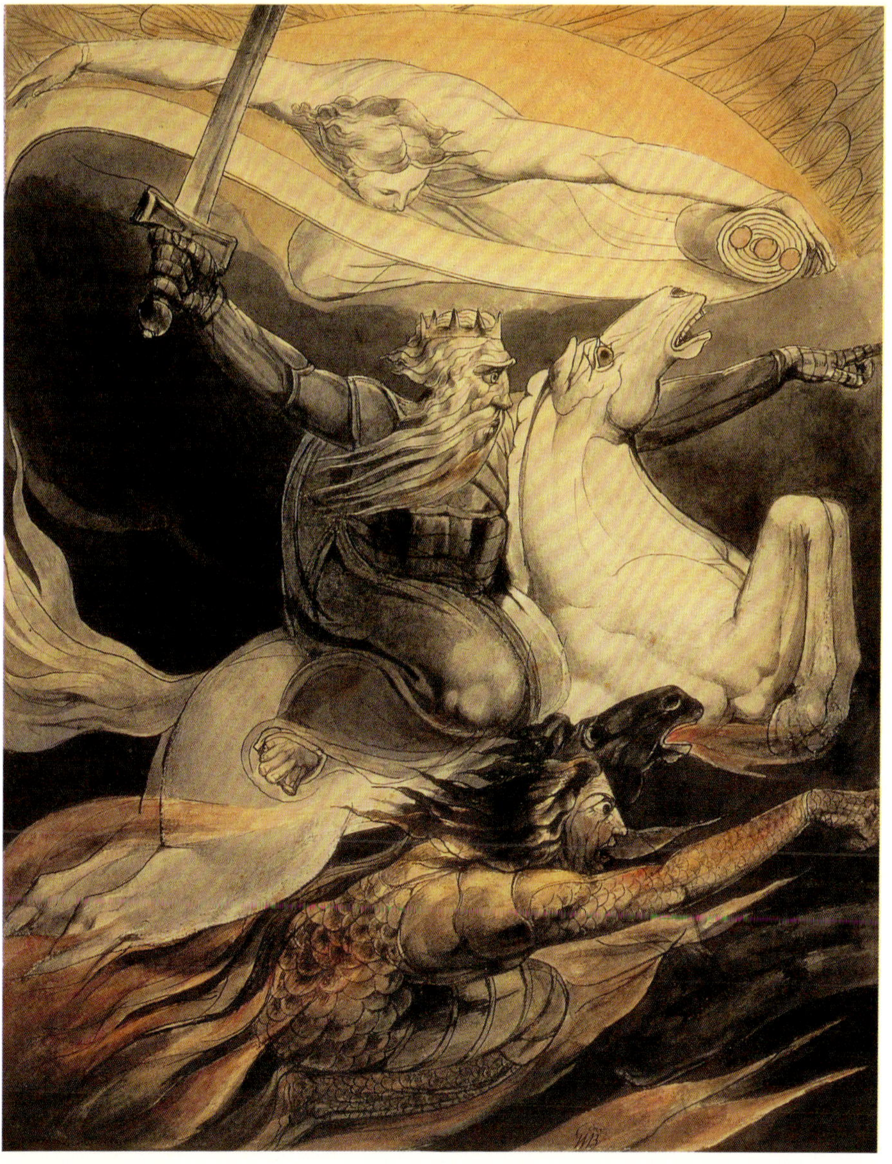

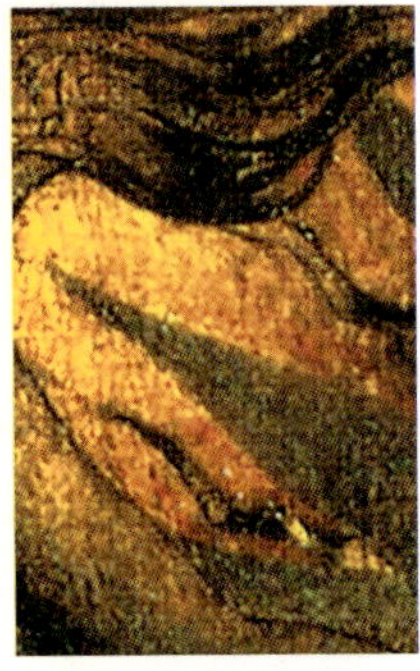

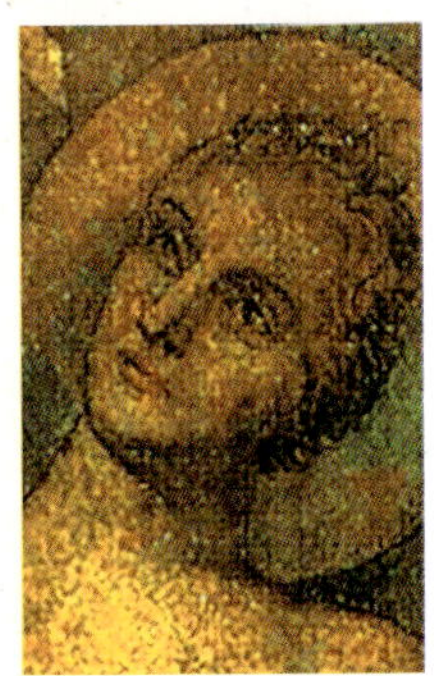

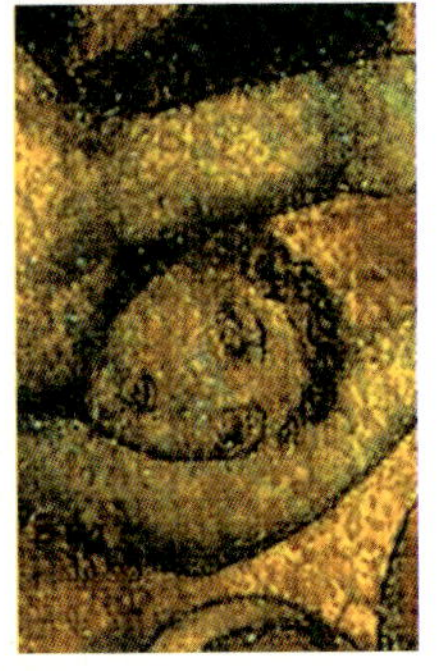

Is not the cry of this child the cry of humanity? So long as eclipses were not known to be the natural consequences of the motion of the moon about the earth, and before it was understood that their occurrence could be predicted with the utmost precision, it was natural that they should have produced a deep impression and been associated with the idea of the end of the world.

The Spiritual Form of Nelson Guiding Leviathan

William Blake, c. 1805-1809
Tempera on canvas, 76.2 x 62.5 cm
Tate Gallery, London

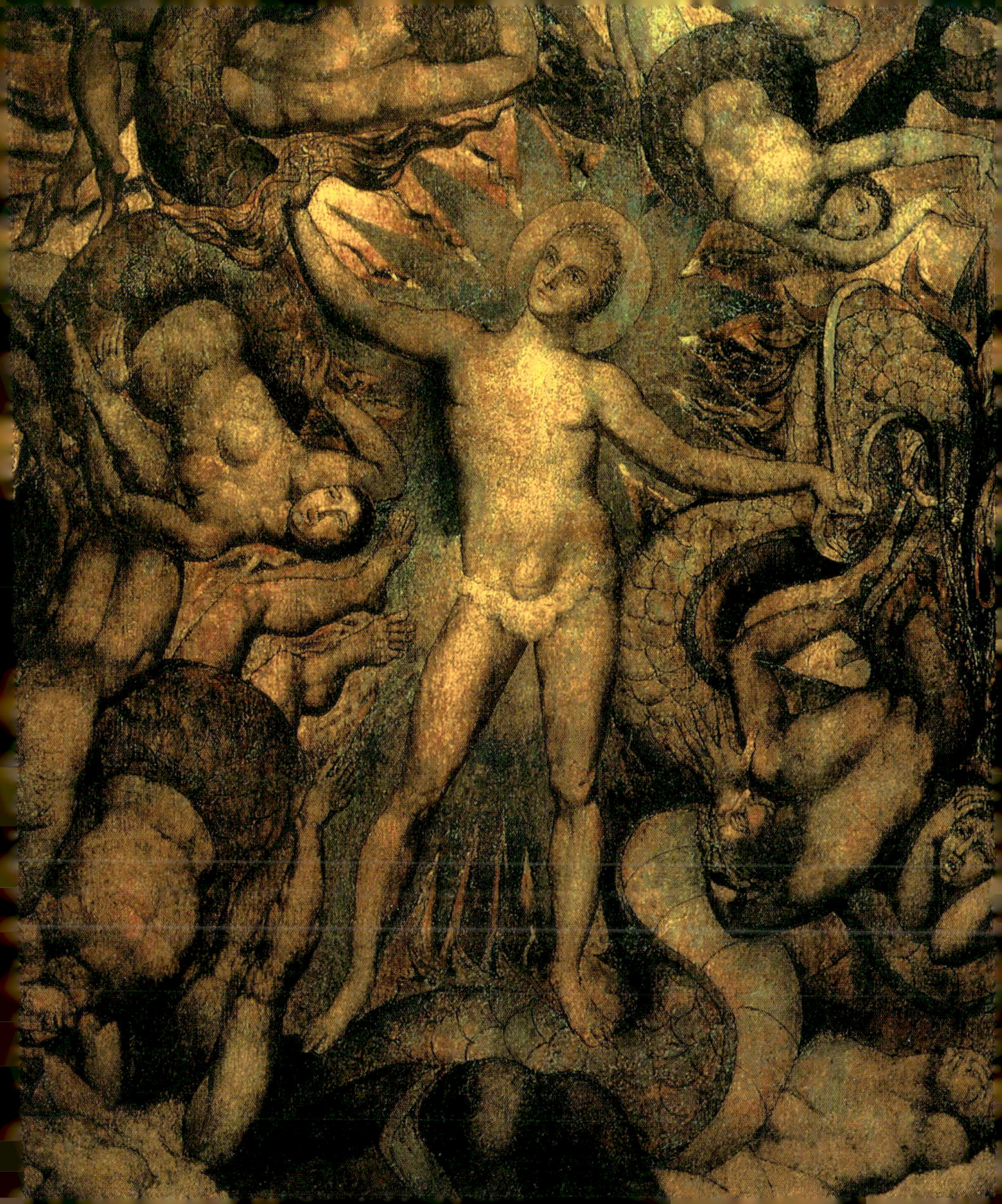

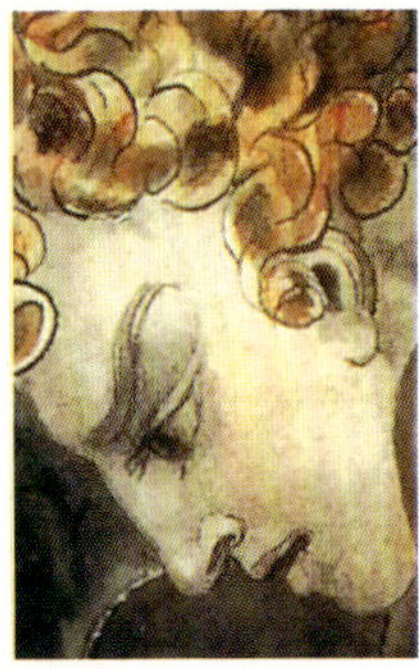

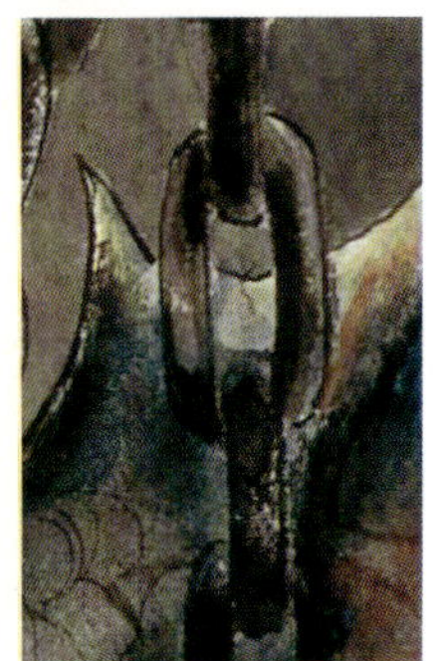

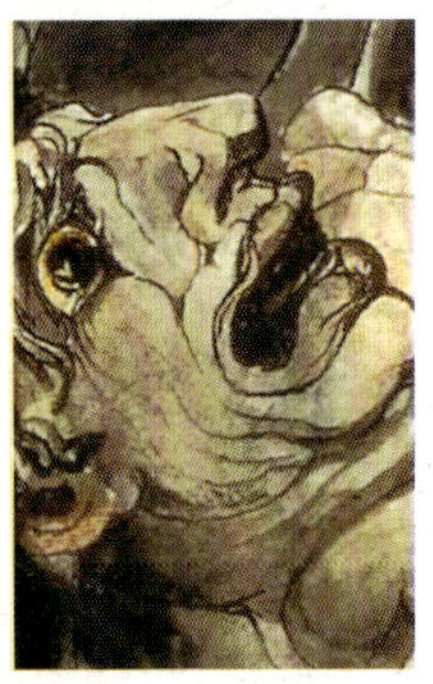

The same is true of other celestial phenomena and notably of the sudden appearance of unknown suns, an event much rarer than an eclipse.

The most celebrated of these appearances was that of 1572. On 9 November of that year, about a month after the massacre of St Bartholomew, a brilliant star of the first magnitude suddenly appeared in the constellation

The Angel Michael Binding Satan ("He Cast Him into the Bottomless Pit, and Shut Him Up")

William Blake, c. 1805
Drawing with watercolours, black ink
and graphite on off-white paper, 35.9 x 32.5 cm
Frogg Art Museum, Harvard University Art Museums

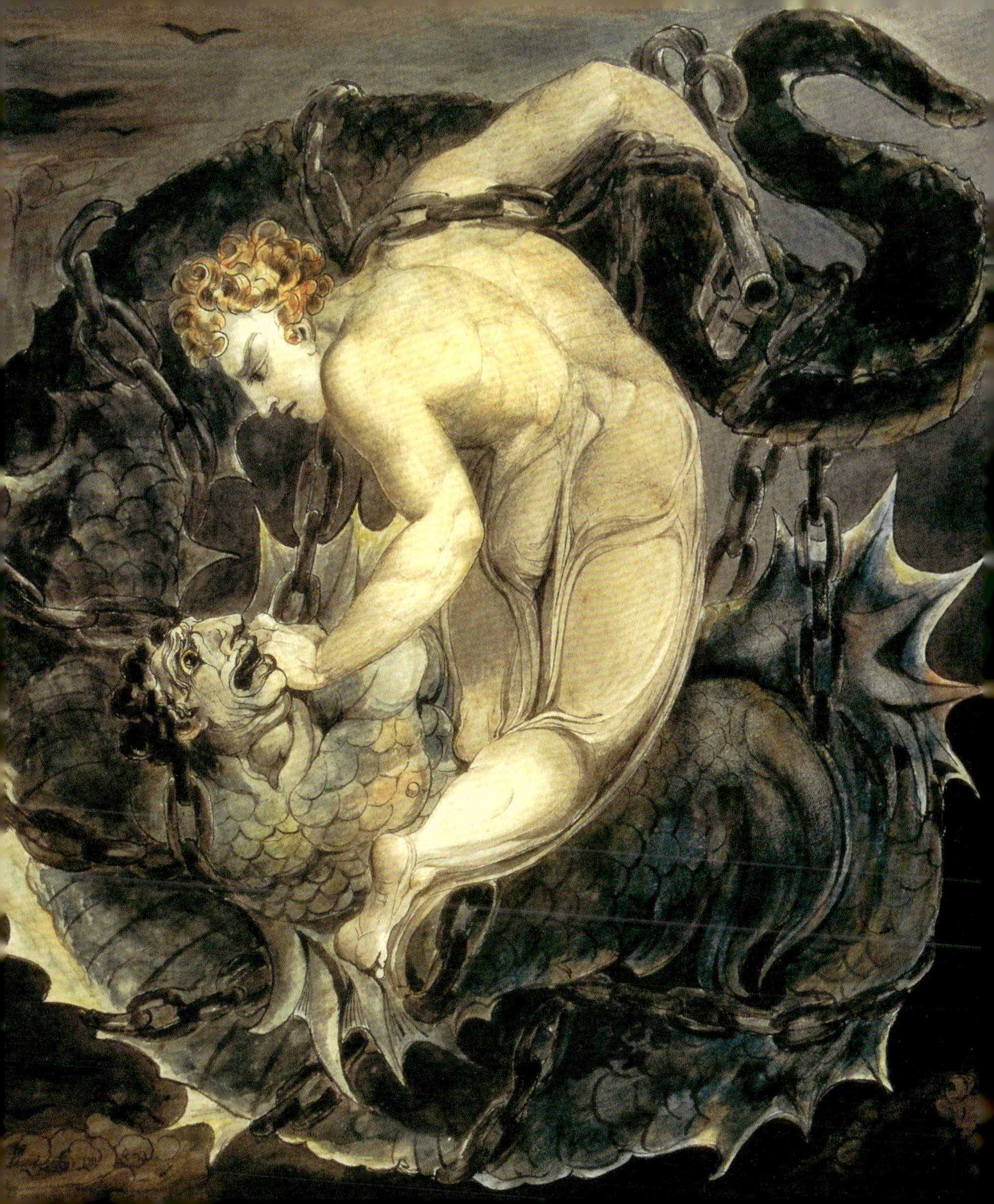

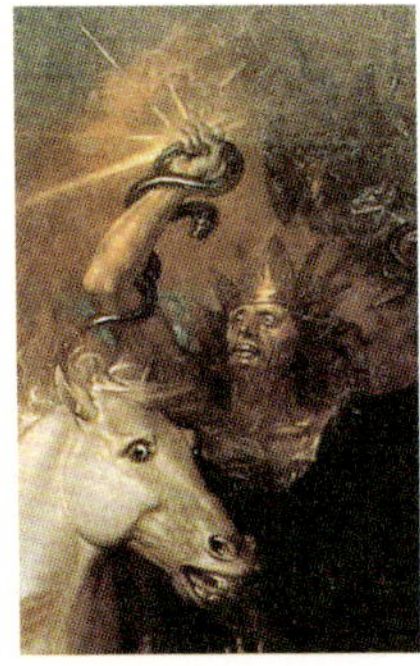

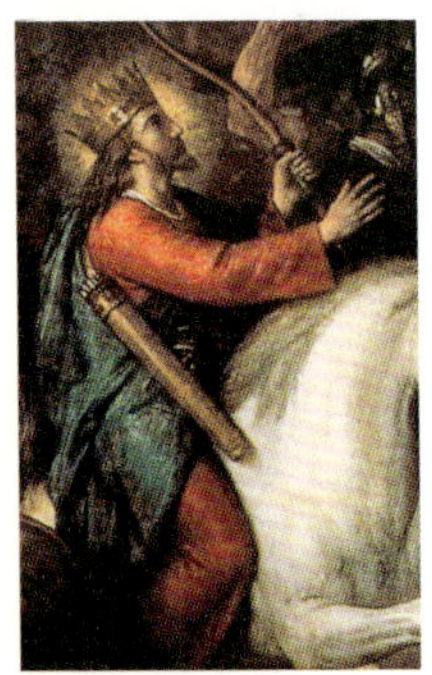

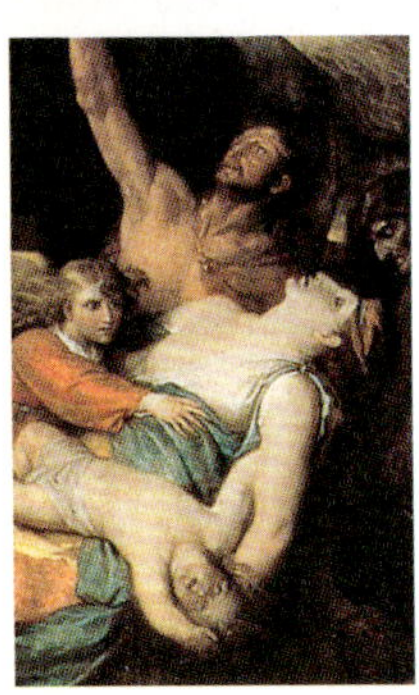

of Cassiopeia. The stupefaction was general, not only on the part of the public, to which it was visible every night in the sky, but also on the part of scientists, who could not explain its appearance. Astrologers found a solution of the enigma in the assertion that it was the star of the Magi, whose reappearance announced the

Death on a Pale Horse

Benjamin West, 1817
Oil on canvas, 447 x 764 cm
Pennsylvania Academy of the Fine Arts, Philadelphia

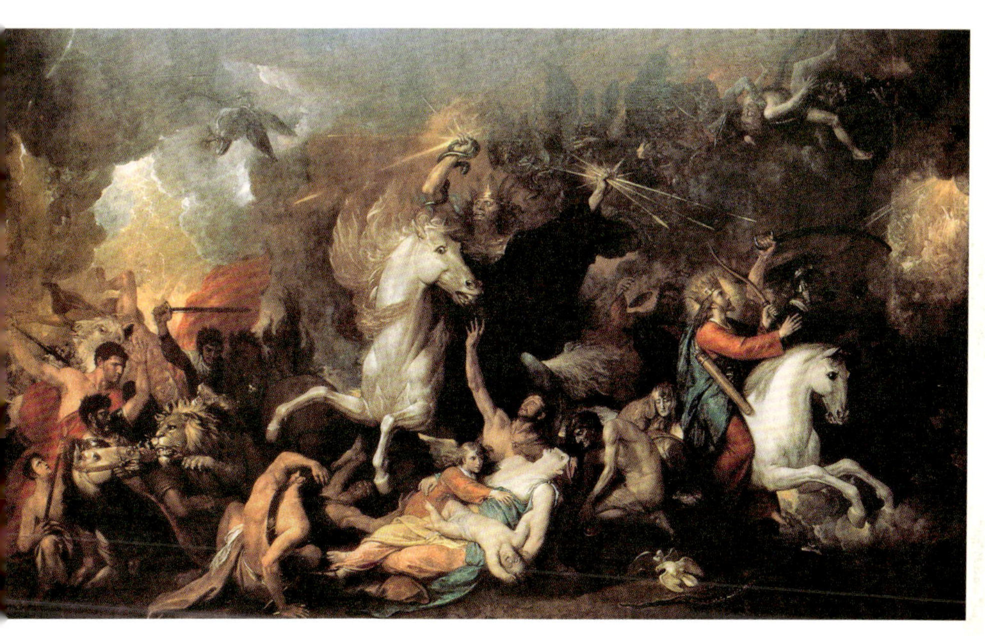

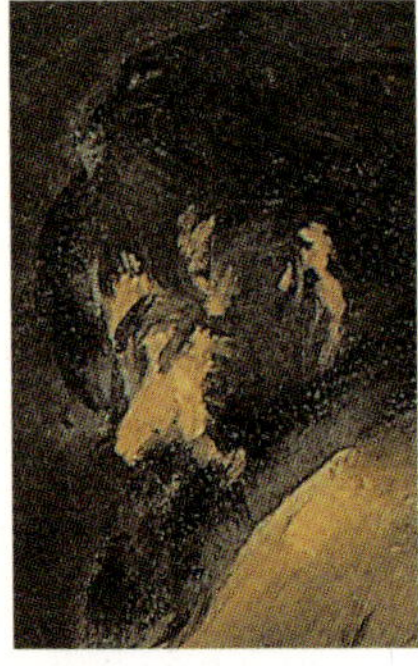

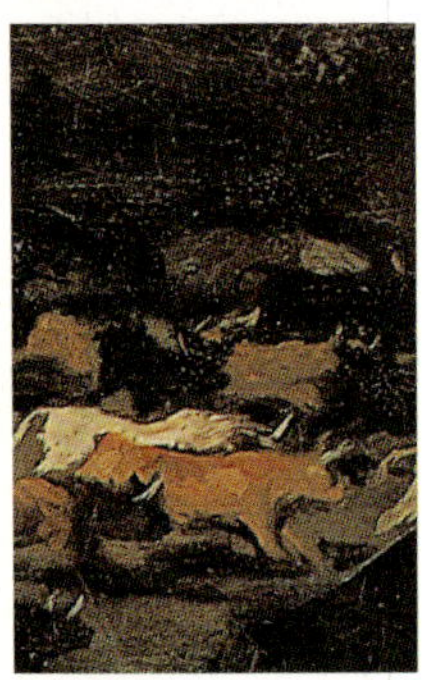

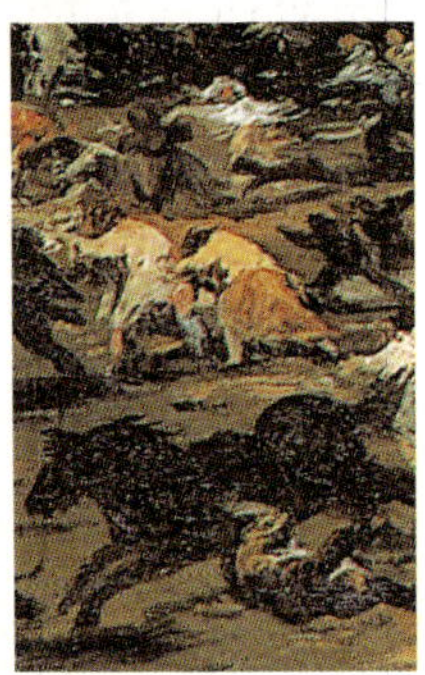

return of the Son of God, the Final Judgement, and the resurrection. This statement made a deep impression upon all classes of society. The star gradually diminished in splendour, and at the end of about eighteen months went out, without having caused any other disaster than that which human folly itself adds to the misery of a none too prosperous planet.

The Colossus

Asensio Juliá (wrongly attributed to Goya), c. 1818-1825
Oil on canvas, 116 x 105 cm
Museo Nacional del Prado, Madrid

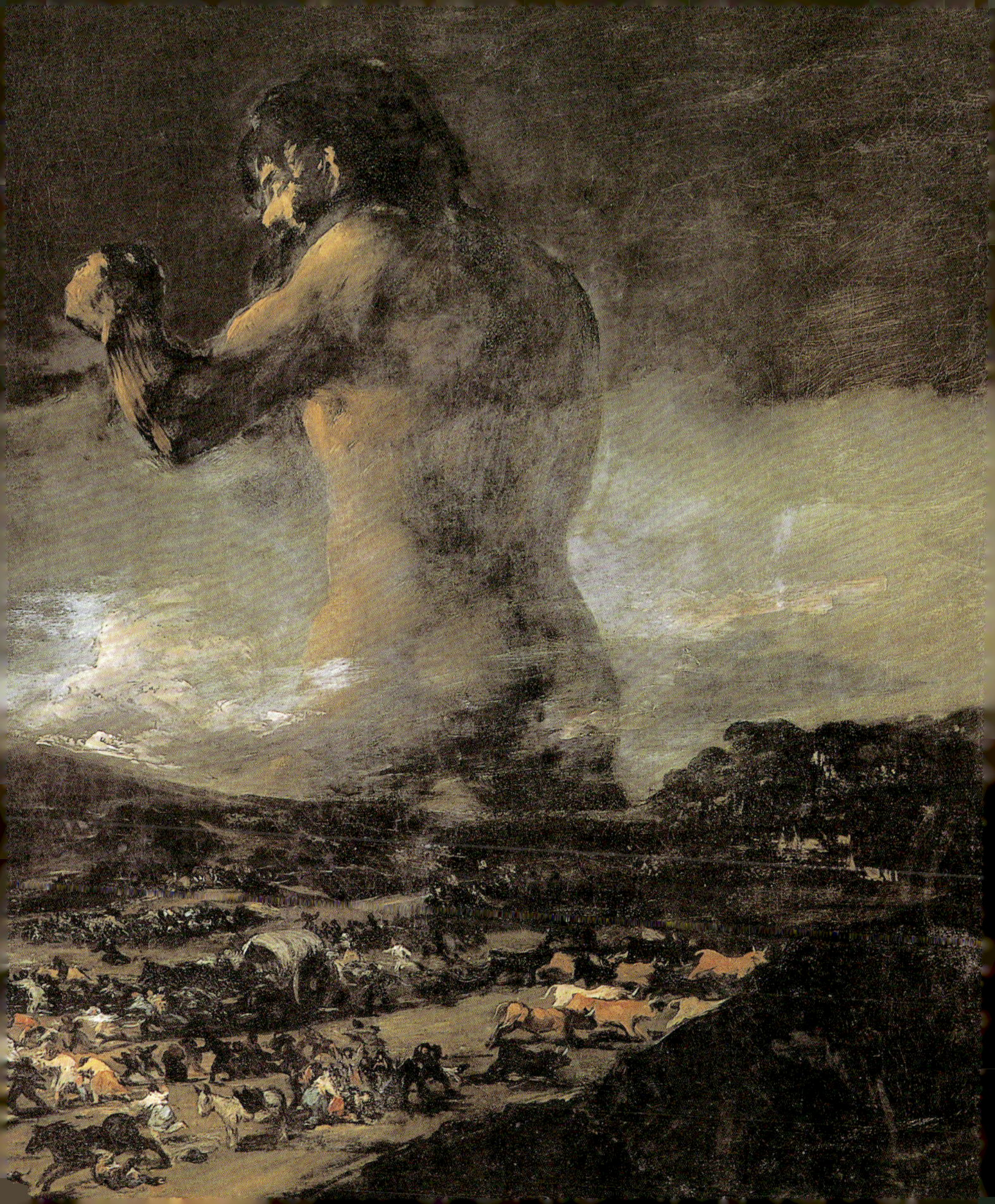

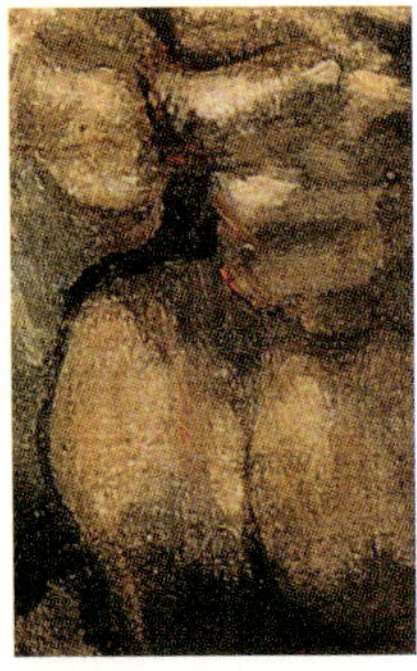

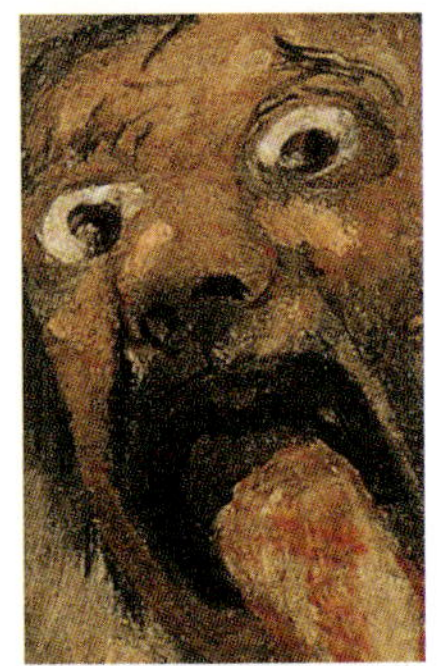

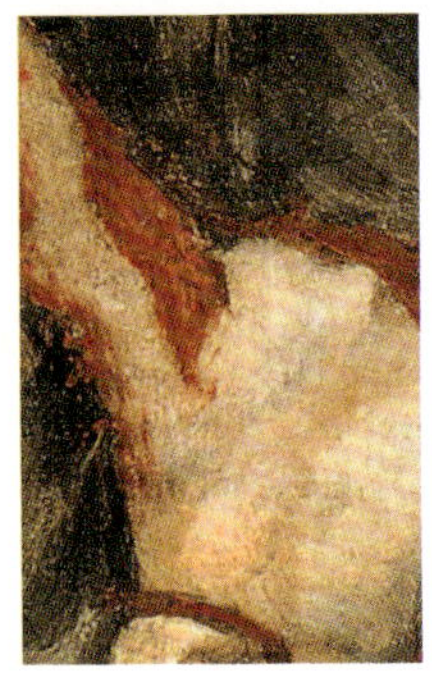

Science records several apparitions of this nature, but the above was the most remarkable. A like agitation has accompanied all the grand phenomena of nature, especially those which have been unforeseen. In the chronicles of the Middle Ages, and even in more recent memoirs, we read of the terror which the aurora borealis, showers of shooting stars and the fall of meteorites,

Francisco Goya, 1820-1823
Oil on canvas, 146 x 83 cm
Museo Nacional del Prado, Madrid

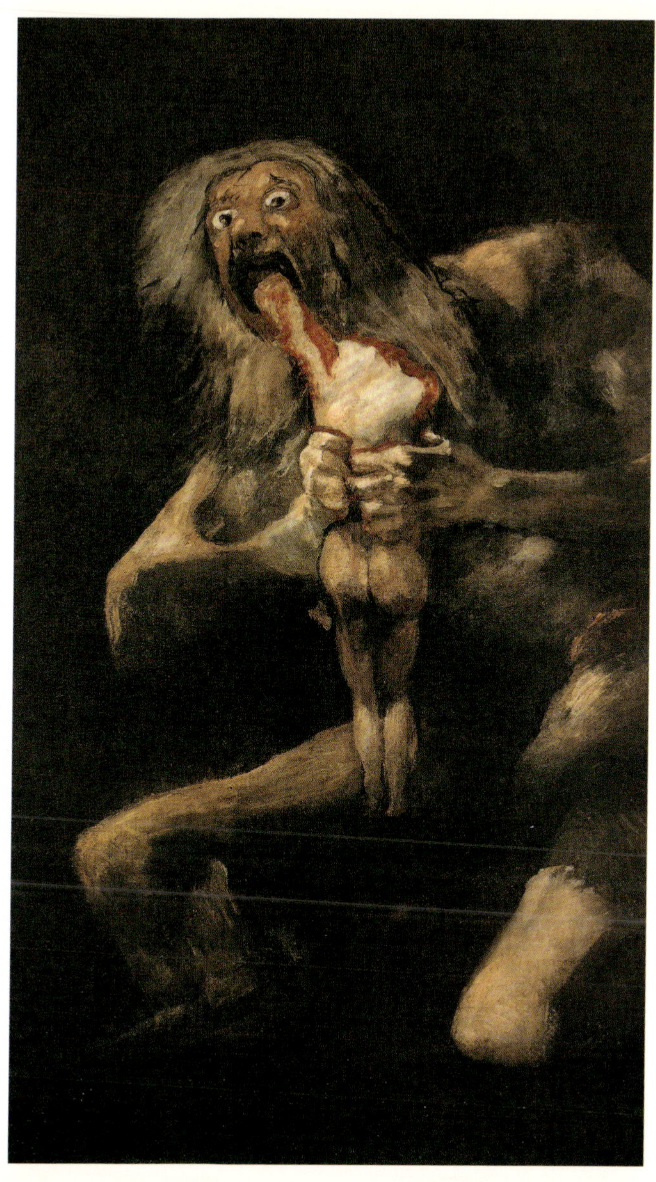

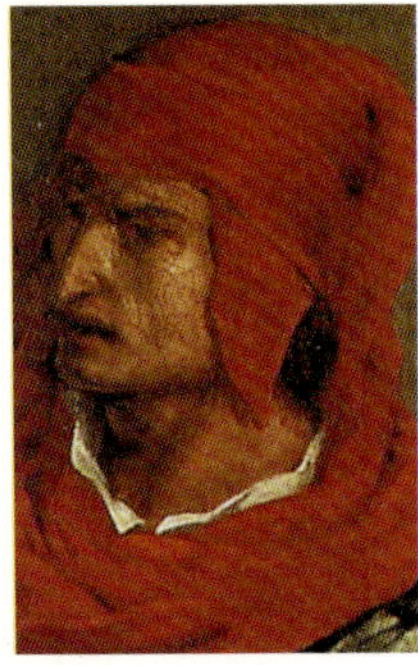

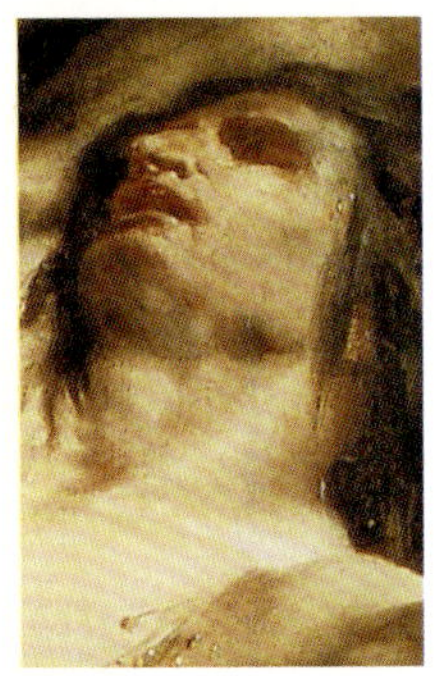

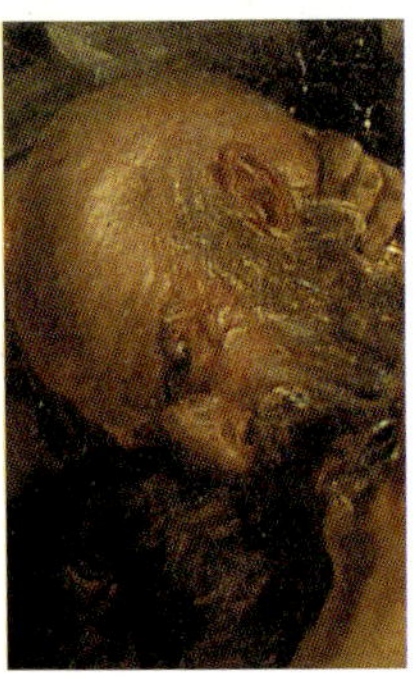

have all produced among the alarmed spectators. During the meteor shower of 27 November 1872, when the sky was filled with more than 40,000 meteorites belonging to the dispersed comet of Biela, women of the lower classes, especially in Nice and Rome, in their excitement, sought information of those whom they thought able

Dante and Virgil in Hell
called The Barque of Dante

Eugène Delacroix, 1822
Oil on canvas, 189 x 241 cm
Musée du Louvre, Paris

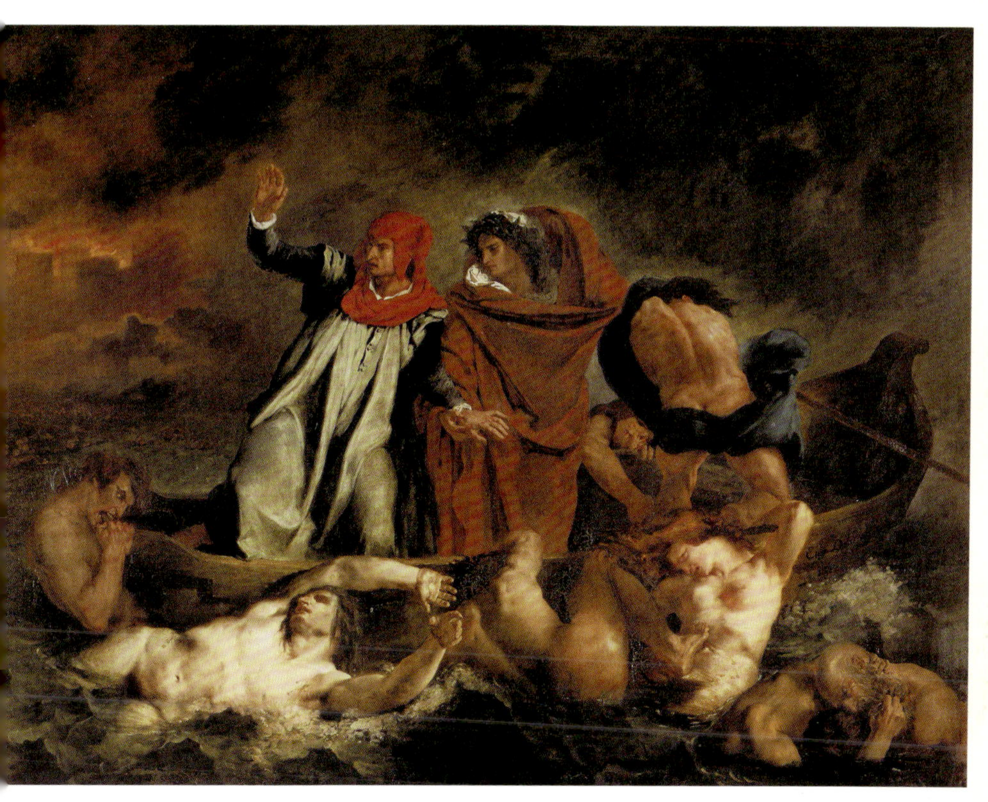

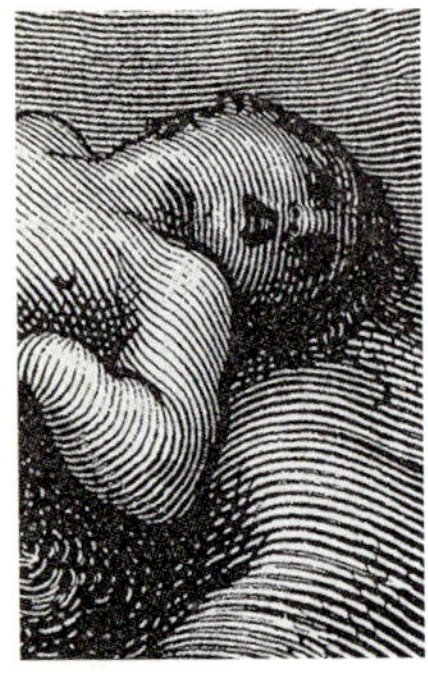

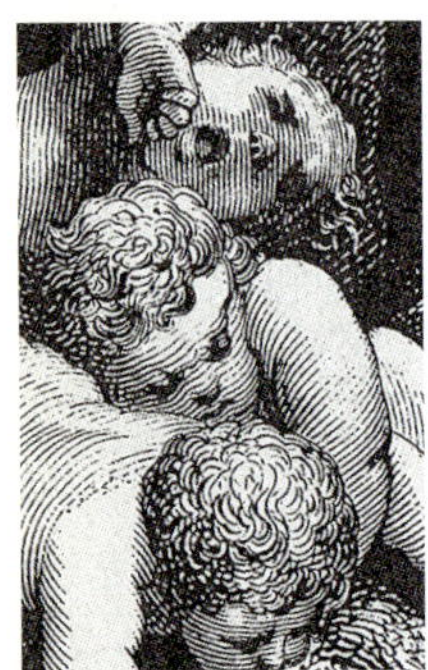

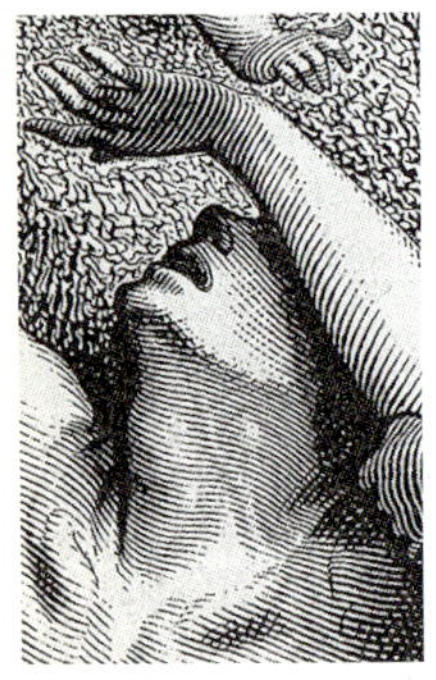

to explain the cause of these celestial fireworks, which they had at once associated with the end of the world and with the fall of the stars, which it was foretold would usher in that last great event.

Earthquakes and volcanic eruptions have sometimes attained such proportions as to lead to the fear that the end of the world was at hand. Imagine the state of mind of the inhabitants of

The Deluge

Gustave Doré, 1866
Illustration from The Holy Bible
with illustrations by Gustave Doré
Engraving
Private collection

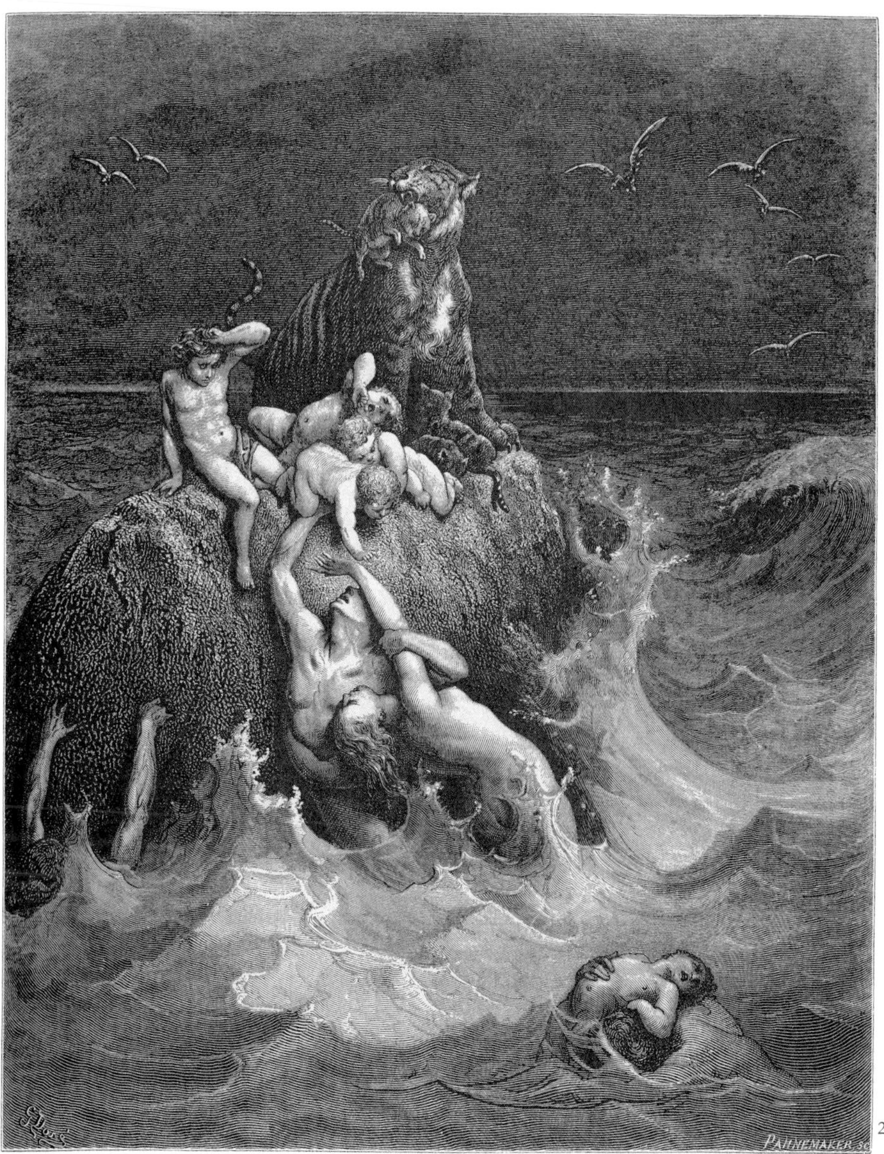

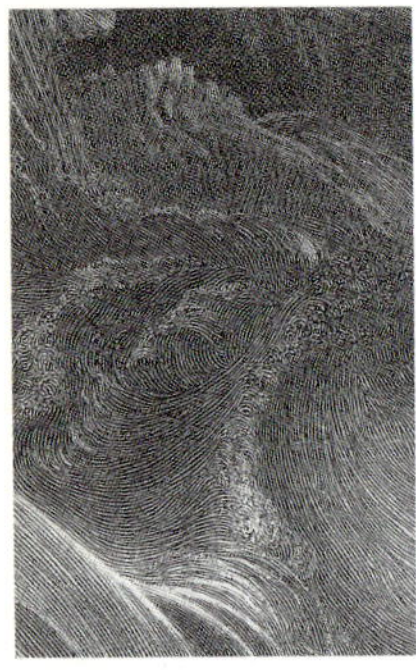

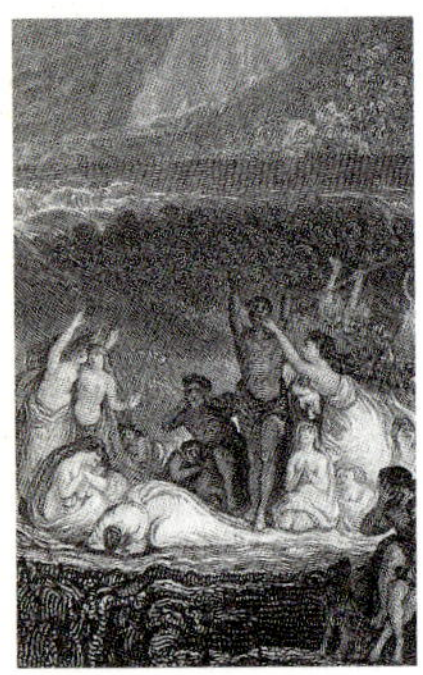

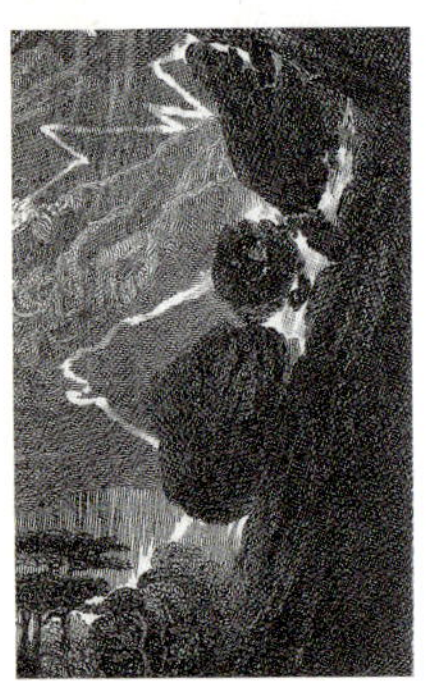

Herculaneum and of Pompeii when the eruption of Vesuvius buried them in showers of ashes! Was this, for them, not the end of the world? Were those who witnessed the more recent eruption of Krakatoa not of the same opinion? Impenetrable darkness lasting eighteen hours, an atmosphere like a furnace, filling the eyes, nose, and ears

The Deluge

———————

William Miller (after John Martin), 1844
From the The Imperial Family Bible
According to the Authorised Version
Engraving
Private collection

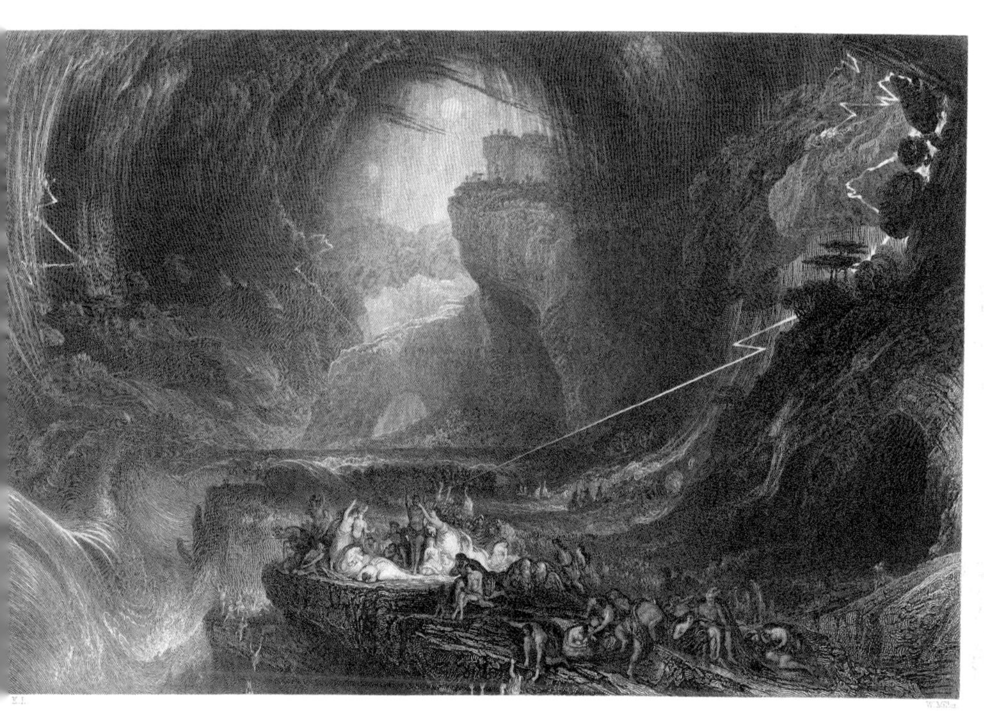

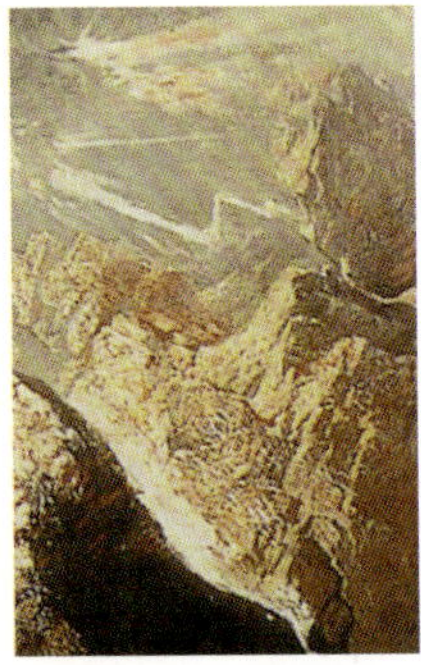

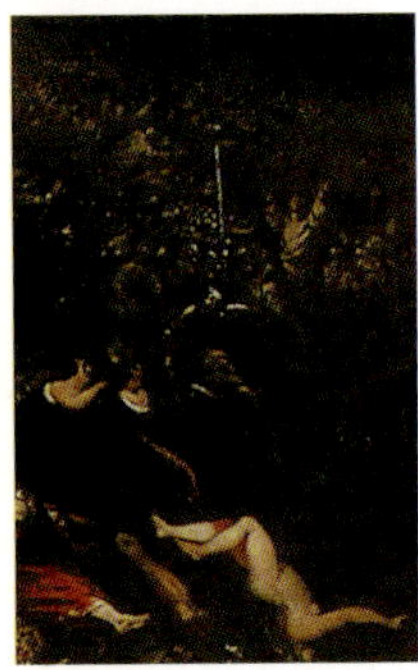

with ashes, the deep and incessant cannonade of the volcano, the falling of pumice stones from the black sky, the terrible scene illuminated only at intervals by the lurid lightning or the fire-balls on the spars and rigging of vessels, the thunder echoing from cloud and sea with an infernal musketry, and the shower of ashes turning into a

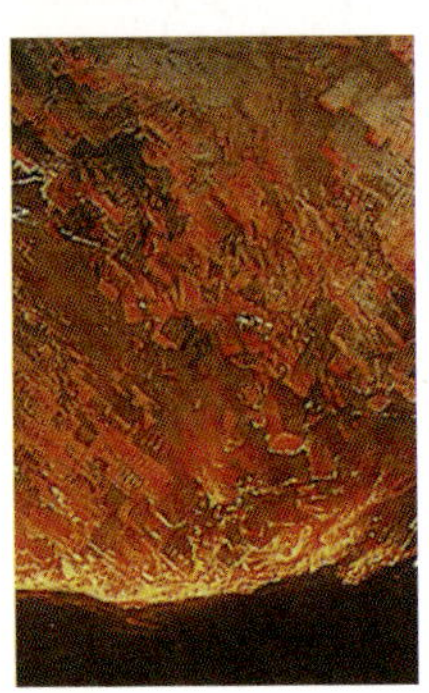

John Martin, 1851-1853
Oil on canvas, 196.5 x 303.2 cm
Tate Gallery, London

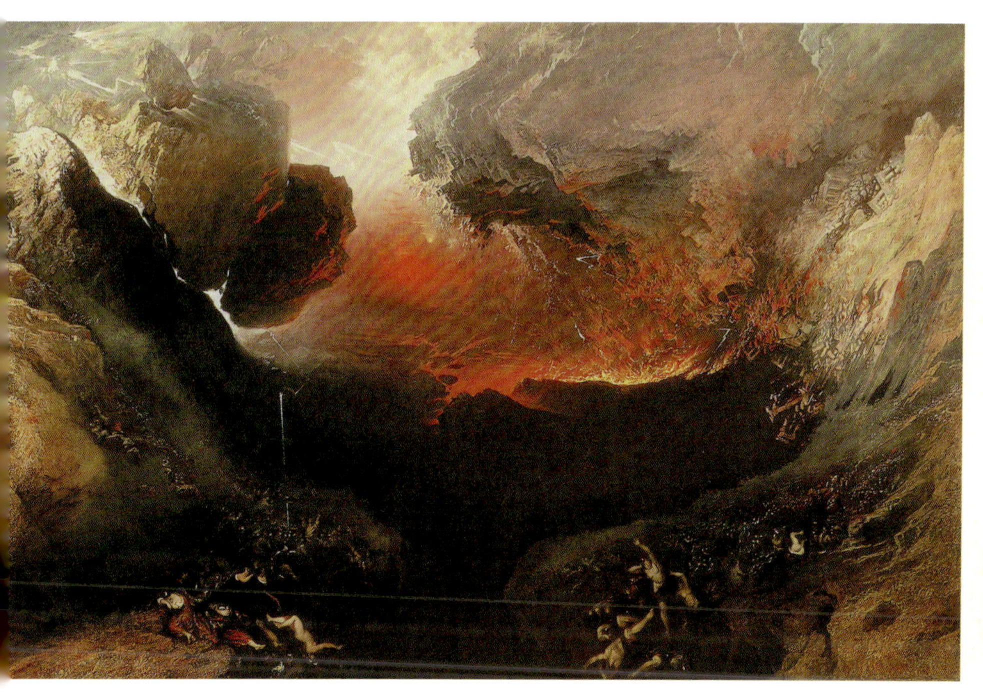

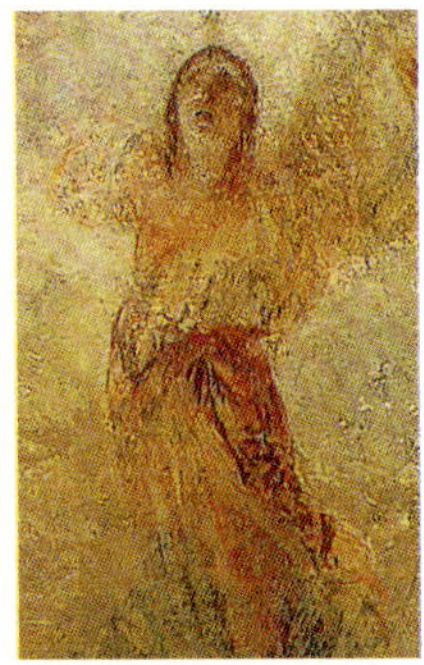

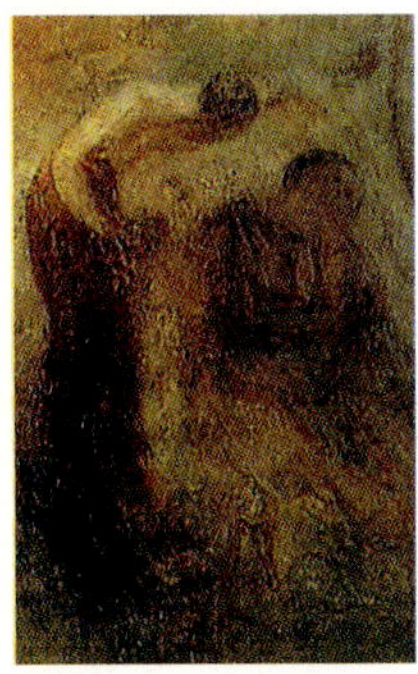

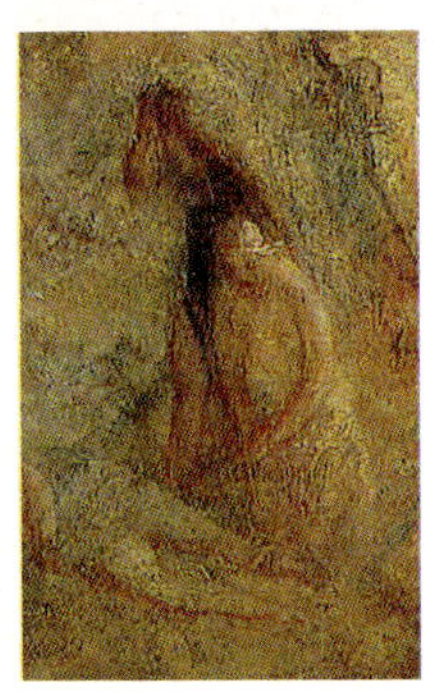

deluge of mud. Thus was the experience of the passengers of a Java vessel during the night of eighteen hours, from 26 to 28 August 1883, when a portion of the island of Krakatoa was hurled into the air, and the sea, after having first retreated, swept upon the shore, with waves over a hundred feet high, to a distance of up to six miles inland over

The Angel Standing in the Sun

Joseph Mallord William Turner, 1846
Oil on canvas, 78.7 x 78.7 cm
The Clore Collection, Tate Gallery, London

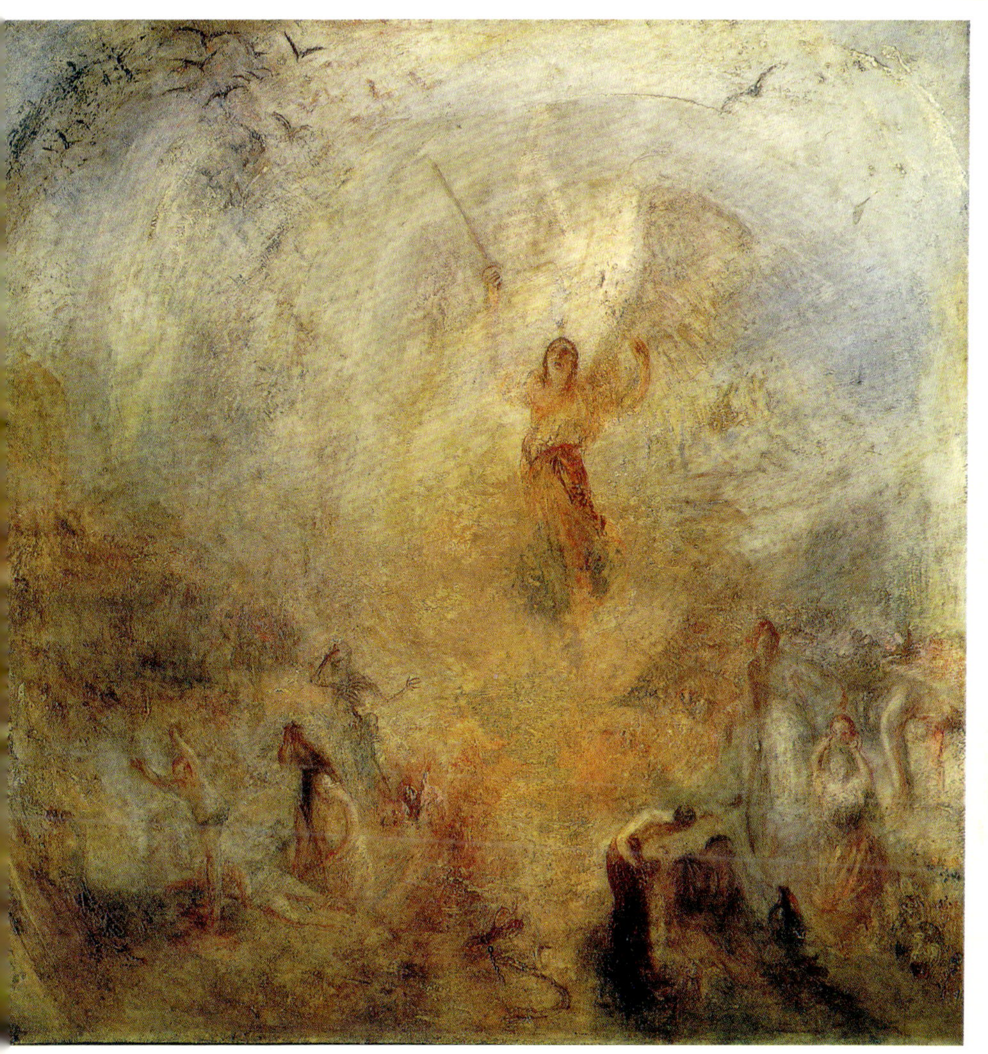

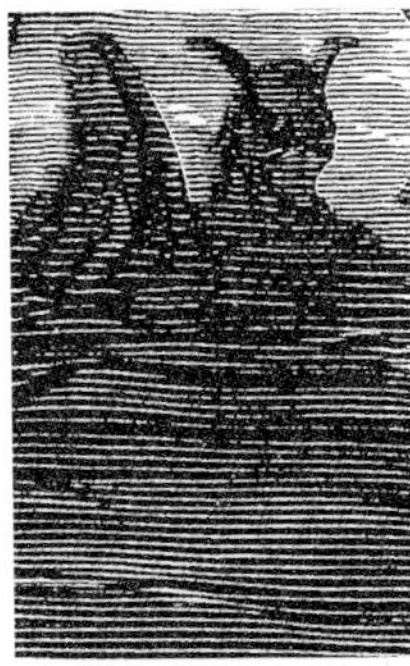

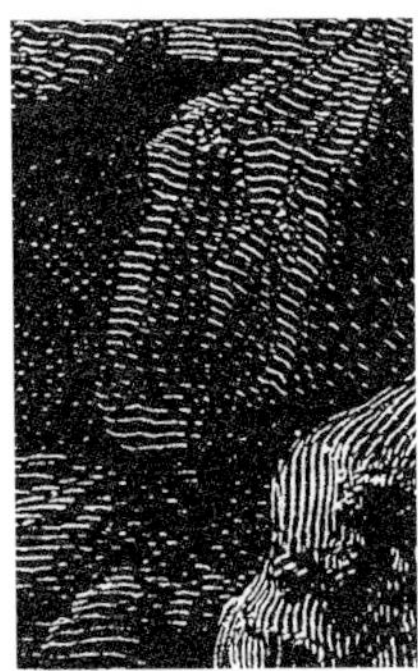

a coastline over 300 miles long, and in the reflux carried away with it the four cities, Tjiringin, Mérak, Telok-Bétong, and Anjer, and the entire population of the region, more than 40,000 souls. For a long time the progress of vessels was hindered by floating bodies inextricably interlaced; and weeks later human fingers, with their nails,

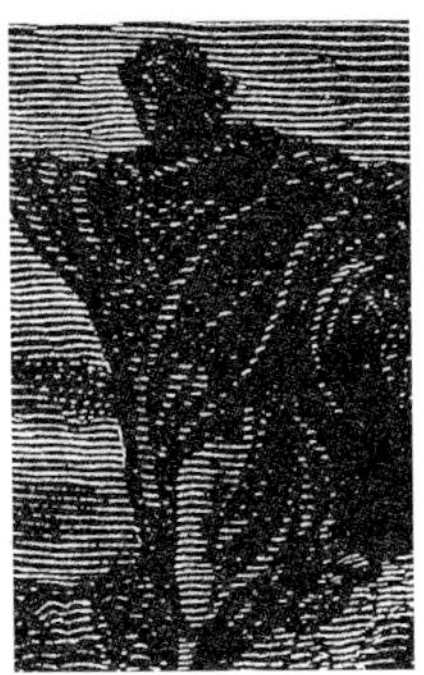

Gustave Doré, 1866
Illustration from The Holy Bible
with Illustrations by Gustave Doré
Engraving
Private collection

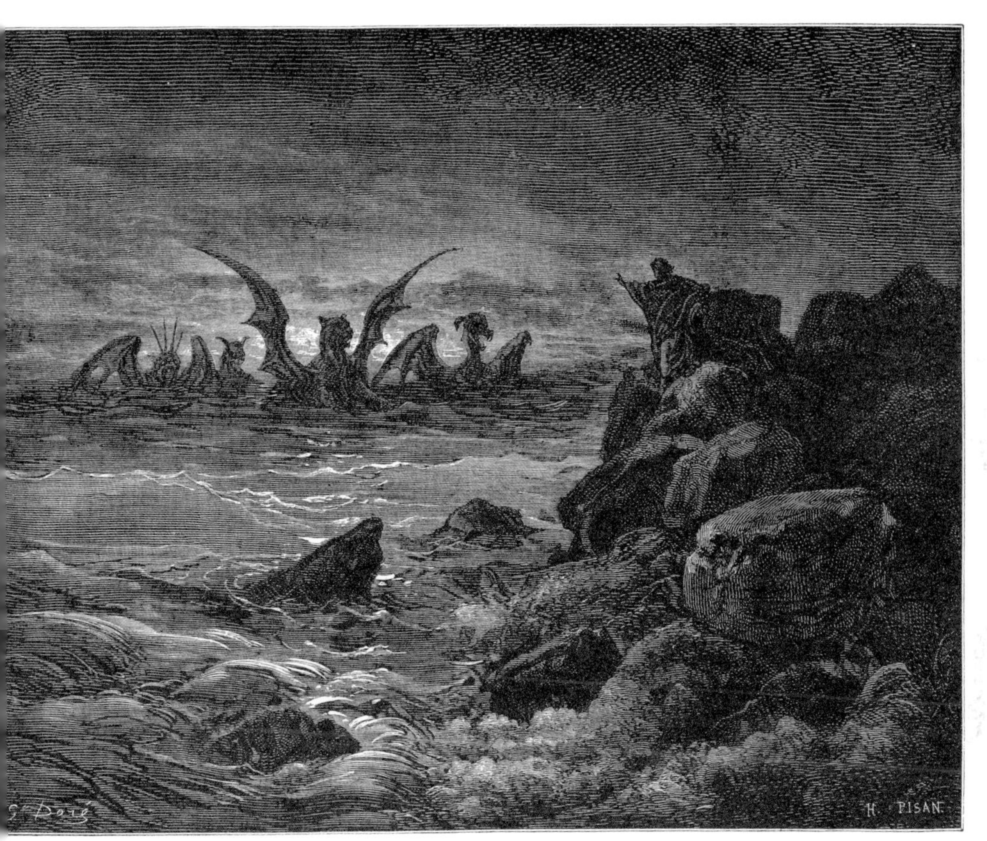

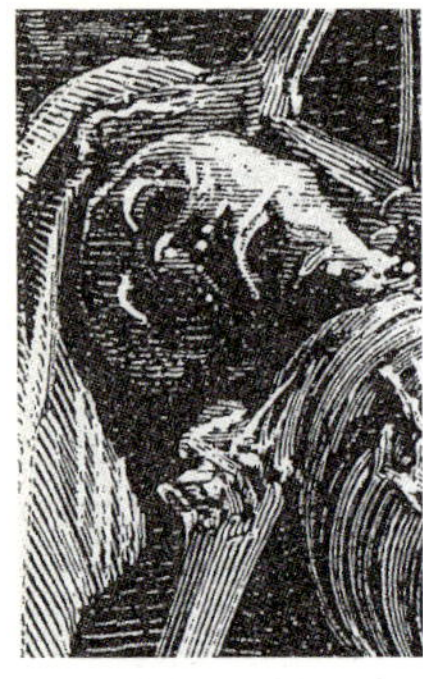

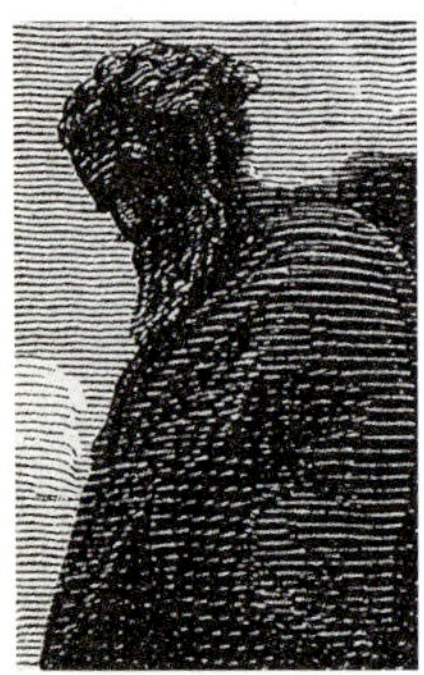

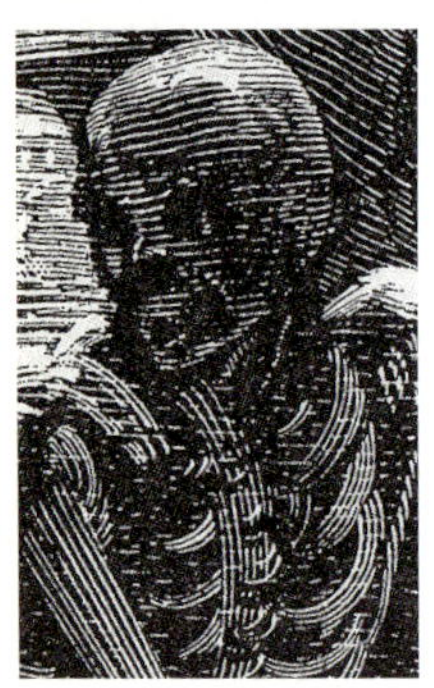

and fragments of scalps, with their hair, were found in the stomachs of fishes.

Those who escaped, or who saw the catastrophe from some vessel, and lived to welcome again the light of day, which had seemed forever extinguished, relate in terror with what resignation they expected the end of the world,

The Vision of the Valley of Dry Bones

Gustave Doré, 1866
Illustration from The Holy Bible
with illustrations by Gustave Doré
Engraving
Private collection

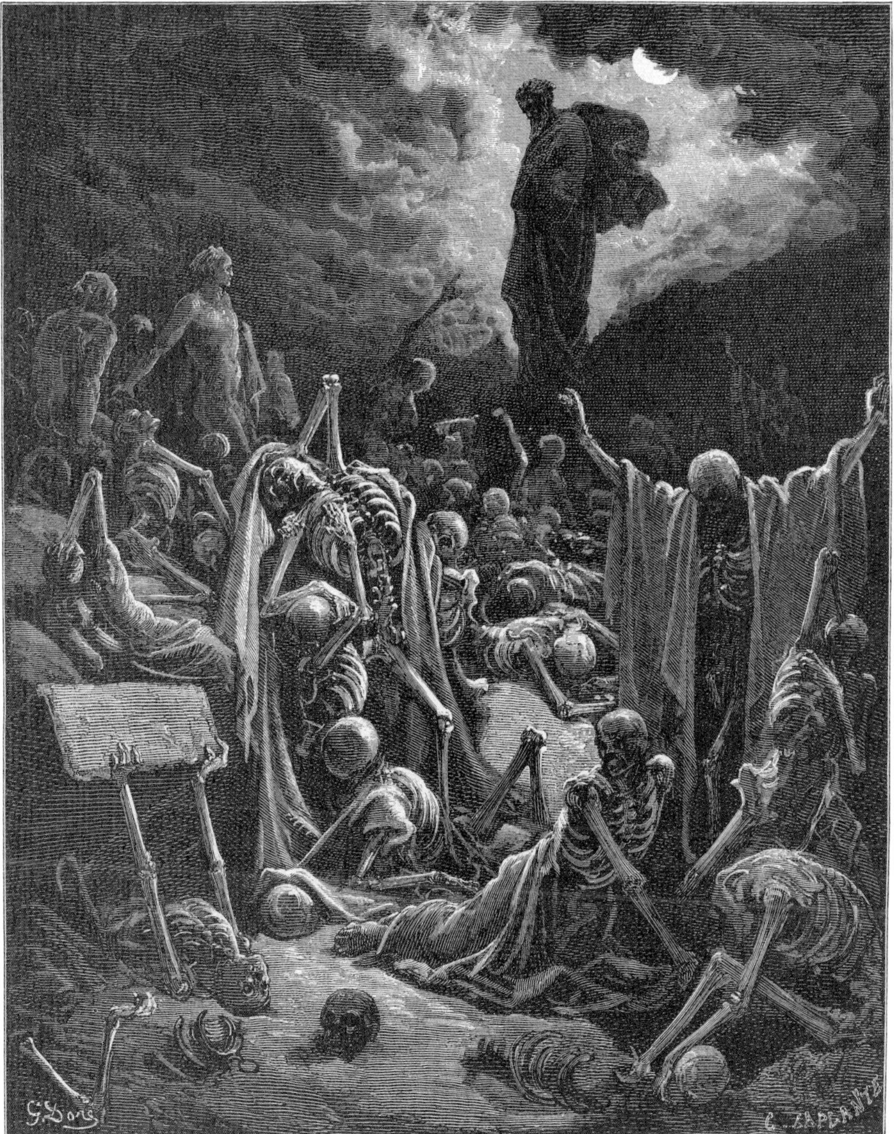
G. Doré
C. LAPLANTE

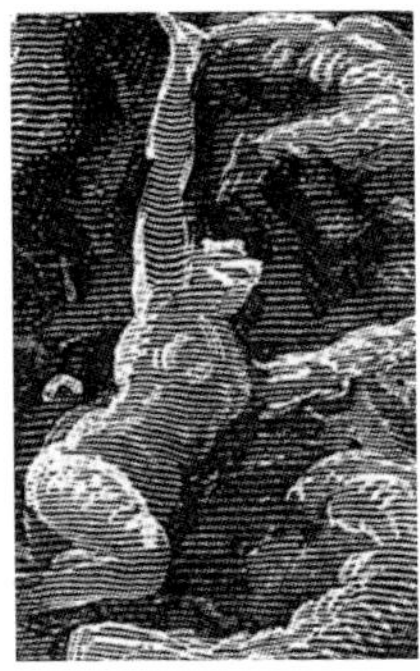

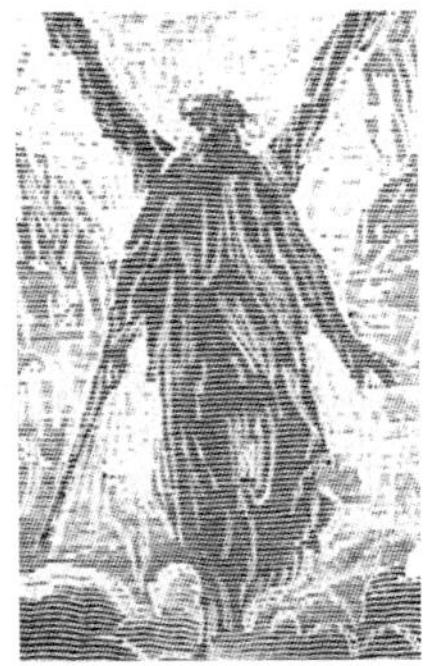

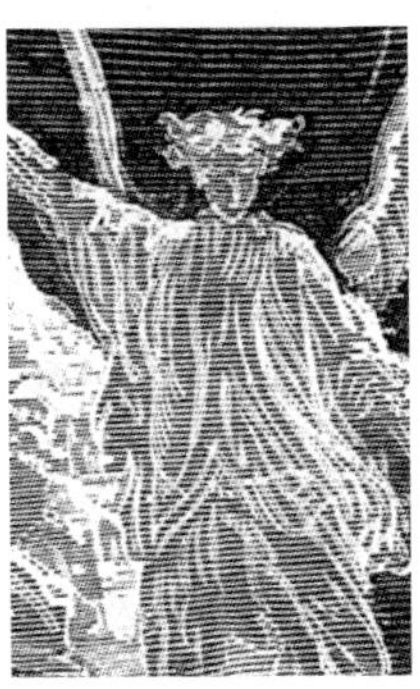

persuaded that its very foundations were giving way and that the knell of a universal doom had sounded. One eye-witness assures us that he would not again pass through such an experience for all the wealth that could be imagined. The sun was extinguished and death seemed to reign sovereign over nature. This eruption, moreover,

The Last Judgement

Gustave Doré, 1866
Illustration from The Holy Bible
with illustrations by Gustave Doré
Engraving
Private collection

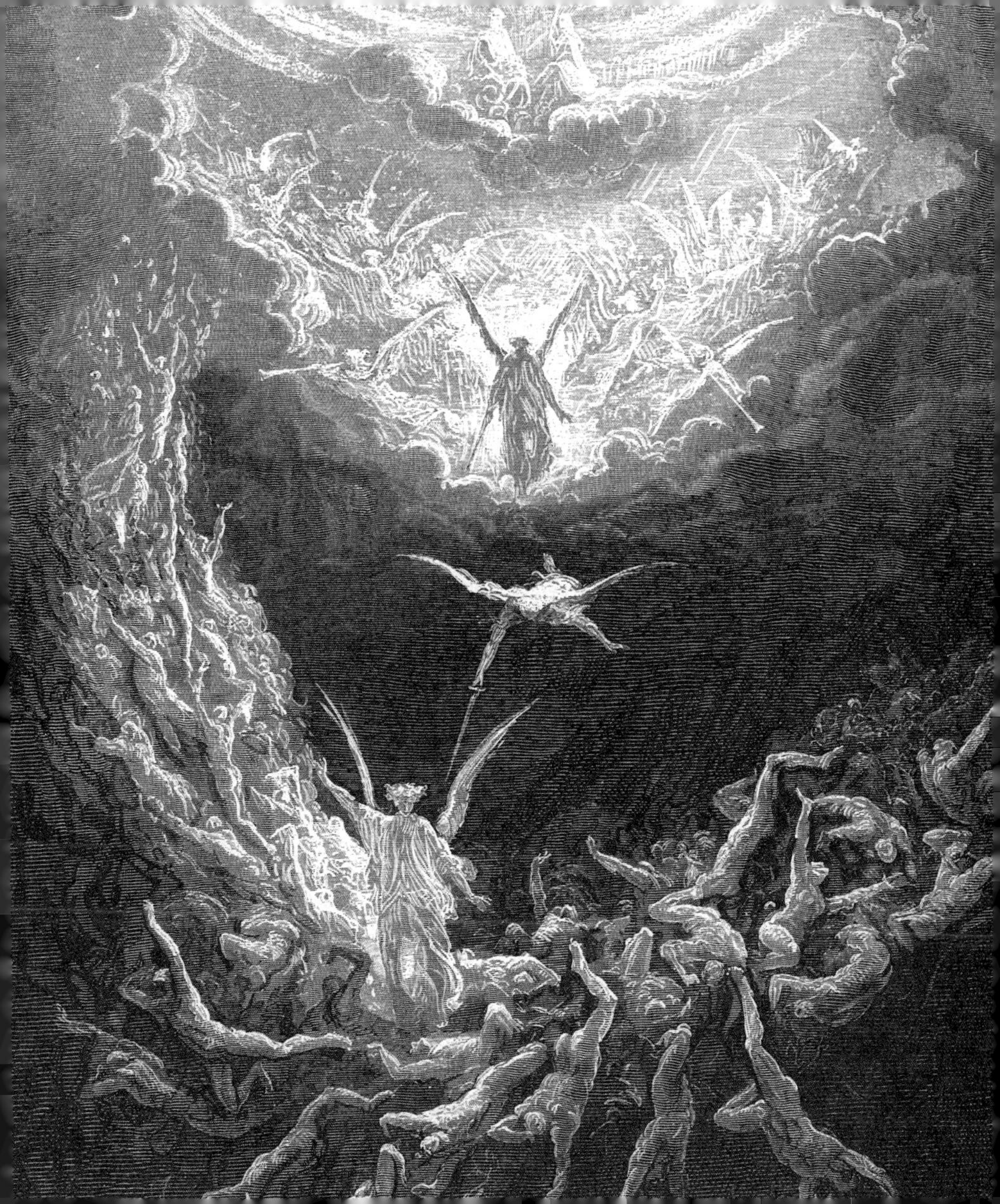

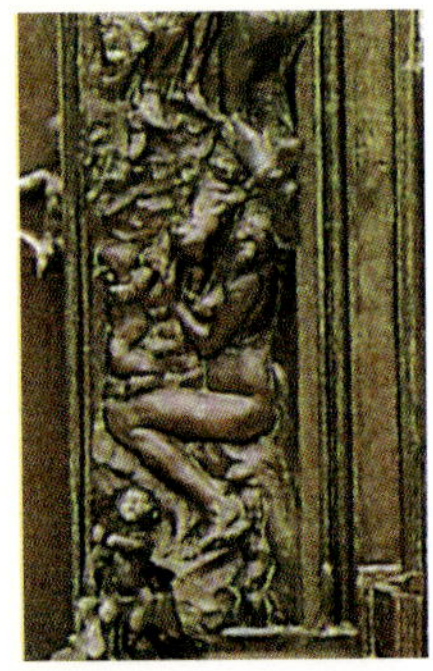

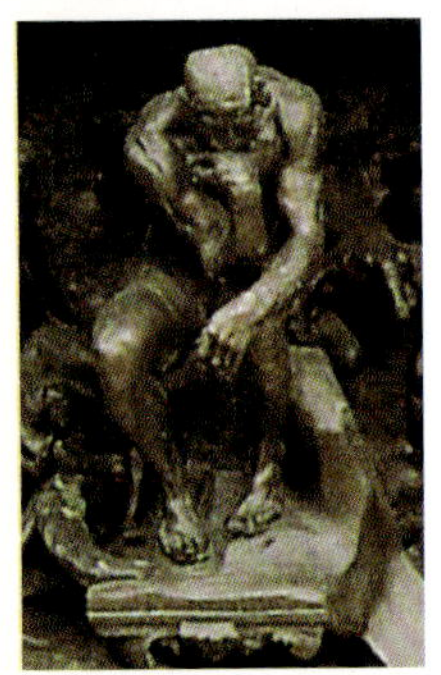

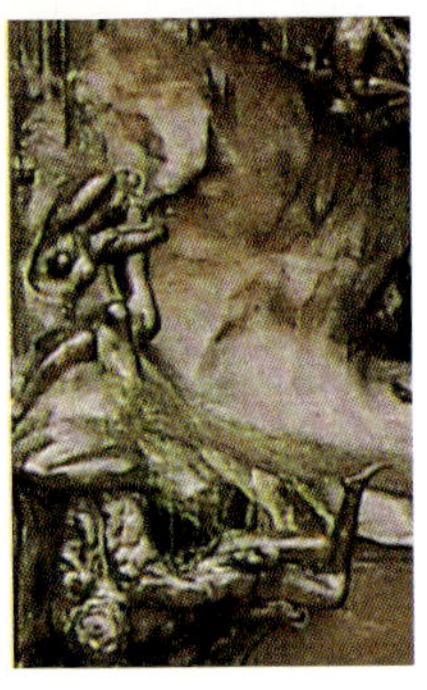

was of such terrific violence that it was heard through the earth at the antipodes; the resulting ash cloud reached an altitude of over 65,000 feet, circling the entire globe in 35 hours (the barometer fell four millimetres in Paris even), and left a fine dust in the upper layers of the atmosphere for more than a year which,

The Gates of Hell

Auguste Rodin, 1880-1917
Bronze, 635 x 400 x 85 cm
Musée Rodin, Paris

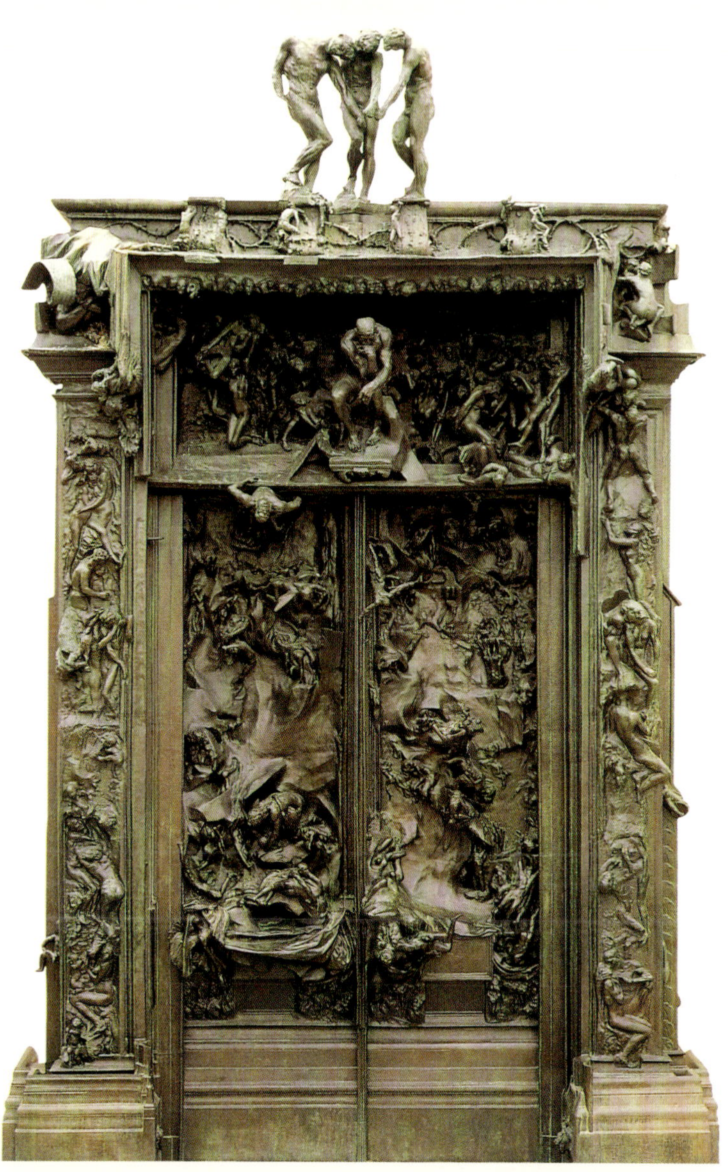

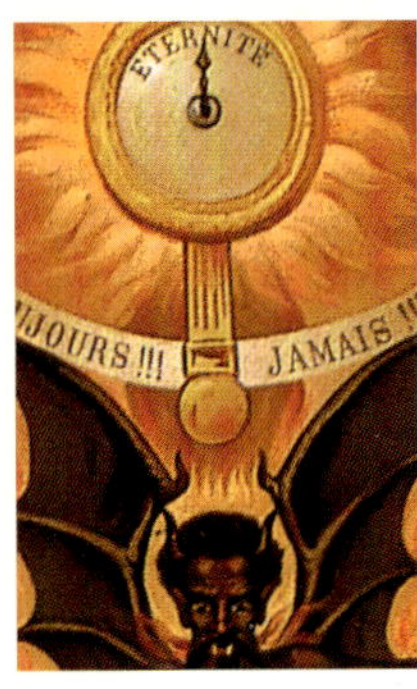

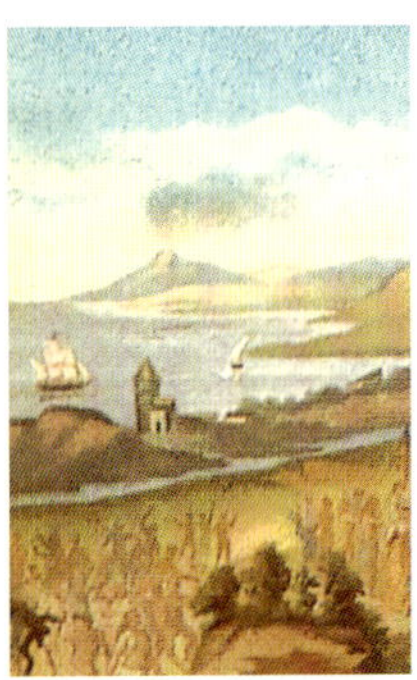

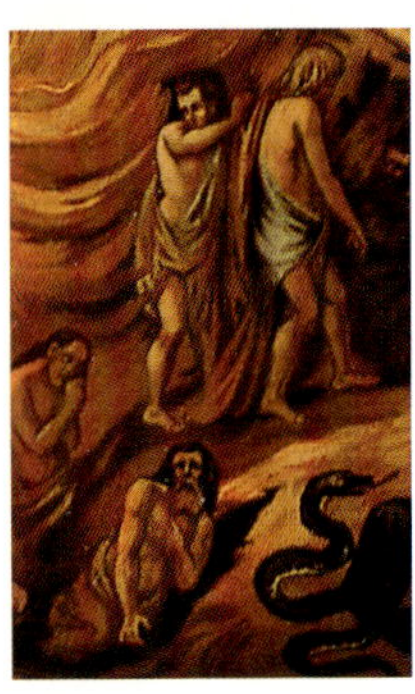

illumined by the sun, gave rise to those magnificent twilight displays admired so much throughout the world.

These are formidable disturbances, partial ends of the world. Certain earthquakes deserve citation with these terrible volcanic eruptions, as their consequences have been so disastrous. In the

Hell and the Seven Deadly Sins

Published by La Bonne Presse, end of 19th century
Private collection

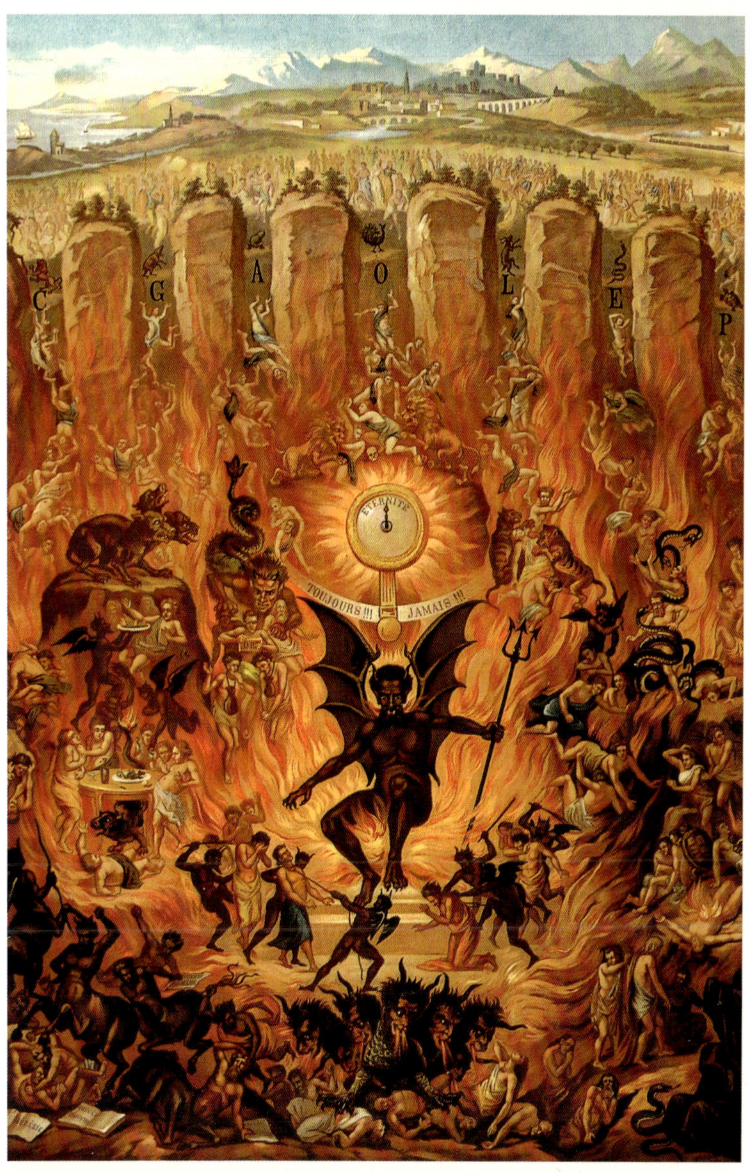
C
G
A
O
L
E
P
ÉTERNITÉ
TOUJOURS !!!
JAMAIS !!!

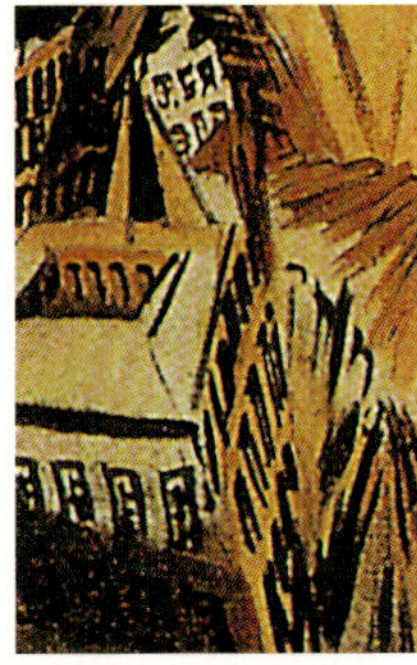

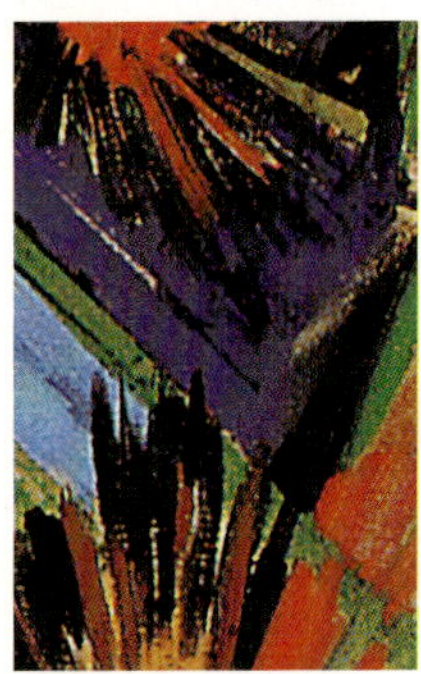

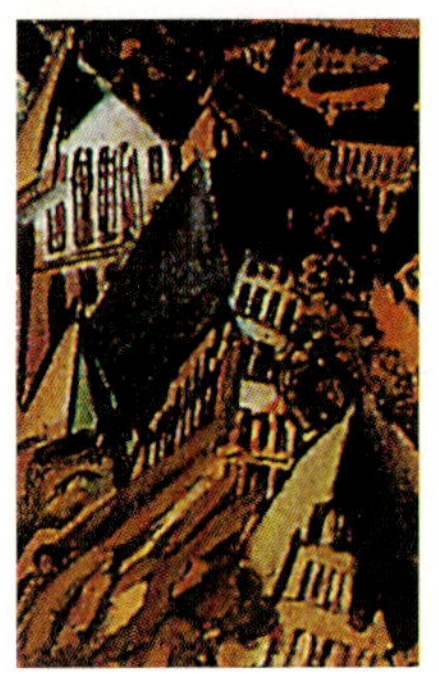

earthquake of Lisbon, 1 November 1755, 30,000 people perished; the shock was felt over an area four times as large as that of Europe. When Lima was destroyed, on 28 October 1724, the sea rose 88 feet above its ordinary level, rushed upon the city, and erased it so completely that not a single house was left. Vessels were found in the fields

Apocalyptic City

Ludwig Meidner, 1913
Oil on canvas, 79 x 119 cm
Landesmuseum für Kunst und Kulturgeschichte, Münster

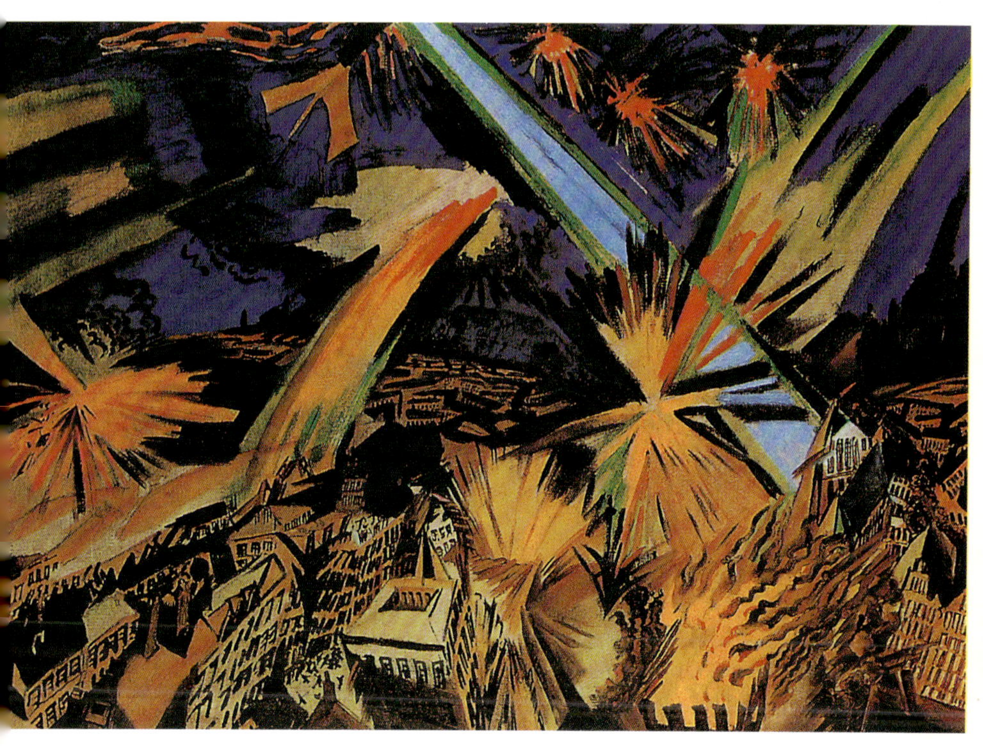

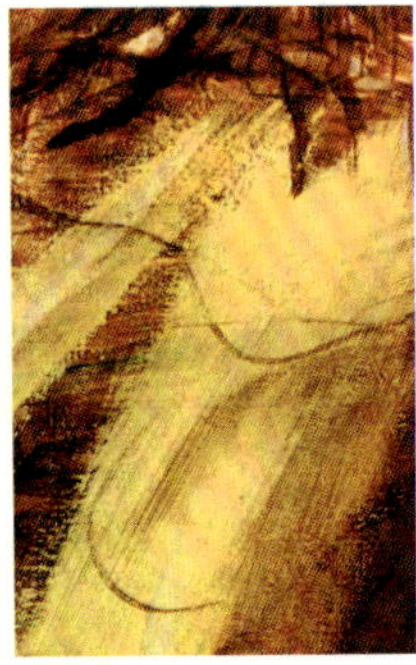

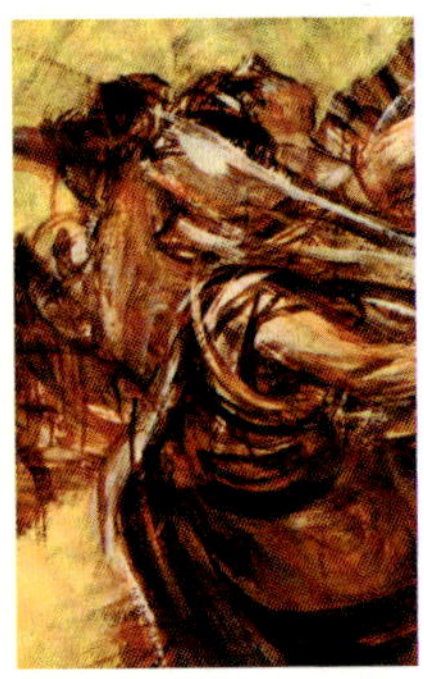

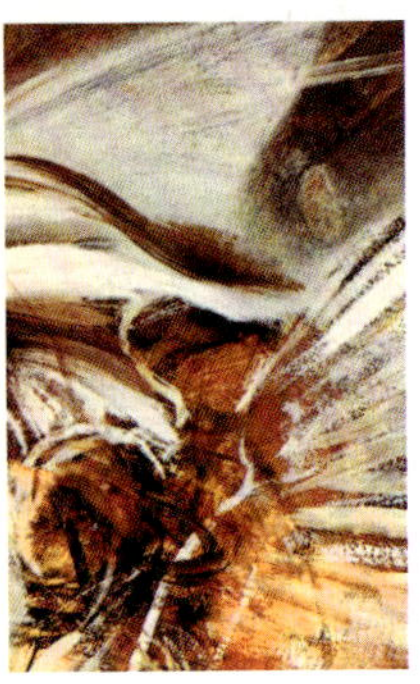

several miles from the shore. On 10 December 1869, inhabitants of the city of Onlah, in Asia Minor, alarmed by subterranean noises and a first violent trembling of the earth, took refuge on a neighbouring hilltop, whence, to their stupefaction, they saw several crevasses open in the city which within a few moments entirely disappeared in the

Angel

———

Giovanni Boldini, 1924
Oil on canvas, 82 x 100 cm
Collezione Boldini, Pistoia

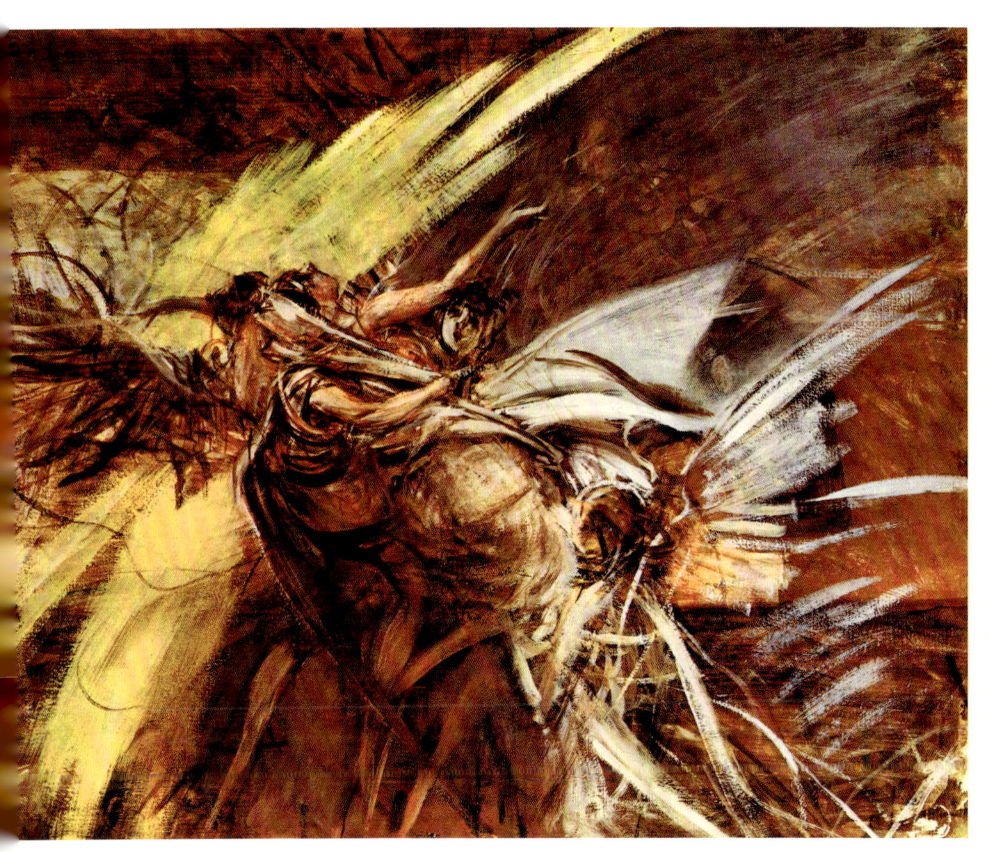

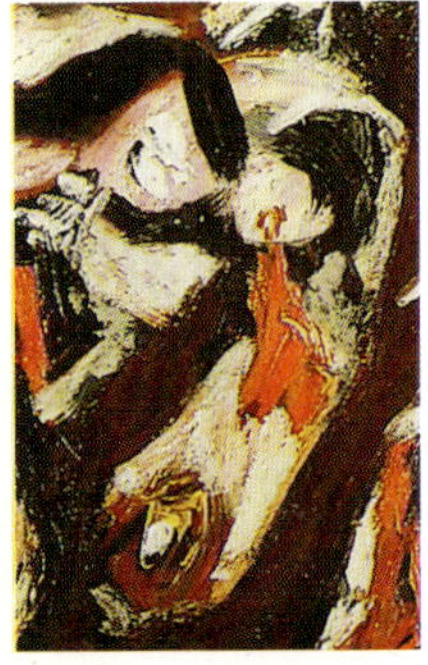

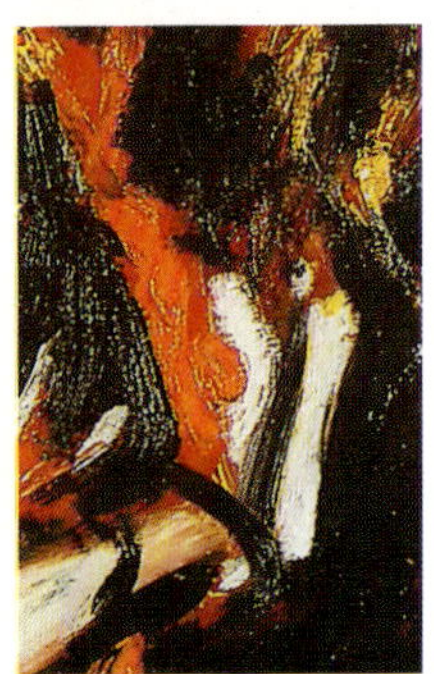

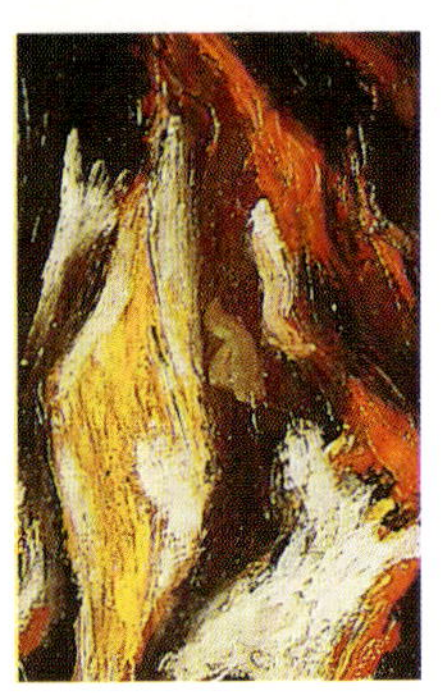

bowels of the earth. We have direct evidence that under circumstances far less dramatic, as for example on the occasion of the earthquake in Nice, 23 February 1887, the idea of the end of the world was the very first to come to mind.

The history of the earth could offer us a remarkable number of similar tragedies, partial cataclysms and threats of final destruction.

Jackson Pollock, 1934-1938
Oil on canvas mounted on fiberboard, 51.1 x 76.2 cm
The Museum of Modern Art, New York

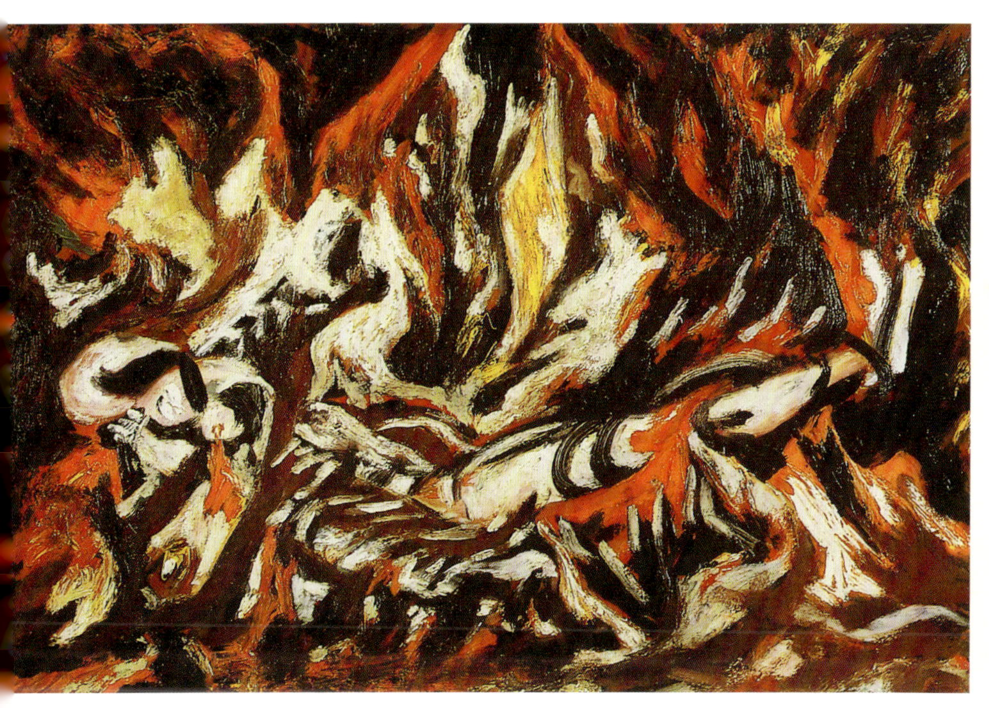

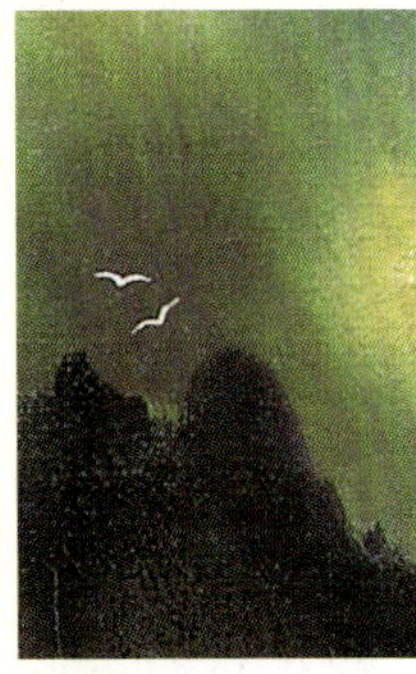

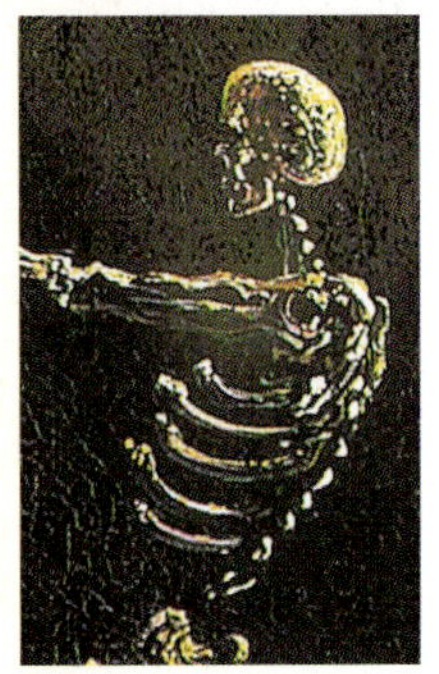

It is fitting that we should devote a moment to the consideration of these great phenomena, as also to the history of the belief in the end of the world which has appeared in every age, though modified by the advancement of human knowledge. Faith has in part disappeared; mystery and superstition, which struck the imagination of our ancestors and has so curiously

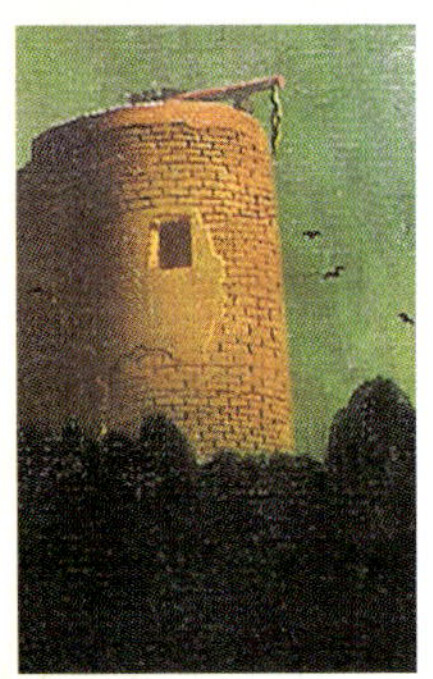

The Horseman of Death

Salvador Dalí, 1935
Oil on canvas, 54 x 64 cm
The André-François Petit Collection, Paris

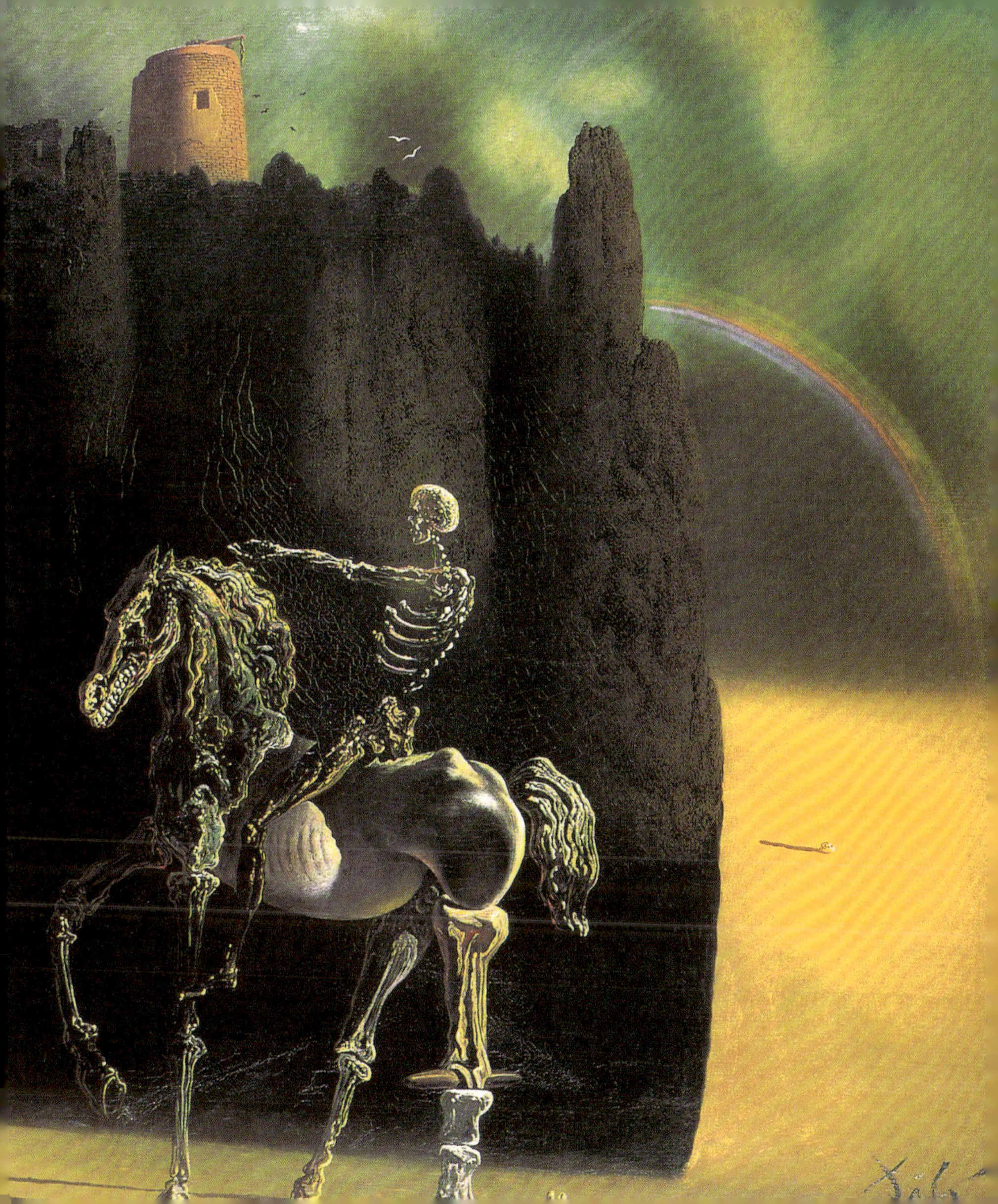

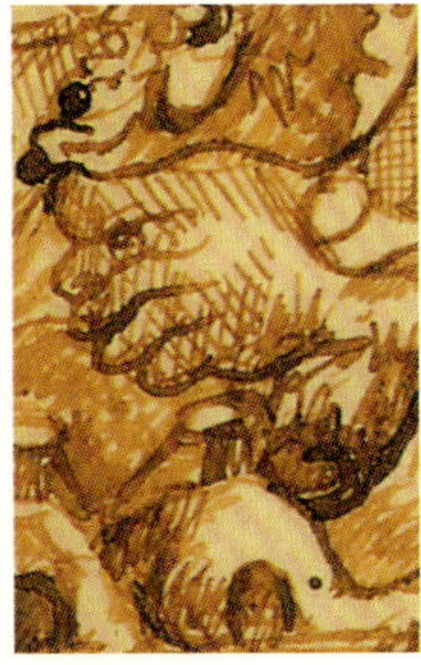

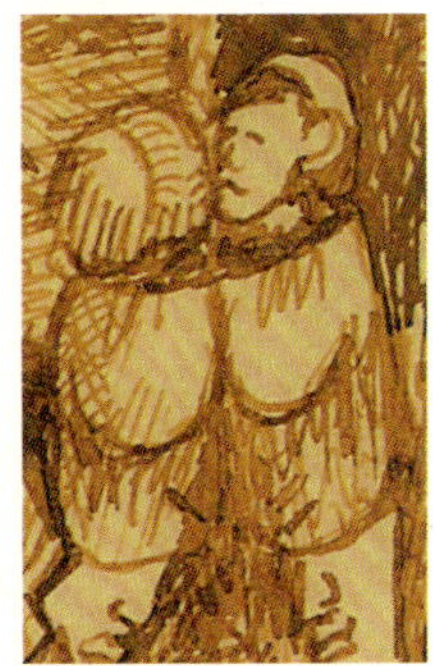

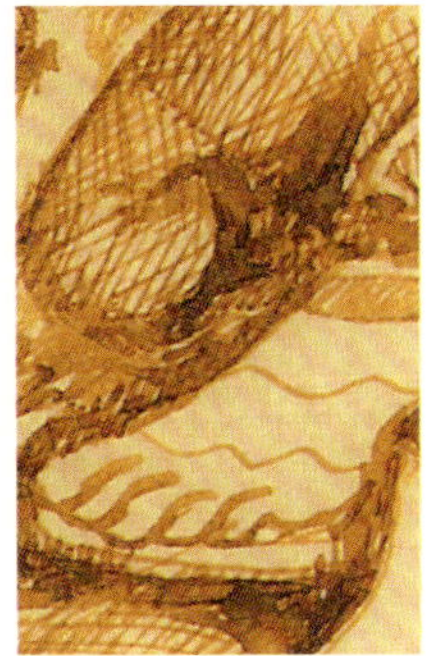

been represented in the portals of our great cathedrals, and in the sculptures and paintings inspired by Christian traditions, this theological aspect of the last day of the earth has given way to the scientific study of the duration of our solar system. The geocentric and anthropocentric concepts of the universe, which makes man the centre and end of creation, has gradually transformed and

Untitled drawing with cataclysmic theme

Frida Kahlo, 1946
Sepia ink on paper, 18 x 26.7 cm
Private collection

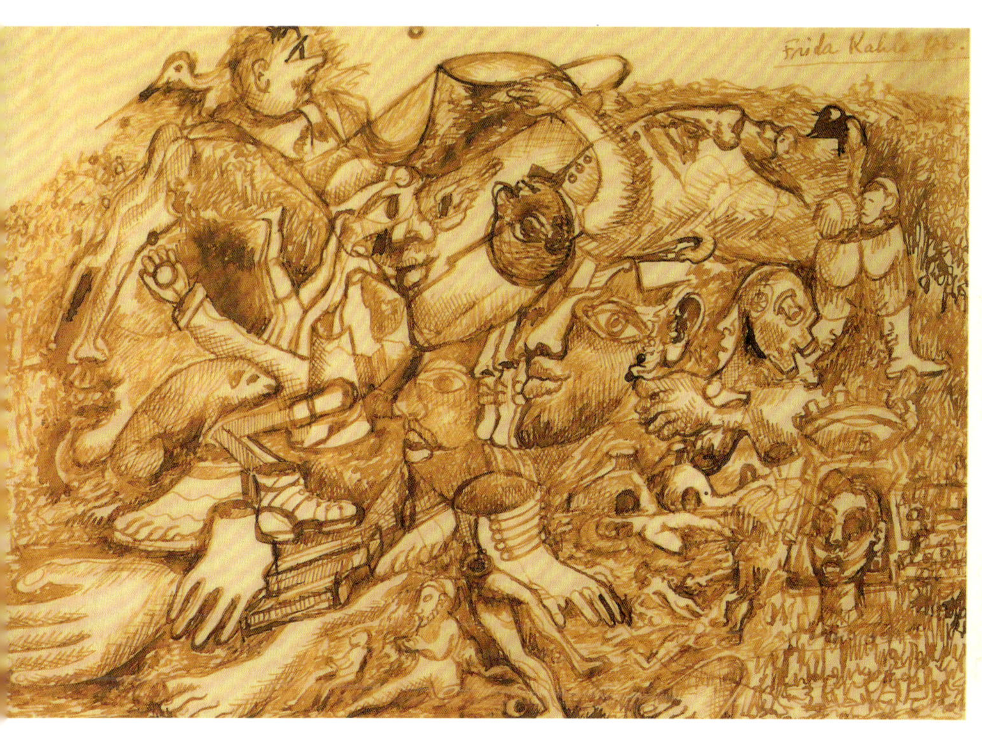

Frida Kahlo

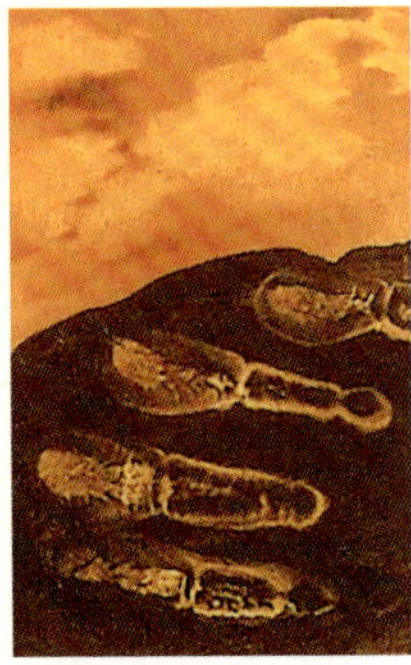

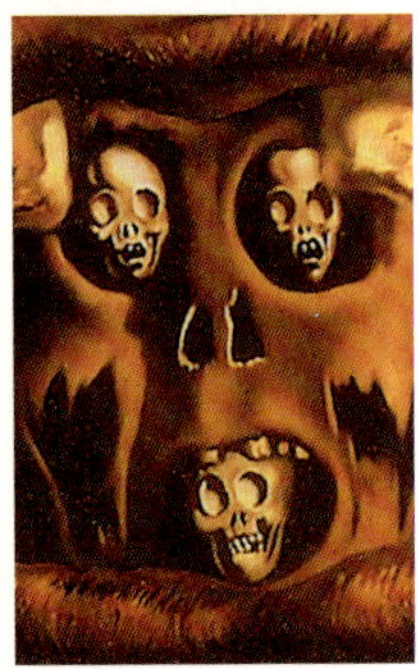

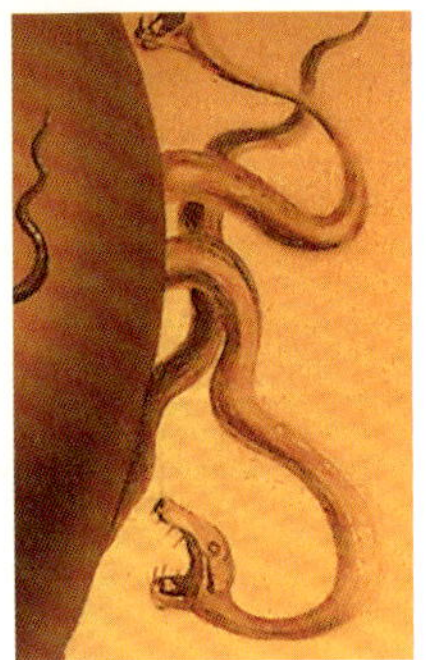

eventually disappeared, for we know that our humble planet is but an island in the infinite, that human history has thus far been founded on pure illusions, and that the dignity of man lies in his intellectual and moral worth. Is the destiny and sovereign end of the human mind, the exact knowledge of things, not the search for Truth?

Visage of War
____

Salvador Dalí, 1940
Oil on canvas, 64 x 79 cm
Museum Boijmans Van Beuningen, Rotterdam

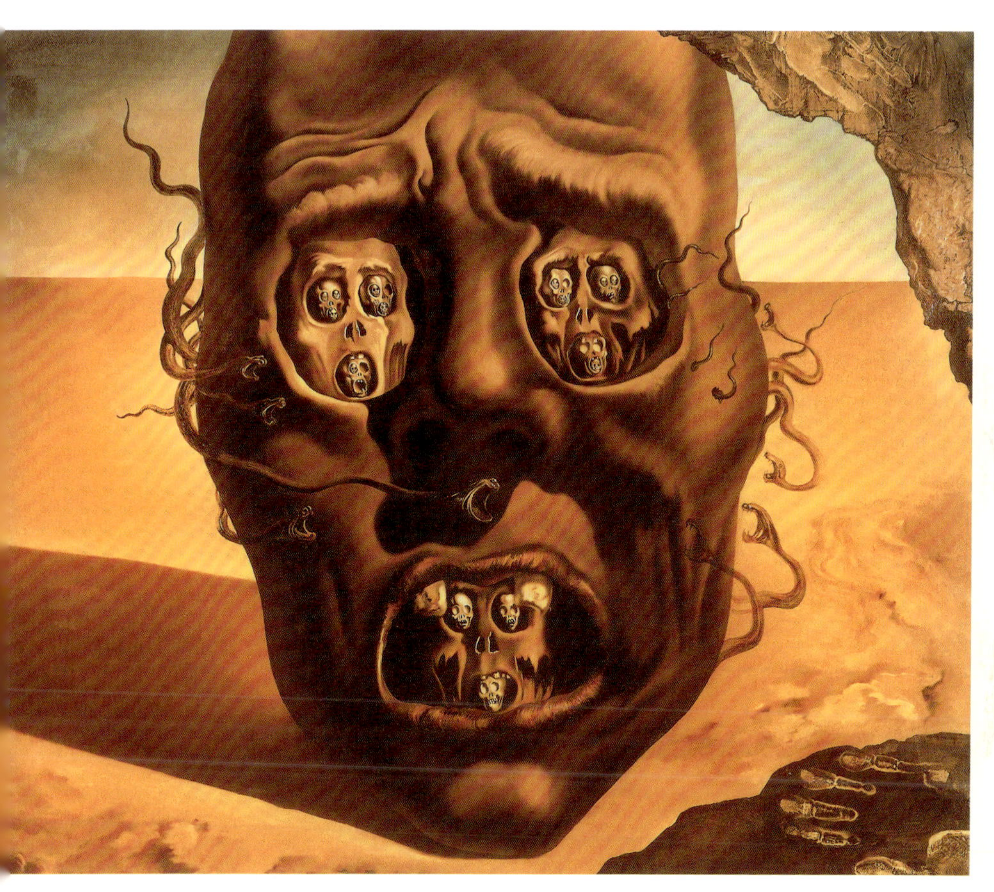

Index

M/N/O